INSIDE OMB

AMERICAN POLITICAL INSTITUTIONS AND PUBLIC POLICY

INSIDE OMB

Politics and Process in the President's Budget Office

SHELLEY LYNNE TOMKIN

M.E. Sharpe
Armonk, New York
London, England

Library of Congress Cataloging-in-Publication Data

Tomkin, Shelley Lynne, 1950– .
Inside OMB: politics and process in the President's Budget Office /
by Shelley Lynne Tomkin.
p.   cm.—(American political institutions and public policy)
Includes bibliographical references and index.
ISBN 1-56324-454-3 (alk. paper).—
1. United States—Office of Management and Budget. 2. Budget—United States.
I. Title. II. Series.
HJ2051.T63   1998
352.4′0973—dc21
97-46969
CIP

Printed in the United States of America

BM (c)   10   9   8   7   6   5   4   3   2   1

Contents

Foreword

They are the president's surrogates, the executive branch's nemeses, and the Congress's competitors. Responsible for budgets, management, some statistical services, and procurement, they coordinate policy initiatives of the executive departments and agencies, provide liaison on budgetary and appropriation matters with Congress, and oversee the executive branch's regulatory activities. They enforce precedent, meet bottom lines, and find buried bones all over the government. Often regarded as the people who say "NO," they are the feared overseers of presidents, and their executive branch enforcers. They are the 500+ policy analysts, managers, and political appointees who comprise the Office of Management and Budget (OMB).

The OMB is the largest single unit in the Executive Office of the President. Created in 1921 by the Budget and Accounting Act, it was moved from the Treasury Department to the Executive Office in 1939 when the latter was created by President Franklin Roosevelt. It has been part of the presidency ever since. A very powerful agency, its influence stems largely from the ongoing support it receives from presidents, from its closed-door mode of operation, and from the critical nature of its central concerns—policy making, implementation, and budgeting.

Presidents have found the OMB to be a useful constraint on the executive departments and agencies, reining in the latter's turf-building and advocacy tendencies, countering their clientele's pressures, and impacting on the resiliency of the bureaucracy's standard operating procedures. They have also found the OMB's informational and analytic capabilities essential for their own decision making and decision defending, and its institutional memory a valuable beacon for navigating unchartered waters, particularly at the beginning of their administrations. The OMB has also served as a convenient target for criticism aimed at presidents, as a "fall guy" for the administration.

That the OMB lacks as much public visibility, media scrutiny, or interest group accessibility as other executive branch offices, including the White House, contributes to its reputation and clout as the most powerful nay-sayer in government. Operating largely behind closed doors, armed with extensive information sources and policy expertise, buttressed by the computational and analytic skills of its personnel, located near the West Wing alongside the president's policy aides and linked to them by partisan ties, the OMB speaks and acts for the president. Rarely is it circumvented in the policy process, although executive departments and agencies and their clientele can and do challenge its decisions.

One would think that an institution so central to the operation of government, one that has had such a long and continuing impact on substantive and budgetary policy, an office so vital to the exercise of presidential power and so important to the coordination of executive branch activities, would have been thoroughly dissected and analyzed by scholars, journalists, and political practitioners. But alas, it has not been.

The last book-length institutional history of the OMB was published in 1979. The last insider's account, *The Triumph of Politics*, which retold the contentious story of budgetary politics during the early Reagan years from the perspective of one of the principals, budget director David Stockman, is now over a decade old. And although there have been several journal articles on the politicization of the agency and its impact on public policy, there have been no comprehensive studies that examine the structure, style, and *modus operandi* of this powerful, professional, political presidential instrumentality, much less assess its impact on governmental decision making and public policy.

Why not? Why has this critical agency remained in the shadows of government for so long? The principal answer to these questions is that the OMB operates largely out of the public view. Although its circulars, bulletins, and occasional studies are published in government documents and now are also available at its website, its internal decision-making documents are not public nor are they easily attainable during the course of an administration. One has to go into the bowels of the archives to get them. Even the executive agencies are not privy to internal OMB memoranda and analyses of their policy positions, congressional testimony, and budgetary requests, although executive departments and agencies are apprised of the OMB's final judgment on *their* issues.

So how can we find out how this particular executive office works? How can we gain a perspective on the OMB's evolving role, on its political interaction with other critical policy-making units, and with its impact on public policy? Beyond the OMB's own self-studies, which may eventually become part of the public record, the only way to understand the OMB is to talk with those involved, the people who collect and analyze the data and make the recommendations to the president, the participants themselves.

That is precisely what Dr. Shelley Lynne Tomkin has done. Over a twenty-year period, she has interviewed and reinterviewed over a hundred OMB officials, both civil servants and political appointees, including two directors, Alice Rivlin and Franklin Raines, as well as others with whom they interacted on a regular basis in the Executive Office of the President and in the Congress. She has also gained access to a vast array of internal documents which have enabled her to construct an institutional history of this agency's operations from 1971 to the present.

What follows is a detailed examination of the OMB: the changing roles of its budget examiners and management specialists, the differing criteria they have used to assess policy decisions, and its growing role in legislative activities. Dr. Tomkin explores the age-old debate within the OMB between giving presidential advice on the substantive merits or the politics of a proposal, the tension between nonpartisan careerists and short-time political appointees, the organizational reforms that have been instituted to promote efficiency and accountability, and the friction within the agency as well as between it and other presidential offices, executive departments and agencies, and increasingly, the Congress and its committees—friction over the OMB's roles, missions, and policy judgments.

If you want to know how the OMB has changed, particularly since the 1980s, how it functions today, how its influence has been affected by powerful White Houses, tight budgets, and increased congressional oversight, and how powerful external forces have challenged its internal policy and budgetary judgments, then you will need to read this book. It is a comprehensive account, one that finally opens the OMB to the outside world and, by doing so, provides its readers with an understanding of the politics and processes of presidential policy making, budgeting, management, and other aspects of policy implementation. It is a must read for the serious student of American government.

Stephen J. Wayne
Georgetown University

Preface

The Office of Management and Budget (OMB) stands at a critical point within the nerve center of the federal government and holds a key position in the communications network that links the President, the rest of the Executive Branch, and the Congress. So positioned, it can exert a significant impact on public policy outcomes through its budgetary, legislative, managerial, and regulatory review mandates.

In spite of OMB's importance, there is little public awareness of the scope of OMB's involvement and influence on federal governmental policy making. There are some, like Paul O'Neill, a former deputy director of OMB, who believe that OMB is not only little known, but is also little understood. In a memorable speech to OMB staff in 1988, he remarked that he considered OMB to be "unexplainable to everyone who lives outside the Beltway and misunderstood by nearly everyone who lives inside the Beltway."[1]

O'Neill's point still holds. That OMB and its predecessor, the Bureau of the Budget (BOB), have always been less than visible institutions is partially attributable to their central mission to provide nonpartisan advice to presidents of different party affiliations as anonymously as possible. Even though OMB evolved into a more recognizable institution in the late 1970s and 1980s, it is generally not understood with even a rudimentary level of sophistication among those who are not students of American government, or who do not work in federal agencies, Congress, interest groups, or law firms inside or outside the Beltway.

As O'Neill also observed, the reactions surrounding OMB among "inside the Beltway" participants in Washington's governmental, political, and bureaucratic circles are quite different. They are often hostile, a response which stems from personal experience with OMB's roles as nay-sayer to agency entreaties for funding or "enforcer" of presidentially driven management improvement. These reactions contribute to the OMB being widely "misunderstood."

Moreover, the literature on OMB is out of date. There have been no texts primarily devoted to examining OMB since the early 1980s. Yet, from 1981 through the mid-1990s, important changes in the budgetary prerogatives of the President and the Congress and a rising federal deficit altered OMB's roles and responsibilities in significant ways.

Thus, the overriding objective of this book is to fill a gap in the existing literature by providing an updated guide to the inner workings of the OMB in as comprehensive a way as possible. The book attempts to examine many of the "stereotypes" and images of OMB held by those who directly interact with it. I have tried to provide a guidebook for staff and officials in the Executive Office of the President and the White House, particularly those who are "new" to Washington and unfamiliar with this important agency. The book is also meant to give those inside of OMB a view of themselves and those who have gone before them. Finally, it is designed to inform all students of the policy-making process interested in the Presidency's role and influence in that process.

The book is organized into eleven chapters. Some chapters explore broad historical trends and cycles experienced by BOB/OMB from its creation in 1921 to the present and some provide a more detailed and close-up description of OMB's decision-making processes and staff role orientations. Chapter 1 presents a brief introductory description of OMB's functions as they exist today and explains why OMB's roles in governmental policy making are so significant. It also summarizes trends such as politicization, institutional overload, and role conflict, which have affected OMB recently or in the past. Chapter 2 describes OMB's organizational layout, the functions handled by different OMB offices, and the role orientations assumed by its staff today. Chapter 3 provides a capsulized account of BOB/OMB's institutional history from BOB's creation in 1921 through the 1970s. It highlights some repeating patterns in BOB's institutional behavior and the congressional and presidential responses to BOB that influenced its capabilities over the duration of these years. Chapter 4 examines OMB career staff role orientations and decision-making dynamics during the mid to late 1970s. It serves as a reference point for Chapter 5, which provides an overview of institutional transformations that occurred in OMB during the 1980s. Chapter 5 also examines the legacies of the OMB Directors who served during these years and draws linkages between external demands and conditions experienced by OMB (increasing visibility and politicization of the surrounding budget process, the growing deficit, and divided government), and their outcomes, such as new and changing roles, added work-load, and erosion of career staff influence.

Chapters 6, 7, and 8 respectively describe the steps involved in OMB's budget formulation process, its legislative responsibilities, and its regulatory review and administrative management roles. Specific institutional practices and procedures are described in some detail with explanations of how they changed during the 1980s and 1990s. Chapters 7 and 8 also serve broader objectives. Chapter 7 illustrates how the Budget and Impoundment Control Act of 1974, and later the contentious budgetary politics of the 1980s, shifted OMB's focus away from the analysis of individual programs in the Executive Branch and preparation of the President's budget, toward greater emphasis on the tracking of the congressional stages of the budgetary process. Chapter 8 provides a comparison of OMB's relationships with federal agencies in the past and present by contrasting the modes of OMB–agency communications and information gathering in the 1960s, 1970s, and 1980s, and by providing an institutional history of BOB/OMB's Executive Branch management roles from 1921 through the 1980s. A similar treatment of OMB's more recently acquired regulatory review role follows. Chapters 9 and 10 offer a detailed account of OMB's institutional evolution during the first term of the Clinton administration, a time when OMB was reorganized and when it was required to adjust to a party change in the White House. Chapter 11 presents a summation of OMB's institutional experience from 1993 to 1996. It focuses on how the Clinton era differed from the previous twelve years in OMB, at the same time that many of its long-standing external pressures and its adaptations to them had remained the same. Finally, Chapter 11 offers recommendations for addressing a number of problems that have continued to impede OMB's ability to serve the Presidency.

The completion of this book represents the end of what has been a long personal journey. My avocation as an "OMB watcher" first began during the mid-1970s while I was conducting a study of OMB budget examiner roles that ultimately evolved into a doctoral dissertation. The research involved about ninety interviews with OMB officials and staff that were conducted in 1976, 1979, and 1980. Some of my findings squared well with those of scholars who had written about OMB's posture in the late 1970s, and helped to fill in some of the particulars surrounding the general trends they had noted. Other findings were new, in that I was conducting the research just as the early implementation of the Congressional Budget Act of 1974 was beginning to unfold and to lead to the modification of some of OMB's "traditional" operating procedures and norms.

Frequently changing conditions and demands were to become a constant for OMB in the years to come. In the spring of 1981, even as I presented and defended my findings, the epicenter of influence in OMB and the roles of its staff were already shifting away from the institutional patterns I had observed during the previous five-year period. The "Reagan–Stockman" budget revolution had already been in progress for some three months. It soon became clear that, if my research was to serve a useful purpose, it would have to do so as a benchmark to be placed in comparative perspective with new and rapidly changing institutional realities in OMB. I would have to continue returning to OMB to chart the transformations that were taking place.

While OMB was not as accessible as it had been in the 1970s, I was still able to talk with some of my previous contacts there, and with time I fell into a habit of interviewing OMB staff on a periodic basis. I was able, in this manner, to keep track of new developments that affected OMB as they occurred. When more dramatic shifts occurred, such as those that came with the appointment of a new director, the election of a new President, or the appearance of altered OMB responsibilities, I would conduct larger-scale interviews. This became my "habitual behavior" for the next twelve years.

The election of President Clinton in 1992, and the resumption of unified party leadership on both sides of Pennsylvania Avenue, presented an opportunity to examine how the institution would adapt to yet another combination of new pressures and roles after a decade when OMB had already experienced significant transformations. Would OMB career staff be trusted by the new administration after twelve years of Republican Presidents? What uses would be found for OMB by an administration that sought to "put people first," at the same time as it faced a federal budget deficit of unprecedented proportions?

Originally this book was intended to cover OMB's institutional experience through the first year of the Clinton administration. As events unfolded, however, I became convinced that it was crucial to continue my research beyond that point, to determine how OMB had adapted to its reorganization in 1994, the resumption of divided government later that year, and the government shutdown in 1995. Thus the bulk of the ninety-some interviews for this segment of the book were conducted from April of 1993 until the spring of 1996. About ten additional interviews were conducted in the summer of 1996 to provide further verification for some sections of the book that handled OMB's institutional evolution during the 1970s and 1980s as well as to keep current with preliminary discussions that were taking place in OMB as it prepared to produce a strategic plan for the future.

Though the 1970s interviews and those conducted in the 1980s and early 1990s were largely confined to OMB staff and officials, those conducted from 1993 to 1997 were broader in scope. They included Executive Branch agency officials and personnel, National Performance Review staff and officials, a larger number of political appointees from both OMB and the Executive Office of the President, and congressional staff as well as OMB civil service employees.

For the past twenty years, I have primarily used open-ended questions in one-on-one interviews that have probed the respondents' perceptions about relevant events occurring at the time as well as longer-term institutional cycles. I have often gained new insights or leads during the course of an interview which I followed up on in succeeding interviews. The interviews lasted on the average an hour to an hour and a half and sometimes longer.

Particularly after 1981, when OMB became more visible and controversial, I found it necessary to make extra efforts to assure respondents that their confidentiality would be protected. That meant giving assurances that my research was for academic purposes, that I was not connected with any press organization, that they would not be quoted by name, and that my questions would focus upon broad institutional patterns, processes, and role orientations, but not include queries concerning specific issue areas that they could not discuss.

Since OMB interacts with so many individuals in government, private organizations, and law firms in the nation's capital, I discovered over the years that a number of friends, family members, and professional colleagues would have been useful sources for the book due to their current or previous professional positions. I decided to refrain from interviewing any of these persons in order to avoid potentially placing them in compromising positions with their institutions or co-workers.[2]

Along with the interview data, I drew from a variety of other primary and secondary sources, including but not limited to internal OMB documents, congressional hearings, testimony, and reports, scholarly journals and convention papers, press sources (including newspapers, *Congressional Quarterly* publications, and the *National Journal*), and studies prepared by the General Accounting Office and by private groups such as the National Academy of Public Administration. In my discussion of OMB's history prior to the mid-1970s, I drew heavily from two books: Larry Berman's *OMB and the Presidency*, and Frederick C. Mosher's *A Tale of Two Agencies: A Comparative Analysis of the General Accounting Office and the Office of Management and Budget*. I also used references to OMB in numerous books on the Presidency and other topics.

During the last couple of years, survey research and public opinion polls have been yielding findings that point to increasingly low levels of public information on democratic institutions. These trends are not new, but they seem to be getting worse. Moreover, the fact that voter turnout in the 1996 presidential election was the lowest in decades, was yet another alarming development. If our democratic system is to effectively meet the challenges of the future, an increase in the amount, sophistication, and availability of information on pivotal governmental institutions such as OMB, is one necessary first step among the many required to begin to address these problems.

Acknowledgments

OMB stands on the cutting edge of three worlds: the political world that produces presidents to lead the nation; the world of the "permanent government" which serves the political will by implementing it; and the world of the academy which seeks truth for its own sake. My understanding of OMB's institutional persona has been greatly enhanced by personal and professional exposure to all three of these cultures. Thus, it seems fitting to recognize those individuals from whom I have learned so much in the context of these different spheres.

To begin with, I have gained an appreciation of those who work in the permanent government from my own family. My husband is a career civil servant, as was my father. My father was a living embodiment of the integrity, honesty, and dedication to non-partisan government service that all too often today is not appreciated in public discourse. My husband exemplifies the same qualities. Without the many dedicated individuals like them who toil out of the public's view, many of the policy initiatives forged by popularly elected officials would come to naught.

My respect for public servants has also been reinforced many times over by the numerous civil servants and policy officials in OMB and other agencies with whom I have spoken over the last twenty years. I have found these individuals to be professionals of the first order, persons with incisive intellects, keen understanding of complex policy puzzles, and enthusiastic dedication to public service. I owe a great debt of gratitude to all those who gave of their time in the midst of their own grueling schedules to speak with me, often repeatedly. Their insider knowledge and perspectives are woven throughout the book, and in a sense this is their story. The conclusions, however, are my responsibility, as are any factual errors or omissions.

I also owe a debt of gratitude to Alice Rivlin for granting me two interviews while she was deputy director at OMB and one interview after she left the institution. From these conversations and all that I have read about her, I have found her to represent the very essence of what public service is all about.

It was probably during my childhood, as my mother regaled me with stories about Franklin and Eleanor Roosevelt, that the study of the presidency began to hold a distinctive fascination for me. She described to me how the President and First Lady gave her hope at a time of peril for the nation and the world; the thrill of meeting Eleanor Roosevelt twice during World War II; and a day she would always remember when FDR smiled and tipped his hat to her as his car drove by. As she remembered the past with such feeling, I began to view the presidency as a potentially compelling force capable of triggering growth in the nation's collective spirit.

In becoming a political scientist and student of the presidency, there has been no more significant influence on my intellectual development than my former professor and dissertation advisor Stephen J. Wayne. Indeed, without his guidance some twenty-two years ago, the first seed for this book would have never been planted in the first place. He suggested at that time that I write a paper on the roles and responsibilities of the OMB budget examiners for a graduate seminar on the American Presidency. This was not a research focus that I would have pursued on my own had it not been for his guidance. As I hope is illustrated in this research, the study of OMB turned out to be an extremely fruitful avenue through which to better understand the national policy-making process as a whole. As editor of one of M.E. Sharpe's series on American Politics, he continued to advise me during the writing of this book. His meticulous review and comments on drafts of this book have been invaluable. Steve Wayne's intellectual integrity, discipline, and emphasis on excellence have served as benchmark standards for me throughout my academic career.

For the last twenty years, I have taught in the areas of American government, constitutional law, and political process at Trinity College in Washington, D.C. I will always be grateful to Betty James for hiring me for my first full-time teaching job at the school. Trinity College has been ahead of its time, from its creation as the first Catholic women's college in the United States a little over a hundred years ago, to the present, as it prepares students to meet the challenges they will face in the twenty-first century. My life has also been enriched immeasurably over the years by the many wonderful colleagues and students I have known at Trinity. Kathy McGinnis, my mentor and colleague in the political science department, in particular has been a trusted friend and professional colleague for two decades. I have been enriched by her wise counsel, sound judgment, and friendship during this time. I also wish to express my gratitude to Willie Kitchens and Sylvia Steed, of Trinity College's faculty support services department, who, on their own time, labored over the early drafts of the book, typing and retyping it more times than I care to remember.

It has been a pleasure to have worked with those at M.E. Sharpe who have transformed my drafts into a book. I particularly thank Executive Editor Patricia Kolb for her encouragement, her professional advice, and for her insightful comments. She was unfailingly patient and understanding in the face of my numerous delays in completing the book, which were created in part by the rapid changes in budgetary politics from 1994 to the present. Steven Martin has been more than a terrific production editor. He has patiently and repeatedly answered my questions about each step of the publication process and has painstakingly and carefully reviewed the final drafts with me. Thanks also go to Elizabeth Granda for her assistance throughout the period that I was writing the book.

Finally, I owe more than can be expressed here to my husband Ross, my son David, and my parents, David and Henrietta Tomkin. My father, who passed away in 1987, was one of the most loving and balanced persons I have ever known. He taught me about integrity, honesty, commitment, and patience, all of which served me well. My mother is an "original." She is a visionary creative force, a free spirit, an independent thinker. She was a liberated woman before there was a women's movement, and she spoke up against all forms of prejudice before it was politically correct to do so. She taught me that one must often venture down uncharted paths to find solutions to problems. To the degree that I am inclined to try to find new and untried ways of addressing recurring institutional dilemmas in OMB or in our civil and political life, it is largely due to her influence.

My husband and my son seem to me to be rather unique. I certainly could not have finished this book without their encouragement, support, and love. Ross read the final drafts of the book and made many valuable substantive and editorial suggestions. If he had not been a full partner in raising our son and then some, I could not have finished this book. If he had resented all the weekends and evenings that I spent hunched over the computer, then I could not have finished the book. If he had not been as committed to my personal and professional growth as he is to his own, then I could not have finished the book. If I had not been married to him, then I would be out looking for him and not writing the book.

Last, but not least to be acknowledged here, is my nine-year-old son, David. Many authors dedicate their books to their young children, but few, I suspect, would have occasion to express gratitude to the child for his or her *assistance in preparing the book.* In this case, however, that is exactly what must be acknowledged. David has been computer-literate since he was six years old and seems to have been born knowing how the inside of a computer operates. I, however, am not endowed with similar skills, and until a few years ago was still writing and rewriting on yellow pads and cutting and pasting manually. At the age of seven, David willingly and enthusiastically offered to change all that. First, he set me up on the computer. Soon he was teaching me to reach for more sophisticated capabilities like cutting and pasting and typing end notes on the computer! If this was not enough, he just loved to accompany me on stack searches at university libraries and particularly relished working with microfilm. He is a terrific child and I am a very lucky mother. Thus, it is to Ross, David, and my parents that I dedicate this book.

Shelley Lynne Tomkin
May 1998
Washington, D.C.

List of Abbreviations

AFDC	Aid to Families With Dependent Children
BEA	Budget Enforcement Act
BOB	Bureau of the Budget
BRD	Budget Review Division
BPS	Budget Preparation System
CBMS	Central Budget Management System
CBO	Congressional Budget Office
CCMA	Cabinet Council on Management and Administration
CFO	Chief Financial Officers Act
CR	Continuing Resolution
EOP	Executive Office of the President
FAR	Federal Assistance Review Program
FY	Fiscal Year
GAO	General Accounting Office
GNP	Gross National Product
GPRA	Government Performance and Results Act
GSA	General Services Administration
HEAF	Higher Education Assistance Foundation
HEW	Health Education and Welfare Department
HHS	Health and Human Services Department
HUD	Housing and Urban Development Department
LA	Legislative Affairs
LRD	Legislative Reference Division
MBO	Management By Objectives
NEC	National Economic Council
NAPA	National Academy of Public Administration
NPR	National Performance Review

OBRA	Omnibus Budget Reconciliation Act of 1990
OEM	Office of Executive Management
OFFM	Office of Federal Financial Management
OFPP	Office of Federal Procurement Policy
OIRA	Office of Information and Regulatory Affairs
OBR	Office of Budget and Review
OMB	Office of Management and Budget
OMO	Office of Management and Organization
OPM	Office of Personnel Management
PACGO	President's Advisory Committee on Government Organization
PAD	Associate Director or Program Associate Director
PAYGO	Pay-As-You-Go
PCIE	President's Council on Integrity and Efficiency
PCMI	President's Council on Management Improvement
PMI	Presidential Management Initiative
PPBS	Planning Programming Budgeting Systems
PPSSCC	President's Private Sector Survey on Cost Control
PRP	President's Reorganization Project
RARG	Regulatory Analysis Review Group
REGO	Reinventing Government
RIA	Regulatory Impact Analysis
RMO	Resource Management Office
SAP	Statement of Administration Policy
VA	Veterans Affairs Department
ZBB	Zero-Based Budgeting

INSIDE OMB

1

OMB: A Presidential Advisor "For All Seasons"

OMB: A Unique Bulwark for the Presidency

OMB's Major Responsibilities

Why have an Office of Management and Budget (OMB)?

The OMB is staffed by career civil servants who remain from one administration to the next regardless of the partisanship of the President, and is therefore able to offer advice and assistance that benefits from long-term knowledge and experience rooted in institutional memory of federal governmental activities and programs. It is thus able to offer recommendations based primarily on the merits of the issues at hand. As a presidential advisory office, OMB is unique in these respects. In the words of Paul O'Neill:

> As our society and government become more complex, it is of the greatest importance that there be a point of institutional memory and neutral competence—better yet, neutral brilliance—available to the President and the Presidency. We are doomed to repeat the mistakes of the past if we lack a trusted cadre of experts who can span the issues of partisan politics and survive the transition between parties in power. This is the role that is the raison d'être of this office.[1]

In practical terms, OMB can only succeed in providing such high caliber advice to the President through the skillful and wise implementation of its multifarious roles and responsibilities. The first and most fundamental of these functions is to assist the President in preparing an annual budget to be presented to Congress. That means assembling budgetary requests for funding from every federal agency, analyzing these requests, and recommending to the President how he should shape his congressional submission.

OMB also operates as a clearinghouse for legislative proposals that departments and agencies wish to see introduced into and passed by the Congress. Such initiatives must receive OMB's approval as conforming with presidential policy guidelines. When legislation is passed by both houses of Congress, OMB offers recommendations to the President on whether to sign or veto it. Since 1981, OMB has also served as a screen through which proposals for government regulations of the public, industry, or other government agencies must pass muster. It also reviews questionnaires, forms, and other paperwork prepared by the government for itself and the public.

Supervising the implementation of presidential initiatives directed toward improvement of general and financial management and program delivery in Executive Branch agencies has also been an important OMB responsibility for many years. One of the prime motives for the reorganization of BOB into OMB was President Nixon's desire to place greater emphasis on the institution's management role.

Since the mid-1970s, when Congress assumed a greater role in the budget process, OMB has also been called upon increasingly to support the President in his efforts to negotiate and pass his budget proposals after they are transmitted to Congress and to help decipher and implement a number of statutes that have reconfigured budgetary rules and procedures. These include the Gramm–Rudman–Hollings Acts I and II, the Budget Enforcement Act, and, most recently, the Line Item Veto Act.

After Congress and the President approve the budget, OMB has the responsibility to release or "apportion" the appropriated funds to the departments and agencies. This process is known as budget execution. OMB distributes appropriated funds to agencies either on a time-based schedule (often quarterly), or at different rates dictated by the functional classifications of the spending.[2] These OMB apportionment controls are designed to prevent agencies from depleting their funds prematurely, and to foster efficiency in agency operations in order to promote savings.

While the epicenter of OMB's institutional activities can usually be traced to its budgetary mandates, to succeed as budgeteer-in-chief it must also be an evaluator of programs, a management expert, an informational repository, and a communications network. "If you are responsible for advising the President about numbers, you are—de facto—in the stream of every policy decision made by the federal government," according to Paul O'Neill.[3]

Although the OMB's influence to affect presidential, agency, and congressional actions has ebbed and flowed over the years, its presence at the center of policy making has remained a constant. Thus, in many respects this small organization, which ranges in size from 400 to 600 staff members, assumes a key position in the communications network that links the President, the rest of the Executive Branch, and the Congress. It has a hand in shaping legislation that molds many governmental activities; it assesses and constrains costs of the governmental services and the mandates that ensue. By exercising these responsibilities wisely, OMB can serve as a guardian of the American people in their roles as recipients of government services and as taxpayers.

OMB's Overarching Purpose: To Advise and Assist the President

OMB's significance is also derived from the role it can play in helping Presidents do their often impossible jobs in ways that other presidential support offices and advisors cannot. Indeed, Presidents have all manner of staff and officialdom to advise them and to provide information and analysis to them. These include their Vice Presidents, White House staffs, their Cabinet and sub-Cabinet officials, their allies in Congress, political consultants, pollsters, and of late, highly politically knowledgeable spouses. Yet in all of the above cases, the requisite institutional memory of specific programmatic issues may be lacking in whole or in part. With the possible exception of the presidential spouse, there is also an ever-present potential in each to skew the information and advice they relay to the President.

White House staff often depend on the President for their present and future careers. They can be hesitant to bring the President the "bad news" even though he needs to hear it. Cabinet members and other political appointees may have their own agendas and interest group attachments that will tend to color the advice they offer the President. All of these advisors may also have incentives from time to time to leak damaging information to the press. Internal White House and outside "presidential image makers" may have little motivation to remain strictly faithful to objectivity in the information they transmit to the President, particularly if that information implies the need for unpopular presidential decisions. While some of these sources of presidential advice may at times be able to marry their roles and interests with objective information, all too often they will not, and even if these information sources are inclined to present balanced and objective assessments, they may lack the background to do so.

OMB can also be particularly valuable to "new" Presidents in the early months of their administrations if they and their political advisors appreciate and understand the subtle roles OMB can exercise and if they trust the institution. Over the years, some administrations have not appreciated, trusted, and therefore used OMB. This kind of assistance is especially significant because, as is often observed by Presidents themselves, nothing can quite prepare them for what they will face once they are seated in the Oval Office. Moreover, in recent years, the demands of campaigning for the presidency have further contributed to the difficulty of making the transition from seeking the office to governing in the office. The sheer physical exertion involved in winning the key to the Oval Office, the simplistic exaggerations that presidential candidates often believe they must make to hold the public's attention and to prevail in the election, and the contentious climate remaining after many elections, are frequently antithetical to the brand of informed governance the American electorate claims to want.

Certainly some Presidents are more prepared than others and in different ways. Former governors have "executive" experience in administering state agencies and handling budgets, but may enter the presidency with a false sense of confidence that is dashed when they find that the political and administrative complexities that a President faces are of greater scope and magnitude on the national level. Presidents entering office from the vice presidency, the Senate, or national appointive office may have a clearer appreciation of the challenges they will face in exercising presidential leadership, but even they emerge from a limited experiential base that may well have been slanted by its own intrinsic biases.

Given OMB's momentous responsibilities and potential, it is not surprising that the following individual descriptions of OMB's "most significant raison d'être," which were recently offered by several OMB staff veterans, focused on service to the presidency rather than on the narrow mechanics of preparing budgets.

> The President needs OMB to narrow the bounds of ignorance in decision making . . . to have at hand all the facts on any given issue and the judgments to make recommendations on resource allocation.

> The President needs a mechanism that is able to make the analytic trade-offs because some Cabinet members will always have their own agenda.

> If the President uses OMB it can help keep him out of trouble . . . to keep him from proposing failing strategies that were tried before.

> OMB can clear out the underbrush so that political appointees can make the bigger decisions. . . . OMB questions at the first level . . . no President can master that level of detail.

> The President needs OMB for the adjudication of agency disputes—there is no other forum for this.

> OMB is a living encyclopedia for the President.

OMB's "Necessary" Institutional Capabilities

OMB's major contribution to the presidential decision-making process is thus its capability to present "more" objective information and advice than other sources, which is based in its longer-term institutional memory. In this sense it acts as both a "check and balance" and a reinforcement to all of the President's other advisory systems. To be most useful, OMB's information and analysis must be grounded in solid knowledge of the budgets, institutional histories, and in recent years the nature of Executive Branch agencies' relationships with the leadership and the committees within the Congress. To achieve its important missions, OMB must also command a high level of respect and authority with other governmental institutions.

OMB staff need to be able to absorb and understand the frameworks of changing administrations by completely transforming to the new value set of each presidency. This skill, however must not prevent OMB from assertively communicating independent facts and analysis that might lead to conclusions that the President and his political adjuncts do not want to hear. At the same time, the assertiveness necessary to be "heard" must not transform into an institutional or personal arrogance that will undermine OMB's objectives by shutting down communications channels to and from the White House, the agencies, and the Congress.

If and when OMB is able to be skillful in these ways and thereby to offer genuinely informative and seasoned analysis to the President, it has performed a function of superlative importance to the presidency. This is so, even if in the final equation, the President and his political staff arms reject all of OMB's recommendations. Presidents *need* the "whole" case presented to them "on the merits" before they factor in other considerations.

When OMB is unable to be "neutral" and "analytically capable," or if Presidents distrust its objectivity, then OMB's ability to help Presidents govern wisely is vastly reduced. It will still be an important institution in the sense of fostering complex budgetary mechanics (putting the budget together and playing various staff roles that Congress has given it over the years), but it will not be significant in the loftier sense of assisting Presidents in the pursuit of "wise" governance.

Internal and External Trends Charting OMB's Course

There are three major problems that have affected BOB/OMB's ability to implement its roles and responsibilities and to serve the presidency in the ways already described. These are institutional overload, role conflict, and politicization. While they have been particularly pronounced in the last twenty-five years, these institutional dilemmas also proved troublesome before that time as well.

Periodically, OMB has been called upon to shoulder new and changing responsibilities, while its staff size has remained constant or has been reduced. It often has not had the requisite time or resources necessary to adjust its organizational training, recruitment, or career patterns to cope with these challenges. One recent origin of these institutional demands has been the growing emergence of the Congress as more of a coequal partner with the President in steering the entire process whereby the federal budget is produced, modified, and negotiated to passage. This development forced Presidents to look to OMB to increasingly track and communicate with congressional staff during legislative consideration of the budget. Such involvement had been minimal in the Bureau of the Budget before 1970. As procedural efforts to contain the mounting deficit were concocted by the Congress, these responsibilities became even more complex. Some of these process changes delegated substantial authorities to OMB career staff even as it added to their work load. The most current example of this is the Line Item Veto Act, which is discussed at some length in Chapter 11 and in the epilogue to this book.

Another case in which the demands on the institution exerted stress on its capacities probably originated back in the Truman Administration when BOB began to be criticized for allowing its governmental managerial roles to be overshadowed by its budgetary imperatives. This is a pattern that continues to the present and will be considered more exhaustively in Chapters 3 and 8.

OMB's second major institutional trend, politicization, is in part related to overload. A growing politicization in OMB can be traced back either to the Truman administration, the Johnson administration, or the Nixon administration, depending upon which scholarly assessment one is examining or how one defines politicization.[4] It is safe to say that by the end of the 1970s, politicization was an important issue for OMB that was to become even more significant a "potential" dilemma during the 1980s. This "politicization" meant that BOB/OMB began to be used in various ways by Presidents and their surrogates to help advocate, sell, or argue for politically favored policies in a way that sometimes conflicted with BOB/OMB's traditional mission to provide "neutral" information to the President.

This tendency toward politicization, which will also be examined throughout this book, may be attributed to a variety of external pressures on the presidency itself which at times have been paired with personal proclivities of individual Presidents. Some of the "politicizing" roles that some in OMB exercised conflicted with or at least complicated BOB/OMB's other purposes. Thus, role conflicts emerged for everyone in BOB/OMB from its directors to its most junior employees. This tension between two different kinds of institutional mandate tended to exacerbate the overload problem, since it compounded OMB's evolving platter of responsibilities.

Other Historical Patterns and Cycles: BOB/OMB as "Crisis Manager," "Whipping Boy," and "Protective Cover"

BOB/OMB has become repeatedly entwined with other behavioral cycles throughout its history that are related to the broad scope of its responsibilities, and during the last twenty-five years to the trend toward greater politicization. One of these is that it has generally lacked the time and opportunity to plan ahead and reflect on its overall institutional mission because it has so often been preoccupied with crisis management. Another is that BOB/OMB has at times been used as a scapegoat by Congress, and thus when it has needed resources to support its growing responsibilities, it did not receive them and was often afraid to ask. Later it would be criticized by Congress, study commissions, and think tanks for failing to adequately meet the mounting demands. In fact, there is a "Washington insider" game that has cast BOB/OMB as a convenient "whipping boy" for the Congress to use as a foil to blame for unpopular budget decisions. OMB has also been used in a similar way to strike back at the President. The White House has furthered this whipping boy syndrome by using OMB as a protective cover or lightning rod to blame for unpopular budget cuts or to save face in retreating from policies that receive too adverse a public reaction.

OMB career staff are good soldiers when being used in these ways. Not only do they not complain about their whipping boy stance, but they sometimes bemoan the fact that various administrations have not understood how to use them in their "protective cover" capacities. Moreover, one will seldom hear OMB staffers complaining about OMB's "overload." They seem to relish their self-image as a group of wunderkind who are also good and loyal soldiers. They also almost never lament heavy work loads, staffing constraints, or treatment by Congress, and are generally ready to take their own medicine of budgetary constraint.

This staff stoicism notwithstanding, institutional overload, politicization, role conflict, and the "whipping boy" syndrome can still undermine OMB's ability to carry out its many tasks effectively and its capability to serve the long-term needs of the presidency. One avenue of inquiry throughout this book will be to examine the degree to which OMB has been able to realize the lofty objectives cited at the beginning of this chapter in light of these institutional trends and historical cycles. Before these issues are explored from a historical vantage point, however, a description of OMB's current organizational structure, functions, and staff role orientations will follow in Chapter 2.

Office of Management and Budget, After OMB 2000

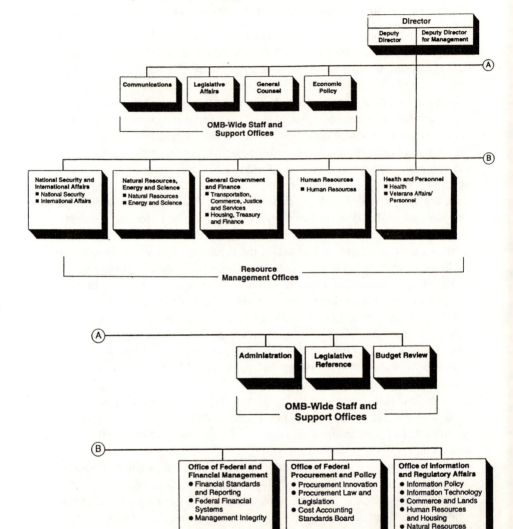

Legend
■ Divisions
● Branches

Source: General Accounting Office, "Office of Management and Budget: Changes Resulting from the OMB 2000 Reorganization, " GAO/GGD/AIMD-96-50 (December 1995).

2

Learning the Institutional Map: OMB Organization and Staff Roles

Organization and Functions of OMB

OMB as Part of the Executive Office of the President

OMB's physical location across the street from the White House and its adjacent Old Executive Office Building goes far toward explaining where it fits into the larger presidential advisory entity called the Executive Office of the President (EOP). The EOP includes the White House staff, the Office of the Vice President, OMB, the National Security Council, the Council of Economic Advisors, the National Drug Control Policy Office, the Office of the U.S. Trade Representative, and a number of other units. OMB's $56 million budget and 518–person staff stand as both the largest appropriation and largest staff size of any one office in the EOP, which has an overall annual budget of $212 million and a staff of about 1,600 persons.[1] The White House Office stands second with a staff of 400 and an annual appropriation of $40 million.[2] Presented in this light, it is easy to understand why few are willing to plead too forcefully for sizable increases in OMB's resources in spite of its significant functions.

Pennsylvania Avenue separates the New Executive Office Building where OMB is housed from the Old Executive Office Building, where staffs of other EOP units reside. The divide is significant in a symbolic sense. Those in the Old Executive Office Building are almost all political appointees, including OMB's twenty or so political appointees; those in the New Executive Office Building are virtually all OMB civil service staff.

Two other important units that are creations of the Clinton administration should also be cited, since in certain significant ways they have shared some of OMB's traditional roles. They are the National Economic Council (NEC), which is jurisdictionally considered part of the President's White House staff though many of its staff are physically located in the Old Executive Office Building, and the National Performance Review (NPR), which is considered to be part of the Vice President's Office.

The Resource Management Offices

The Resource Management Offices (RMOs), as depositories of agency-specific programmatic information, operate as collective intelligence centers for other units in the OMB to draw from, as they perform their other budgetary, legislative, and management-related responsibilities. These OMB divisions, which until 1994 were called "program divisions," house the "program examiners" whose official moniker was also changed from "budget" examiners at that time. These changes reflected an OMB reorganization that was intended to integrate programmatic and managerial considerations into budgetary decision making.

The program divisions/RMOs have been the "heart and soul" of the institution, perhaps since the end of the 1940s, when BOB's budget divisions took a back seat to its Office of Administrative Management, which had played a central role in supporting President Roosevelt during World War II. Budget process demands have dominated the work of the program divisions over efforts to improve management and delivery of services to the public.

The RMOs are divided into five major functional subject-matter areas. These are the National Security and International Affairs Division; the General Government and Finance Division; the Human Resources Division; the Natural Resources Division; and the Health Division. Three of these divisions are broken down into subdivisions. Each of these units reviews the budgets and legislative proposals of several Cabinet-level departments and/or independent agencies.

These offices are each directed by one of five noncareer political appointees formally designated associate directors, but commonly referred to as the PADs or "program associate directors" by OMB staff. They are further segmented into subdivisions headed by deputy associate directors, commonly referred to as "division chiefs," or in OMB parlance, "DADs." Some also have intermediary deputies. The RMOs are further divided into branches of anywhere from five to ten program examiners, with most totaling about eight professionals. The division chief's position as well as all subordinate offices (the branch chiefs and the examiners) are not political appointments, but career positions. The crucial line between political and civil service personnel falls between the division chief and the PAD. Therefore, the division chiefs often remain in their positions over the span of several administrations while the PAD will be replaced with each new incoming President.

Practically speaking, the PAD's tenure is usually shorter than the entire span of a four-year administration. Since the introduction of the position in the early 1970s, many areas have experienced a turnover of two or more PADs over any four-year term. PADs remain in OMB an average of eighteen months, but it is not unknown for a PAD to stay an entire four-year period, or into a second presidential term.

Below the division chief level in the hierarchical organization of OMB are twenty-five branch chiefs, each supervising several program examiners who review functionally related programs and agencies and/or programs falling under the same Cabinet-level department. In summer of 1997, there were 164 program examiners listed in the EOP telephone directory.[3] This number excludes a few economists, procurement analysts, and one or two lawyers who were integrated into the RMOs by virtue of the reorganization in 1994.

The program examiners are critical foot soldiers for the entire organization. They are, in general, responsible for review of a discrete agency-area or subject-matter assignment and do so on an individual basis rather than sharing responsibility with other examiners. Institutionally, this contributes to their accountability. Such individual responsibility, however, does not always result in examiners reviewing only one agency. Many budget examiners are responsible for review of several small independent agencies, while others review several programs within the same Cabinet-level departments, and still other examiners review a combination of one or more small independent agencies as well as parts of a Cabinet-level departmental budget.

In addition to the agency review assignments, examiners in several but not all branches receive functional subject-matter assignments that cut across agencies and departments. The general rule of discrete examiner assignments is also not without exception. In large departmental review areas requiring a high degree of coordination, examiners will sometimes work in team arrangements with other examiners.

Both the organizational structure and the internal decision-making process within OMB allow the program examiners to play an integral role in OMB's annual legislative and budgetary cycles. They are responsible for keeping abreast of all budgetary, legislative, and program issues involving their review areas. They offer verbal or written analysis of agency information and discuss how it relates to administration policy. They serve as frontline external information conduits between their assigned agencies and OMB. Thus the program examiners assume three major institutional roles: the information gathering role, the analysis role, and the information conduit and communicator roles. To add to that, examiners must be proficient as translators of broad presidential policies into specific programmatic applications in order to be able to explain presidential policies to the agencies and to be able to make the analysis and recommendations they offer the President useful in light of his agenda. Examiners are responsible for developing issues related to the "formulation" of the budget proposals for their account areas and the "execution" of appropriated funds to their assigned agencies once they are appropriated by Congress. The OMB examiner also plays important roles in clearing proposals for legislation before they are sent to Congress. To more of a varying degree, examiners also clear testimony of Executive Branch agency political appointees or career civil servants before it is delivered before congressional committees.

Examiners will occasionally receive short-term information requests from upper levels of OMB or the White House. This will occur most frequently in visible areas beset by press coverage or congressional activity. A certain portion of the examiner's time is spent in drafting responses to correspondence related to his or her functional review area. This correspondence comes from three primary sources: congressional committees, congressional constituent requests for information, and letters to the President or the White House that require more detailed replies connected with a specific agency budgetary matter. The magnitude of such demands is in part related to whether or not the White House and Congress are controlled by the same party. If they are, the volume of inquiries may increase, as occurred during the Carter administration and the first two years of the Clinton administration.

Finally, examiners are occasionally asked to participate in interagency task forces, study commissions, or presidential task forces or commissions, if it is felt that their institutional memory, knowledge, or insights would contribute to the deliberations. While OMB was not "institutionally" included in the deliberations of the Health Care Task Force, chaired by First Lady Hillary Rodham Clinton, there were a couple of OMB staffers with expertise in health-related programs who were detailed to work on the task force.

Much has been added to these core roles in recent years. Now RMO examiners, branch chiefs, and division chiefs to varying degrees also track the legislative, appropriations, and other budget processes in Congress that involve their account areas, and contribute to the preparation of aggregate and programmatic cost and economic projections more than they did twenty-five years ago. To accomplish these duties, they have had to develop personal contacts with congressional staff and members to a greater degree than in the past.

The promulgation of administrative managerial initiatives that have originated in the White House or the Congress is not new and has been a part of the BOB/OMB story since the 1940s. The degree of program division/RMO involvement in these endeavors varies widely. Moreover, since Presidents tend to look to BOB/OMB for help on matters that do not seem to fit elsewhere, examiners may often find themselves with ad hoc analytic and research tasks atop their other established duties. One recent example is staff support related to the Clinton White House's attempts to formulate proposals to address financial and management-related crises in the District of Columbia government.

OMB veteran Bernard Martin eloquently captured the complexity, subtlety, and significance of the program examiners' roles in a public administration and budgeting journal in 1995.

> One of the ways I think about it is like pointillism in French painting—a good budget examiner on a daily basis will be involved in a legislative clearance item, maybe something to do with a financial statement, a budget exercise in figuring out outlays. You do enough of that—you get involved in all levels of detail and all kinds of questions involving your program—and after a while, you really get to know the program inside out and backwards. If you are intelligent and you read—more than just internal OMB stuff—that constant immersion in the program really keeps you on top of it, so when a policy or program issue comes along, you can think it through.
>
> People may develop a great policy idea, but have no idea how to carry it through to the budget; for example, they have no idea that they are violating The Budget Enforcement Act. A good budget examiner can avoid that because he or she understands how the whole system works.[4]

With all of these roles, it is not surprising that the examiners and their career staff bosses have often been exceedingly influential role players in government although they have tended to experience different degrees of influence from one administration to the next. Their clout varies with the particular PAD they serve under, the stage of any four-year term, and the nature of the issues being considered.

The RMOs and program divisions have varied in their internal cultures, norms, and in some of the procedures they follow. The variation is driven by their dissimilar issues, the level of requisite expertise needed to understand these issues, their public visibility, their political and bureaucratic environments, and the nature of the relationships their assigned agencies have with the Congress and interest groups.

The Budget Review Division

Next to the Resource Management Offices, the single biggest OMB unit is the 70- to 75-person Budget Review Division (BRD), which encompasses two subdivisions, the Budget Analysis and Systems Division and the Budget Review and Concepts Division. These offices are responsible for coordinating the budget process for the entire Executive Branch and for compiling and assembling the budget proposals that the President submits to Congress.

BRD has long been an indispensable arm of OMB. With the creation of new budget requirements and procedures for both the Congress and the Executive Branch in the mid-1970s, BRD became increasingly engaged in preparing aggregate economic projections. When the deficit increased in the 1980s and executive-congressional relations became more contentious, and as interactions between Congress and OMB became more necessary, BRD became a central link between the two branches of government. Moreover, as Congress passed legislation designed to constrain the deficit and spending, BRD became OMB's lead civil service–level statutory interpreter, implementer, and arbiter with regard to these laws in those instances where Congress had left its intent open to interpretation.[5] Moreover, when the deficit continued to mount and the concern of many budget process participants on both sides of Pennsylvania Avenue focused more on aggregate deficit and economic projections and less on individual programs, BRD's influence within OMB, with Congress, and with the agencies grew, some say at the expense of the program divisions.

Thus, some observers believed that at times during the 1980s and early 1990s, BRD exercised a "gatekeeper" role with the examiners having to go to BRD "for validation." As the congressional budget process became increasingly complex, and the technical requirements for influencing that process turned highly technical and arcane, a handful of top-echelon career officials in BRD could be counted among the few budget process participants in Washington who best understood its technicalities and nuances. BRD's chief, an assistant director, is the highest ranking career official in OMB.

While BRD has substantial institutional clout, its significance should not be overstated. Like other parts of OMB's career echelons, it will only be as powerful as OMB's directors and PADs wish it to be, particularly if the directors are both technically and politically sophisticated. Moreover, OMB's programmatic institutional memory involving specific agencies throughout the government resides in the RMOs, not BRD.

A breakdown of the responsibilities and staff profiles of BRD's four component branches begins to convey the reach of its responsibilities. The Budget Analysis Division, which was known as the Fiscal Analysis Branch before the early nineties, is staffed by about twenty financial and fiscal economists and policy analysts. It produces aggregate economic and fiscal analysis and estimates that cross-cut individual programs and helps to project accurate economic assumptions which will in turn drive its deficit, economic, and budgetary forecasts. This unit, along with a politically directed OMB office called the Office of Economic Policy, is the central OMB participant in what has for years been an economic policy-making "troika" for the President which included OMB, the Treasury Department, and the Council of Economic Advisors. (During the Clinton administration, the National Economic Council was added and must now be considered a fourth key participant.) The Budget Analysis Branch is also a central participant in presidential interactions with Congress when economic and budget estimates of the Executive Branch and the Congress are under discussion. Since presidential-congressional budget agreements "seemed" to have often hinged upon economic forecasting differences between the two branches in recent years, the Budget Analysis Branch has become all the more significant. As part of its responsibilities, this unit also acts as an OMB liaison with the Congressional Budget Office (CBO) and the House and Senate Budget Committees.

BRD's Budget Review Branch, which is staffed by about eighteen "budget preparation specialists" has two main responsibilities: to coordinate preparation of the President's budget in final form before it is transmitted to Congress, and to track the appropriations process in Congress. As part of its responsibilities, it "monitors each stage of congressional action on appropriations" and prepares position papers to be used by OMB and EOP policy officials.[6] The Budget Concepts Branch prepares the budget process instructions and guidance that will determine the formats agencies must use when they submit their budget requests to OMB. It also reviews appropriations bills to make certain they are consistent with accounting and budgetary principles and statutory guidelines. It is staffed with fifteen budget methods specialists.

The Budget Systems Branch houses OMB's central computer system—the MAX System—and is staffed by about ten information management and computer specialists. The MAX System was introduced in 1994 when OMB's two previous central computer systems—the Budget Preparation System and the Central Budget Management System—were integrated into one system. It tracks agency budget formulation processes and budgetary activity on Capitol Hill through one system.

The Legislative Reference Division

LRD and Legislative Clearance

BOB/OMB has played three legislative roles for many years—the first responsibility, legislative clearance, involves the screening of agency initiated legislative proposals for compliance with presidential policies. The second role is to provide information and advice to the President concerning bills that have passed both houses of Congress during the ten-day period he has to act on these enrolled bills. In both cases, OMB's Legislative Reference Division (LRD) assumes central coordinative responsibilities. The level of LRD influence in a third area, formulation of the President's legislative initiatives, has varied over the years.

More "recently" acquired LRD roles include preparation of "Statements of Administration Policy" (SAPs)[7] on legislative bills scheduled for House or Senate action, and the responsibility to monitor agency preparation of commemorative proclamations. In addition, as OMB became more involved in tracking congressional activity during the 1980s, so too did LRD.

LRD was created in 1945 and has remained relatively small over the years. It is staffed by 10 to 20 legislative analysts,[8] who tend to hold master's degrees and law degrees.[9] This largely coordinative division is subdivided into three branches. These cover, first, labor, welfare, and personnel-related agencies; second, resources, defense, and international agencies; and third, economics, science, and general government-related agencies.

LRD has worked in tandem with the program division/RMOs for many years. Its role in legislative clearance today and in the recent past is primarily "coordinative," with the RMOs assuming the primary responsibility for the insertion of substantive programmatic intelligence into clearance decisions.

Any proposal for authorizing legislation that a department or agency drafts must be cleared by OMB before it may be submitted to Congress. In its review of the legislative proposals, OMB seeks guidance and comments from the governmental agencies affected by the proposals, as well as other parts of OMB and the EOP as appropriate. In those cases where a number of agencies are affected by a proposed bill, the coordination of sometimes conflicting agency positions and the designation of an administration position can be a challenging task. As OMB indicates in its training materials, "clearance can be completed in days or may take months, depending on the urgency, complexity, and importance of the proposal."[10] After OMB prepares comments on the legislative drafts, it takes the agencies from one to thirty days to resubmit their reactions.[11]

OMB also provides positions on legislative proposals that do not originate in the agencies. LRD, for example, will clear authorizing legislation drafted "to implement budgetary requirements written into law," as well as authorization bills drafted in congressional committees.[12] In the latter case congressional staff are usually "testing the waters" with respect to how a particular bill will conform to presidential policies. Legislative proposals requiring OMB approval can emanate from other sources such as the Cabinet Councils that were used during the Reagan administration.[13]

Agency testimony pertaining to legislation is also submitted to OMB for clearance and comments. This process is much less formal than is the clearance of legislative proposals for a number of reasons. First, in cases where testimony or agency reports involve "matters that are significant for the agency, but not for the government as a whole," the agencies do not necessarily have to change their positions to comply with those of OMB.[14] In many such cases, however, the OMB position must be transmitted to Congress along with the agency views.[15] Second, certain statutes governing some agencies either require that agency testimony not be prereviewed by OMB before submission to Congress or that "uncleared" reports or testimony indicate "that they do not necessarily reflect the Administration's views."[16] A final factor which necessitates that testimony clearance be less formal, is that the clearance process may be operating under severe time constraints.[17]

While legislative proposals or testimony enter and leave OMB through the Legislative Reference Division, in most cases the RMOs play a far more pivotal role in the central clearance process than does LRD. For many years, LRD's role has been a primarily coordinative one; it is the examiner who plays the key role.

The Legislative Clearance Process generally operates in the following way: The program examiner receives the draft proposal from the Legislative Reference Division, where it "formally" enters OMB, and either clears it, or makes remarks and changes on the draft copy and prepares an accompanying explanatory letter. The examiner then communicates these modifications to the pertinent agency personnel in meetings and/or phone conversations. After the examiner offers a clearance recommendation on the legislation, makes any changes, and checks with the supervisor if necessary, the proposal is returned to the Legislative Reference Division to be officially cleared. The agency receives formal notification of OMB's disposition of the proposal from the LRD, though in most cases the matter would already have been discussed by the examiner and the agency official. Assuming OMB approval, the agency will then transmit the proposal to Congress. Some higher priority legislation, however, will be sent to Congress from the White House. In these cases, OMB "forwards" a presidential transmittal message, and a "fact sheet suitable for issuance by the White House press secretary," along with the legislative proposal.[18]

Testimony involving congressional committee inquiries into Executive Branch activities but no particular legislative proposal is handled differently. The Legislative Reference Division is not required to sign off on the clearance of such testimony. It may have come through the LRD and be routed to the examiner or may come directly to the examiner. LRD may become involved if more than one agency has commented on the issue at hand or if the testimony is expected to lead to submission of a legislative proposal.

LRD and the Enrolled Bill Process

An enrolled bill is one that has been passed by both houses of Congress and awaits a presidential approval or disapproval within a ten-day period. OMB provides guidance to the President concerning the enrolled bill by preparing what are termed enrolled bill memoranda. These include veto or approval recommendations by all interested agencies, an OMB analysis and summary of significant issues involved, and an OMB recommendation to the President.

LRD receives the copies of the original parchment bill even before it is sent to the White House. It in turn sends copies to all Executive Branch agencies affected by the legislation as well as the pertinent program examiners, who offer their comments and opinions. LRD then compiles all of the views, prepares a file for the President, and formally recommends whether he should sign or veto. If the recommendation is to veto, a draft veto message must accompany the packet.

The budget examiner's involvement in the enrolled bill process is limited because of time constraints. Since the President has only ten days, excluding Sunday, to approve or disapprove legislation, OMB is usually given the first five days to prepare its enrolled bill memo. The Legislative Reference Division analyst regularly performs this function. Occasionally, when LRD has a flood of enrolled bills at one time, the examiner responsible for reviewing the program area at hand will be asked to assist in drafting the enrolled bill memo. Under normal circumstances, however, the drafting of enrolled bill memos is not to be considered one of the examiner's typical duties.

The Management Divisions

As of 1997, the OMB offices that were exclusively devoted to the promulgation of government-wide management improvement efforts were the Office of Federal Financial Management (OFFM) and the Office of Federal Procurement Policy (OFPP), but since the management divisions have long been highly susceptible to reorganizations and alterations in their functions, these structural designations might change at any time. A third division that has been considered part of OMB's management side since its creation in 1981 is the Office of Information and Regulatory Affairs (OIRA).

At this writing OFFM is staffed with about fifteen management and policy analysts who are responsible for "developing and coordinating government-wide financial management policies."[19] This office is about half the size it had been (forty-one authorized positions) before a 1994 OMB reorganization abolished one of its branches and moved some of its staff into the RMOs.[20] Several responsibilities, which had been delegated previously to OFFM, were also transferred to the RMOs during that reorganization.

OFPP was established by Congress in 1974 to provide leadership to the departments and agencies with respect to "procurement policies, regulations, procedures" and to "improve the quality and performance of procurement personnel."[21] It is now composed of about twenty professionals. Ten of its staffers were transferred to the RMOs as part of the aforementioned reorganization to be jointly managed by OFPP and the RMOs.[22]

The Office of Information and Regulatory Affairs (OIRA) was established in 1981 by the Paperwork Reduction Act of 1980 and will be discussed at length in Chapter 8. It is charged with oversight of "management of information resources and reduction of unnecessary paperwork," as well as analysis of regulatory proposals that have originated in the departments and agencies.[23]

The Legislative Affairs Office (LA)

OMB has a tiny legislative relations office consisting of about five professionals. Its staff almost completely consists of noncareer staffers with the exception of one individual who has served in several administrations and has preserved his civil service status. This career position has played a highly useful role in maintaining institutional memory with respect to congressional relationships and procedures from one administration to the next. The Legislative Affairs Office is headed by a politically selected associate director.

LA is concerned with structuring OMB-congressional relations with the House and Senate Appropriations Committees. This activity includes serving as a liaison between the appropriations committees and the White House staff, providing the director and other political appointees in OMB with analysis on the appropriations process, and assisting in OMB and White House negotiations with the Congress.[24]

The Economic Policy Office

The Economic Policy Office, which is structurally separate from BRD, also prepares economic modeling constructs that are used to determine the economic indicators and assumptions that OMB will use in arriving at its economic and fiscal forecasts. The Economic Policy Office is small, with seven or eight senior economists who are directed by a politically appointed OMB associate director. It stands rather high in OMB's pecking order with regard to decisions involving aggregate and cross-cutting economic projections.

Completing the Organization Chart: The Office of Administration, the Communications Office, and the Office of the General Counsel

OMB has an Office of Administration of about fifteen professionals to attend to internal OMB management matters, housekeeping, and personnel issues, and a General Counsel's Office of about five attorneys to offer legal guidance to OMB officials and staff as needed.

OMB's tiny Communications Office deals with press and public inquiries. This office has existed for a number of years under different monikers such as "External Affairs" or "Public Affairs." It provides an example of OMB's transition from a shielded and insular institutional staff arm for the President to an institution where directors play visible and public roles as spokespeople for the President, where associate directors often engage in partisan warfare on Capitol Hill and elsewhere, and where career staff can no longer prepare analysis in an ivory tower atmosphere devoid of political and ideological influences. Thus, an institution that once had no public image now has to take heed of its image both apart from the individual President it is serving at any given time and in examining how that image might affect the President's stature and budgetary policy choices.

The staff size and organizational proximity to the Director's Office varies somewhat. For example, in 1984 under David Stockman the unit was called Operations and Communications and housed twelve professionals, while from 1985 to 1989 its name was changed to Public Affairs and it was structurally located under the Director's Office.

OMB Officialdom and Staff

The Political Echelon

OMB's political-level officials and staff number approximately twenty to twenty-five "policy officials," as they are referred to inside OMB, and their noncareer adjunct support staff. This policy officialdom includes six positions requiring Senate confirmation. These are to date: the Director, the Deputy Director, the Deputy Director for Management, the Controller, and the administrators of both the Office of Information and Regulatory Affairs and the Office of Federal Procurement Policy. Prior to 1974, BOB/OMB directors and Deputy directors did not require Senate confirmation and the other positions listed above did not exist.

The "PAD" position was added in the early 1970s. These officials can potentially exercise significant influence over OMB decisions because of their strategic placement between the OMB Director and Deputy Director and OMB's central programmatic memory bank in the RMOs. For this reason, their existence has always been somewhat controversial among students of the institution and career staff within OMB. This debate will also be fully aired in later chapters.

Other noncareer officials include associate directors over the Offices of Economic Policy, Communications, Legislative Affairs, and Administration just discussed. The remainder of the noncareer staff in OMB are made up of support staff for the aforementioned officials, including a small number of "special assistants" or "senior advisors" to the director and the deputy director. These positions may be occupied by staff brought in by a new director or deputy director, but it is also not unknown for these positions to be held by former OMB career staff who have converted to noncareer status. The wisdom of maintaining this relatively sizable contingent of political appointees has been debated along much the same lines as has the existence of the PADs. The chief concern is that these noncareer layers of supervision will politicize the objectivity of advice reaching the director and the President.

OMB Career Staff: Their Profiles, Training, and Career Patterns

OMB's 1997 career staff numbered about 520, a size that had been relatively constant for the past seven years, plus or minus anywhere from ten to thirty employees. Most staff tend to hold graduate degrees in public policy, public administration, or MBAs. Some are generalists with highly honed analytical and writing skills or specialties in scientific or technical areas. OMB has a fair share of economists in BRD, its Economic Policy Office, and in the RMOs, and a number of lawyers in units such as OIRA or OFPP. The fact that accounting degrees and CPAs exist, but are not the most commonly found degrees, provides one illustration of how OMB is much more than a collective "green eye-shade" agency for the President.

Overwhelmingly, incoming staff are young and recruited from graduate schools. In fact, it is somewhat unusual for mid-career or senior civil servants from the departments and agencies to come to work at OMB, for reasons that will be discussed in Chapters 5 and 11. From most reports, OMB is currently able to attract the best and the brightest graduates from prestigious graduate programs. Former OMB directors attest to the high quality of the recruits. Alice Rivlin found the new staffers she interviewed to be a "remarkable group of young people." Former Director James Miller described OMB career staff as "the elite of the government's civilian corps," and found "competition for analyst and budget examiner positions at OMB" to be "fierce."

Career mobility in OMB has been characterized for some time by rather rapid turnover at the junior levels, averaging about a three-year tenure from the point of entry to the point of departure.

A not atypical career pattern in recent years has been for OMB to hire talented professionals in their late twenties or early thirties with the understanding that they will be required to work long hours and sometimes be subjected to intense pressures, but that their experience will serve them well in securing responsible positions in federal agencies, the private sector, and more and more in recent years on congressional staffs and committees. Coexisting with this quick turnover among junior staff is what has been, at least up to the present, an echelon of experienced branch and division chiefs with longer tenure and institutional memory. The downside to this longevity on the part of senior staff is the salary ceiling it creates for young staff, which may account for a part of the turnover rate.

Whether by circumstance or by design, there currently appears to be a glass ceiling for women in the managerial levels of the institution, with only six women serving as branch and division chiefs and forty-six men working in comparable positions. Gender representation is more even among program examiners, policy analysts, and budget technicians, with women serving in slightly fewer than half of all of such positions. This was apparently not always the case. One elderly retired career staffer recounted a story of how at some point before the 1970s, BOB employed virtually no women in professional positions and thus lagged behind other federal agencies in this regard. Purportedly, at that time an effort was launched to bring women professionals into the organization.

The demanding work schedules, coupled with the preponderance of young staffers, many of whom may have young children, might also in some cases explain the rapid turnover. OMB Director Alice Rivlin, in particular, attempted to make the institution more "family friendly" by promoting the use of flex time or alternative work schedules for parents of either gender. Given OMB's high-pressure atmosphere and external demands, it is unclear how much of this will be workable in the future.

With the exception.of a several-day central training session offered once a year for all new employees, OMB's professional personnel are trained and socialized on the job to OMB's institutional norms by their direct supervisors, and with somewhat of a sink-or-swim philosophy. There are some important reasons for this mode of training, not the least of which is that program review areas differ so widely and that time is generally limited due to the demands and pressures that surround OMB's responsibilities.

OMB Staff: The Cultural Climate, the Role Perceptions, and the Personality Profiles

One of the intangible qualities that OMB observer Hugh Heclo believed had made the BOB of yesteryear a unique institution was a distinctive esprit de corps that prevailed among its staff to a greater degree than might be found in other American governmental settings.[26] This was portrayed as a sense of genuine pride and teamwork in serving the missions of the institution among the staff and a willingness to be anonymous outside of BOB/OMB's enclaves. How well today's OMB culture lives up to this "institutional ethos" cannot be easily evaluated. The reality presents a variegated picture that closely approaches the ideal in some regards and misses the mark in others.

One sign that some of this esprit de corps still exists in OMB is an institutional ritual of recent vintage. For the last few years, OMB has annually celebrated "budget examiner's day," when OMB's political echelon attends a musical revue composed and performed by the career staff. The show either "roasts" or pokes fun at the directors and other political appointees or vents annoyance or sarcasm through satire and humor that cannot be aired outside the institution. OMB's staff units can also be quite analytically competitive with each other and do not always forge cohesive institutional teams easily. One external agency observer went so far as to characterize the RMOs and program divisions before them as driven by a "lone ranger" philosophy and culture. The up side to this "individualism" is that it fosters a climate that is supportive of spirited debate in which diametrically opposing views can be articulated.

If it were possible to provide a composite modality of the OMB staff as a whole, it would exhibit smart, knowledgeable workaholics who tend to resist politically motivated tinkering with the "facts" as they see them, but stand ready and anxious to serve the President through many avenues short of that. Most remain prepared to dispute what they believe to be ill-thought-through proposals wherever they come from, but to accept and implement contrary policy decisions gracefully when their advice is disregarded. It is a clearly perceived taboo among OMB career staff to leak information or to even speak with the press, unless directed to do so by OMB policy officials. There are few if any incentives and plenty of strong disincentives to impede career staff from breaking this code.

With other personality characteristics and institutional role perceptions, OMB staff vary more widely. The "nay-sayer" image of BOB/OMB staff has persisted since the creation of the institution in 1921. Certainly, BOB/OMB has always been in some part a bastion for fiscal constraint. As one long-time OMB official remarked, "there are many others in the White House and the agencies who can be cheerleaders for the programs." Moreover, as the deficit mushroomed from the early 1980s into the 1990s, many staff in OMB perceived their mission there to be as guardians of the taxpayer's dollar; many still feel that way. Thus, some at times seem to be uncomfortable when aspects of an administration's agenda in any way departs from "waste-busting" and "belt-tightening" into the development or design of new programs that might lead to more as opposed to less spending.

But, while the historically resilient BOB/OMB "nay-sayer" bias appears to be alive and well in OMB, it is neither uniform nor uninformed. This prevailing institutional "instinct" is balanced out by many accounts of career staff who assertively make the case for funding those programs they consider to be of critical public value and reflective of the President's policy agenda or that they believe will result in less public expenditure in the long run. Most staff also assume new roles, change their mindset, and produce excellent results when an administration requires them to do so.

Finally, there has been the image of "arrogance" in some OMB career staff. The relative youth of the staffers, coupled with their significant authority, has indeed proven to be an irritant to agency personnel for years. This view is illustrated by one long-time agency budget official who believed that, institutionally, OMB "wants OMB examiners to be arrogant, hard and directive," with the outcome being "some 29 year old kid going to a budget hearing and talking to a political appointee as if he knows it all." Not all OMB career staff elicit a perception of arrogance in the agency officials with whom they deal, and obviously such reactions also vary with the individual personality proclivities of the OMB staffers in question.

The OMB Director: "The Second Most Powerful Job in Government"

Presidents have characterized the OMB Director's position as one of the most difficult and significant jobs in government.[27] They are not alone in this assessment. Former Chair of the Senate Committee on Governmental Affairs Senator John Glenn tended to begin confirmation hearings for the OMB Director with a description of the appointment as "the second most powerful job in the Executive Branch of government."[28] Glenn sometimes followed up on this introduction with the assertion that he did not believe that he was overstating the budget director's significance at all.[29] Former President Gerald Ford also appeared to realize the importance of the job when it was included as one of the authorities he wished to control should he accept the vice presidential nomination as then candidate Ronald Reagan's running mate.[30]

What makes OMB Directors so critical and their mandates so challenging? The OMB Director stands at the helm of an exceedingly powerful institution with a multiplicity of mandates. Indeed, it is not hard to conclude that in recent years, the directorship has grown in responsibility to the point that it could be considered to encompass at least two separate roles. A description of each follows.

The "Traditional" Directorate and the "Modern" Directorate

For purposes of identification, these two different and often conflicting jobs will be termed the traditional and the modern directorates. In the first instance there are elements that have been part of the job since the Bureau of the Budget was created in 1921 that remain to the present. These are the responsibility to lead BOB/OMB in preparing the President's budget and in translating his policies into specifics. So, too, the BOB/OMB Director has been the institution's chief liaison with the President of the United States. As former OMB Director Alice Rivlin describes, "the Director must bridge the gap between the OMB and the White House."[31]

As head of BOB/OMB, the incumbent of this position has been most directly responsible for assuring that the President is provided with thorough and objective information and analysis that is also politically sophisticated but not slanted toward partisan considerations. To accomplish this, the director must assume a role as an intermediary, ensuring that both the OMB career staff and political-level staff are able to provide and communicate that advice to the President in digestible and useful dosages. Another job requirement for the "traditional director" is the ability to represent and to defend the President's policies and priorities with Cabinet officials and the departments and agencies. Alice Rivlin has said that she believes the OMB Director's job to be two jobs. She sees the "running of OMB internally as a job in and of itself." The other mandates she found quite consuming were facilitating communications between OMB and the White House and "interfacing with the Cabinet agencies."[32]

What qualities does an individual need to have in order to succeed in the traditional role? Certainly, with all of this "bridge building" between different organizations, the director is helped by being a communicator par excellence, with all of the necessary personality characteristics that go with that. Even in years past, the individual also had to have a fundamental understanding of the political realities involved in governing. Today, competence, communications facility, integrity, and loyalty[33] appear to be necessary but not sufficient qualities for a budget director to possess, if OMB's institutional advice is to be used and taken seriously by Presidents. The "modern" director's job includes two other substantial demands that sometimes also conflict with the requirements of the traditional roles, particularly during a deficit era. They are, first, that directors be the President's very public and visible representatives, and second, that they act as strategists and negotiators on behalf of the President when he interacts with Congress on budgetary matters, which these days is practically all the time.

Out of the Protective Cover of the Ivory Tower

Scholar Frederick C. Mosher wrote in 1984 that "the relative anonymity of the BOB/OMB outside the government itself was, until recently, matched by the low public profile of its leadership—its directors and deputy directors."[34] That had already been changing when David Stockman's directorate ushered in a new era of public visibility for OMB Directors and "such anonymity and political immunity as had once shielded OMB and its leaders from the public spotlight had disappeared."[35]

Today, OMB Directors are expected as a matter of course to appear on evening and weekly news interview programs as advocates of administration policies and are called on to debate these policies with congressional opponents of the President. They may even find themselves arguing positions that they only recently argued against within the administration.

Depending upon personality and inclinations, OMB Directors today can become public figures almost apart from the Presidents they serve, a reality that creates more than a few problems for both the President and the director, as well as the long-term interests of the presidency. David Stockman first and best personified this evolution of the director's role, but it did not stop with him. Richard Darman had a reputation as an exceedingly powerful budget director, particularly in the arena of domestic policy making.[36] Darman, though he gave public speeches very rarely, did on one occasion offer his centrist visions for a broad national policy-making agenda in an address to the national press club entitled, "Beyond the Deficit Problem: 'Now-Nowism' and the New Balance." When the Bush administration showed little support for Darman's public ruminations, he, in his own words, "abandoned cultural commentary for awhile."[37]

OMB Directors must now operate as both consummate strategists and/or consensus builders with Congress on budgetary and other matters all year round. That is true for many other professionals within OMB as well and has been since the early 1970s, when BOB Directors testified on behalf of the President's budget after its transmission to Congress and then returned to the job of formulating the next budget and advising the President. The selling and negotiating of the President's budget package in those days was largely left to other Executive Branch participants. All that has changed. Today, in-depth substantive and procedural knowledge of the Congress and a number of broad-based contacts among congressional leaders and rank-and-file members are now important job qualifications sought by Presidents when they are "hiring" OMB Directors. The issue of whether OMB, its directors, and its staff can handle both their traditional and modern roles effectively will be discussed at various points throughout the remainder of this book.

3

The Bureau's First Sixty Years: Ancient History or Not?

The President Becomes "Budgeteer-in-Chief"

This institutional history of the Office of Management and Budget (OMB) and its predecessor the Bureau of the Budget (BOB) begins and ends with deficit eras. In fact, BOB might never have been created in the first place, if not for a surge of public pressure to eliminate several years of deficits during the first decade of the twentieth century.[1] At the time, agency budget requests were mechanically siphoned through the Treasury Department before being submitted to Congress. With several notable exceptions,[2] few Presidents before Taft had involved themselves to any degree in reviewing this budget package, since no statute required that they do so.

With no laws mandating that the President take actions to stem the tide of rising costs of government services, and no permanent office in either the Congress or the Executive Branch to appraise broad budgetary issues with any analytical sophistication, the task was left to congressional appropriations committee members. The public, in turn, perceived that these representatives tended to favor their own constituencies to a disproportionate degree in the budget decisions they reached.[3] Mosher writes that the "public budget movement" that was spurred to action by this set of circumstances espoused the view that rationality, accountability, comprehensiveness, and accuracy of information be introduced into the budget process that existed at the time.[4]

President Taft's steps to respond to this outcry, including the appointment of a Commission on Economy and Efficiency, in 1910, did not culminate in congressional enactment of the commission's recommended reforms.[5] It was to take the nation's involvement in World War I and its resulting postwar deficits to reinvigorate public and congressional interest in pursuing budgetary reform.[6]

While Congress usually does not relish the delegation of its prerogatives to the President, in the face of mounting public pressure, many congressional members began advancing toward acceptance of the position that the President be given the responsibility to prepare a comprehensive federal budget for submission to Congress. Both the House and Senate proposals to design this new system included the notion that a staff office was required to support the President in his newly conceived role as budgeteer-in-chief.[7] A disparity between a House plan, which envisioned that this unit be housed directly in the President's office, and a Senate bill, which located it in the Treasury Department, was settled by a compromise in which the new Bureau of the Budget was placed in the Treasury Department but was to be headed by a director and assistant director appointed by the President but not subject to congressional confirmation.[8]

While the bureau was to be "directly responsible to the President,"[9] its placement in the Treasury Department would presumably make it somewhat more subject to congressional oversight than if it had been housed in the President's office.

The Budget Bureau 1921–1932: The Beginning of a Tradition

Many of BOB's core budgetary roles were set forth in its enabling legislation, the Budget and Accounting Act of 1921. For example, that law had emphasized that BOB would not only compile and submit budgetary requests of departments and agencies, but would be authorized to reduce or increase them.[10] The act had also established the foundation for BOB/OMB's management role by authorizing BOB to conduct administrative studies in the executive bureaucracy.[11] The precedent for OMB's legislative clearance role was set through a presidential directive in 1921. It required that agency proposals to Congress that "might later affect appropriations," be transmitted to the Budget Director, who would in turn make recommendations to the President as to whether the proposal should be approved.[12]

While BOB's basic authorities originated in statute, the role orientations of the individuals first implementing them began to create the roots of a BOB "culture." BOB's first director, Charles G. Dawes, played a pivotal role in shaping BOB's early persona and institutional identity during the first year of the new institution's existence. Moreover, Dawes's conceptions of "how" BOB should exercise its congressionally mandated roles would set enduring precedents for some of BOB/OMB's institutional behavior patterns that were to recur repeatedly in the years to come.

First and foremost, Dawes promoted the notion that BOB's fundamental raison d'être extended beyond the reduction of expenses and budgets to the promulgation of "impartial, impersonal, and non-political"[13] advice to the President and Congress. Mosher notes that Dawes's background as a military professional drew many of BOB's first staff members from that arena and set a tone of military-style dedication to mission during BOB's first year of operation.[14] From these emphases on impartiality and esprit de corps would grow the more variegated concept of "neutral competence" that would become BOB's much vaunted emblem in the future.

As a trusted advisor to President Harding, Dawes set a firm precedent for future Budget Directors to assume positions of similar stature. One indication that the President supported the conception of a strong budget director was his willingness to support the notion that a BOB Director had the authority to be quite directive toward Cabinet officials. This included the director's right to "convene two or more cabinet members on his own initiative in the Cabinet room."[15] This would prove to be a comforting model for future BOB Directors engaged in the power struggles with Cabinet members that would follow in later years.

Ironically, at the same time that Dawes was acting to establish a firm foundation for an influential BOB, he assumed the almost servile public stance that BOB's role was to be entirely restricted to administrative matters that were characterized as being completely divorced from policy making.[16] This supposition disguised the reality, even then, that BOB was too centrally placed at the vortex of critical governmental activities to avoid exerting an influence on the shaping of policies.[17]

Dawes's stated restrictive focus did prove to limit the institution's scope of activities, particularly with his two successors. Director Herbert M. Lord (1922–1929) and Director J. Clawson Roop (1929–1933) appeared to draw from Dawes's pronouncements against waste and extravagance, as opposed to his statements promoting BOB's broader advisory role for the President. Larry Berman reports extreme and almost comical manifestations of this tendency in Director Lord, who had been taken to checking "employees' desks for excessive use of official stationary, paper clips and other government supplies." Lord had also instituted a " 'Two Percent Club' for agency heads who trimmed that amount off their estimates" ... and the "Loyal Order of Woodpeckers," whose "persistent tapping away at waste will make cheerful music in government offices and work shops the coming year."[18]

These somewhat amusing accounts of early BOB parsimony represented the beginning of the BOB/OMB "nay-sayer" orientation that was to surface during later administrations alternatively supporting or conflicting with the aims of the administrations at the time. The position that BOB had to set an example of economy in its own organizational activities and thus "take its own medicine," was also an outgrowth of this orientation. In its early years from 1921 to 1939, this limited BOB's size to only forty-five staff members and to a relatively simple organizational structure.[19]

BOB's potential to exercise an administrative management role remained dormant for the bureau's first twenty years. President Harding and Director Dawes had also set this precedent. Mosher reports that they had found competing units in both the Executive Branch and Congress, with mandates that overlapped BOB's statutory role to conduct administrative studies, and had agreed to exclude BOB from participating in these activities.[20]

BOB's Benchmark Years: 1932–1952

Introduction

When presidency and public management scholars nostalgically hearken back to a time when BOB reflected a set of ideals now considered at least partially lost, they are in large part focusing on a twelve-year period in that institution from 1939 to 1952. It was during these years that a number of historical circumstances converged that allowed BOB to experience an era marked by swift and pronounced growth, outstanding productivity, and an almost idyllic institutional esprit de corps. It was also during this period that BOB's often touted "ethos" of neutral competence had the opportunity to develop and mature.

The institutional transformations that ushered in this "golden era" in BOB might never have materialized if not for several preconditions. These included a President who assiduously sought straightforward information wherever he could find it, a government reorganization commission with the foresight to grasp BOB's potential to strengthen the presidency, and profound demands on the presidency generated by a rapidly expanding federal government and later a world war. To these circumstances should be added the lack of any competing presidential advisory units to use as springboards for the "help" the President now needed to manage his burgeoning responsibilities. With these elements in place, a "visionary" BOB Director serving a seven-year term under both Franklin D. Roosevelt and Harry Truman, was able to successfully consolidate this evolutionary process.

A Slow Beginning, Brownlow's Revolution, and a BOB Takeoff

Most of these momentous changes did not take hold immediately with the beginning of FDR's presidency, and for the first few years of his administration, BOB operated generally as it had since the 1920s. Some part of this might have been due to the fact that FDR's first budget director, a fiscal conservative, had resigned in 1934 after a difficult period during which the President had found the director to be philosophically opposed to his own thinking. Berman reports that this had led to FDR's decision to "circumvent" BOB in many matters and to appoint career civil servant Daniel Bell as acting director. (Bell would serve until 1939.)[21]

From 1933 to 1938, new mandates were created for BOB and some of its roles that had been dormant or restricted to the service of "economy" were redirected and broadened. In 1933, through Executive Order, FDR conferred the power on BOB to supervise and modify the apportionment of agency appropriations.[22] Between 1934 and 1936 BOB's legislative clearance function was expanded to include all legislative proposals and appropriations.[23] Of equal significance was the establishment of BOB's enrolled bill process in 1938.[24]

With a rapidly expanding federal government to administer and little direct staff assistance, Roosevelt appointed a Committee on Administrative Management headed by Louis Brownlow to provide recommendations to the President on meeting these spiraling demands. It was the Brownlow Committee Report in 1937 that ultimately spearheaded BOB's rapid development. With no comparable institutional base from which to build an advisory support system for the President, the Brownlow Report argued for BOB's enlargement in scope and size to fit the modern-day demands on the presidency. BOB was deemed by the Committee to have failed to live up to its potential due to its lack of adequate staffing and organization, its placement in the Treasury Department as disconnected from the President, and the narrow view of BOB's mission that had been adapted by its past directors.[25]

The Brownlow Committee's vision for the BOB of the future was not exclusively as a guardian of "economy" but as a repository of objective information and institutional memory for the "presidency." The broadened spectrum of BOB tasks recommended by the committee included "fiscal policy and planning, execution, as well as preparation of the budget, administrative research, information services, coordination of field activities, assistance to the departments and agencies with their internal organization and management, and clearance of proposed legislation, testimony, reports and presidential directives."[26] These functions would become BOB's core roles when two years later the Brownlow recommendations were finally codified into law and the reconstituted Bureau of the Budget was transferred to the newly created Executive Office of the President (EOP).

As driven by the Brownlow recommendations, BOB's metamorphosis included the addition of a number of "new" roles, a changed organizational structure, a staff that would grow over tenfold, and a sustained personnel recruitment effort. Most significant among BOB's recently advanced roles at the time was the green light for BOB to pursue its administrative management role, but BOB's legislative clearance and enrolled bill processes would also prove to enhance BOB's service to the presidency for years to come.

The organizational arrangements[27] devised to house these functions can be considered to be the foundation for OMB's modern organizational structure. The Estimates Division, which reviewed agency budgets and was organized on an agency-by-agency basis, was the largest unit and can be considered an early predecessor to today's RMOs. The Fiscal Division, which was the forerunner to BRD, advised the Estimates Division on matters related to micro- and macroeconomic policy making. The Legislative Reference Division was the central unit responsible for legislative clearance as it is today. The new Division of Administrative Management was of considerable significance, in that it was destined to set a benchmark standard for excellence that none of the BOB/OMB management units to follow in future years would equal. A fifth division was designed to assist the agencies with respect to statistical analysis.

In order to shoulder new roles in a more evolved institution, both a larger and more diverse staff was needed. Both the Mosher and Berman accounts accord much credit for assembling and holding exceedingly high-quality BOB employees to the wisdom and foresight of Harold Smith, FDR's third BOB Director. Smith had built on what the Brownlow Commission and President Roosevelt had already started in 1937 when they managed to convince Congress to increase BOB's funding and size. BOB enlarged to over 600 staff persons by the end of Smith's tenure as director. The meticulous care he took in recruiting and socializing BOB staff would prove to be a critical element in making BOB the unique agency it became in the 1940s and 1950s.

Larry Berman's descriptions of Smith's organizing principles on personnel matters, as derived from his diaries, shed much light on how the man thought and why he was so successful. Smith was described as valuing "quality" above "quantity" in recruitment, often leaving staff slots vacant for months before finding the "right person" for the job.[28] His desired qualities in the staff he chose included "balanced outlook and judgment concerning governmental problems," "planning types of minds," and social science skills.[29] He particularly sought persons "who valued the good of the organization over their personal goals."[30] According to Berman's account,

Smith also attended to the institutional socialization of his recruits by continually stressing their service to the presidency as an "institutional career staff, distinct from personal White House aides" and not as merely a "'budget' staff."[31, 32] Since many of these original staff members remained in BOB for years thereafter, these norms became institutionalized and provided a firm organizational reservoir for excellence and a sense of purpose for years to come.

Both the Berman and Mosher books' portrayals of Harold Smith fit well as a "quintessential" model for what has been labeled the "traditional director" in Chapter 2. Even though he was a registered Republican at the beginning of his term as Budget Director,[33] Smith was able to win the trust and confidence of FDR. Smith's early role model is one instance in which the principle of neutral competence and the mission of service to Presidents and the presidency alike superseded personal political leanings.

How did Smith define both his role as Budget Director and BOB's mission for the presidency? In Berman's analysis of Smith's views, both roles, if properly exercised, presupposed a sophisticated understanding of the difference between a President's need for personal, politically oriented advice and the kind of objective institutionalized support only BOB could offer. Berman wrote, "the future tendency of Presidents and Directors to blur or ignore this distinction . . . created role dilemmas for the BOB and deprived the President of a desperately needed perspective. Harold Smith understood what some of his successors did not—that the political interests of the President and the long-term interests of the presidency as an institution are not the same."[34]

From Smith's own thoughts as recorded in his diaries, Berman distilled a number of ways in which the newly envisioned BOB would be able to help the President. These were to provide objective, knowledgeable assessments of agency budgets and legislative initiatives, and to review the President's own ideas as well as those proposals that originated with other presidential advisors.[35] Both of these mandates provided the checking and balancing of the information sources that FDR required. Smith also viewed it to be incumbent upon the budget director to attend to the long-term institutional well-being of BOB, and to educate the President on BOB's appropriate roles.[36]

The War and the Truman Years

With the outbreak of World War II, BOB and its Division of Administrative Management in particular were to find its staff and resources diverted into support of the President's war efforts. Berman noted that "between 1940 and 1943 the Budget Bureau constituted the sole staff support for the President in managing the defense and, later, the war effort," with commensurate staff increases in the Division of Administrative Management, which had climbed to seventy-seven employees in 1942,[37] and to over 100 employees by the end of the war.[38] Mosher's historical account opines that the Division of Administrative Management may have had "the finest staff of management analysts ever assembled."[39]

With President Roosevelt's death, the transition to the Truman administration was to elicit certain patterns of presidential response to BOB that would repeat themselves in later administrations. While President Truman was not at all hostile to BOB's institutional presence, Berman describes how he initially entered office convinced that he would use his Cabinet as a more significant advisory source than had FDR,[40] and how he viewed BOB's chief utility to be in budget making as opposed to policy making.[41] Both orientations were to markedly change when Truman began observing some of his Cabinet members delivering advice he considered to be more in keeping with departmental interests than with his own.

Thus, President Truman subsequently concluded that he needed competing sources of advice. Berman quotes Truman as remarking to Budget Director Smith, when comparing him favorably to certain Cabinet officials, "You have been interested in doing a job. That's the difference."[42] Berman also recounts that Budget Director "Smith informed Truman that the President was not getting maximum production from BOB staff because practically no one in the White House understood Bureau responsibilities."[43] This lack of sophisticated understanding of BOB/OMB's role of service to the President among White House staffers at the beginning of new administrations would also recur in many succeeding presidencies.

James Webb, Truman's first Budget Director, broke new ground in a number of respects, even while extending many of the institutional norms and role orientations set in place during Harold Smith's tenure. Innovations or role shifts in BOB/OMB often come as a result of specific presidential predilections or new external demands on the President. In this case, the still relatively small White House staff needed help in developing a number of legislative initiatives such as the Employment Act of 1946, the Social Security Amendments of 1950, and the Housing Act of 1949. Soon learning to appreciate BOB career staff capabilities, the White House looked to BOB for support.[44]

Director Webb and BOB staff responded with enthusiasm, showing an institutional flexibility in their ability to transform the "nay-sayer" roles assumed by BOB's legislative clearance staff previously, into more "positive" program development roles.[45] Moreover, Webb moved BOB career staff into personal interactions with White House staff, a practice that his predecessor Smith had eschewed.[46] Many of these staffers were to impress those in the White House to the point that BOB eventually was to lose them to full-time positions there.[47]

With a Democratic President and a Republican Congress in 1947, the Legislative Reference Division (LRD) was also called upon to perform the additional task of providing the administration's positions on proposed legislation to congressional committees.[48] This expanded the scope of LRD's reach into a congressional liaison function that facilitated communications between the two branches of government as well as the opposition political parties. In addition, Truman used LRD head Roger Jones, who was a registered Republican, to serve as a liaison with the 80th Congress to establish an "institutional relationship with an opposition Congress."[49] Berman cites from Jones's oral history a description of the nature of this BOB liaison role, showing it as one that could be safely played by career staff. Jones had explained, "We were expositors, explanatory people. We were not peddlers of doctrine."[50]

By the end of the 1940s, BOB was beginning to exhibit strains from the weight of its new burdens and to experience external and internal criticism for its inability to fully shoulder its increasing responsibilities. The well-regarded Office of Administrative Management had received its share of criticism, particularly after the war. A task force on budgeting of the Hoover Commission on Administrative Management had criticized it for failing to communicate and coordinate with the Estimates Division, and recommended merging the two divisions.[51] The final Hoover Commission Report's recommendations fell short of merger, but did propose including management personnel in all stages of the budget review process.[52]

Related problems were articulated and solutions proposed in a series of three internal BOB self-studies in 1947, 1948, and 1951, and also through the Hoover Commission Report.[53] The 1948 self-study sought to find ways to integrate BOB's management and budget functions (as did the Hoover Commission's Report), and to "provide opportunities for changing habit patterns and installing new points of view" in staff.[54] This study also recommended a separate Office of Program Review to respond to the President's need for staff work related to his broad programmatic goals.[55]

In 1952, BOB was reorganized in response to these critiques by merging staff into five functional divisions organized along agency lines. These were the Commerce and Finance, International, Labor and Welfare, Military, and Resources and Civil Works Divisions. The Office of Administrative Management was replaced by a much smaller Management and Organization Division. The Fiscal Division, which had been staffed by economists, became the Office of Budget Review. LRD and the Statistical Standards unit remained generally intact.[56]

According to Mosher, the architects of the 1952 reorganization hoped to integrate the personnel expertise necessary to address the different functional problem areas that tended to beset particular agencies. This reshuffling was also intended to facilitate communications between BOB and the agencies and to prevent duplication of work activities across BOB. The grouping of related agency review areas (i.e., Welfare and Labor) under one divisional umbrella and one division chief was also meant to provide the capability to analyze issue areas that cross-cut individual programs. The hope was also that personnel with experience in the administrative management and fiscal analysis areas could nourish the process by expanding the budget examiners' knowledge, while the examiners in turn could share their programmatic knowledge. Workload considerations were also at issue. Since the budget examiners' work was "seasonal," it was intended that their services be used for additional projects at times when their budget-related responsibilities dwindled. Finally, the relatively small Office of Management and Organization was to be used to address government-wide administrative management issues.[57]

This reorganizational design seemed well suited to addressing BOB's new institutional demands at the time and it established a rough blueprint for OMB's organizational structure today. In later years, some observers were to believe that this kind of institutional structure, in which budget and management functions were merged, had ensured the preeminence of BOB/OMB's agency-based budgetary functions over its broader potential to be a government-wide manager and long-term planner.

BOB in the 1950s and 1960s: Two Contrasting Case Studies

Introduction

Selected synopses of developments in the Bureau of the Budget during the Eisenhower and the Johnson years are presented together to compare BOB's responses to presidencies with starkly contrasting sets of orientations and demands. In the Eisenhower case, fiscal discipline constituted a prevailing presidential objective, while LBJ's central domestic objectives revolved around the development and enactment of new government programs to address societal inequities existing at the time.

The Eisenhower Years: BOB Doing What It Does Best

A review of both the 1950s and the 1960s shows that it is probably less of an institutional strain for BOB/OMB to serve economy-minded presidencies than it is to serve activist presidencies devoted to program development and formulation. Clearly, BOB career staff had an easier time serving President Eisenhower as an institutional staff responsible for advising him how government could run for less money. Through its established legislative clearance routines, BOB was also able to generate ideas for the President's legislative programs as they "bubbled up" from the agencies.[58] In both instances BOB was able to deliver services required by the President and in neither task did it overload the institution's capabilities.

But the Eisenhower administration also provides examples of potential hazards that may surface during nonactivist economy-minded presidencies. One such hazard is the tendency for budget directors and Presidents to feel compelled to "take their own medicine" in the sense of subjecting BOB/OMB to the same fiscal constraints they are promulgating in the agencies. The resulting staff and funding reductions create the risk of limiting BOB/OMB's capabilities for future administrations with different goals. This is precisely what would happen in the Eisenhower administration. Larry Berman recounts how Eisenhower's first Budget Director Joseph M. Dodge reduced appropriations requests for BOB and eliminated four of its field offices even as a key appropriations committee member counseled him otherwise.[59] A second potential inclination is for an unimaginative "nay-sayer" orientation to become entrenched in BOB/OMB,[60] thus leaving it ill prepared to serve future activist administrations. Berman reports examples of political appointees during the Johnson administration who found BOB's view to be "not creative" and "just analytical of the agencies." One political appointee had complained that, "this adding more and more programs just sort of strikes them as wrong."[61]

Some of this orientation might well have been inculcated in BOB staff during the Eisenhower years. Even so, such "nay-sayer" roles should not be viewed as monolithic for all BOB staff at any time. Aaron Wildavsky, in his seminal work, *The Politics of the Budgetary Process,* confirms a prevailing institutional philosophy of budgetary constraint in the BOB of the 1950s and early 1960s, but acknowledges that there would always be "some people in the Budget Bureau who identify more closely with an agency or program than did others," or who have a "creative urge" and "see themselves as doing the right thing by pursuing policies in the public interest."[62] Therefore, overall institutional staff orientations were more variant and complex than is suggested by descriptions such as "negative" and "nay-sayer."

In the Eisenhower case the intervening variable of the quality of the Budget Director also influenced the "state of the institution" by the end of the 1950s. While two of Eisenhower's Budget Directors, Joseph M. Dodge (1953–1954) and Maurice H. Stans (1958–1961) were highly regarded, Berman quotes a "senior official" as characterizing the intervening terms of Rowland R. Hughes (1954–1956) and Percival F. Brundage (1956–1958) as "four awful years."[63] Hughes purportedly neither trusted nor communicated with BOB career staff.[64] Brundage did attempt to promote BOB's interests, but had been purportedly overpowered by White House Chief of Staff Sherman Adams and Treasury Secretary George Humphrey.[65] Generally, while BOB was able to serve President Eisenhower's limited mission, this four-year period probably also did much to contribute to the erosion of staff creativity during the 1950s.

The Whipping Boy Syndrome I: BOB and Program Formulation

Introduction

The case of the Johnson administration presents an entirely different model of presidential demands and BOB responses, in some respects similar to institutional patterns observed during the Truman administration. Berman reports LBJ to have been extremely impressed with the high quality of BOB's assistance to him during his transition and in particular its help in reducing the 1965 agency budget requests in order to free funds for a planned tax cut.[66] While this was a task that BOB was quite comfortable with, results flowing from the President's "admiration" were to break new ground for BOB in the sense of producing new roles. This process began with the recruitment of BOB staff into the effort to formulate Great Society Programs through service on LBJ's numerous task forces and through ad hoc assignments from various units in the White House. The haste with which the Task Force policy development process was conducted and the magnitude of policy initiatives being introduced, with time, overloaded BOB's analytic routines almost to the breaking point. And, of course, one of BOB's central dilemmas would apply: It could not reject the demands of its chief patron.

The LBJ Task Force Treadmill

The Johnson Task Forces,[67] which were comprised of both federal agency officials and outside participants such as university research units, were used to generate specific legislative proposals and programmatic initiatives. They were ordered around a schedule that culminated in the production of proposals for each legislative year.

The schedule began in the spring with requests for ideas from the departments and agencies, continued with visits to universities and the private sector, and culminated in the production of "Program Development Books" containing the proposals for new programs. A presidentially appointed Task Force would then review the books and formulate final recommendations.

BOB staff entered the Task Force process at practically every stage.[68] The BOB Director and LRD chief were part of the group reviewing the program development books in the summer. When the actual Task Force was created, a BOB staff member would usually serve on it. After the Task Force Reports were issued they would be sent to the Legislative Reference Division as well as the relevant program divisions for comment. Factors to be assessed by BOB included impact and cost projections of how the proposals would affect the next budget and how each recommendation as a whole related to the affected agency's budget.

This BOB involvement overloaded its staff capability since the time afforded to the Legislative Reference Division and the Program Divisions to make comment was insufficient for staff to thoroughly analyze the proposals.[69] Some BOB staff found that there was inadequate guidance on how to project or measure program costs. To add to these problems, the removal of BOB staff to serve on the Task Forces in liaison and executive secretarial roles diverted the institution's talent and energy away from its established jobs.

As BOB's "systems" thus became overloaded, White House "admiration" turned to dissatisfaction with BOB as political officials started characterizing it as unresponsive and too slow to meet the President's needs. As cited in the previous section, political appointees charged that BOB staff lacked creativity and a sense of perspective. Some were believed to have harbored fundamental antipathy to spending increases needed to implement new programs.[70] While these deficiencies in part may have been rooted in the entrenched attitudes BOB staffers had developed during the Eisenhower administration, the unrealistic demands that had been placed on BOB during LBJ's administration also partially explains these institutional weaknesses.

As BOB appeared to be unable to keep up with the demands, the policy development process became more top-down, often emanating from Joseph Califano's Domestic Affairs staff.[71] This contrasted with the policy-making processes that prevailed during the first two years of the Johnson administration when BOB advice "bubbled up." With this came concerns that White House Domestic Policy Offices were circumventing the BOB director's authority by seeking information directly from the budget examiners.[72]

The Whipping Boy Syndrome II: BOB's Executive Branch and Intergovernmental Management Roles

Introduction

Neither the Eisenhower administration nor the Kennedy and Johnson presidencies had been strongly committed to investing their energies in governmental management endeavors.[73] Yet in both cases BOB was to receive criticisms from outside governmental study commissions for failing to adequately address federal bureaucratic or intergovernmental management problems to a sufficient degree.[74] Such criticisms and certain of the recommendations that would be offered for their resolution were to become familiar refrains in administrations to follow. Some part of these debates usually revolved around the question of whether BOB/OMB's management and budget roles should be merged or integrated or whether BOB/OMB should have a management role at all. These debates often did not adequately take into account the significant role the President plays in the success or failure of government-wide management prescriptions and the fact that Presidents have tended not to consider bureaucratic management a top-priority concern at all, or have abandoned it as more "pressing" problems arise in their administrations.

Further complicating this cycle was the propensity for Cabinet officials or members of Congress who considered themselves once aggrieved by OMB's meddling to retaliate against BOB/OMB by joining in these denunciations of its "institutional" failure in the management area.

In the Eisenhower administration the criticisms came in 1956 for BOB's failure to attend to administrative management problems in a growing federal bureaucracy. Their source was the President's Advisory Committee on Government Organization (PACGO), chaired by Nelson Rockefeller, which recommended that a new office of administration be established in the EOP encompassing all of BOB's managerial responsibilities.[75] Later a compromise proposal was put forth that recommended the establishment of an Assistant to the President for Management.

The PACGO–BOB "relationship" presents an early example of the cycle just described. Rockefeller, who was described by Mosher as having been "very critical of the bureau's management work,"[76] may have had some motivation to institutionally limit BOB's "management" authority over the agencies after having served as undersecretary of Health, Education and Welfare (HEW). One can speculate looking back in time as to whether or not the PACGO recommendations and Rockefeller's views had been driven by the desire to make proposals that would better serve the presidency or whether they may have been somewhat colored by Rockefeller's personal frustration with BOB-directed budgetary constraints on HEW. BOB's action with respect to HEW may have reflected President Eisenhower's orientation of "fiscal constraint," but at the expense of programmatic improvements Rockefeller wanted to make.

Whipping Boy Fights Back

Before leaving the PACGO story, it is instructive to note another example of a behavioral "response cycle" in BOB that was destined to recur in the future. When BOB/OMB has perceived a threat to its institutional influence, whether genuine or exaggerated, it has at times taken actions designed to preserve its authoritative institutional posture. Such actions may originate with the Budget Director, career officials, or both. Consider the Eisenhower case, which provides an early example of both this institutional resistance and resilience. Director Brundage had been able to successfully halt the creation of the PACGO-recommended EOP Office of Administration, or White House Assistant for Management. Both of these were viewed by BOB as undermining its authority because they would interpose a staff layer between BOB and the President.[77] According to the Berman account, even when new Budget Director Maurice Stans had agreed on a compromise option with PACGO that BOB would be reorganized and renamed the Office of Executive Management, there had been vehement resistance offered by BOB Assistant Director William Finan. When Assistant Director Finan was "directed" to draft a plan for this reorganization, his product purportedly did not reflect the plan Stans and PACGO had agreed upon.[78] Berman reported that the staff director of PACGO believed at the time that "the Budget Bureau staff was trying to sabotage the reorganization plan" and that PACGO had been "out maneuvered by the budget staff."[79] Mosher writes that "the impression prevailed among PACGO's staff that the bureau's staff was negative, obstructive, and anxious to preserve its status."[80] In the end, Eisenhower sided with "BOB" and refrained from moving toward a major BOB reorganization. Immediately thereafter, Stans undertook a BOB self-study, which Mosher characterizes "partly as a defense against PACGO proposals."[81]

The Management and Implementation of Good Intentions:
BOB Tries to Manage the Great Society

In the mid to late 1960s, as the Great Society Programs went from the "drawing board" to implementation, inevitable difficulties arose in attempting to assure their effective management and delivery to the public. Many of the programs had been underfunded due to the "disconnect" between the budgetary and legislative processes during their development and design phases. The administrative management of these programs was further complicated due to the fact that many of them required more interdepartmental coordination and/or linkage between federal agencies and state and local governmental units than did existing programs.

This reality generated the establishment of two study groups commissioned to attempt to determine how Great Society Programs could best be managed. They were the Bailey Task Force on Intergovernmental Program Coordination in 1965, appointed by Budget Director Charles Schultze, and the President's Task Force on Government Organization (known as the Heineman Commission), appointed in 1966–67 by President Johnson. The administration's third way of addressing budget- and management-related problems in the new programs was the introduction into the domestic agencies of the Defense Department's administrative management fixative, "Planning-Programming-Budgeting-System" (PPBS).

An examination of the fate of the Bailey Commission's recommendations and BOB's role in promulgating PPBS in the agencies is instructive in that each highlights a different facet of BOB's "checkered history" as federal "manager-in-chief."

The Bailey Commission recognized that BOB's staff and resources would have to be replenished if it was going to be able to spearhead efforts to improve coordination in the Great Society Programs. It recommended that BOB's management staff be increased or that a BOB office for interdepartmental coordination be established and that the field offices eliminated during the Eisenhower administration be restored.[82] These recommendations acknowledged the reality that since 1950, while the size of the federal budget had more than quadrupled, and BOB had been given new roles, its staff size had dropped.[83]

Congress refused to heed these recommendations, however, denying BOB appropriations requests to recreate the field offices,[84] for fear that "a BOB with field offices would become a high-level ombudsman, federal czar, umpire, or decision-maker in the field, and not a catalyst for working out agreement."[85] This "perhaps" exaggerated apprehension among some members of Congress rendered BOB handicapped in attempting to solve government management problems.

After Congress had denied the necessary resources required to do an effective job, it branded BOB as inherently incapable of succeeding in its management role. In 1968, for example, Senator Abraham Ribicoff, Chair of a subcommittee on Executive Reorganization of the Senate Government Operations Committee and a former secretary of HEW, asserted that "much of the problem and the blame of what happens in the executive branch falls on the shoulders of the Bureau of the Budget."[86] Ribicoff, like Nelson Rockefeller, had emerged from an HEW post as no admirer of BOB. He was to continue his attacks on BOB later during the Nixon administration. Both Ribicoff's subcommittee and the Heineman Task Force concluded that BOB was not the most effective office from which to direct efforts to better manage the Great Society Programs. The Heineman group recommended the creation of an Office of Program Coordination to be in the EOP, but outside of BOB.[87]

Even without the needed infusions of staff support, BOB attempted to respond to its new challenges. Its relatively small Office of Management and Organization (OMO) surveyed federal, state, and local government officials as well as academics to discern the depth of coordination problems and duplication of efforts in federal grant programs. They found extensive problems centering around the complexity of the state application process for federal funds and inadequate communications among different federal agencies administering federal grant programs. BOB then coordinated and simplified the application process for grants-in-aid programs and created an information exchange procedure among several anti-poverty programs.[88]

BOB succeeded less well in its implementation of PPBS. PPBS involved an annual agency process to set and prioritize programmatic objectives, create action plans to implement these objectives in the most effective and least costly manner, and to evaluate the results. BOB's budget examiners were charged with reviewing PPBS-related analysis prepared by their assigned agencies.[89] Both Mosher and Schick suggest that BOB's role in maintaining the momentum of the PPBS process left much to be desired. Mosher writes that examiners generally did not have adequate time to devote to this task and also suggests that some examiners would have resisted their PPBS role even if lack of time had not been a deterrent.[90] Schick maintains that part of the problem stemmed from the separation of BOB's PPBS responsibilities from its budget formulation processes. He wrote, "for all its preaching about an integrated planning and budgeting system, the Budget Bureau steadfastly kept the two apart, quarantining its tiny PPB operation from the powerful examinations and budget review staffs, and promulgating separate PPB and budget instructions."[91]

1959–1969: The Self-Studies and the Reform Commissions

The recommendations and findings pertaining to BOB in the PACGO and the Heineman Commission and those emanating from two BOB internal self-studies, conducted in 1959 and in 1967, provide a useful point of historical comparison for the analysis of the OMB that will follow. Some of their assertions were generally held in common and others differed.

The studies all acknowledged to one degree or another that significant improvements were needed in the centralized management and coordination of proliferating federal programs. They differed as to whether this effort should take place in rejuvenated BOB units or in EOP offices outside of BOB. Most of the studies also concurred on the necessity of upgrading BOB's program evaluation capabilities.[92] The Heineman Commission viewed program development as an appropriate role for BOB and issued a recommendation calling for the establishment of a Program Development Office inside of BOB.[93]

The writers of the 1967 internal BOB self-study were less sanguine about such a prospect after weathering the program development demands of the Johnson administration. They maintained that responsibility for program development should remain in the White House and that "BOB should provide only support services."[94] The 1959 and 1967 self-studies also offered conclusions on other topics worth noting. Both cited the need for greater flexibility,[95] and more planning for changing conditions and presidential demands, a departure from the "nay-sayer" style of doing business and more effort directed toward the adaptation of more creative and positive approaches to the implementation of BOB assignments.[96]

A major theme of the 1967 study was that BOB had become overburdened with too many "nontraditional" demands and roles including but not limited to "ad hoc problem solving, the exercise of immediate coordinating authority, and political communication and liaison."[97] To address this problem the study recommended the prioritization of some tasks and the elimination of others.[98]

As part of the 1967 self-study, BOB had commissioned a consultant— Merrill J. Collett—to examine BOB's personnel systems and socialization processes among other issues. Collett concluded that BOB's personnel patterns did not allow for sufficient mobility of staff within the organization.[99] The self-study of which Collett's research was a part recommended that BOB's training be "extensively" overhauled and updated.[100] Overall, Collett cited the lack of attention to internal management issues in BOB as a significant institutional problem.[101]

The BOB Organization That President Nixon Would Find

This institutional soul-searching did lead to a partial reorganization of BOB. OMO was abolished and replaced with an Office of Executive Management (OEM) with a number of new staff members directed by a noncareer assistant director.[102] While this office did not include any permanent auxiliary field offices, Mosher notes that starting in 1969, it was to develop a highly effective program to better manage and simplify Great Society Grants Programs requiring coordination between federal, state, and local governmental units. He writes that this Federal Assistance Review Program (FAR) "proved to be the most energetic and effective program of innovation in the field of management that BOB had undertaken since the 1940's."[103]

Other organizational changes reflected the concerns of the 1967 self-study. These included the establishment of small resource planning and program evaluation units under assistant directors who reported to the Budget Director.[104] A new Human Resource Program Division was created so that Great Society Programs (HEW, HUD, LABOR, VA) could be reviewed under one institutional umbrella.[105] A senior career official was asked to advise the director on internal management issues.[106]

Whether these reforms would have significantly enhanced BOB's ability to serve the needs of the presidency if they had had sufficient time to evolve and develop is unclear. As it turned out, they did not. With the 1970s and a new Republican administration, far-reaching transformations in BOB and in the surrounding budget process at large were to overshadow the impact of these institutional adjustments.

BOB/OMB During the Nixon Years: New Names, Roles, and "Political Controls"

The Ash Commission: BOB Becomes OMB

The Nixon presidency was to be a pivotal one for the Bureau of the Budget. Both its name and its organization chart would be altered while its credibility would be challenged in more damaging ways than ever before. These momentous organizational changes began with an apparently straightforward attempt to "pick up" where the Johnson administration had left off with regard to bureaucratic management improvement efforts. President Nixon had appointed an Advisory Council on Executive Organization under the direction of Roy Ash, former head of Litton Industries. This group recommended the reorganization, upgrading, and expansion of BOB's management capabilities to the point of transforming BOB into an entirely new organizational entity. The Ash Council's initial proposal that BOB be renamed the Office of Executive Management was changed due to opposition from some members of Congress who insisted that the institution's central budgetary responsibilities be acknowledged in its title.[107] Thus it was to be designated the Office of Management and Budget.

A major objective of the commission's plan to reorganize BOB was to remove any significant "policy-making" responsibilities from BOB's purview and to vest such authorities into an EOP level domestic policy unit, that would later become the Domestic Council. The new OMB was to "implement" and "manage" policies reached by the Domestic Council and the White House. The following characterization of this institutional arrangement offered in the President's message to Congress accompanying the plan is often cited as best describing the Nixon administration's original intentions: "The Domestic Council will be primarily concerned with what we do; the Office of Management and Budget will be primarily concerned with how we do it and how well we do it."[108]

This plan in its initial conception had the affect of reversing the recommendations reached by the Heineman Commission that an Office of Policy Development be established in BOB and an Intergovernmental Program Coordination role be vested in another EOP unit outside of BOB.

From the outset, the Ash Commission recommendations were quite controversial among some OMB staff who saw the reorganization as potentially undermining their budget formulation roles and institutional authority.[109] The fact that President Nixon was generally considered by observers to have viewed civil servants in both the bureaucracy and BOB with pronounced suspicion,[110] contributed to some of this BOB staff uneasiness, particularly at the beginning of his term.

In a repeat performance of the "whipping boy fights back" syndrome, various quarters of BOB either attempted to undermine the whole proposal, or to eliminate certain of its features. Robert Mayo, the Budget Director at the time spoke against provisions in the plan for staff of the new domestic policy office to be included in BOB's budget reviews.[111] BOB resistance did not stop here. Berman describes how some observers believed that BOB was able to influence the House Subcommittee on Executive and Legislative Reorganization to eventually vote against the reorganization.[112]

Conversely, the Senate Subcommittee on Reorganization viewed the proposal in a more positive light in that its chairman, Abraham Ribicoff, "hoped" the new plan would limit BOB's reach and authority. In his own words, Ribicoff believed that "The Bureau of the Budget [had] become power hungry and power crazy. This is an opportunity to take some of the function of the Budget Bureau and put it in the Office of the Presidency where it belongs."[113]

Berman attributes such intensity of feeling to "general frustration with the inability of institutional machinery to solve administrative problems."[114] Ribicoff's experiences at HEW may also have colored his views.

The Transformation and Its Outcomes

The executive reorganization plan passed the Senate and, with an intense lobbying effort, the Nixon administration was able to steer it through to passage in the House of Representatives as well.

On July 1970, OMB was officially established by Executive Order 11541. OMB's management offices were expanded to number over 140 staffers,[115] an action which vastly enlarged the management arm of the institution. The management side was made up of divisions dealing with Program Coordination, Organization and Management Systems, Statistical Policy, and Management of Information Systems, as well as the Legislative Reference Division.[116] Each of these "management" divisions was headed by an assistant director who reported to an Associate Director of Management. Four assistant directors who would report to OMB's deputy director were superimposed over the Program Divisions and BRD.[117] The added layers of executive management throughout the organization particularly stand out when comparing the 1967 BOB organization chart with OMB's first organizational schema.

As events unfolded in the Nixon administration, the functions of the Domestic Council and the new OMB would evolve in unanticipated ways. Most striking was the fact that both the Domestic Council and the new OMB would be drawn into activities and roles intended for the other unit.[118] For example, OMB became involved in the policy-making realm with the appointment of Nixon's second Budget Director, George Shultz, who was soon afforded the status of a trusted presidential advisor and was physically housed in the White House. Conversely, John Erlichman, the first Executive Director of the Domestic Council, was called upon to monitor bureaucratic management issues in the departments and agencies. In these endeavors, Erlichman would need to enlist the assistance of OMB staff.[119] This role reversal may be attributed in large part to President Nixon's growing belief that agencies including both civil servants and some Nixon Cabinet and sub-Cabinet appointees could not be trusted to implement presidential policies adequately. Thus, "policy development" in the White House and the Domestic Council could not be entirely separated from OMB's management of those policies in the departments and agencies as the Ash Council had originally envisioned. These administration "concerns" led to efforts on the part of the Nixon White House to place firmer "political" controls on policy implementation in the executive bureaucracy. According to Richard Nathan, who introduced the concept of an "administrative presidency" strategy to describe these actions, it was implicit in this approach that "management tasks can and should be performed by partisans."[120] With the Nixon administration having reached these conclusions and with OMB career staff already involved in supporting Domestic Council enforcement efforts, it was not long before the Nixon administration took additional steps to make OMB an even more effective agent for its policies. This was accomplished by devising yet another reorganization plan designed to place OMB under stricter political controls.

The 1973 Malek Reorganization

Roy Ash, the former head of the "Ash Council," had become President Nixon's third Budget Director in 1973. He and his Deputy Director, Frederic Malek, developed and implemented the second major OMB reorganization of the Nixon presidency. The reorganization placed four politically appointed Program Assistant Directors between the career budget examining staff and the Director. These "PADs," as they came to be called, were also granted direct supervisory authority over the program divisions.[121] In a reversal of the 1970 action which bifurcated OMB's management and budget functions, those staff specializing in the management issues were "once again" housed within the program divisions.[122] Many of these management units, which were housed adjacent to the budget examining divisions, were staffed with newly recruited MBAs.[123]

One of the ostensive purposes of this further alteration of OMB's management staff organization was to assist in introducing the Nixon administration's formal palliative for bureaucratic management problems, Management by Objectives (MBO), into the departments and agencies. MBO was a centralized management tool that sought to direct Executive Branch programs by promulgating administration objectives to the departments and agencies in a "top-down" fashion and in so doing to elicit compliance with these goals from successive levels of government managers.[124] According to some observers, however, bureaucratic management improvement was not the major driving force behind these actions. They were instead intended to ensure bureaucratic responsiveness to Nixon administration policy objectives. As Richard Rose later wrote about MBO: "The Nixon innovators did not see this new technique as a mere management tool, but rather as a way of coming to grips with central problems of political direction and government performance."[125]

The placement of political appointees over the newly integrated program divisions was directed toward the same goals. OMB's involvement in these bureaucratic "troubleshooting" roles began to assume a distinctly politicizing tone for the institution. For example, Larry Berman, quoting from the Senate Watergate hearings, noted instructions from Fred Malek to a PAD "to ensure that politically sensitive grants receive special consideration, with OMB communicating the administration's 'political priorities.' "[126]

The Nixon administration's allegedly illegal impoundments were also among the litany of abuses showcased in the Watergate revelations that later undermined OMB's institutional credibility. These impoundments involved the withholding of appropriated funds in unprecedented proportions and in ways that altered congressional intent. Louis Fisher in his seminal work *Presidential Spending Power,* described how OMB (whether willingly or unwillingly) had appeared to be playing accomplice to these administration actions. Fisher showed how OMB had underestimated the amounts of money that were "impounded" in certain domestic programs.[127]

The White House's efforts to control policy implementation from the "top" generally collapsed for the most part during the Watergate period. White House officials and some Domestic Council staff became increasingly immersed in the crisis and were thus rendered dysfunctional in efforts to steer routine policy-making and implementation-related activities. Under the direction of Ash and Malek, OMB stepped into the power breach and OMB took on the appearance of "running the government" for a few months.

This "power" only further tainted OMB's image of institutional integrity. While Roy Ash is quoted as telling Larry Berman in an interview that the government was "probably better managed in terms of government function than it [has] been in any other time in American history, except not by the President,"[128] other OMB watchers of the time interpreted this period differently. These individuals perceived OMB to have been merely interfering with trivial bureaucratic details and to have been borrowing presidential authority in attempts to force agencies into submission on significant matters.[129] Other observers concluded that these efforts were unsuccessful anyway, since they believed the agencies were merely feigning compliance with OMB directives, while waiting for the demise of the administration.[130] To those subscribing to this view of OMB during the Watergate period, the major outcome of this phase of "better government management" was an unprecedented antagonism toward OMB within many federal agencies.

The Ford Administration: A Transitional Time

OMB's image had emerged from the Nixon administration tarnished to the point that the Ford administration transition team had been willing to pay lip-service to the notion that OMB had to be put in its place.[131] This position had constituted in some part an effort to placate some departments and agencies whose anger was still simmering over OMB's attempts to discipline them into compliance with Nixon administration directives. The battle over questionable impoundments had not helped either. The assault on the stature of the presidency that had been created by Watergate disrupted OMB in other ways as well. Hugh Heclo reported that by 1974 almost two-thirds of OMB's career staff had less than a year's experience in OMB.[132]

The proposition that OMB could be an effective bureaucratic manager had also been cast into doubt during the Nixon administration. Even though OMB's "management" staff had been greatly increased, various studies had already observed that bureaucratic and intergovernmental management improvements had not taken hold to any significant degree. These disappointing outcomes had been documented by outside study groups under both OMB's "bifurcated" management–budget staff arrangement and the Malek-driven integration of management associates into the budget-examining program divisions.[133]

In a general sense, the Ford presidency was a time of healing for OMB as it was for the political system as a whole. Ford's OMB Director, James Lynn, made symbolic gestures at the outset of his term intended to restore OMB's credibility as an objective presidential staff agency, including the moving of his office back to the Old Executive Office Building from the White House.[134] Agency–OMB routines resumed "normal" patterns of activity, and OMB was not subjected to any major reorganization. While President Ford had talked about reducing OMB's "policy-making" role, one year after the transition it did not appear to some observers that OMB's influence had declined or that its role had been altered to any significant extent.[135]

Three congressional actions taken directly before or during the Ford administration would exert a significant impact on OMB in the future and therefore merit mention. First was the establishment of an OMB Procurement Policy Office that was designed to be "virtually autonomous" and whose Director would be subject to Senate confirmation. The creation of this office reflected the belief among some members of Congress that centralized policy review of procurement had been neglected in OMB in the past.[136] Second, the Nixon-era abuses had spurred Congress to require that future OMB Directors and Deputy Directors receive Senate confirmation.[137] This action further distanced OMB from its role as a unique institutionalized advisory system that almost exclusively served the presidency.

Perhaps most significant of the three was the passage of the Congressional Budget and Impoundment Control Act of 1974 in the last days of the Nixon administration. This act and its impact on OMB will be thoroughly discussed in Chapter 7. Here it will suffice to note that the passage of this statute started a process of moving OMB career staff into accelerated information-gathering roles on Capitol Hill to keep track of new budget units and staffs authorized by the statute. Moreover, by the mid-1970s, Director Lynn and his PADs were already expending much time and energy on congressional liaison activities, a development that in itself was beginning to reorient the duties of many OMB career staff.

Motivated by the questionable impoundment actions that were taken during the Nixon administration, the framers of the Budget Act also restricted the President's authority to withhold appropriated funds from the departments and agencies either permanently or temporarily. "Rescissions" that would permanently cancel funds could be overturned by Congress within forty-five days. Even temporary "deferrals" of spending were to be reported to Congress and Congress was given the authority to direct that the funding in question be released. The rescission and deferral processes were to be implemented through the apportionment process by OMB.

Another notable action in OMB at the time was the production of an advocacy-like "explanation" to accompany the President's budget submission to Congress.[138] The stepped-up congressional liaison activities and this more polemical section of the budget were to be characterized later as examples of an increased institutional politicization that had allegedly taken hold in OMB.

OMB and the Politicization Debate in the 1970s

"Politicization" became an important buzzword in serious discussions of OMB in the mid-1970s.[139] The notion that OMB had become "politicized" and could no longer play the unique role it had once served for the presidency revolved around the concern that the new layer of politically appointed PADs might prevent "objective" advice from reaching the OMB Director and the White House and that the PADs might draw OMB career civil servants into the political fray while lobbying on behalf of the President's budget or programs in Congress. A related risk was that OMB's career staff might lose the "anonymity" that had traditionally allowed them to provide presidential advice "on the merits" without threatening their personal career statuses in any way. Too much visibility could compromise that institutional capability by connecting individual staff members with particular policies or administrations.

The seeds of politicization probably took root much earlier during the Truman administration when Director Webb started the precedent of bringing BOB career staff to the White House to assist in drafting legislation, or later when LBJ tried to use BOB staff to achieve politically motivated ends in the agencies. Concerns about politicization in BOB might have become more intense in the 1970s because of the rapid increase of political appointees in OMB that took place between 1970 and 1980. Before 1968, other than the Director and Deputy Directors there had been no more than four noncareer officials in BOB, and BOB's civil service hierarchy was organized so that communications channels were all directly connected to the Director's office.[140] By 1975, there were four PADs and a noncareer assistant director. Moreover, these five officials held line positions that internally constituted a new supervisory layer between the OMB Director and the OMB career staff, and between OMB career staff and the agencies.[141] In addition, the Watergate revelations probably also played a role in fueling trepidations that OMB was at risk of losing its neutral status.

In one of the earliest and most thoughtful discussions of this issue, scholar Hugh Heclo cautioned that if OMB's capacity for "neutral" competence were to become too seriously eroded, OMB could be transformed into just another politically motivated presidential advisory office and thus lose its unique stature. Heclo's own description of this "neutral competence" best captured the institutional capabilities and qualities that he feared could be lost. He wrote in his 1975 article "OMB and the President—The problem of neutral competence,"[142] that "neutral competence"

> envisions a continuous, uncommitted facility at the disposal of, and for the support of, political leadership. It is not a prescription for sainthood. Neutrality does not mean the possession of a direct-dial line to some overarching, nonpartisan sense of the public interest. Rather it consists in giving one's cooperation and best independent judgment of the issues to partisan bosses—and of being sufficiently uncommitted to be able to do so for a succession of partisan leaders. The independence entailed in neutral competence does not exist for its own sake; it exists precisely in order to serve the aims of elected partisan leadership. Nor is neutral competence merely the capacity to deliver good staff work to a political superior, for a major part of this competence lies in its ability to gain compliance from lower-level officials. The competence in question entails not just following orders but having the practical knowledge of government and the broker's skills of the governmental marketplace that makes one's advice worthy of attention. Thus neutral competence is a strange amalgam of loyalty that argues back, partisanship that shifts with the changing partisans, independence that depends on others. Its motto is "Speak out, shut up, carry up, carry out."[143]

Heclo further expressed concerns for the survival of certain institutional qualities that had historically sustained this "neutral competence" in the BOB of the past. These included institutional memory, impartiality, fluidity of communications between BOB's career staff and its Directors, a consensus-building capability, and credibility to the White House and external institutions such as the Congress and the Executive Branch agencies. Heclo's thesis was built upon the concern that these institutional capabilities had already been compromised during the early 1970s and could be undermined further in the future due to the introduction of the politically appointed PADs. He feared that the pronounced career staff turnover at the end of the Nixon presidency could portend a loss of institutional memory in OMB. He was concerned that the PADs could potentially filter out "advice on the merits" before it even reached the OMB Director or the White House.

Another series of concerns involved the potential for more externally visible OMB career staffers to become publicly identified with one administration and thus lose their utility for later presidencies. Agencies, long ready to grouse about BOB/OMB's oversight authorities would thus have added ammunition to neutralize OMB's "legitimate" disciplinary role in this regard.[144]

Heclo also worried that White House staffers might convert OMB career staff into blatantly partisan bag-carriers during the many crises of the moment that administrations often face. On this point Heclo had quoted one examiner who had described such experiences and had recounted: " 'The White House wanted to make decisions and you were supposed to give them the reasons.' " According to Heclo, when those decisions were "the heavy-handed use of impoundment or the dismantling of OEO, for example, independent OMB advice was unduly compromised by close and ingratiating ties between White House and OMB staff."[145]

Finally, "politicization" of OMB could potentially impede both upward and downward communication in OMB. With too many power centers in the EOP and White House offering policy guidance to OMB, political appointees could become negligent in their responsibility to communicate policies with one "administration voice" to career staff and in particular to those who remained unpoliticized. Upward communications could also suffer if career staff ceased to produce and communicate objective analysis to OMB's political echelons out of the belief that such analysis was not heard or listened to.

Heclo's concerns were thought-provoking at the time. One objective in the chapters to follow will be to gauge to what degree these concerns were to turn into institutional realities for OMB in the coming years.

President Carter: Four Years of Contrasts

OMB veterans today recall the Carter transition as an unusually difficult one in terms of the amount of initial distrust harbored among Carter administration appointees and directed toward OMB career staff. This is not surprising coming on the heels of eight years of Republican presidencies, two of which had included the Watergate debacle. In a relatively short time, however, this suspicion not only evaporated, but OMB career staff were to experience a greater degree of influence in the budget formulation process than they had known for perhaps two and a half decades. This influence arose in part from the direct exposure to President Carter that some OMB civil servants experienced during the first two years of Carter's presidency. Both Colin Campbell and Larry Berman report that OMB civil service staff were invited personally into the White House to defend their budget recommendations to the President.[146] This unusual degree of direct career staff exposure to their principal client emanated from Carter's personal interest in delving into the details of the budget process in combination with Bert Lance's lack of desire to micro-manage his own agency.[147] Campbell characterizes the budget formulation process under President Carter as analysis driven and points to a "surge in OMB morale" during the first two years of the Carter administration.[148] He writes,

> If OMB best fulfills its mission by keeping a weather eye for long-term issues and developing analysis based options for the president, the agency reached its apogee during the first two years of Carter's term.[149]

The incidence of such contacts declined in the second half of the Carter administration when the President became increasingly preoccupied with international matters including the Iran Hostage Crisis, though even then the OMB career staff continued to enjoy a substantial amount of influence in the budget formulation process.

President Carter also afforded OMB significant leverage in the "management" realm by allowing it to assume a major role in his President's Reorganization Project as described in Chapter 8. Once again OMB's management staff were "reorganized" by separating them out of the budget-examining program divisions and placing them under a politically appointed Executive Associate Director. Management staff numbers were also replenished.[150] The rationale for this reshuffling was similar to the previous budget–management separation: to energize OMB's management capabilities, which were thought to have been overshadowed by the pressure of budgetary schedules and routines.

Observers at the time differed in their interpretations of the nature of OMB's input into President Carter's domestic policy-making process. One view was that OMB and White House advisors worked well and cooperatively in a team-like fashion.[151] Another was that the Domestic Policy Staff had become "an institutional rival of OMB in the routine business of government."[152] Nonetheless, OMB at least had a seat "at the table" on the policy-making front as one point of a domestic policy staff triumvirate that also included representation from other White House/EOP units and the agencies.

While it can be asserted that OMB career staff were "influential" during the Carter administration, such clout does not necessarily correspond to overall OMB influence among other institutions. At the end of the Carter administration many students of the presidency believed that the Carter

OMB represented just another stage in a continuing process of institutional decline that had begun during the Kennedy/Johnson years.

The status and stature of the OMB Director appears to correlate more directly with OMB's ability to project a posture of authority to Congress, agencies, and Washington clientele groups than does internal OMB career staff influence. But the experiences of the two Carter Budget Directors illustrate the two sides of a dilemma modern OMB Directors were beginning to face. Bert Lance, as an inner-circle presidential advisor, carried more weight both with the President and within Washington's inner power circles. This enhanced OMB's institutional aura for a while, but when Lance faced allegations of improprieties in his former banking endeavors and resigned, it bruised OMB's institutional image. President Carter's second Budget Director, James McIntyre, was able to pare down the deficit by 8 billion dollars,[153] but was viewed as deficient in President Carter's eyes for lacking the public relations skills that were now part of a more visible OMB Director's job description.[154] Hence, under McIntyre, OMB's posture eroded further.[155]

Certainly, on the surface, actions were taken during the Carter administration that maintained and in some cases even furthered the trend of politicizing OMB. Two new politically appointed Executive Associate Directors were superimposed over the PADs, thus creating two political supervisory staff layers separating OMB career staff from the Director. An 180–page summary of the Carter administration's major accomplishments which accompanied the 1981 budget[156] followed the advocacy tone taken in President Ford's *Seventy Issues Monograph*. OMB Directors had become more visible since President Nixon's first term, in that they were routinely expected to "give speeches, even campaign speeches on behalf of the President."[157]

BOB/OMB's First Sixty Years: From Distinction to Decline

For much of BOB/OMB's first sixty years it won respect from both Republican and Democratic administrations for its service as an elite, institutionalized advisory office for the presidency. It had also received a fair amount of criticism from time to time for being uncreative, inflexible, and excessively negative.

By the end of the 1970s, OMB had lost stature as a presidential staff agency. This decline can in part be attributed to pressures that had been inflicted upon the institution by the White House and other external sources. These include politicization, the unrealistic and onerous demands made by some White Houses, and the casting of BOB/OMB as a scapegoat for unsuccessful administrative management initiatives, and/or failures on the part of the White House to plan ahead or "pace" its efforts. BOB/OMB's institutional staff also shared some of the blame for this loss of stature when they exhibited change resistance or inflexibility when shifting from "economy-minded" presidencies to activist administrations or vice versa, or when some budget staffers refused to integrate management initiatives into their budgetary routines.

Budget process scholar Allen Schick partially attributed this decline of influence to a tendency among Presidents since World War II to use BOB/OMB less as a significant policy-making participant and more for routine "accounting" tasks and as a reservoir for informational support for White House and EOP staff.[158] In this, Schick found the declining size of OMB's program divisions to be both a cause of its alleged inability to prepare more sophisticated analysis, and an effect of the existing scaled-down expectations for what it was supposed to do.[159] He suggested that a diminished OMB might offer hidden payoffs for White House officials and EOP units. Such policy-making competitors of OMB could more easily "tune out when OMB representatives launch into their explanations as to why something will not work or should not be done."[160]

To Schick, OMB's primary functions for the presidency at that juncture were to handle issues not considered critical enough to be handled in the White House or at times to handle those matters of direct concern to the President that could not be housed in any new or existing agency.[161] He believed that OMB program division staff tended to de-emphasize many auxiliary management-related tasks at their own peril, given that they would "need new functions . . . to regain presidential esteem."[162]

Schick also agreed with those who had observed that OMB's politicization had already eroded its capability to provide first-rate information and analysis to the President. (Though he acknowledged that OMB still offered "solid, objective service as well.")[163] In this final analysis, Schick concluded that OMB could not do it all in the sense of providing "both institutional and personal-political service from the same group."[164]

Others, such as Aaron Wildavsky, found other reasons for OMB's decline. To Wildavsky, the increasing size of government expenditures, which demanded large-scale aggregate budgeting solutions, had deprecated the significance of the kind of small-scale analysis-based micro-budgeting that had been BOB/OMB's forte.[165]

Colin Campbell's research on OMB during the Carter administration would later qualify some of these pronouncements of OMB's decline. He cited both the Schick and Wildavsky assessments as having "overstated somewhat the demise of [OMB's] executive-bureaucratic clout and analytic salience."[166] His interviews during the Carter administration did not bear out reports of a severely compromised OMB analytic and informational capacity due to the superimposition of political appointees over career staff.[167] Finally to the view that most decision making at the time actually took place outside of BOB/OMB's budget "routines," Campbell found that at least during the Carter administration, OMB's budget procedures had been honored in a disciplined fashion.[168]

Chapter 4 will discuss the findings from my study of OMB's program divisions in the late 1970s, which provided a close-up view of career staff role orientations and OMB decision-making processes. The study made it possible for me to evaluate OMB's overall status at the time and the degree to which the career staff had become politicized, from a different vantage point. While the study unveiled a number of specific examples of politicization in OMB, I came to view many of these indicators of OMB's institutional politicization as OMB's "inevitable" institutional responses to a changing congressional budget process as well as having been derived from the need to provide realistic advice and information to the President. Moreover, I would eventually reach the conclusion that the transmission of neutral information and politically sophisticated advice from OMB to the President were not *necessarily* mutually exclusive. To provide such service to the presidency, OMB's political and career staff would be required to perform delicate and difficult balancing acts and would often have to negotiate their way through troubling role conflicts.

4

Institutional Service to the President, 1976–1980: The Roles of the Budget Examiners

Introduction

The study I conducted from 1976 to 1980 specifically examined the budgetary and legislative roles of the budget examiners, their degree of influence on OMB decisions, and how the examiners related to OMB's decision-making and internal and external communications processes. I also attempted to gauge whether advice to the President from OMB civil servants had become politicized, to what degree, and with what potential implications. The research filled a gap in the existing literature at the time, since unlike other studies of the institution, it provided a then up-to-date and in-depth treatment of OMB's career staff levels.

This research presented a snapshot in time of a highly productive analytical staff arm for the presidency. OMB career staff used a variety of innovative techniques to obtain information on federal programs, produced high-quality analysis, and exerted a marked influence on the ultimate dispositions of OMB decisions.

The study also yielded evidence that OMB had become politicized in the preceding decade, and not only because its analysis was being politically sensitized by the PADs. "Encouragement" to produce more politically sensitive analysis had been transmitted to many career staffers as well. To this degree, my research could be interpreted to have further confirmed Heclo's observations in the mid-1970s. It would be in my conclusions regarding these "politicization indicators" that I was to part company with some of the scholars at the time who viewed this OMB "politicization" with significant trepidation. I reached these determinations slowly as the research introduced me to OMB staffers who in many cases could be considered extraordinary in their ability to maintain the necessary balance needed to produce objective advice that would still be politically realistic enough to be useful to the President.

Demographic Characteristics, Career Patterns, and Training of OMB Career Staff

The budget examiners in the sample tended to be young, well educated, male, and moderate with regard to ideology and party identification. Branch chiefs followed suit on these characteristics, except not surprisingly they tended to be older. Both populations varied in approximately similar proportions with respect to the nature of their advanced degrees, previous experience in the federal bureaucracy, stated party identification, and educational or professional experience related to program review area.

Examiners' ages were overwhelmingly in the twenty-five-to-thirty-five-year age range. Their immediate supervisors were on the average a decade older. Their career patterns reconfirmed a high staff turnover rate cited by Heclo as well as by the Collett study ten years earlier. Eighty-six percent of the examiners had been with the institution for less than eight years (in 1975), and 55 percent for three years or less. Only 14 percent indicated seniority levels of more than eight years.

The educational level of OMB staff had risen since the mid-1960s. Among the 1970s sample, only 17 percent of the examiners and branch chiefs cited the B.A. degree or less as their highest level of educational attainment, as compared with approximately 41 percent falling into this category in the mid-1960s. The typical degree for both examiners and branch chiefs was the M.A. or M.S. degree, with examiners having a slightly higher percentage of Ph.D. degrees than had branch chiefs.

The study also examined whether that staff had previous experience working in federal agencies before coming to work in OMB, and whether they had previous educational or professional experience that was related to the programs they reviewed. This was thought to be useful data since previous experience in the federal bureaucracy might have helped to provide the examiners with general procedural references to better facilitate OMB– agency information gathering and communications. Related experience also might have potentially increased the examiners' effectiveness when they analyzed complex programs. Conversely, related experience also could imbue examiners with favorable or unfavorable biases regarding the agency under review. The findings that over half of the examiners and branch chiefs interviewed had previous bureaucratic experience and that about 40 percent of the total career staff had some kind of professional experience related to his or her programmatic review area, offered some evidence that a knowledgeable career staff had been assembled at that time but that entrenched biases might have been a problem in some cases.

With respect to party and ideological self-identification, most examiners and branch chiefs appeared to be attempting to maintain a neutral and moderate image in their responses. Over 75 percent of the interviewees rated themselves as "moderate" or "middle of the road," compared with 37 percent of the general population at the time who perceived themselves as moderate. Of the staffers choosing between a liberal or a conservative label, 18 percent chose the liberal label and 7 percent the conservative.

Responses with regard to party identification among the staffers echoed the same general trends. Fully 40 percent of the interviewees either refused to indicate a party identification or indicated none. This compared with 2 percent of the general public who classified themselves as nonpolitical. Twelve percent of the staffers classified themselves as independent as compared with 36 percent of the general population. Adding the independent self-identifiers with those who refused to offer a party identification totaled a subpopulation of 42 percent of the OMB staff not labeling themselves as Democratic or Republican compared with 38 percent of the general population.

Those examiners reviewing high-visibility program areas were even less likely to indicate a Democratic or Republican party identification. Most examiners reviewing highly visible program areas offered no party identification, while most reviewing less visible programs did so. Perhaps, the more politically controversial or visible the program, the more the examiner wished to maintain a neutral and nonpartisan image.

Several examiners indicated that they were hesitant about indicating a party identification even though they were protected by the Civil Service. As one commented, "if some study was published showing that 90 percent of OMB staff was Democratic and we were under a Republican administration or vice versa, we wouldn't lose our jobs, but we'd certainly lose our effectiveness for that President."

Two observations were drawn from these findings: First, examiners and branch chiefs particularly, those reviewing high-visibility areas, were still trying to present a neutral, moderate image notwithstanding claims of increased politicization. Another somewhat speculative but seemingly viable conclusion concerning these data is that exposure to OMB probably tended to modify any previously held strong ideological or party stands on either side of the spectrum. Several respondents indicated that when exposed to the substantive complexities of programmatic issues in government, ideological and party labels began to appear too simplistic. This along with an institutional norm of neutrality and fear of losing effectiveness probably explained the respondents' avoidance of party and ideological labels.

With respect to OMB's approaches to staff training, ten years after Collett's recommendation that BOB's "training program should be extensively over-hauled and updated," institutional training had not changed much. From the staff interviews, it appeared that newly hired budget examiners learned the intricacies of their budgetary and legislative duties with the assistance of a procedural guide entitled the *Examiner's Handbook*. Occasionally, they also participated in one- or two-day seminars designed to introduce them to certain procedural aspects of their budgetary duties such as those involving the apportionment process. However, with respect to the bulk of the examiner's job functions, there was no formal training program. Examiners absorbed institutional norms, job techniques, and role orientations informally by on-the-job training in much the same way as Collett described in the 1960s. Most staffers asserted that a formal training program for any but the most procedural and technical aspects of the job would not be viable given the nuances of the examiner's roles and the differences between individual program areas. Several, nonetheless, expressed the view that there were deficiencies in the then present system and that more formal training would have been helpful.

The Competence Factor in "Neutral Competence"

How well did the budget examiners fulfill their analytic and information-gathering functions for OMB and the President? The investigation of the examiners' analytic priorities and strategies yielded a picture of presidential advice at the career staff level that was multifaceted and had a good deal of depth. When performing analysis, examiners considered several cognitive criteria of primary importance with no one aspect dominating to the exclusion of all other factors. Cost–benefit constructs and "rational" decision-making models were balanced out by an appreciation for considerations in the Congress that might ultimately impact OMB's decisions. This lent a degree of "realism" to the analysis. Other criteria emphasized by examiners suggested an analytic capability to provide generally "complete" information to the President. With regard to their information-gathering roles, examiners exercised initiative and employed very innovative techniques in extracting information from the agencies concerning their programs. The approaches OMB career staff used when preparing analysis will be further described in Chapter 6, and their information-gathering strategies will be covered in Chapter 8.

Politicization in OMB: Had Civil Servants Really Joined the Game?

Introduction

My interviews uncovered a number of career staff analytic and information-gathering activities that appeared partly "political" in nature, but were also in significant ways dissimilar to the type of work performed by political appointees in the White House or the EOP. They were different in large part because they were balanced out by strong, institutionally endowed role orientations that supported and demanded objectivity and neutrality. For those reasons I labeled them "quasi-political." A discussion of each follows.[1]

Careerists as Quasi-Political Analysts

Information in the Body of Analysis

OMB program division civil servants prepared written issue papers on legislation, legislative proposals, budgetary policy options, and enrolled bills that were processed through the supervisory channels of OMB. As part of their analysis and recommendations, careerists frequently made assessments of how a particular budgetary or legislative program would be received by Congress, clientele groups, or other selected constituencies. This analysis usually appeared as a paragraph to the side of the bulk of the analytic arguments, which were based on objective programmatic information.

The interview data indicated that over 80 percent of the budget examiners surveyed included such analysis within their issue papers. This analysis was described as projecting the potential effect of congressional and interest group reaction, the electoral reactions of key congressional members' constituencies, and the character of particular agency-congressional relationships on a proposal's chance for legislative enactment. One example, "congressional head counts," would attempt to predict potential voting patterns on a given budgetary or legislative measure.

This type of analysis was termed "quasi-political," since it did not encompass "political" analysis in the sense of assessing how a measure would specifically affect presidential popularity or "the President's chances of electoral success," but rather how it might affect a budgetary proposal's chances of being acceptable to the Congress. The use of such analysis was more prevalent in highly politically sensitive or visible issue areas.

Here is one examiner's description of this "quasi-political" analysis:

> Political assessments were usually indicated in some way. There is a tradition that if it is important enough to be sent up, you have to indicate what the opposition is. The politics of the situation is very often the easiest part of the job. It doesn't take much knowledge to know that agriculture is important to a certain state.

The transmittal of such politically oriented information was not considered by examiners, branch chiefs, and division chiefs to comprise an invasion of the civil servants' politically "neutral" roles, since most viewed it merely as a means to inform OMB political appointees of all the ramifications of alternative options; the actual decision being left to OMB's political strata.

A number of Ford administration PADs interviewed for the study found examiners' assessments related to congressional activity sometimes necessary and useful as an information support system. Given a high turnover rate among PADs, such information might have provided a necessary support for PADs unfamiliar with program specifics. That PADs oftentimes needed the examiner's substantive expertise on particular political facets of programs to assist them in their decision-making process is illustrated by the following comment offered by one branch chief:

> Generally, when you get a new political associate director (PAD), in particular, one from outside the government, he would give instructions that he didn't want any political decisions or influences on recommendations. He wanted us to be objective analysts. But, most of these people, after some months experience, will find that they didn't have the knowledge to make the political assessments that they needed to make and would end up coming back to the branches and divisions for guidance. They had the right theory, but the problem is that they had no expertise in OMB on the political realities of the situation except from the examiners, branch chiefs and division chiefs. . . .

One plausible explanation for the origin of these "quasi-political" footnotes in the margins of analysis might have been that they represented a response to criticisms in a 1967 study that had faulted OMB for not producing analysis that was politically sensitive enough.[2] Had such quasi-political analysis increased since 1970? Division chiefs with tenure spanning this time period were split concerning whether this kind of analysis had increased in recent years. Some division chiefs indicated that such analysis had always been "standard operating procedure," while several others felt that it had indeed increased.

One such division chief said:

Yes, we get this more than we used to in the past. This has slowly evolved and it is hard to pinpoint an exact time. In the "old days," examiners wrote issue papers that were sterile on the political side and were just on the merits of the case.

Cognitive Consideration of Political Factors in Examiner "Recommendations"

A more subtle and perhaps more indicative distinction to be drawn than whether such political analysis was included in the body of the analysis paper was whether the examiner cognitively took these political factors (interest group or "Hill" reactions) into account when making "recommendations." Reaching recommendations only on the merits was defined as utilizing cost–benefit considerations, policy guidance from political levels of OMB, substantive programmatic information received from the agency, and outside research. Under this approach, while political factors might be mentioned in the analysis, the examiner made a recommendation without factoring in its potential reception in Congress or with interest groups. Inclusion of such quasi-political factors in an examiner's final recommendation, in lieu of making recommendations based solely upon the merits of the case, could comprise an indication of examiner involvement in politically motivated aspects of decision making more decisively than would instances where he or she merely provided such information to alert political appointees, who could then factor it into their decisions.

Career staff in the Program Divisions varied widely in their views with regard to the appropriateness of such cognitive inclusion of political factors into recommendations. Over 60 percent considered this approach as unacceptable and as compromising their "neutral" role, but well over a third of the sample disagreed. These staffers often argued that they considered it of little use to the President to recommend a policy option that would meet with probable demise upon reaching Capitol Hill, just to make an "ivory tower" judgment. The following are several contrasting staff views on this issue. One examiner said:

> If I know the Congress, and it's going to be completely unacceptable to them, I don't recommend it. Or I might phrase the recommendation on the merits we believe best, but because of the political ramifications, we would modify the recommendation. You'll find it varies quite a bit from examiner to examiner, from branch to branch, how examiners include political considerations. If you had a scale, you'd find that most examiners would tend to ignore political considerations. I am more attuned to that in my recommendations than most people. This is mainly because of the importance of the program. It's such a political program. I'd be completely ineffectual if I ignored the political ramifications.

A branch chief said:

> If I began worrying too much about congressional reactions . . . who wanted this and who didn't want that, I think we'd wind up in a state of paralysis. I tend to keep my examiners looking at the projects on their merits, leaving political assessments aside, even though I know which Senators are for and which are against the project.

One division chief said:

> An examiner came in here a couple of years ago with an issue paper. . . . I told him the budget recommendation he came up with wasn't supported by the analysis. He agreed but said that his analysis led him to a recommendation that was too low politically. I told him—don't make that judgment. That's not your job or my job. That's my boss's job. . . . We do try to avoid mixing the two together. It is not only important at the division level, it is important to OMB as an institution. I've had some disagreement among some political officials within OMB about what our role is. I think as an institution, if we have political views even beyond the division level, we should carefully indicate what analysis shows and try to vote on that basis.

One PAD commented:

> It is not "either–or." I think it's more the job of the PAD or the Director to make independent political assessments. But I don't think it's feasible to ask an examiner to ignore them. I think if an examiner is preoccupied with them, he's a lousy examiner because he's not doing what he does best and he's doing too much of what he doesn't do well. That's not why he's there. But I think they have to take it into account. As an example, you can't just march through the government doing analysis on the problems you think are the greatest without regard to whether or not the five items which fall out of the analysis all turn out to be sacred cows.

What relationship existed between the examiner's willingness to cognitively include political assessments in final recommendations and the propensity of those recommendations to be accepted? From the responses, it appeared that the inclusion of cognitive political assessments in recommendations clearly corresponded to a higher rate of complete recommendation acceptance. The approximate average percentage of "estimated" recommendation acceptance for those examiners not including cognitive political factors in recommendations was 61 percent, while the average rate of acceptance for examiners who did cognitively include political assessments in recommendations was approximately 77 percent. A review of "recorded" budgetary recommendations showed that 80 percent of the recommendations that were approved at the Director's level originated in examiner account areas where the examiner in question had indicated that he or she cognitively included quasi-political factors into recommendations. Of those recommendations that were not accepted, half emanated from examiners who did not take the political factors into account.

These findings suggested that inclusion of political assessments in recommendations makes the recommendations themselves more palatable to upper-level management. This is not surprising since addition of political assessments into the equation before final decisions are reached is the primary role of the politically appointed strata in OMB. If these considerations had already been taken into account by career staff members, the recommendations would automatically become more readily acceptable to the "political" people. Moreover, if further recommendations were being accepted from examiners who cognitively took political factors into account in their final recommendations, then one must conclude that these examiners were successfully impacting upon final decision making by offering certain political assessments that "political" and not career staff were institutionally designated to make. This finding provided further evidence of politicization among a minority of OMB career staff at the time.

Whether supporting inclusion of political assessments in recommendations or not, supervisors above the examiner level indicated that the "basis" for the recommendations needed to be completely explained in the issue paper so that the decision maker knew all the factors that went into the recommendations. Without a complete explanation, decision makers ran a risk of misinterpreting the staff recommendations. Several division chiefs and PADs indicated that occasionally this lack of communications could be a problem with regard to decision making at all levels of OMB. Objective cost–benefit arguments might not have received a "fair hearing" if decision makers mistook a "politically motivated" recommendation for a recommendation made only on "the merits" or vice versa.

The responses suggested that more examiners and branch chiefs with professional or educational experience related to their program areas tended to exclude or encourage subordinates to exclude cognitive political assessments in recommendations, while those without such related experience tended to divide evenly on this issue. This relationship might be explained in that previous related experience gave the staffer an additional experiential basis from which to judge program issues that the individual without previous experience did not have. Without such a knowledge base, there was more room for the examiner or branch chief to consider the potential political outcome of recommendations. On the other hand, the budget examiner with experience might have been more concerned with providing the political appointee with a more thorough picture of the program's substantive issues.

Careerist Quasi-Political Information Sources: "Congressional Contacts"

Another quasi-political indicator derived from the analytic roles just described was the fact that OMB career staff were interacting with congressional staff to a greater degree than they had in the past. With a greater need to know what was transpiring in Congress in order to prepare the aforementioned analysis, OMB careerists increasingly found themselves participating in personal and telephone communications with congressional staff and occasionally members of Congress, and personally attending congressional committee hearings. With no formal institution-wide policies governing these practices, a little over half of the examiners interviewed were cultivating personal contacts in Congress and the majority of branch chiefs and division chiefs either encouraged the practice or allowed the examiner discretion with regard to cultivation of congressional contacts.

Those career staff who were opposed to the practice had three major fears regarding staff communications with Congress: (1) it removed the careerist from the protective cover of internal analyst to the role of administration spokesperson; (2) it consumed a great deal of time and detracted from the careerist's pursuit of longer-term studies and in-depth program analysis; and (3) it could potentially slant the examiner's mindset from emphasis on cost–benefit criteria to concern for congressional priorities.

On the other hand, the substantial number of OMB civil servants who supported more careerist–Hill contact argued that career staff were better able to provide realistic and complete analysis to the political levels of OMB if they developed congressional contacts. They argued that in order to make their case on Capitol Hill effectively the political appointees needed the "combined" program expertise and political knowledge of the civil servants as an informational support system.

Interest Group Contacts

A third politicization indicator was the finding that many OMB career staffers were communicating on a regular basis with interest group representatives. Traditionally, interest groups had directed their energies primarily toward influencing congressional and bureaucratic decision making. The "presidency" and its support staff were considered to be somewhat more insulated from interest group pressure than was the Congress. However, the days when previous budget offices functioned in a relatively isolated atmosphere were a thing of the past by the 1970s when OMB careerist–interest group contacts appeared to be an established part of many an examiner's informational reservoir. Approximately 50 percent of the examiners utilized information from clientele groups. In the main, the branch and division chiefs encouraged examiners to cultivate such sources if relevant, but left the extent of such information gathering largely up to the examiner's discretion.

Examiners who actively sought assistance from outside interest groups did so for several reasons. Several examiners indicated that their agencies were reluctant to supply them with adequate information, so they turned to outside sources. Some examiners also expressed the opinion that certain interest groups were in a better position to research the agency's activities due to larger staffs. In such cases, it behooved the examiner to make use of interest group reports, data, and representatives whenever possible in order to make the analysis more realistic, complete, and useful to the President and to provide a check on agency-supplied information.

Did such contacts increase since 1970? While a couple of division chiefs thought that their staffers had been approached by such groups both pre- and post-1970, most others believed that such contacts had increased. This was thought to be due to the increased visibility of OMB during the 1970s which had attracted the attention of certain of these groups who a decade earlier would not have considered the Budget Bureau as a likely lobbying ground. As one division chief commented, "BOB might have had all the power but before 1970 nobody knew who we were." Indeed, interest groups not only contacted OMB for information, but hoped to influence executive decision-making at a crucial stage in the process. Another division chief said:

> Yes, we get information from them and they try to get information from us. We've established a line of communication with most of these groups. A representative group of them will come in and tell us where they're from and how they stand on particular issues hoping to influence us just before going into the budget process. Next to the President himself, we're here making recommendations. If they can interdict the line of communication at this level it beats dealing with their old counterparts in the agencies.

Given this, there was an obvious danger of the examiner becoming overly influenced by the interest group pitch or becoming a prisoner of such information. Examiners might have weighted interest group information or positions too heavily in their analysis, thereby diluting the overall objectivity and "public interest orientation" of OMB's presidential advisory system. Conversely, if handled "correctly," interest groups could provide useful information to help staffers make their analysis more meaningful and representative of all alternatives. Which direction were they taking in the 1970s? The study's findings showed that interest group sources, while utilized, were of secondary importance, suggesting that at least during the mid-1970s, career staff–interest group contacts were not an institutional problem.

The Nature of Communications Between the Political and the Career Levels of OMB

General Communications Dynamics

Communications between the budget examiners and the PADs were generally indirect. When processing issue papers and memoranda up through the OMB hierarchy, examiners usually transmitted them through the branch chief and division chief levels before they reached the PADs. The majority of the examiner's actual work assignments were directly communicated to the examiner from careerist supervisory levels within OMB rather than from the political levels.

Budget examiners received both specific and general policy guidance concerning their assigned program areas. The conceptual distinction between "specific" and "general" policy guidance rested with how detailed the policy directive was and whether or not it was aimed at an individual program or agency. One example of a "specific" guideline might have been a written memo or telephone communication from a PAD or the director containing clear instructions to reduce or increase the budget or personnel in a particular program or agency. General guidance, on the other hand, was offered in the form of budget ceilings or "general" administration philosophy involving a broad category of programs (i.e., reductions in all research and development programs, etc.), which might be communicated to an entire division or branch. Another form of "specific" as opposed to "general" guidance might have been clear-cut instructions for the examiner to focus on and develop certain specific program issues as opposed to others.

With only general guidance, determinations of which programs received recommended increases or reductions and how these adjustments were structured would largely be left to the careerists' discretion. With "specific guidance," the examiner's analysis and recommendations would merely be a reflection of the guidance that had been communicated.

Most budget examiners rarely or never received guidance concerning the specific nature of administration policy as it related to particular program issues from politically appointed officials within OMB or the White House *before* these examiners had an opportunity to provide their initial information and recommendations. When examiners did receive such specific communications it usually concerned only those areas considered to be highly politically sensitive. This was attributed to the overall complexity of most issues, and the lack of necessary expertise and time constraints on the part of the PAD or other political appointees.

As one examiner said:

> I asked what is the President's view on a certain program since I had to write a legislative report on the subject. The answer was, "whatever you say it is." There is relatively little that is decided at the top and then gets passed down. . . . In my area, there is nothing that is decided at the top. If I want an issue raised, I have to raise it myself. I always have the first shot. That is what is good about my job.

The policy guidance that examiners did receive was usually of a general nature, taking the form of budgetary expenditure ceilings. Within these ceilings, the examiners were then left to fill in the details. Such general guidance was communicated to examiners in branch- or division-level meetings and through individual verbal communications with branch chiefs, division chiefs, or PADs. Since most policy guidance communicated to examiners was only of a general nature and not always that encompassing, it became the responsibility of the examiner to seek out potential policy guidance and translate the "general" administration policies into specifics. As one examiner described, "No matter what administration is in office, the examiner should completely transform to the new value set of that administration. He should learn to see everything that way. He should read what the President and policy people have said (if they haven't said anything, find out what they think), and then translate it to fit the specific program."

When policy guidance was offered, was it communicated directly to the examiner from the political levels of OMB? Guidance from political levels that was communicated to the examiner through the branch chief or division chief levels stood a greater chance of not completely reflecting presidential or politically set views, but of representing the perceptions and biases of the division chiefs and branch chiefs. As Heclo had written, the more political level participants who became involved in giving policy signals, the greater the chance for miscommunications.[3] So too, the more levels that policy communications traveled through, the more chance for incorrectly communicated messages.

I found that specific and/or general policy guidance was generally communicated to examiners through career supervision; namely branch chiefs and division chiefs. In only a few cases did examiners state that such communications frequently occurred directly from the PAD level or higher. This indicated that when specific messages were offered from political levels of OMB to the examiner, they more often moved through hierarchical channels and thus did not take place directly.

The following quotes from examiners indicate that these communications dynamics may have been somewhat problematic in certain parts of OMB. One examiner said,

> Last year in budget review meetings all indications were not to add personnel, but to keep down the size of the federal government. The division chief had given the branch chief instructions to add no personnel and therefore I worked with that personnel constraint on me. Later I learned from the political associate director that this personnel policy hadn't been presidential policy at all but had been the division chief's decision. All the time I was under the constraint, thinking it was presidential budgetary policy. No budgetary policy was involved. Political people should be making political decisions. Sometimes the branch chief level has too much autonomy and uses their staffs to enforce their biases.

Another examiner observed,

> The lack of communication in OMB is frustrating from level to level. Last year we were told by the division chief it was going to be a tough budget season and that we had to cut budgets and we did. Then the political associate directors came back and said, "Why did you cut the budget?" We had been working at cross purposes since the division chief didn't communicate with the political associate directors and vice versa. The communications problem is a major dilemma.

It should be emphasized that only a small minority of examiners indicated that personal agendas of career managers played a role in distorting political-level policy stances. However, the potential for garbled communications, as a consequence of excessive layering of supervisory staff, was considered to be an institutional problem worth monitoring by these individuals.

How Career Staff "Sought Out" Policy Guidance

Since most policy guidance communicated to examiners was only of a general nature, and because communications could be compromised as they moved from political levels to the examiners, the examiners used a number of methods to "seek out" potential policy guidance and translate the "general" administration policies into specifics.

Presidential Speeches and Political-Level Statements

Examiners kept abreast of the relevant statements and speeches of presidential candidates even before the President was elected and was sworn into
office. The process would begin from the time a presidential candidate
received his party's nomination in the summer through the general election
in the fall. Examiners closely followed all presidential candidates' speeches
bearing any relevance to their particular program areas for both the Democratic and Republican candidates during the general election campaign. As
one branch chief indicated,

> We are probably a group of people who are more interested in presidential
> campaigns than most other people in the country. Because one of these people
> is going to be our boss, we probably follow the campaign a little more closely
> than your average person does so that we can start building our understanding
> of what the President's policy might be right from the beginning.

After presidential elections, some administrations have transmitted com-
pilations of all the President's campaign statements and speeches to OMB
as a means of introducing career staff to the overall thrust of the
administration's policies. For example, one branch chief said, "when the
Carter administration assumed office, the domestic policy staff put out a list
of campaign statements which everyone in OMB latched onto."

After the election, presidential statements, speeches, and documents
would continue to serve as a valuable means for providing policy guidance
to the examiner throughout the presidential term. Examiners perused *Presidential Documents,* a weekly journal containing all presidential statements
made in a given week that was circulated to all examiners so that they could
explore its contents for material that was relevant to their areas. Available
memoranda and statements articulated by the Director, PADs, or other politically appointed officials were similarly used by examiners as a means for
understanding an administration's policy direction.

Policy Testing as Means for Policy Guidance

As one examiner suggested, "OMB is the one place in town where policy
bubbles up and percolates from below." "Percolating," or testing policy
from below, was a second means cited by examiners to extrapolate administration policy as applicable to their particular program areas. When issue
papers were forwarded to OMB's political levels, the examiner was able to

obtain indirect policy guidance by observing the political-level reaction to the alternative options and recommendations that he or she had submitted.

This type of back-and-forth testing out process was usually more prevalent during the early stages of an administration (usually for the first six months to a year), since it was during this period that examiners needed to become familiar with new policy directions. It was through this "policy-testing" process that examiners were also able to reconcile seemingly contradictory positions taken during the presidential campaign or early stages of the administration.

As the presidential term continued past the first year or so, the examiner would slowly begin to rely on precedents set and cues offered during this early period in the administration without having to seek policy guidance that often. A PAD summed this up as follows:

> The nature of policy guidance differs with respect to the administration and the age of the administration. Some administrations initially establish an ideological position and over time a very consistent body of policy. In that kind of situation after that has been "laid" down, the vast majority of our work is policy policing. But if a new administration does not have an ideology established then every decision is in effect a new policy. You start with no policy, and we start building policy, smoking out policy and understanding policy and we attempt to make assumptions of how the decisions might be made if they were bucked upstairs.

Pre-Checking of Policy

While most examiners indicated they utilized the "testing-out" approach as their primary method of seeking specific policy guidance, some examiners also sought specific policy guidance by contacting and questioning supervisors before they processed issue papers. These individuals hoped to "grease" the way for their analysis and recommendations by gauging policy direction before the issue paper was processed. The danger of this approach was that critical information might have been screened out before ever reaching the "political levels" of OMB by career staff seeking to curry favor with political-level managers.

Those examiners who did not pre-check policy, but who merely sent issue papers up the OMB hierarchy without prior attempts to seek guidance from supervision, felt that such "pre-checking" compromised the quality, substance, and neutrality of their work. For example, one commented, "You don't make a recommendation because you think it will get through but you make a recommendation because you think it will be the best decision. If I ask for guidance, I'm running a risk that they're going to tell me what to do. Everything else being equal, I do not want to do that."

Almost half of the examiners interviewed neither sought nor received policy guidance prior to sending their issue papers up the OMB hierarchy. They merely received guidance as a result of feedback or decisions made after the fact. Since most of those examiners who did seek policy guidance before sending issue papers to supervisors, mainly did so by contacting career and not political-level staff in OMB, the risk of self-censorship did not appear to be a major problem at the time.

Feedback Involving Policy Communication

Career staff often experienced difficulty when trying to obtain feedback on policy decisions from political appointees in OMB, the EOP, and the White House. The following are some illustrative observations from career staff: "It's rare that there is good feedback from upper levels on specifics." "The main problem is that it is so hard to get the political people to make a decision, that once it's been made such guidance is used beyond its original intent." Approximately half of the examiners perceived that they did not always receive adequate feedback from political levels of OMB, a finding that suggests somewhat of a potential communications problem in this area. Given the variation in frequency of feedback received by examiners, it was possible to further investigate whether there was evidence to indicate that those careerists who tended to be least politicized would be more likely to experience communications problems with the political levels of the administration than would other more politicized staffers, as Hugh Heclo had feared.

Whether or not the examiner cognitively included quasi-political assessments in recommendations, was used as a measure of examiner politicization, and frequency of receipt of feedback from political levels was held as a measure of communications clarity. Based on data obtained from examiners offering responses on both items, it appeared that examiners who did not take quasi-political factors into account and therefore could be considered to be less politicized, did not appear to receive feedback any less frequently than did other examiners.

Two other factors, however, did appear to relate to whether career staffers experienced direct communications with political officers with respect to work assignments and receipt of policy guidance and the frequency and adequacy of feedback they received on policy stands of the administration. The most striking of the two was the communications style of the individual PADs. With respect to three of the four PAD supervisory areas, generally clear and direct communications prevailed in one area and generally indirect communications in two others. In addition, all of the division chiefs interviewed confirmed that individual PADs set the tone in this regard.

The second important determinant of whether career staff experienced direct communications with PADs was their level of educational attainment, but was not tied to longer tenure in OMB. Staff with only B.A. degrees experienced the least satisfactory and direct communications with PADs, staff with MPA or MBA degrees did better and those with Ph.D.'s or LL.B.'s averaged the highest scores on a number of communications indicators.

Several tentative conclusions could be drawn from these findings. First was that the "upward" communications dynamics through which information and advice were transmitted from the career to the political levels of the institution positively contributed to the airing of "objective" presidential advice that "generally" was not pre-censored for its "acceptability" to OMB's political strata. The examiners' efforts to aggressively seek out the administration's reactions to their position papers after a case had been made "on the merits" appeared to allow for a workable policy-making system where political appointees could integrate political considerations into the primarily objective information offered and then determine more specific policies to communicate back to career staff. Since such presidential policy was usually not "spoon-fed" to examiners and communications with the political levels were often not direct, such examiners exercised much personal initiative in "seeking out" policy direction from their supervisors and other internal sources. These talents and efforts on the part of most budget examiners significantly contributed to the utility of the presidential advisory system at their level.

The findings that many career staff were exclusively processing information to superiors "on the merits," that "initial" policy guidance was general rather than specific, and that so few career staff actually pre-censored information and recommendations on "political grounds," suggested much evidence that career staff still viewed their roles as those of neutral analysts and that merits arguments were still being presented to OMB's political appointees.

The problem was that feedback from political appointees was often slow in coming back to civil servants, or did not materialize at all. High levels of career staff discretion appeared to derive from unclear or nonexistent communications from political levels, where lack of policy or inadequately communicated policy placed the examiners, branch chiefs, or division chiefs in "de facto" policy-making roles. Lack of clarity in "downward" communications also made it more difficult for OMB staff to translate presidential positions to apply to specifics regarding individual program areas.

In all of this, the responsibility rested with political appointees in OMB and the White House. The broad discretion afforded to PADs also added to the dilemma, since they usually could control to what degree policy feedback was provided to career staff, as well as whether objective information and "merits" arguments emanating from the career levels of the institution would be communicated to other EOP policy units, the White House, and ultimately the President. That the wisdom of various PADs in these and other matters was such a significant factor, and the fact that the average PAD turnover rate at the time was under two years, suggested at least in some instances that the concerns of Hugh Heclo and others were not completely unfounded.

OMB Career Staff Discretion and Influence on Decision Making

While OMB career staff examiners generally did not assume formal decision-making powers, they perceived themselves as having an unusually high degree of discretion when performing their assigned duties. This was generally confirmed by their supervisors. One interviewee in OMB commented: "The budget examiner virtually has more discretion than anyone in Washington except those at the Assistant Secretary level." Another careerist further elaborated on the delimitation to this discretion. He said,

> Budgets are the President's decision. Not ours. In this institution, it is not the role of career staff to make decisions. That becomes readily obvious very soon. We should have no autonomy as far as decision-making is concerned but we should have complete autonomy in as far as how we seek and gather our information. OMB is an invisible government and to some extent, we are responsible to no one but the President. Because of that, we should have no sort of authority in the policy area.

On five measures of institutional discretion—the degree of supervision, degree of self-initiated information gathering, degree of discretion regarding clearance of testimony and legislative guidance to agency personnel, and discretion in determining small-dollar pricing issues—levels of career staff discretion varied within OMB, but overall were found to be relatively high. The level of discretion was even higher for examiners who reviewed technically complex program areas or independent agencies, or who held advanced degrees or specific public administration training. Tenure did not seem to be as significant a factor in determining discretion levels as might have been expected.

A strong emphasis on the examiner's "personal assessments" of the value of programs in their analysis indicated an independent attitude on the part of most career staff. These attitudes, to be discussed further in Chapter 6, presented a potential danger for unaccountable civil servants to make policies on their own, particularly when policy guidance was vague or nonexistent. On the other hand, since the data indicated that such personal assessments were just one analytic criterion among many utilized in examiner analysis, this "independence" might have contributed to the airing of additional facts, even if such facts did not conform to politically set policy constraints.

Career staff not only enjoyed a great deal of discretion in doing their jobs, but also exercised pronounced influence on shaping OMB decisions at whatever level they were "finalized" before leaving the institution.[4] In a number of respects, the career levels of the institution were clearly influencing what the political appointees decided.

Much of this influence was derived from the "bubbling up" decision-making process just described and the fact that specific policy guidance from the political levels of OMB was rare. Another source of this institutional clout emanated from the examiner's traditional role as information conduit. Budget examiners were exposed to a vast amount of data that was elicited or received from departmental, agency, and other sources and were required to make choices with respect to which data and issues were worth considering and which items were to be ignored and excluded from the analysis. Information that was not included in the process of analysis changed the outcome of the final decision. As experts who understood the intricacies of programs well enough to generate or not generate issues that might otherwise remain unnoticed by supervisors, examiners wielded influence by virtue of subject-matter expertise. For example, one PAD said:

> The examiner is really the foot soldier of the whole organization. With something as vast as the federal government, you have to depend on other people to analyze it. Therefore, the examiner is the key person in the whole operation.

A branch chief commented:

> The examiner may come in and say, "Here's an issue—what should I do about it?" My response is: "If I knew what to do about it, I wouldn't need the examiner. You have to tell me what you think about it. . . ." They ought to be out doing analysis, beating the bushes, discussing the whole problem with agencies and coming up and telling me what should be done.

A second source of influence held by the examiner was one that was built into his or her role as information analyst. It was the examiner who structured the analysis, created the options, and made recommendations that were forwarded to the OMB Director. It was the examiner who defined the scope of the arguments.

A third source of influence was derived from institutional norms allowing examiners and other careerists to register disagreement with politically set policy stances. During the mid to late 1970s, such expression of dissent was perceived to be part of the examiner's institutional role. As one examiner put it, it was the examiner's responsibility to be the "eyes and ears" of the President vis-à-vis his assigned program area. If the examiner felt that some stated policy thrust presented hazards, it was his responsibility to "make his views known." One examiner explained:

> That's the best part of OMB, we do not refrain from attacking programs that are hallowed presidential programs. There have been times when we have seriously questioned some major administration efforts. I have never known any examiner to be criticized for raising issues like that.

It is evident that there was an overall institutional norm that allowed, if not encouraged, the expression of dissent on the part of the examiner. Eighty-eight percent of the examiners and branch chiefs interviewed on this point expressed the willingness to disagree with politically set policy and to allow such expression by their subordinates.

Examiners also perceived the acceptance rates of their recommendations to be quite high. The average examiner estimate for complete budgetary and legislative recommendation acceptance annually was approximately 70 percent. The branch chief estimates were even more generous than were those of their subordinates. While roughly half of the branch chiefs were unable to place a numerical percentage rate on average examiner acceptance of recommendations, of those who did, no branch chief estimated an average examiner's complete recommendation acceptance rate of less than 80 percent. Division chiefs also estimated generally high recommendation acceptance rates.

A group of recorded recommendations for expenditures and the recorded decisions made on those recommendations were examined in order to provide an "empirical" check on both the examiners' and branch chiefs' perceptions of examiner recommendation acceptance. The criterion for measuring the rate of recommendation acceptance was whether the examining division's recommendation was accepted by the OMB director or changed. This was established by comparing the division recommendations for (individual examiners') program areas with the final expenditure recommendation decided by the OMB director for presentation to the President.

The results of the recorded recommendation and decision data further substantiated the perceptual data by indicating a 66 percent rate of complete acceptance of budgetary recommendations for the two years studied.

Rates of Recommendation Acceptance in Complex Programs
and Independent Agencies

Examiners reviewing highly technical or complex programs and/or independent as opposed to Cabinet-level agencies tended to report higher recommendation acceptance rates. As one branch chief indicated with respect to program complexity:

> There is an inverse relationship between size and complexity of programs and the extent to which recommendations are changed. In the simple programs everyone can understand, they all think they are experts. In the very complex programs few people would pretend to understand, they would be concerned about making the wrong decisions without proper knowledge and therefore are reluctant to make changes in the program division's recommendations.

Examiners reviewing programs they perceived to be highly or very complex averaged a perceived recommendation acceptance rate of 75 percent, while those examiners reviewing programs they did not consider complex averaged a perceived recommendation acceptance rate of 65 percent. In 1975 and 1976, over 70 percent of the approved program recommendations occurred in areas rated as highly or very complex by the pertinent examiner, whereas only half of the recommendations that were changed at the Director level did so. With respect to Cabinet-level versus independent agency review, the interview data suggested that the examiners reviewing independent agencies also had higher rates of recommendation acceptance. While those examiners reviewing only agencies within Cabinet-level departments reported an average of 64 percent recommendation acceptance, those reviewing independent agencies indicated an average recommendation acceptance rate of 76 percent. Again, the recorded recommendation and decision data confirmed this trend.

The Institutional OMB at the End of the 1970s

Career Staff Influence

As the decade of the 1970s drew to a close, OMB career staff were influential participants in OMB's internal decision-making processes as measured by their impact on decisions and policies before they were finalized and left OMB to be scrutinized in the White House. These findings did not address OMB's overall success in shaping policies once they were considered significant enough to be discussed in the White House, EOP, or by the President. They did suggest that on most issues OMB's career staff were "leading" its new political strata and not the other way around. The "bubbling up" policy-making process that prevailed at the time suggested that the fears of a completely politicized OMB that had been voiced by some observers had not yet been borne out.

Still, the study's findings provoked other questions. Did "influential examiners" serve the purposes of the institution? Should career as opposed to politically appointed personnel have been exercising such a large measure of influence on institutional decision making?

In the end, the study yielded evidence that pointed to an affirmative answer to these questions for several reasons. First, OMB's mandates necessitated a high degree of influence and discretion for those front-line staff members providing presidential advice. Information had to be evaluated and filtered, and issues prioritized and simplified, since the President and his politically designated advisors could not possibly be aware of or scrutinize all the expenditures or legislative proposals for the entire governmental establishment. In addition, few incoming administrations at the time had knowledge of most bureaucratic issues, let alone predetermined policies on them.

The high quality of the career staff, as marked by their enhanced levels of educational attainment and their sophisticated, innovative, and balanced analytic and intelligence-gathering approaches, also lent confidence that OMB was serving the presidency as an advisory system offering a unique perspective shared by no other. So did the finding that the staff still maintained strong institutional role orientations supportive of "neutral competence." This was not to say that OMB career staff had not been touched by institutional politicization. Indeed, the study's findings illustrated that they had been so affected.

Politicization and Its Uses

The variation in staff attitudes regarding activities and career staff role orientations that were dubbed as "quasi-political," and the lack of institution-wide policies guiding them, revealed an institution in flux that seemed to be struggling to find its appropriate roles. Alternating demands on career staff shifted between the need to convey expert and neutral advice to the President, and to make certain that the advice be realistic enough to be of use to him without screening out important "merits"-based information and arguments. The staff divides on these issues were obvious throughout the interview process, as were their efforts to maintain a balance between the two seemingly contradictory roles. The study's findings yielded evidence that the career staff were generally successful in maintaining that balance.

Moreover, a return to an "ivory tower" orientation was not a viable option for OMB anyway, if it was going to be able to serve the presidency at the time. Increases in many of the quasi-political activities described in this chapter had occurred as a consequence of a genuine need on OMB's part to adapt to changing environmental demands. To ignore these would have been to reduce OMB's utility for the President.

These changes included first and foremost the passage of the Congressional Budget and Impoundment Control Act of 1974, which had provided the Congress with the means through new resources, committees, and processes to play a more meaningful role in the federal budgetary process than it had in the recent past. The Congress would now be more of an equal partner with the President when it came to the federal budgetary process, and OMB would need to monitor the congressional budgetary arena if it was to be of genuine assistance to the President. A second development was the growth and increasing sophistication of available information in Washington-based lobby groups that OMB could use as informational sources.

With respect to institutional analytic capability, inclusion of quasi-political analysis in careerist issue papers provided needed information to political officers already overburdened by the ever-increasing complexity and size of government. OMB careerist-congressional contacts, when properly controlled, contributed to the maintenance of better communications between the President and the Congress. Insulation of OMB careerists from congressional information sources would have detracted from the quality of presidential advice at the OMB careerist level and the influence of OMB generally.

Even though the OMB "picture" was considered generally to be a very positive one, there were still some concerns that remained. Certain OMB staff role perceptions and attitudes, even though they were expressed by only a minority, were troublesome. So too were the lack of clear institutional policies on such issues as congressional and interest group contacts.

Personal communications with congressional staff by OMB careerists presented the danger of the OMB careerist tipping the President's hand in the executive–congressional bargaining process at too early a stage, or providing a premature or inaccurate picture of policies that had not been fully developed with agency and OMB political-level input. There was also a potential for some congressional–careerist contacts to lead to an involvement of careerists in "negotiating or selling" roles on Capitol Hill. The lack of clear institutional policies left too much to the discretion of the examiners. Conversely, there was some evidence to suggest that in the absence of clear policies with regard to congressional contacts, the more politically charged the area was perceived to have been, the less willing were many examiners to deal with the appropriate congressional committees. Yet, it was in just such areas that examiners needed congressional information to an even greater degree in order to monitor agency activity on Capitol Hill and provide the President with related information. The "potential" danger of co-optation of OMB civil servants by interest groups was also real.

The findings that some examiners cognitively included political factors in recommendations as well, and that those examiners were more likely to have their recommendations accepted, was problematic because political-level decision makers were not always certain which assessments had or had not been taken into account. Without a complete explanation of the bases for recommendations, decision makers were at risk of misinterpreting the recommendations.

To address these various quandaries, I recommended the promulgation of clear and uniform institutional policies with regard to all of these matters. Guidelines for congressional contacts needed to be somewhere between total isolation on the one hand, an option chosen by many examiners in light of unclear policies, and an involvement by careerists in "negotiating," "selling," or other such activities on the other hand. The former would have diminished the value of the examiner's analysis to the decision maker, and the latter and would have placed the civil servant in danger of compromising the President's interests as well as diluting neutral competence within OMB. One suggestion to address this dilemma was that requests for explanations of unclear administration policies from Congress or interest groups be automatically routed to the PAD or in some cases to division chiefs and that OMB preclude careerists from attending congressional or interest group negotiating meetings without the attendance of a political appointee. In addition, given their high turnover rate, it seemed prudent that new PADs be thoroughly briefed on the limits of what civil servants could be expected to do with respect to congressional involvement.

Finally, to prevent misinterpretations of analysis, clear policies needed to be agreed upon by PADs and their subordinate careerists on whether political considerations were supposed to be factored into recommendations. Since this might have varied with the specific issues, institutional norms were needed to mandate that the bases for all recommendations be identified in staff analytic papers.

Discrete Agency Review Areas

The prevailing rule in OMB of generally discrete agency review areas for each examiner suggested a potential problem for OMB when attempting to coordinate the increasing number of interagency programs. By affording the examiner greater autonomy, discrete agency review areas also increased the likelihood for the development of positive or negative examiner biases and the possibility for agency or interest group "co-optation" to take root. This was found to present an even greater hazard in high-complexity or independent agency review areas where examiners appeared to exercise even more discretion and influence on OMB's decision-making process. In such areas some examiners had enough discretion to be able to wrap program issues in technological jargon so that upper-level managers would end up deferring to the judgment of the specialist. This could "potentially" serve the agency or related clientele group interest more than that of the President.

I recommended that these potential institutional problems be approached by rotating most examiner accounts periodically within and between divisions when practical, and by using examiner "teams" to review agencies. Such institutional arrangements would have provided greater coordinating capability to OMB's examining divisions by familiarizing examiners with more agency review areas, and also would have allowed for a consistent institutional method of controlling the potential growth of examiner biases in an institution that admittedly required a high level of discretion for its lower-level professional echelons.

5

Onslaught in the 1980s: Causes and Effects for OMB

Introduction

The institutional transformations within OMB that occurred in the 1970s proved to be precursors to developments that would unfold in the 1980s. If the "potential" for OMB politicization existed in the 1970s, it was to increase sharply in the decade to follow. External pressures on OMB precipitated by divided government, a changing congressional budget process, two visible White House insider OMB Directors, and a rapidly escalating structural deficit created a web of new roles for OMB to deal with in addition to its traditional mandates.

OMB was also to slip further out from its cloak of anonymity, becoming quite visible, but not for the attributes of neutral competence for which it had traditionally prided itself. And indeed, during that era, it often seemed that the BOB ethos of an institution with a passion for anonymity had become the forgotten artifact of a bygone era.

Chapters 6, 7, and 8 provide detailed views of what transpired within OMB during that time with respect to its budget formulation process; its legislative, management, and regulatory roles; and its relations with departmental agencies. This chapter offers an overview of the OMB story during the decade of the 1980s.

The Reagan–Stockman Budget Revolution: Implications for OMB's Institutional Persona

Stockman's Entrance: Early Reactions in OMB

With OMB Director David Stockman at the helm, the Reagan administration produced and negotiated to congressional passage a budget and economic plan that reduced discretionary domestic program budgets by an unprecedented $38 billion,[1] while at the same time setting in motion actions that were to change the budget process and make Director Stockman and OMB's institutional persona more visible to the public. Depending upon whether one was an adherent or critic, OMB came to symbolize either a key player in a "holy war" to reduce government spending, bureaucratic waste, and burdensome government regulations, or a cruel crusader in the dismantling of Great Society social programs. Chief among the means by which the Reagan administration was able to achieve its early victories in 1981 were ingenious legislative strategies employed by Stockman to gain passage of budgetary proposals. In a break with tradition, Stockman squired the executive budget throughout the congressional phases of the process and set a precedent for dexterity of congressional maneuvering that later directors would be expected to follow. As part of these strategies, OMB was used to supplant agency legislative affairs offices in the monitoring of administration-supported budget proposals on Capitol Hill.

Hints of some of what would follow emerged even before the 1980 presidential election was over, when OMB was discussed in Republican Party campaign documents. In what may have been an unprecedented action by a national political party organization, the Platform Committee of the Republican National Committee in an ostensive effort to signal support for defense modernization and buildup, issued an indictment of OMB's National Security Division.

The party plank read as follows:

> The Republican party pledges to reform the defense programming and budgeting management system established by the Carter Administration. The ill-informed, capricious intrusions of the Office of Management and Budget and the Department of Defense Office of Program Analysis and Evaluation have brought defense planning full circle to the worst faults of the McNamara years.[2]

According to OMB career staff veterans, there were other indications that the transition from a Democratic to a Republican Presidency would prove to be a difficult one. Various Reagan administration appointees were said to distrust OMB career staff and to believe OMB to have been largely composed of "liberal Democrats" who were either still in OMB or who had migrated away from the institution and were "entrenched" in senior career positions in the departments and agencies.

This particular unease among OMB career civil servants was to be short-lived, however, when their new director gathered the staff together. From the recollection of more than one OMB civil servant, Stockman told them of his profound respect for their institution and of his elation with his new position as its director. Thus, he primed his recently acquired troops for battle. Indeed, during the first few months of the Reagan administration a heady feeling of excitement prevailed among many career staff who reviewed domestic agencies because they believed they would now be afforded an open season to question previously politically untouchable programs. Much of this climate, however, would soon change.

The atmosphere in the National Security Division was much different even from the beginning. That the Republican campaign platform was not to be forgotten would become obvious to National Security staff, whose measured efforts to recommend moderate actions to conform to the administration's desire to "build up" the defense establishment were to be cast aside by the administration in favor of more pronounced spending. One of scholar Colin Campbell's interviewees is quoted in *Managing the Presidency: Carter, Reagan, and the Search for Executive Harmony* as recalling:

> We were quite disappointed in the first year. There was no big assessment of defense. It was like they just didn't want to do it. They just wanted to add dollars, which they did. Our advice to the administration when they came in was . . . add a few billion bucks—from five to ten, depending on how far you want to go—then do a big study and decide how to allocate. . . . But they didn't follow that advice. They just added twenty-six or so billion. This was beyond our wildest imagination. It probably was even beyond the wildest expectations of the defense establishment.[3]

This atmosphere led to a demoralized National Security Division staff, a rapid decline in detailed review of defense spending, and a loss of key National Security staff, whose slots would not be refilled. The National Security Division was to shrink by almost one-third.[4]

On the domestic side, staff euphoria began to fade as well when it became evident that Stockman already had a clear vision of what he wanted to accomplish. Since the administration had determined that reduction of domestic programs was to constitute a central priority, policy and policy development in OMB became top-down as opposed to bottom-up, and policy guidance from OMB's political appointees became increasingly more specific. This change in OMB's communications dynamics was one of the most striking institutional reversals that I observed in my 1982 and 1983 interview data.[5] The responses revealed that a trend had been set in motion for budget examiners to be used to justify or fill in details on decisions that had already been reached by political appointees, rather than to provide advice and information to support decision making in progress.[6] This contrasted dramatically with what I had observed in the late 1970s.

Consequently, career staff were to lose their former influence on the budget formulation process as compared with the institutional realities they had experienced in the late 1970s. Policy guidance from Stockman became so specific that it left little space for career staffers' informational input and advice of the "bubbling-up" variety described in Chapter 4. Such "specificity" denigrated the traditional career staff role to provide a uniquely honest informational resource to be factored into decisions. Moreover, OMB career staff would often not be informed of decisions reached by Stockman in concert with agency political officials. Such decisions would frequently be made without the benefit of career staff analysis as well. A number of division chiefs also observed that OMB career staff recommendations that were offered were overturned much more often than had been the case in the recent past. It seemed to some interviewees that Reagan political appointees were not interested in receiving careerist analysis even if it was directed toward supporting the attainment of administration goals.[7] Hugh Heclo and Colin Campbell cited similar findings with respect to top-down budgeting and changes in OMB's institutional decision-making dynamics.[8]

It should be noted, however, that staff perceptions pertaining to Stockman's personal interest in and use of career staff analysis were not monolithic in my interviewees over the years. Stockman had devoted admirers among OMB career staff, some of whom offered their most complimentary assessments years after Stockman had left the institution. One recently described him as having literally "soaked up" analysis. Others continued to be impressed with his interest in career staff analysis as well as the depth of his own knowledge during Director's Review sessions described in Chapter 6. But no one disputed the fact that policy guidance was generally more specific and decision making more top-down than it had been in the past. And almost no one denied that career staff analytic and information-gathering roles were changing as a consequence of the new ways Stockman was using OMB.

New staff roles included the year-round preparation of rationales, facts, and figures in support of decisions Stockman had already reached, and quantitative projections, estimates, and other informational backup for the director to use while he "worked the Hill." It was on these kinds of issues that Stockman communicated frequently with career staff. Since much of this involved the manipulation of aggregate estimates, the Budget Review Division (BRD) was to become more and more of an important part of OMB during the 1980s. As an outgrowth of these developments, many staff feared that the career staff's agency-based analytic and intelligence-gathering roles and skills were in danger of falling into disuse.

The alleged lack of Reagan administration interest in analysis was, however, only part of a potential long-term institutional problem. The increase in OMB tracking of congressional activity and its congressional liaison workload in support of the director's activities had diminished staff energies available for information gathering in the agencies, field trips, preparation of long-term analysis and special studies, and one-on-one training of new examiners by seasoned managers. This was tough, time-consuming work not to the liking of seasoned analysts, some of whom only a couple years before had been able to present their views directly to the President.

Some of the "down sides" of the institutional dynamics that prevailed during the late 1970s comprised a few of the "up sides" for career staff during the early 1980s. If careerists now had less of a chance to influence policies than in the past, at least Stockman's policies were made easier to decipher than they had been in the immediate past. In that sense, clarity of political to staff-level communications had improved markedly. In addition, a few OMB staffers who admitted after the fact to having experienced discomfort at being thrust into congressional negotiating roles during the Carter administration recalled that with Stockman playing such a one-man show on Capitol Hill, such incidents did not occur as often.

Many of these developments reflected the view held by some observers that Stockman believed that he was sufficiently cognizant of the programmatic intricacies of federal budget accounts to play the role of "budget examiner in chief" during the budget formulation process and certainly during congressional negotiating. Whether reality, myth, or a bit of both, the view prevailed that Stockman's knowledge was of such unprecedented depth that his was a "special case" and that he did not need the analytic support from career staff required by other directors.

Paradoxically, while many career staff were becoming demoralized at their reduced influence, the institution was becoming more well known and visible than ever before due to David Stockman's personal prominence in the administration. Even though OMB's career staff believed that their clout to shape policies was waning, to outside observers a large part of Stockman's aura had carried over to the institutional staff. The late Aaron Wildavsky, in particular, implied that OMB's upgraded focus on aggregates and on the congressional arena was reflective of broader changes in the budget process anyway, and that "so far as loss of agency supervision was concerned, it was compensated for by greater OMB influence with Congress."[9] With respect to the egos of OMB career staff, it was a question of whether they wanted to be "big fish in a smaller pond" or "smaller fish in the biggest show in town."

It should also be pointed out that Stockman *needed* OMB's institutional assistance to pursue his multifaceted activities. Even though OMB civil servants often found the continuous numbers crunching grueling, as Bruce Johnson later wrote, OMB was the only Executive Branch institution capable of responding to the need to alter the budget to respond to financial markets and to track changes to the president's budget during the congressional budget process as a result of "negotiation and compromise."[10]

OMB staff also began exercising greater control over their assigned agencies. As those reviewing domestic programs began to perceive a loss of clout in the budget formulation process, some had begun taking a tighter hold of the reins in their budget execution responsibilities through the apportionment process, where they stood a greater chance of exercising "discretion" and at the same time could claim to be serving the administration's aims and policies. This use of the budget execution process involved OMB examiners in delaying release of agency funds (to the degree allowable by statutory and appropriations language) as a means of policing agency conformity with administration policies. But because the administration and the Congress diverged so widely on the direction policies should take, OMB's role in the apportionment process became an object of controversy between the two branches. Bruce Johnson observed that this contentious climate tended to complicate the examiners' apportionment duties and to make them more burdensome.[11]

What was the verdict on OMB politicization under Stockman? In the larger sense, the answer would have to be that OMB had become *more* politicized. While some career staff may have been placed in uncomfortable positions on the Hill less frequently than before, the more significant development was that OMB was not getting the adequate opportunity to do its most important job of delivering a uniquely objective view of budgetary and programmatic issues to the President. It was too busy doing "other things."

David Stockman as Budget Director: Beginning of the "Post"-Modern Directorate

David Stockman's directorate ushered in many of the new expectations, requirements, and dilemmas that his successors were to face for the next fifteen years. The combination of Stockman's personal talents and single-minded pursuit of what he personally acknowledged was a grand plan to reduce the size and scope of government set in motion a series of events that resulted in spurring significant changes in the institution he had led. Many of the evolutionary changes in OMB that are chronicled in this book were to grow out of these events and actions, from "top-down" budget formulation processes, to the undermining of OMB's credibility, to the expectation that future OMB Directors would be required to be skillful congressional negotiators.

David Stockman was a powerful and compelling figure who in a sense put OMB on the map and introduced the general public to its existence. He was considered brilliant by many observers, and to have invested abundant energy and commitment into his job as President Reagan's budget director. He also was bestowed with perhaps unparalleled power and discretion to shape administration budget policy during President Reagan's first year in office. Stockman's power had for a while surpassed the authorities of the Cabinet and the domestic White House policy councils. Other than his unyielding positions on tax cuts and the need to disregard the price tag required to bolster U.S. military capacities, President Reagan had left the details of domestic government to Stockman. Frederick Mosher captured the feel of OMB's role at the time. He wrote:

> Except in the fields of foreign affairs and national defense, statements and releases from OMB seemed more authoritative than those emanating from the heads of departments and major agencies—or indeed from the White House itself. . . . For a considerable period in 1981, OMB was *the* voice of the executive branch of the government; its word was *the* policy.[12]

Stockman's large-scale ideological designs to reduce the size of government programs including political "sacred cows," were of such primary importance to him that they led him into breaking some fundamental rules that Budget Directors should follow.[13] By his own admission, he failed to completely communicate to the President the unvarnished facts surrounding budget decisions, their projected outcomes, the assumptions upon which they rested, and the probability that Congress would agree to them.[14]

Moreover, since he believed he was leading a revolution, he needed a witness. Ergo, he engaged in a series of free-wheeling conversations with William Grieder of *The Atlantic.*[15] The outcome was that the public was afforded an unusually candid picture of what was transpiring behind the scenes at the highest levels of government. The implications for OMB Directors who would come in the future and for OMB's institutional credibility were in part deleterious. Institutionally, OMB was pulled further away from its mantle of protective cover and was thrust more into the public eye. The image projected of OMB was not that of a "safe haven" to help presidents find honest information, but that of a useful tool and informational storehouse for independent directors to use to pursue their independent agendas.

Even more destructive were Stockman's admissions of "cooking the books" to achieve his ends.[16] In so doing, he inadvertently muddied the reputation of the institution. This would mean that in the budget wars that followed over the next fifteen years, congressional combatants would feel free to question OMB numbers and projections for both valid as well as nefarious reasons.

Stockman also set the wrong role model for directors that would come after him; one that undermined the trust that must exist between a President and his OMB Director. Stockman created the role of an independent director who felt free to cavort with the press, and pursue independent agendas in the Congress against the wishes of the President, moving by his own admission toward "out-and-out subversion—scheming with the congressional leaders during the first half of 1985 to force a tax hike."[17]

In light of the Stockman experience, four rules of thumb for future Budget Directors can be suggested. First, the Budget Director needs to be not only an honest communicator to the President, but a teacher, translator, and interpreter as well. Second, the Director should not be an ideologue with an independent agenda. The Director's policy perspectives should be as close as possible to the President's or at least within the President's comfort zone, and must be flexible enough to bend with the alterations in the President's mindset that occur during any four-year term. Third, the director should be loyal and not leak to the press behind the President's back. Yet, he/she must be assertive enough to relate honest assessments of the implications of policy options to the President, regardless of how they might be received by him. Fourth, as with any important presidential advisor, the Budget Director should have a high level of maturity.

The Reagan Regulatory Revolution

During the Reagan administration, another initiative was going to exert a long-term impact on OMB's institutional image. In 1980, even before the Reagan administration came into office, OMB's Office of Information and Regulatory Affairs (OIRA) had been mandated by Congress to review and reduce burdensome requests for information that government agencies promulgated to the private sector and to other government agencies. On entering office, the administration immediately used OIRA to lead another revolution intended to decimate the number of federal regulations the private sector would be subjected to in the future. Before long, OIRA was to become a publicized focal point for clashes between a free market Republican President and a Democratic House of Representatives. Critics claimed the Reagan administration had expanded OIRA's authorities beyond original congressional intent and that OIRA's regulatory review activities supplanted legitimate agency regulatory review authorities. OIRA's internal decision-making processes as determined by executive order during the Reagan administration, were faulted as being shielded from public scrutiny and were characterized as causing inappropriate delays in the regulation review process. While OIRA was directed by a political appointee, future OMB Director James Miller, its staff was composed of civil service employees. It was unclear at the time whether this newly constituted OMB staff saw itself as deeply rooted in the traditions of objective analysis as were staff members from other more long-standing sectors of OMB. In any case, critical press pieces at the time accused OMB of seeking out interest group contacts that favored industry representatives as opposed to public interest groups (see Chapter 8). When seeking input during the regulatory review process, some "bureaucrat" in OIRA would be blamed for allegedly egregious actions, which were probably directed by political-level staff and the White House. In any case, OIRA and its surrounding controversies sometimes became equated with the whole institution in the public mind.

The Era of Continuous Budgeting and "Dead-on-Arrival" Executive Budgets

After 1982, many congressional Democrats and some Republicans had rebelled from the Reagan–Stockman juggernaut, thus ushering in an era of stalemate and deadlock between Congress and the Executive. From 1982 to 1990, presidential budgets, which once had served as definitive foundations for congressional decision making, were frequently considered moribund on arrival to Capitol Hill. They were at best, as Allen Schick described, an "opening maneuver" in a presidential-congressional budgeting process,[18] where budgetary decision making became a continuous year-round proposition often marked by White House–congressional summitry and the failure to complete passage of appropriations bills in time to fund the government. Continuous resolutions became a frequent means for keeping the government operating, and huge omnibus reconciliation bills negotiated behind closed doors at the eleventh hour provided cover for hidden political trade-offs in the final budgetary decisions reached. This budgetary deadlock, plus a large military buildup and a tax cut, would contribute to rapid escalation of the federal deficit, which climbed to more than $200 billion dollars in FY 1983[19] from about $74 billion dollars in 1980.[20]

Each of these developments triggered a continuation of "top-down" and centralized decision making in OMB and created new roles and responsibilities for OMB career staff. Since the initial presidential budget had ceased to be a defining document, the Executive Branch shifted into continual oversight of an increasingly convoluted congressional budget process. Even with David Stockman's departure from OMB in 1985, these conditions had institutionalized an intensified congressional tracking role for OMB. Since executive budgets were frequently disregarded and superseded by White House–congressional agreements, Allen Schick would come to call the traditional processes whereby agencies and OMB recommended budget levels, a "casualty" of this era.[21]

In many areas, OMB PADs continued to supplant agency legislative affairs offices in negotiating administration proposals in Congress, with OMB career staff providing the backup support. Bruce Johnson, a former OMB watcher, noted this OMB "negotiator role" as he observed the Reagan administration's effort to weaken cooperative relationships among federal agency bureaus, congressional committees, and interest groups known as "iron triangles." According to Johnson, OMB's strategy to accomplish this was to appeal "to Congress as a whole by packaging and negotiating the budget as a whole through the various pieces of omnibus budget legislation , . . ." as OMB began more often to deal "directly with the subcommittees and interest groups, instead of dealing with them through the agencies, to influence the political process."[22]

Consequently, OMB career staff were now interacting with congressional staff at more points in this ever-changing congressional budget process. With Stockman's departure, the "potential" for the blurring of OMB staff analytic support roles with "negotiating and selling" roles was now greater than it had ever been before. Certain stages of the process created more ambiguous situations for career staff than others. OMB staff support during the highly politically charged reconciliation process was particularly problematic in this regard.

The Miller Years

Ideological Purity in OMB, or, How to Stick to Your Guns and Get Nowhere Fast

When James C. Miller III was sworn in as OMB director in 1985, the deficit had reached crisis proportions and the President and the Congress seemed to be hopelessly deadlocked. President Reagan's insistence on keeping tax increases and defense cuts off the table and relying almost exclusively on domestic programmatic reductions to decrease the deficit was at loggerheads with a Democratic Congress and, by 1986, a newly elected Democratic Senate that presented little realistic possibility of acquiescing to such presidential entreaties.

At the end of 1985, Congress had crafted Draconian methods for meeting planned annual deficit reduction targets in the Balanced Budget and Emergency Deficit Control Act of 1985, better known as the Gramm–Rudman–Hollings Act. When Congress and the President failed to meet the targets in 1987, they were lowered in a second Gramm–Rudman–Hollings legislative effort. To arrive at budgetary compromises in this climate, the White House and congressional leadership resorted to budgeting strategies involving agreements that specified across-the-board reductions in broad areas, but did not specify where cuts would be made.

Due to both Congress's and the President's inability to reach Gramm–Rudman–Hollings targets, both institutions often factored unrealistically optimistic economic assumptions into their deficit projections to produce estimates of future deficit growth that proved to be low when compared with the actual deficit figures that evolved later on. OMB's estimates often proved to be more out of line with the economic indicators that actually materialized than did those of the Congressional Budget Office (CBO). In the process, OMB's reputation as a purveyor of honest information continued to suffer. Now that the deficit and the machinations of the federal budget process were becoming known to a wider and wider audience, it was again, often through alleged "cooking of the books," that OMB became publicized.

Director James Miller was following in the footsteps of perhaps the most clever, informed, and influential modern OMB Director up to that point. Thus, at their very kindest, observers rated Miller as much less knowledgeable about government programs than Stockman had been,[23] and as substantially less agile when entering into congressional negotiations. Miller was not characterized, therefore, as having been a particularly influential OMB Director with the White House or the Congress.[24]

The most common characterization of Miller, both in interviews and in press accounts, was as having been excessively "ideological," but unlike Stockman's original ideological visions, Miller's ideology was seen to fit the President's budgetary and economic world view rather closely. In this, James Miller's directorate illustrates just how difficult it is to reach the correct balance when you are sitting in the Budget Director's seat. Where Stockman had gone too far in one direction, Miller went too far in the other. Miller's seemingly rigid ideological loyalty to President Reagan's budgetary and economic orthodoxy may have prevented him from initiating any substantive internal debate with the President. This adherence to certain principles also considerably weakened his potential as a congressional negotiator and contributed to producing a series of dead-on-arrival budgets to the Congress.

As part of this ideological bent, a new potentially "politicizing" advocacy role for OMB staff was encouraged.

As Bruce Johnson describes:

> Under Director Miller OMB has taken a more active interest in speech making before interest groups and the placement of favorable "op-ed" pieces in various newspapers and magazines. . . . Under Miller the development of "op-ed" pieces has been guided by its own tracking log that follows each proposed article in various stages as it is prepared. In some cases these speeches and pieces have been composed entirely by political appointees. In other cases these advocacy documents have been reviewed by career staff to supply factual data to support the arguments and to review the accuracy of other factual assertions. In other instances the articles or speeches may be drafted mostly by career staff with final editing by the political leadership.[25]

These activities constituted an even greater foray for career civil servants into political posturing. Johnson worried at the time that these activities might further undermine the "sense of objectivity and nonpartisan detachment that may be necessary for first class policy analysis," and that OMB staff might become "taint[ed]" and "less useful to the next administration if that administration does not share the same political objectives as its predecessor."[26] Another troubling indicator of potentially insidious OMB politicization was that by the end of the second Reagan administration, the number of political appointees had grown to eleven not counting their noncareer support staff.

Miller's personal account of his years as budget director casts some doubt on claims that he had politicized OMB's career echelons to any significant degree, particularly with respect to its budget review process. He wrote that on budget review decisions for the 1987 budget, he "directed that calls be made on the merits of the programs and that the merits should consist of the analytic merits, not the political feasibility."[27] If so, ironically, his failure to factor political realities into decisions at any point in the process might further explain the dead-on-arrival budgets he submitted to Congress. Thus, while David Stockman's reputation had elevated OMB's influence in its relations with agencies and the Congress, James Miller's directorship presented a different case of unwavering loyalty to an unbending "party line" and a reduced clout with the Congress. OMB's overall status also diminished accordingly.

OMB During the Bush Administration

Richard Darman: Policy Wonk, Strategist, and "Game Player"

At the beginning of his term as Budget Director, it appeared that Richard Darman possessed an almost "ideal" combination of personal talents and experience (in the Reagan White House and as Deputy Secretary of the Treasury) to fulfill both the traditional and the modern-day director's roles. It quickly became evident that as the new director, Richard Darman would become a central participant in policy making, the crafting of administration strategy, and in "dealing" on Capitol Hill. But in a number of ways, Darman's leadership was to take different turns from those of both of his immediate predecessors. His vision at the outset of his tenure at OMB was to reduce the deficit as a necessary means to the end of "investing" in the economy through education, space exploration and other research and development efforts.[28] In this, he perhaps revealed a greater appreciation for enhanced investment in government programs than did his two immediate predecessors.

With respect to preserving the neutrality of OMB's career staff advice to the President, Darman's early confirmation testimony left room for some optimism that he both understood "what OMB was about" and grasped the breadth of its many responsibilities. He indicated the following in his written responses to the Senate Committee on Governmental Affairs:

> It is imperative that the President receive the most competent advice possible from his staff at OMB. . . . If confirmed, I intend to ensure that the competence of OMB staff is maintained at the extremely high level necessary to serve the President as effectively as possible. As Director, I would satisfy myself that OMB's analyses are as accurate, tough-minded, and as objective as possible (within the inherent constraints of operating in policy areas where much is uncertain and time demands are always enormous). At the same time, I would expect to advise the President on policy matters and advocate the policies and priorities he has chosen. In my view, however, proper advice and effective advocacy cannot be based on erroneous or biased assumptions; I will seek to ensure that this does not occur.[29]

At his confirmation hearings, Darman also showed sensitivity to OMB's institutional overload and its accompanying drain on the long-term analytic capability of the institution. He remarked, "It is very difficult to do a responsible job analytically of long term issues. . . . It takes human resources. The people within OMB work, I think, as hard or harder than almost anybody in Government. They are always under enormous time pressure."[30]

While both the author's interviews and other observers suggest that staff continued to experience that time pressure during Darman's tenure, he did argue for and win a moderate increase in overall staff numbers and made some efforts to listen to and respond to workload-related grievances of new staff members.[31]

Darman's abilities were in a league with those of Stockman. Some OMB staff observed that while Darman may have fallen slightly short of Stockman in his knowledge of the mechanics of the budget process, his analytic reach was broader and more "subtle." There were those who were dazzled by his intellectual and analytical acuities, and the word "brilliance" has been used to describe him more than once. One OMB careerist recalled Darman as having an ideal combination of policy sense and political sense, which he integrated rapidly when reaching decisions. Since he could assess the political factors so well himself, he had little need or desire to politicize OMB staff.

There were also those interviewees who believed that Darman understood OMB's roles and the need to balance them better than any director they had worked with. Such retrospective views from civil servants thus lend credibility to Darman's promises at his confirmation hearings to preserve OMB's neutral competence. Along these same lines, descriptions in Darman's book *Who's in Control?* portray him playing the traditional OMB roles of providing the President and top White House officials Sununu and Brady with budgetary options that included assessments of their prospects for success in Congress.[32]

These descriptions, however, only capture one dimension of this complicated public figure. Another characterization of him often emphasized in the press was that of a consummate game player and a wily Washington insider with the ability to outsmart most of his adversaries most of the time. His capacities as a strategist when dealing with the agencies or the Congress were considered by some to be unparalleled. For example, the *National Journal* characterized him as a "master plotter, a long-range thinker, and a strategist (to critics, a schemer) without peer."[33]

In running OMB, he more or less operated as a "one-man show," exhibiting a penchant for secrecy, centralization, and control-based methods to achieve mastery over the institution he headed. In the beginning of his tenure, Darman generally only interacted with political-level OMB officials and a few career staffers who had gained his respect and/or were expert on policy areas of particular interest to him. In this regard, one interviewee described him as "holding his strategies very close to the cuff" with five or six plans developing in his mind at the same time. The *National Journal* described him as tightly controlling the flow of information in OMB, particularly those communications to be transmitted to the White House, making it clear that "OMB officials [reported] to him—and to him alone."[34]

In interactions with those OMB staff he did deal with, Darman was often said to be at very least impatient and brusque, though these unpleasant portrayals of his style were said to apply more often in his dealings with PADs and other OMB policy officials than with the career staff he saw less of anyway. Purportedly, he did not attend "budget examiner's days," and

OMB legend has it that he drove to a staff picnic only to circle around the picnic site and not get out of his car.

Darman writes in his book that "one of my failings was that I was not gregarious. I was uncomfortable in large social settings," and that his "social unease was often translated into aloofness or arrogance."[35] Yet, to further complicate the picture of this intense man, Darman has been described as charming and delightful by others who knew him who claimed to have been baffled by the other less flattering portrayals.[36]

This appearance of arrogance, abrasiveness, and secrecy may have been projected by design on the part of this master strategist as well as being part of his personality. All of this alleged secrecy and standoffishness appears to have served him well in consolidating power within OMB and within the government in general. In this regard, there are few who would contest the conclusion that Darman was an exceedingly powerful OMB director. Darman admitted that he "sought and was granted influence far beyond what is ordinarily accorded a Budget Director."[37] Within OMB, his tough tone might have been intended to prevent his policy staff in particular from straying from his central OMB agendas (presumably the President's agenda) and from pursuing independent dealings with the White House, EOP, and agency officials.

The methods used by Darman to successfully control internal OMB operations also had down sides. They eroded his ability to foster the independent analytic capability of the institution in its traditional sense. While Darman encouraged and sometimes publicly rewarded stellar analytic efforts by staff, his reputed arrogance also discouraged bottom-up information and analytic communications from any but the stout-hearted. But to add to the difficulty of easily characterizing this complex man, Darman was also credited with making other positive efforts to work with "OMB's next generation."[38] This translated into his taking time to hold luncheon discussions with junior staff and taking actions designed to streamline some of OMB's workload.[39]

Darman was an influential White House insider as well as a somewhat independent public figure in Washington. His speech laying out his policy visions for the future has already been noted. This perception of Darman as independently powerful extended to the next administration to the point that Elizabeth Drew reports that the Clinton White House made careful efforts to prevent "a Darman" from being hired in the EOP.[40] Thus all of this "power" in the OMB Director's office tended to detract from the institution's traditional anonymity, and perhaps its image of objectivity. All this "power" further left Darman's personal reputation open to political bashing. Darman felt this, and believed that "a strong OMB Director, who tries to do his job in times of serious fiscal stress, is bound to have more than his fair share of opponents."[41]

Paradoxically, in a deficit era, Presidents needed powerful figures in the OMB Director's seat if they were to have the job handled with mastery. To do so, budget directors needed to play some of the roles that Darman played so well. And yet, even Darman himself could not bring about deficit reduction in the climate that existed. The Darman case brings to light factors during the Bush administration that both made the OMB Director's job and deficit reduction so difficult. For example, after leaving a White House meeting, he reports having felt like he was required to "square a circle," and do the impossible, after being asked to "flesh out a radically reduced budget 'in a politically acceptable way.' "[42] With respect to the prospect of shared sacrifice on the part of Cabinet officials, Darman observed, "among the Bush cabinet, there was close to zero serious interest in a radical reduction of spending—or any reduction at all when it came to cabinet officers' own departments."[43]

On the Congress he wrote, "as a matter of practical fact, neither party was advocating a workable program to eliminate the deficit. Privately, the leaders of both parties admitted that."[44] In all, paths seem to lead to the electorate. He observed that "polls showed that the public wanted to reduce government only in the abstract, not in the fundamental particulars," and that "the practical political fact was that the American middle class had become addicted to its 'entitlements.' "[45]

In the end, Darman left the job feeling "a sense of [his] own failure."[46] He wrote, "I had let down some terrific professionals at OMB who had sacrificed a great deal in order to serve the public interest."[47] However, the story that unfolded in the account of his experiences during the Bush administration provided less a picture of personal failure and more a description of the crushing strains of the directorship during an era of unprecedented deficits, divided government, and mixed messages from the public.

OMB During the Bush Years: Credibility Issues, Management Actions, and the Budget Deal

For two of the Reagan administration's credibility problems, OIRA and inaccurate economic forecasting, OMB could be credited with making moderate improvements during Darman's stewardship. In the former case, OIRA's credibility may have been somewhat restored, if for no other reason than the fact that it was taken out of the limelight. During the first year and a half of the Bush administration, the President, at least on the surface, appeared to be de-emphasizing the deregulatory crusade, only to change course in 1990 and recharge it again by vesting its leadership within a newly created EOP unit called the Competitiveness Council directed by Vice President Quayle.

With respect to the accuracy of the economic projections and deficit forecasting coming out of OMB during the Bush administration, the record of improvement was also somewhat mixed. While the OMB under Darman was credited with producing more accurate forecasts of economic performance, OMB's deficit predictions were faulted when they turned out to be extremely low when compared with the actual accumulated deficit. Disputes also flared between OMB and Congress over the validity of the economic assumptions that Darman and OMB used when estimating the amount of savings to be derived from administration budget proposals.

OMB experienced other "image" problems during the Bush years. One flap concerned OMB's testimony clearance role, when in May of 1989, NASA's "Dr. James E. Hansen told the Senate Commerce Subcommittee on Science, Technology and Space that OMB had ordered him to soften his conclusions that global warming would cause severe weather in the future and that man-made gases are primarily responsible for the so-called 'green house effect.' " Claiming that Hansen did not appeal the outcome of the testimony clearance process to higher levels in OMB, Darman asserted that he first heard about Hansen's displeasure in the *New York Times*.[48]

While not heavily investing his personal time and energy in management-related activities in OMB, a number of Darman's actions served to invigorate the federal management mandate in OMB, thus making good on the director's promise during his confirmation hearings to emphasize OMB's management role. These actions included a successful effort to increase the size of the management divisions by one-half, and the creation of OMB staff teams to attempt to intervene in those agencies considered to have the most profound financial management problems. Darman also created new units in OMB's General Management Division, which attempted to factor in agency management issues when arriving at budgetary decisions.

President Bush's budget and tax agreement with Congress, the Omnibus Budget Reconciliation Act of 1990 (OBRA), and its accompanying Budget Enforcement Act (BEA), were also to prove exceedingly important to OMB. With the BEA, the administration and Congress were able to temporarily free themselves from having to meet annual deficit targets. Instead, both Congress and the Executive would have to apply discipline to growth in annual appropriations, which the act capped, as well as to control new entitlements, where a "pay-as-you-go" system was applied. Through Darman's shrewd negotiating efforts, OMB was afforded significant enforcement powers in the law. At the same time, OMB staff would need to decipher yet another piece of complex legislation in order to assume new congressionally mandated responsibilities in their budget formulation and congressional tracking duties.

OMB in the 1980s: Institutional Overload and Staff Size

Institutional overload was not a new problem for OMB, but it seemed to have become more pronounced during the 1980s. This is illustrated by considering a "laundry list" of the broad array of new responsibilities that program division staff were performing by the early 1990s that were as-sumed to a far lesser degree in the 1970s, or not at all. These include the tracking of new stages of a more complex congressional budget process (budget resolutions, reconciliation bills, omnibus continuing resolutions, budget committee proceedings); cultivation of personal contacts with com-mittee staff; Gramm–Rudman–Hollings I and II scoring and estimating ac-tivities from 1985 to 1990; and Budget Enforcement Act score-keeping tasks from 1990 to the present.

To these responsibilities can be added sporadic short-term informa-tion requests from the White House or other EOP units, calls for inputs into aggregate numbers exercises as well as more sophisticated eco-nomic analyses and more complex apportionment responsibilities. While the program divisions continued to serve as a wellspring of program expertise for LRD and the various management divisions, some divi-sions would also be called upon frequently to serve in a similar capacity for OIRA. To these duties can be added occasional participation in in-vestigations into agency mismanagement conducted during Richard Darman's tenure. Career staff were responsible for handling all of these charges and others, while at the same time maintaining responsibility for traditional budget formulation activities.

This is not to argue that all program divisions were participating in these activities to the same degree at all times. The variations among the program divisions was a constant in OMB, as described in Chapter 2. Nor is this to imply that other units within the organization were not similarly affected by some of the same factors. It is just to observe that it was the program divisions as OMB's repositories of program expertise that felt to some degree almost any new responsibility mandated to the institution as a whole.

At the same time that OMB had been accumulating these added layers of responsibility, it had also been shrinking in size throughout the 1980s. David Stockman had alluded to this work load increase in his testimony supporting OMB's budget request for FY 1986. He had testified:

I calculate that each budget examiner who actually has an assigned agency, program or account, has to handle $5 billion a year out of our $1 trillion budget. Some have a lot more, some less, but the average is $5 billion. Ten years ago it was less than half that. You can see that we are stretched pretty thin and every one of our budget examiners has an awfully large amount of public money to worry about.[49]

Stockman's entreaties did not appear to have resonated with a Congress that had repeatedly been at loggerheads with OMB. It seems that the "budget-cutters" were expected to "take their own medicine" once again.

In Richard Darman's confirmation testimony Darman also asserted that "whatever OMB has asked for over the last decade roughly, it has received less."[50] In his response to a question regarding the relatively low number of OMB employees at the time, Darman spoke to the dilemmas that OMB directors faced in attempting to increase appropriations for their own agency.

Darman said,

When we have been trying to apply standards of some fiscal stringency to other parts of the Government, I think OMB has been hesitant—and understandably so—hesitant to ask for an increase in its own resources. It would be accused of hypocrisy, no matter how much the resources might be deserved. . . . I do not myself want to be in a position of being accused of being hypocritical, coming up here asking—as I will be at some point, if confirmed—for some very unpopular cuts, and turning around and asking for an increase in the staffing of OMB. I just think that would be foolish. The Congress is not going to give it to OMB, I would expect—it hasn't in the past eight years. So I think we are going to have to live within these tight resource constraints at OMB.[51]

The constraints can be observed both in numbers of employees and in total expenditures. According to a GAO study, total employees had dropped from 614 staffers in 1971 to 598 in fiscal 1981 and to 525 in fiscal 1988.[52] In 1989, at Richard Darman's confirmation hearings, GAO reported that OMB had only 378 employees.[53] Total expenditures had dropped from $35.3 million dollars in fiscal 1981 to $32.2 million in fiscal 1988.[54] Breakdowns of allotments for different sectors of OMB are also instructive. For example, the decrease in staff in the management divisions and OIRA, dropping by 31 percent from 163 to 112, were more pronounced than decreases in the program divisions and BRD, which fell from 335 to 316, a 5.5 percent change.[55] During the first budget under President Bush, for fiscal 1990, staff numbers only rose to 507.[56] Darman was able to convince Congress to improve the overall picture somewhat by bolstering the depleted management divisions. Institution-wide staff numbers climbed to 540 in fiscal 1991,[57] to 553 in fiscal 1992,[58] and to a high of 561 in fiscal 1993,[59] but never reached 1980 levels.[60] These boosts did not, however, address the needs of OMB's program divisions.

Career Staff Recruitment, Credentials, and Turnover in the 1980s

Staff recruitment patterns, turnover rates, and the institutional incentives used to attract career staff to OMB illustrate how OMB was attempting to maintain its capabilities in an era marked by rapidly changing challenges and demands. In the mid-1980s and early 1990s, the prevailing recruitment pattern for career staff was to hire well-recommended and usually young MPPs or MBAs who were recent graduates of prestigious educational institutions but did not generally have experience working in federal agencies or particular expertise related to the programs they reviewed. As one departmental agency budget official with twenty-five years of experience described it,

> Recruiting methods changed in OMB in the mid-1980s starting in 1985 and more pronounced after 1987. They used to recruit people who had the intellectual skills but also had agency experience. Then they started recruiting people with intellectual skills from graduate schools in public policy but not the operational technical detail/skills. They had the smarts but not the experience.

One inducement, which enabled OMB to recruit such bright young staffers, was the hope that they could parlay a couple of years of experience in OMB into fast-track positions in the government and/or the private sector. Moreover, some of the entering staff were told at the outset to expect to work in OMB less than three years and then to plan to move on to other professional pursuits.

There were several reasons that OMB employed these recruitment strategies. First, because of the nature of their graduate training, the incoming staff that came to work in OMB during the 1980s were generally better able to use the sophisticated quantitative analytic techniques that were needed in OMB during an era of continuous aggregate budgeting than staff in the past had been.[61] Second, the relative youth of the recruits was attractive to the institution because such staff would be more willing and able to work long days and weekends if required. Third, it was difficult, expensive, and problematic for OMB to recruit mid-level or senior agency staff to assume work paces considered to be far more demanding than most agency work schedules. Interest in such career movement among likely candidates was not easy to elicit. Fourth, OMB was able to save money by bringing entry-level staff who turned over quickly into the institution at lower salaries.

These approaches to recruitment and the underlying institutional pressures that drove them led to exceedingly rapid turnover rates among entry-level staff. A review of OMB telephone directories from 1984, 1986, 1988, 1989, 1990, 1992, and 1993 showed that new staff entering a program division branch from 1986 to 1990 spent only an average of 2.8 years in the unit. (This composite figure comprised an average of accumulated time spent in the branch of entry for 155 staffers entering the program division budget examining branches from 1986 to 1990.) To look at this question another way, only about 14 percent of fifty-two staffers entering the program divisions in 1988 (new from 1986) were still present in their branches or divisions in 1993. About one-third of thirty-two new entries in 1989 were still present in 1993. Program division branch chiefs, however, had lower turnover rates and higher levels of institutional tenure. The average branch chief tenure among program division chiefs from 1984 to 1994 was 4.5 years, and the overwhelming majority had served in the branch they headed for several years before becoming a branch chief.

To further examine staff turnover rates as one indicator of the health of OMB's institutional memory, comparisons with other units in OMB were drawn. BRD, as a nerve center in the aggregate budgeting wars of the 1980s, was relatively stable, still housing 30 percent of its 1984 staff in 1993. Certain of BRD's branches, such as the critical "budget concepts" branch, was made up of about 60 percent of the staff that had been in BRD in 1984. An image of instability in the management divisions, prompted by frequent reorganizations, is supported by the finding that only 10 percent of the 1984 staff in the management divisions (excluding OFPP and OIRA) were to be found in the newly reorganized 1993 management divisions. With regard to OIRA, the questions of whether the early OIRA staff were in fact as ideological as some observers had claimed at the time was not entirely moot since almost 30 percent of the (1993) OIRA staff had been working in that division in 1984.

OMB's career patterns and recruitment philosophies had both strengths and weaknesses. The "pluses" revolved around maintaining OMB's ability to assure a continuing stream of bright and energetic troops, while providing some check against institutional stagnation or a buildup of entrenched biases involving agencies under review. The "down sides" were threats to the integrity of OMB's institutional memory and to the maturity of its analytic capability that such a "revolving door" can create. Some interviewees in the agencies believed that because of this rapid turnover and the fact that fewer staffers came into OMB with agency experience, OMB's knowledge base and analytic capability had eroded. One such interviewee commented that new staff "were able to do the quick analysis as called for but didn't have the long-term, in-depth understanding of the agencies. The agency review just became more superficial."

Scholar Walter Williams reached similar conclusions. He particularly questioned the analytic depth of OIRA's young career staff, whom he characterized as having "fared badly against deeper, more experienced agency staffs"[62] resulting in what a NAPA panel had found was a tendency for OIRA to concentrate on " 'nit-picking,' on relatively minor provisions of proposed regulations, on choice of wording, and on other differences that do not seem to have much importance."[63] Williams cited lack of experience in government and its attendant lack of sophisticated program knowledge in many budget examiners as undermining analytic capacity in the program divisions.[64] He did note that the "fallout" resulting from inexperienced staff was somewhat less in the program divisions than in OIRA due to the presence of more experienced branch chief supervisors.[65] This last point would turn out to be a "saving grace" for the institution. As some OMB respondents tell it, the stability of the branch chief level was a critical support in maintaining OMB's institutional memory in the 1980s.

But even taking the stability of the branch chief level into account, the potential loss of institutional memory through retirements of "old timers" who had been able to transmit both programmatic expertise and OMB institutional norms to less senior staff, remained a concern. One agency budget official observed that "the old hands didn't lose the capacity, but they just got fewer and fewer and no longer made up the critical mass." Moreover, the rapid turnover of junior examiners and the "potential" for experienced analysts and technically savvy staff to leave, carried with it the risk of more serious depletion of OMB's all-important institutional memory at some point in the future.

Just such a "brain drain" had occurred in the Natural Resources and Science Program Divisions in 1992. It involved the departure of three veteran branch and division chiefs with tenures of seventeen, fourteen, and nine years respectively, and two budget examiners, all of whom had impressive scientific credentials. Of the five, three held Ph.D. degrees in cellular biology, physics, and nuclear engineering.[66] *Physics Today* characterized these departures as causing "gaping holes in the White House science policy apparatus," with respect to understanding "the costs, risks and benefits of many programs."[67] While the staffers denied any relationship among the reasons that the five staffers left OMB, the article pointed to a loss of "flexibility in dealing with budgets" in OMB, and in particular the constraints of the Budget Enforcement Act, which purportedly "frustrated many OMB staffers" and turned some of them into "bean counters."[68]

Internal Politicization in OMB: Did Civil Servants Get a Bum Rap?

Introduction

The pressures surrounding OMB staff that have been described in this chapter did not provide ideal conditions for neutral competence and reasoned analysis to flourish in OMB. Moreover, by the end of the 1980s, the number of political appointees in OMB had climbed to thirteen.[69] These political officials in turn had from ten to twenty noncareer staffers working under them.[70] What remained of the old institutional ethos and esprit de corps that had marked BOB/OMB during earlier years? Did career staff still support the notion that OMB should provide a "unique" source of advice to Presidents? While these are difficult questions to answer definitively, it was possible to elicit career staff observations about norms and processes in OMB that might have supported the maintenance of analytical objectivity during a period of institutional change.

Institutional Supports for Keeping Neutrality Alive in OMB

> *Norms are passed from one generation to the next, norms that there are certain lines we don't cross. We can explain policy, but do not advocate it. We are information conduits and communicators.*

> —An OMB Division Chief

> *The President needs to know the institutional realities and public policy dilemmas, 80 percent of which don't touch on party politics or ideology to transition from campaigning to governing. Was OMB career staff politicized in the 1980s? No.*

> —An OMB Manager

Discussions with OMB career staff managers from the early 1980s to 1995, as well as with congressional committee staff with tenures spanning much of the period in question, revealed some promising indications that many of the old traditions of neutral competence were alive and well in OMB, particularly in the program divisions.

Throughout the 1980s and to the present, these career staff continued to view the communication of honest and unslanted advice and analysis to the President and his political appointees to be their fundamental responsibility. This was true whether the information was of the traditional "bubbling-up" variety or was in response to short-term requests from OMB political staff or the White House. Career staff recounted many instances when they had been willing to air facts and analytic conclusions that did not tend to support a general direction the administration was taking before that administration had articulated clear-cut policies. Indeed, some staff took pride in recalling situations in which they had been able to persuade an OMB political appointee or Cabinet official to support their conclusions by the sheer force of their "merits" arguments. More telling is the observation by career staff that OMB political appointees did not sanction career staff who "told it as they saw it" or "played the devil's advocate" as policy was being developed. In fact, as an OMB "old timer" indicated,

> All of the policy/political people in the last 15 years have wanted the staff to do good neutral analysis in the beginning but as time goes on some of the more ideological administrations might say—Thank you but we're going in a different direction. Then the staff falls in line—certainly some career staff will not recommend things that are clearly inimical to administration goals, but they don't skew facts.

What of the kinds of advocacy roles OMB staff were playing in the mid-1980s? Did activities such as supplying backup data and facts and sometimes even putting the "spin and rhetoric" on political-level speeches and press pieces, as one OMB manager described it, or providing statistics to support administration positions tend to politicize career staff? If not, what institutional constraints prevented them from evolving into just another "political research staff"?

While these activities always eroded time that could be spent in other ways, career staff attitudes showed little evidence that these experiences had turned them into latter-day "pols." On the contrary, most OMB staff did not relish these quasi-political roles and though they dutifully performed them, they somewhat resented the time taken away from what they considered to be their legitimate analytic and information conduit roles. Others considered that these activities did not consume enough time to really have any appreciable impact.

At least in the program divisions, recruitment and socialization processes also constituted a brake against career staff politicization. OMB civil servants involved in hiring and training staff in their divisions continued to communicate norms of neutral competence to OMB recruits and trainees. In the rare cases when staff appeared to have become too enamored of any one administration, their career supervisors would not hesitate to show their displeasure. Their views are instructive. One division chief cited an intensive interview process where the importance of neutral competence was stressed, as well as "initial suspicion of anyone coming from the Hill or campaigns and institutional rewards for good dispassionate analysis." A second veteran staffer commented, "I tell applicants that if they have a cause, if they have an ax to grind, they shouldn't come to OMB."

A couple of career staffers talked about how the nature of the policy-analysis process itself had mitigated against any personal partisanship or ideology working its way in their analysis. One staffer commented: "The analysis process itself is a check against this. I would go into research and analysis on a topic and end up making recommendations that I would have opposed before going into it. As an analyst you see all sides . . . most issues are not simple or clear cut."

Even though there continued to be no institution-wide policies guiding career staff in their dealings on the Hill, mid-level managers, when describing the guidelines of appropriate behavior that they attempted to inculcate in their staffs, seemed to have maintained a shared understanding. The following are three such typical comments.

> It's a tricky business. We have to get as much information on staff and member positions as possible without giving too much in return. Once the President's policy is clear and stated we can communicate that. It is particularly tricky when congressional staff are trying to get a read on whether the President will veto or not.

> I tell my staff what not to divulge on the administration strategy or numbers that haven't been released.

> In order to do your job you need to get to know people in the area. To find out information and to tell them appropriate information . . . obviously you are not going to be giving out confidential information. The subtle line is that you are not supposed to be advocating policies. It becomes difficult when you get calls from them wanting explanations or advice on what presidential policies will be on X, Y or Z. Only if the position is clear do you tell them.

Even so, did congressional tracking and information conduit roles evolve into actual "selling" or negotiating in spite of supervisory tutelage to the contrary? Again, the answer to that question still appears to be probably occasionally, but not to any great degree. Most program division staff interviewed during the 1980s reported that they were not involved in either selling or negotiating roles at all. Appropriations and Budget Committee staff were interviewed on this issue as a check, and strongly confirmed the OMB staff responses.

Did OMB political appointees or White House or EOP officials leave career staff "alone" with congressional staff to draft legislation or negotiate? There were only rare reports of such situations, usually triggered by a PAD or another political official who did not understand OMB's norms or refused to abide by them. A standard response would be that OMB career staff rarely accompanied policy officials to congressional negotiating sessions and then only as silent partners on hand to provide technical assistance. Other budget process participants during the Reagan administration had also found that Hill staff were able to distinguish between OMB political officials who gained "little trust or respect,"[71] and OMB career staff who were viewed as "highly professional" and "competent."[72]

As with other institutional dynamics within OMB, politicizing forces varied widely from one division to another and from one time period to another. As in the 1970s, the changes often occurred when a new PAD or director assumed office. Directors Stockman and Darman were White House insiders with visible and sometimes controversial presences, which in a larger sense may have politicized OMB's overall image. However, since they often pursued personalized strategies while negotiating in the White House or on Capitol Hill, they placed career staff in fewer potentially compromising roles. Career staff also cited instances where both could be persuaded to a position by the force of objective analysis. The Miller directorate on the other hand is pinpointed by many observers and insiders as casting a particularly ideological tone for the entire institution. The fact that Miller was less personally involved in Capitol Hill negotiating sometimes may have moved OMB career staff into more questionable Hill relations to support PADs who were filling a void created by Stockman's departure. PADs also often had the discretion to set a tone that either discouraged or encouraged civil servants' involvement in congressional liaison or "advocacy activities." Since most program divisions tended to have more than one PAD during any one presidential term, tacit marching orders could be changed markedly within one four-year period.

If any issue related to OMB politicization concerned the career staff most, it was the threat of losing the protective cover of their own civil service status and being unfairly identified with an administration's policies and thus becoming "tainted" when a new administration entered office. One career staffer recalled being cited in a letter to the OMB Director for "making an allegedly reprehensible policy" which the examiner claimed was nothing more than a restatement of a current administration policy in that examiner's area. The letter was written by an opponent of the President at the time who was closely allied with one of the President's chief competitors in the upcoming election. While OMB officials denied the charge, the examiner worried what would happen if the opposing candidate won the election. How effective could that examiner be then? It was this kind of dynamic, of lost public credibility to those outside of OMB, that threatened to prove problematic for OMB as an institution in 1993. Thus, while most OMB career staff did not become personally politicized during the 1980s and early 1990s in most senses of that word, the "appearance" of politicization and a loss of credibility as a neutral broker of policy carried with it the potential to minimize OMB's utility to serve an incoming Democratic administration.

OMB Career Staff Advice in the 1980s: Bubbling Up or Bubbling Down?

No matter how objective and well reasoned the analysis, and no matter how willing career staff are to "tell it like it is," if OMB political appointees, the director, or the White House are not listening, or if career staff–political level communications are blocked through excessive layering in OMB, then "merits" arguments will not ultimately be factored into presidential decisions. As one official observed, "they don't have to accept your recommendations for OMB to do its job, but they do have to hear you."

OMB career staff were still being heard even in the 1970s after political appointees were superimposed over career staff. Not only was there a bottom-up policy development process, but usually only general as opposed to specific policy guidance was offered to career staff before their analysis and recommendations were prepared. Career staff recommendations were accepted by political appointees most of the time. The exception to prove the rule involved recommendations in more politicized areas. In the 1980s, when the whole budget process became more politicized and visible, more issues received White House and political-level scrutiny accordingly. This often occurred before career staff analysis was prepared, thus reducing the career staffer's impact on decisions. In addition, with two budget directors who were considered White House insiders and more layers of political appointees and their support staffers, OMB career staff positions dropped significantly in the overall "pecking order."

While this "loss of influence" cannot be denied, it also should not be overstated. Staff influence was still relative to what had existed before, some career staff were still able to have a significant impact on the process through new congressional monitorship and agency micromanagement roles, and even in cases where broad policies were set from the top down, career staff were often able to fill in important details. The degree to which any career staffer was able to influence any particular decision was highly variable, hinging upon the director's personal stature and decision-making style, the views and influence of individual PADs, the clout of the relevant departmental secretary, the nature of an administration's agenda in an area, and the complexity of the issues involved.

Sources of Career Staff Influence in the 1980s

The complexity of many public policy issues, the bulk of which did not fall into neat partisan or ideological packages, had for many years maintained a respectable level of career staff influence and discretion. This continued to be true in the 1980s, in spite of contrary trends. Even within the aggregate budgeting of the 1980s, career staff analysts still recommended *where* the cuts would be made within any proscribed percentage reduction. Many staff still described themselves as being able to influence decisions around the "margins" throughout the 1980s. Often these "margins" were not insignificant. One BRD career staffer noted in 1988 that "within the ceilings set by Congress and the President they still have to go to the analysts to find out what to cut," and with respect to reaching Gramm–Rudman–Hollings estimates, that "the staff still had plenty of discretion since otherwise they would use machines to do the work."

Other sources of career staff influence were derived from variations in some time-honored OMB roles with the agencies. One of these was an increased discretion to oversee agency management, delegated informally to some OMB staff by the Reagan and Bush administrations to be further discussed in Chapter 8. Other important sources of career staff clout were the congressional score-keeping tasks which political officials delegated to career staff and the significant enforcement powers granted OMB in the Budget Enforcement Act of 1990, many of which were also delegated to career staff. These will be further discussed in Chapter 7.

Staff Influence and the OMB Director

As discussed earlier in this chapter, while David Stockman set in motion institutional dynamics that decreased OMB career staff influence, he is still remembered in OMB by some as being an enthusiastic consumer of facts, figures, and analysis offered by career staff and of enjoying intensive debates during director's reviews. These recollections conflict with others that viewed him as being more disinterested in "programmatic analysis." The variations probably were related to the nature of the issues being discussed.

The fact that Stockman was so detail oriented and knowledgeable about budgetary issues therefore had contradictory effects. It made it possible for him to offer much more specific guidance to PADs and career staff, but it also seems to have made him open to and interested in getting all the information and views he possibly could to integrate into his decisions in certain areas.

Richard Darman's decision-making style and personality presented an interesting point of comparison in this regard. Also an intense, hard-working White House insider who was concerned with detail, Darman was a much more insular decision maker who was uncomfortable working with large groups of people. However, there was a hidden advantage to Darman's decision-making style. Since Darman projected the impression that he was uncomfortable with personal contacts, there was less policy guidance at the outset than under Stockman, so that staff had the opportunity to present their arguments unfettered by political guidance. In these communications as well as face-to-face discussions, Lawrence Haas of the *National Journal* observed that career staff who were able to stand "their ground in exchanges with Darman or in their written work,"[73] were often able to get a fair hearing. Moreover, interviewees in some program division areas believed that Darman's use of analysis had represented a "peak point" which allowed OMB career staff to shape analysis. Those in other areas perceived that analysis was requested and prepared, but not read.

The Miller directorship presents a telling contrast to these models of "activist–insider" directors. Since Miller was perceived as being less knowledgeable about the details of programs than either Stockman or Darman, some staff observed that the guidance coming out of his office was less specific, thereby allowing them to impact outcomes in complex policy questions that did not revolve around ideology.

Other Determinants of Career Staff Influence

Career staff influence also varied with the prominence of the Cabinet secretaries or agency heads in their areas and how it compared with the clout of the director. If such administration officials had the direct ear of the President or a prestigious reputation, it was more difficult for OMB to compete and for career staff to exercise unbridled scrutiny of agency budgets or further management-related disciplines within that agency. In the converse case, where the Cabinet secretary was known to have little influence in the White House and/or had proved to be a less than competent administrative manager, OMB career staff were able to fill the breach.

The 1980s in Retrospect

On the eve of President Clinton's inauguration, OMB career staff had weathered over a decade of new external pressures and demands. On the whole during that period, their counsel had been sought less frequently in formulating policy than in previous periods, and so on the whole their influence in that forum had waned. On the other hand, the institution itself had become increasingly powerful and visible, so paradoxically some of that influence carried over to the career staff. As before, issues below the "political interest level" fell to career staff to resolve and because of the complexity of many programmatic, budgetary, and management issues, this foundation was not insignificant.

OMB career staff juggled a myriad of new roles that strained the capacity of the institution to produce in-depth long-term analysis. Bruce Johnson cited this institutional overload and later concluded, "The multiplicity of institutional roles and functions, together with the sheer volume of work, has overburdened and confused many budget examiners."[74]

OMB's size had declined with time and rapid turnover, and staff inexperience threatened to deplete institutional memory in some parts of OMB. Now more people had heard about OMB and many did not like what they heard.

Yet with all of this, OMB as an institution designed to play unique roles for the presidency had developed coping devices which had enabled it to meet the demands of the 1980s without compromising its institutional integrity. New recruits had the quantitative skills demanded at the time, institutional memory was still maintained among mid-level managers, and bright and gifted people still found reasons to come to work in OMB.

In spite of all the stresses, respect for norms of neutral competence had been preserved and were in evidence in sufficient critical mass, so as to enable this beleaguered institution to fulfill its core mandates, on the condition that its institutional dilemmas be addressed in the future. With the necessary time, training, and leadership, staff could broaden their analytic skills where necessary to enhance the utility of their advice to the President.

But this maintenance of core values would not last forever. And the caveat of more time, space, and leadership for the institution to heal itself presupposed conditions that were unlikely to occur in a deficit era beset with interparty strife and huge divergence in the public mind of what the appropriate role of government should be. In such an environment, it was unlikely that OMB Directors, consumed with keeping their Presidents afloat in rocky congressional waters, would have sufficient time or commitment to attend to OMB's institutional needs or that OMB staff would be relieved of their continuous "firefighting" activities or congressionally imposed responsibilities long enough to take institutional "stock of themselves." At the core of all of this was the central dilemma that somehow future Presidents and Congresses were going to have to resolve; to decide what roles OMB would play for Presidents, which, if any, roles were to be discarded, and whether to give OMB the appropriate resources to "do it all."[75] Only then would it be possible for OMB to serve as a repository of collective budgetary, legislative, management, and regulatory "wisdom" to support the presidency as an institution.

6

OMB's Budget Preparation Mandate Goes Second Tier

Introduction

The Office of Management and Budget (OMB) committed the major portion of its institutional resources to the preparation of the President's budgetary recommendations to Congress prior to the early 1980s. By the 1990s, this institutional emphasis on the Executive stages of the budgetary process had changed. It was replaced by two parallel processes, one directed toward the traditional BOB/OMB mandate to prepare the President's budget, the other toward monitoring and attempting to influence its progress in Congress.[1] This enhanced congressional monitorship role reduced the time and energy available to staff to prepare the President's budget.[2] Top-down and aggregate budgeting[3] and increased centralization and politicization[4] also decreased the ultimate impact that OMB's career civil service program experts could exert on budget formulation decisions as well as the importance of OMB budget preparation procedures.

All of these evolutionary changes in OMB led some OMB watchers to downplay the importance of the ten-month process whereby the President's budget was produced in OMB as sometimes being irrelevant to the outcome of decision making that took place in the White House and among political appointees in OMB.[5] While this characterization did hold true with respect to overall institutional trends from the beginning of the 1980s into the 1990s, it did not entirely take into account the complexity of the federal budget and the diversity of individual programmatic issues. These factors, still, virtually dictated that OMB budgeteers and the processes they followed in producing the President's budget were still of significance in setting the stage for many decisions made in OMB, the White House, and ultimately in the Congress. A detailed examination of those processes and a description of how they have changed in recent years follow.

Timeline of Budget Preparation

It takes about ten months of information gathering, analysis, iterative decision making and compilation to complete the President's budget submission to Congress. From March through May, OMB begins a review of major issues that can potentially affect the outcome of the President's budget. At the end of that period, agencies receive guidance in some form from OMB to aid them in placing their budgetary requests to OMB. These requests are due in OMB at some point from September 1 to October 1.

In October and November those requests are subjected to analysis and several levels of review by OMB career staff, top political appointees, and the OMB Director. This phase of the process usually takes from six to eight weeks to complete. By late November or early December the Director begins to make decisions and recommendations to the President. Presidential decisions are then communicated back to the agencies, which receive a last chance to modify those decisions during a "presidential appeals process." Finally, with the appeals resolved, the final budget documents are prepared at some point from December through January to be sent to Congress.

In the 1980s, in particular, there was a great deal of variation in the timing of this process. From 1981 to 1992, the budgetary transmission to Congress occurred anywhere from the beginning of January to late February for a variety of reasons. Sometimes statutory requirements necessitated an early budget submission, as in the Gramm–Rudman–Hollings Deficit Reduction Act's requirement that the President's budget be submitted to Congress by the first week in January. This resulted in an acceleration of the process after the passage of that legislation, so that the FY 1988 budget was transmitted to Congress on January 5 including an overview of the budget, economic assumptions, and policy changes.

At other times, when White House congressional summit negotiations were not completed until late October, early November, or later, the progress of budget preparation became stalled, because budget options could not be developed and approved until the preceding year's budget was known. In addition, during election years, when the budget would still "belong" to the outgoing President, staff recommendations to the director could not be offered until it was clear who had won the election. Until the fall of 1992, all outgoing Presidents submitted complete budgets for the upcoming fiscal year. This provided a structural foundation upon which the incoming President could "build" his first budget. Given the relatively brief time available to compile the new submission, this proved to be a useful operating procedure for incoming Presidents, particularly those of the same party as the outgoing President. Where there was a change of party, the outgoing administration was able to build some of its policy preferences into the base of the budget. In 1992, the Bush administration was the first to fail to prepare a complete budget and in fact only submitted an abbreviated current services budget.[6] This made it all the more difficult for the Clinton administration to assemble its first transitional budget.[7]

The Stages of the Budget Preparation Process

Spring Planning Review

Prior to the early 1980s a process called Spring Planning Review, which allowed for detailed analysis of departmental agencies, preceded agency budget requests to OMB by several months. During the months of April and May, key issues that would provide the substance for decision making during preparation of the President's budget would be selected and developed. This process began with examiners, branch chiefs, and division chiefs identifying "program and budgetary issues, and current agency plans" they felt would impact the upcoming year's fiscal budget.[8] When this was accomplished, a series of planning review sessions would be held for different governmental agencies and departments. These were conducted by top BRD career officials, PADs, and other political appointees. The relevant budget examiners almost always attended and actively participated in these meetings. The program division staffer making the presentation, be it the branch chief or the examiner, would describe the agency's present program objectives and cite estimates on projected budgetary requirements for the coming fiscal year.[9] After the Spring Planning Review, issues discussed at the review sessions were summarized by the Budget Review Division and presented to the Director and then to the President in late May. These "issues" would then provide the foundation for a series of relatively in-depth programmatic guidelines and budgetary targets for agencies to use during preparation of their budgetary requests, which would be submitted to OMB in September.

In the spring of 1983, the Spring Planning Review was significantly altered. Instead of program issue identification for the upcoming budget, the review involved a shortened analysis of the administration's previous goals from the past budgetary cycle and an assessment of the success rate of those goals. Some OMB staff believed at the time that this abbreviated spring review had the practical effect of eliminating the Spring Planning Reviews as they had formerly been known.

The experience of the next ten years bore that prediction out. Overall, the thorough Spring Planning Reviews of the past succumbed to OMB's newer legislative demands. While during the Reagan and Bush administrations agencies still received budgetary targets on ceilings in the late spring, OMB did not provide in-depth programmatic guidance, since there were generally no formal Spring Planning Reviews to produce such analysis. Bruce Johnson notes that an abbreviated process took its place which sometimes involved reviews of "cross-cutting issues that are not program or agency specific," and were "selected from the top-down." Such analysis usually was not fundamentally influenced by OMB staff analysis or recommendations.[10]

Preparing for "Budget Season" in OMB: Summer Activities

It is during the summer months of the budget cycle that agency and departmental budget offices carry their heaviest burden as they prepare their budgetary requests for the coming fiscal year to be submitted to OMB in September. Therefore, for many years prior to the early 1980s, the work load in OMB slacked off significantly in the summer, thus providing an opportunity for program division staff to investigate budgetary, legislative, and management, issues pertaining to their assigned programs. They would accomplish this by tackling long-term studies and analysis papers that examined issues thought to affect agency productivity and the upcoming budgetary requests.

OMB staff would also travel to regional agency offices (sometimes unannounced) to observe the agency in action. As many staff likened their roles to that of "investigative reporters," many creative and sometimes unorthodox methods were employed to "know their agencies thoroughly" and to "find out where the bodies were buried." While such information-gathering activities were pursued year round, the summer months did provide a window of opportunity for OMB staff to learn about their agencies with some degree of depth. Since the early 1980s much of the time OMB staff once had to devote to such activities has become somewhat dissipated by demands for aggregate budgetary exercises and other congressional tracking activities.

Budget Season in OMB: Submission of Agency Budget Requests

"Budget Season" in OMB is officially ushered in at some point from September 1 to October 1 when departments and agencies submit their budgetary requests for the next fiscal year. For many years, OMB-Circular A-11 has described the required format for the budget requests by outlining in great detail how agencies are to report their employment and personnel needs, justify financing methods for their programs, and prepare financing schedules.[11]

When reviewing agency budget submissions, examiners are advised to check the agency's numerical estimates and projections for accuracy, to consult studies prepared by the agency under review or relevant reports produced by external organizations such as the General Accounting Office, and to look for "weak spots" identified during the previous year's budget process.[12] They are also directed to construct their analysis around two or three issues that have not been examined before if possible. Typically, these might include an examination of how the program in question plans to project "future demand for services," or an analysis of how "certain agency overhead functions compare to other federal/state agencies or private firms."[13]

From October to December, as the President's budget is being prepared, budget examiners are responsible for entering budget estimates into OMB's central computer system. Such estimates will frequently change to reflect ongoing OMB and White House decision making during the fall budget season. OMB's computerized Budget Preparation System (BPS) was updated, improved, and subsumed into the multifunctional MAX System in the early 1990s. MAX now tracks the development of the President's budget as it is being formulated, breaks down budget estimates by budget account and/or program, and calculates technical estimating changes that are driven by statutory budget constraints.[14] The entry of these budgetary estimates by OMB staff is referred to as fall "scorekeeping."[15] This process culminates when the final data that will appear in the President's budget are entered into the MAX System in late December or January.

Hearings

During the next stage of the budget preparation process, examiners engage in fact-finding activities, which include the preparation of questions for relevant officials in the programs under review. In the past this process took the form of formal hearings, which provided an opportunity for key agency officials to justify budget requests to OMB as well as a forum to help agency officials gain a clearer understanding of the President's policies.[16] The format and amount of time consumed by the agency hearings (which were usually but not always held on OMB premises) varied from one area to another, but most hearings included oral arguments as well as presentations of other written budgetary material. The hearings, which were conducted by the relevant examiners and/or branch chiefs and division chiefs, took as little as one hour for smaller agencies or as long as several weeks for larger programs within Cabinet-level departments. For smaller independent agencies, the budget examiner would often conduct the agency hearings alone without the branch chief or division chief being present. PADs and higher OMB officials may or may not have attended, depending upon the agency involved, issue being discussed, and presence of a Cabinet officer or other high-level agency policy official. One common mode of operation was for senior agency officials to come to OMB to be questioned, sometimes by junior OMB examiners. Given obvious differences in status and age, many senior officials (often at the administrator level) found this procedure particularly odious. Today this process may be less formal than in the past, involving only written communications or telephone conversations, but no formal hearings.

In either case, while this phase of the budget formulation process is supposed to provide an opportunity for agency officials to better explain their programs to OMB staff and for the latter to reiterate the President's policy stands on the programs at hand, in reality, many of these positions are already well known by both sides. Whether through correspondence or hearings, this fact finding allows an additional opportunity for the designated agency representatives to make a dent in OMB's decision-making loop and is often enlivened by a good deal of posturing on the part of both sides. Examiners, for example, might send specific questions to the agency stressing the need for some sort of rank-order prioritization of their budgetary requests only to be confronted with elaborate defenses designed to argue the necessity of all requested funds. Such responses sometimes result in follow-up questions from OMB to be answered in writing after the hearings, as well as some degree of antagonism.

Agency representatives sometimes win OMB staff support by presenting sound analytical arguments that stress how increased spending in the short term could lead ultimately to greater savings. If such arguments can be made successfully at this point in the process, the agency can exert some influence on the ultimate configuration of the President's budget, since agency hearings directly precede examiner issue papers and recommendation preparation. A soundly based agency presentation at this point in the process can be important, bringing agency arguments into the first round of OMB review.

Issue Papers and Analysis

During budget season, examiners also prepare "issue" or "decision" papers recommending budgetary levels to be included in the President's budget. OMB training materials advise staff to review a wide range of written information, whether preparing the decision papers or other analysis, in order to keep current on programmatic issues on an ongoing basis.[17] These include programmatic evaluations, performance reports, financial reports, interest group–generated data, agency budget documents from past years, and congressional committee reports, hearings, and floor debates that relate to the program at hand.[18] Staff are also urged to glean information from their relevant personal contacts in the agencies, Congress, interest groups, and the academic community.[19]

The structure of the issue papers has been relatively standard over the years. Following a summary presentation, the examiner outlines two or three potential alternative funding levels and any new legislative action that might be required to support each option. OMB guidelines for the preparation of budget season decision papers direct staff to present the "full range" of "realistic" options and to clearly delineate the potential outcomes and pros and cons of each.

For many years, examiners usually have been expected to include a brief paragraph describing how the agency, interested parties in the Congress, or related interest groups might react to each alternative. This has continued. Instructions found in OMB training materials in the mid-1990s suggest that new staff include the views of interest groups, the general public and other OMB and EOP units.[20] Moreover, those reviewing the decision papers are asked to consider what the general public would think of "the OMB decision-making process" if the paper was to appear in the "*New York Times* or the *Washington Post.*"[21] Such directives represent one example of OMB's quasi-political analytic roles described in Chapter 3 and are indicative of OMB's increased visibility in recent years.

But OMB's traditional role of producing presidential advice that is fundamentally grounded in neutral information is also in evidence in current OMB directives to its staff. Those reviewing decision papers are advised to look for "any assertions not backed up by facts,"[22] and another document in the same packet advises staff to build analysis around an examination of whether a program's goals are being met through objective measures and data collection, and not based on whom the program "serves and how."[23] Moreover, the institution advises career staff to be detached and objective.[24] Training materials urge examiners: "You look objectively at a program. The fact that it 'serves' a 'needy' population is immaterial to you if the service is not effective, is not adequately or efficiently provided, or is not worth the investment. Think about the program in this way. You will be surprised how few people do."[25]

In the overwhelming majority of cases, the examiner is expected to conclude issue and decision papers by offering a recommendation for action.

This recommendation is an important aspect of the examiner's analytic role as it allows him/her a greater degree of cognitive responsibility and accountability than if only an analysis were required. It can provide the OMB Director with a ready-made answer in issue areas with which he or she does not have great familiarity or interest. In other more visible areas, the recommendation still provides a prepackaged answer.

My study of OMB during the late 1970s indicated that OMB program division staff of that period considered four criteria to be primary influences on their analysis.[26] They were, in order of importance: (1) any concrete policy guidance received from political levels of OMB or the White House; (2) necessary budget constraints; (3) the examiner's personal assessments of the intrinsic value of the program; and (4) the nature of agency-generated information. Three other factors—the possibility of creating interdepartmental precedents, rational decision-making approaches, and projected assessments of congressional or interest group reaction—were taken into account but were considered secondary. Interest group information and projected acceptability of analysis to political levels or OMB and/or agency heads were also considered secondary.

OMB's presidential advisory system at the career level was, therefore, primarily characterized by a fundamental emphasis on the assimilation of any policy guidance received from political levels of OMB, a need to guard the taxpayer's "dollar," and, not surprisingly, a reliance on information received from the departmental agencies. It was also distinguished by certain characteristics which suggested an ability to provide generally complete information to its political appointees and the President. A strong emphasis on the examiner's personal assessments in analysis indicated an independent attitude and willingness to personally influence decision making on the part of the examiner. This "independence" at times promoted the airing of additional facts, even if such facts did not conform to politically set policy constraints. In addition, while examiners considered any policy guidance received to be of the greatest importance, they did not appear to spend a great deal of time second-guessing their political superiors when such guidance was not received. This indicated that while concrete guidance was always respected, examiners did not in most cases purposely color analysis for the sake of personal advancement.

Though presentation of objective, substantive program analysis was uppermost in the staffers' minds, theoretical "objectivity" did not appear to eliminate a measure of realism in the analysis. This is illustrated from two vantage points. First, examiners utilized cost–benefit models, but only when the issue realistically fitted into such constructs. Second, assessments of potential congressional and interest group reaction often offered within the body of analysis provided a measure of political sensitivity and realism to that analysis as well. Such assessments, however, did not appear to destroy the examiner's ability to do objective neutral analysis, but merely gave an additional informational dimension to that analysis.

Analysis and Issue Papers: The Reagan–Bush Years

During the first four years of the Reagan administration and the Stockman directorship, changes in institutional emphasis reduced the opportunity for career staff to influence OMB decisions through issue papers and analysis. These changes constituted a marked departure from some of the previous institutional patterns prior to this period.

As the author noted in a 1983 article:

> Policy guidance [became] increasingly more specific than it had been in the past. . . . In some cases, examiners [were] told what options to include in issue papers, a practice that was not prevalent in OMB previously. In other cases, administration policies with regard to specific aspects of programs [were] made crystal clear to examiners prior to the preparation of the examiner analysis. In short, the process [became] "top-down" as opposed to "bubbling-up."[27]

This was one specific manifestation of the overall centralization of the budgetary process cited in Chapter 5.

> At the same time, the demand for careerist analysis by OMB's political appointees . . . waned. While in most branches budget examiners still prepare analytic issue papers and recommendations, there [was] a discernible reduction or output of such analysis in some areas. Even when analysis [was] prepared, some careerists perceived that it [was] not taken as seriously by political appointees as it [was] in former years. Budget examiners [were] being used more and more to justify or fill in the details on decisions that have already been made by political appointees. . . .
>
> More time [was] spent on other types of work assignments such as "numbers exercises." Numbers exercises involve requests from the director and other top OMB officials or the White House staff to prepare numerical projections of program budgets and other figures, taking into account different across-the-board funding cuts. This type of activity understandably fit in with the [Reagan Administration's] emphasis on budgetary reduction, but [reduced] the amount of time examiners had to spend on in-depth program analysis and information gathering.[28]

During this period there were other structural difficulties for OMB staff who sought to provide their political supervisors with realistic budgetary projections and recommendations. Congress's propensity during the 1980s to delay the passage of the current year budget until right before the beginning of the new fiscal year (October 1) or right afterward (using continuing resolutions to fund the government) made it difficult for examiners to develop their issue papers and analysis for the coming fiscal year. In a 1988 article, Bruce Johnson described how this "congressional tardiness" during the Reagan years tended to undermine the accuracy of OMB staff projections and recommendations. For lack of a starting point, in cases where the examiner had no current year budget, he/she would have to use the President's budget requests for the current year. However, as Johnson explains below, such estimates could be largely off the mark.

> Unfortunately, for some programs, about which large policy disagreements exist between Congress and the President, the budget request of the President is not likely to be close to the amount to be appropriated by the Congress.
>
> For these programs the analyst has a hard time choosing a starting point. Programmatic analysis, even in a zero base budget approach, still needs to know what spending and employment levels exist in the current year to plan for the upcoming budget year. For instance, holding even with the President's current year request under consideration by Congress may result in the need for politically-explosive, personnel reductions in force if Congress were to provide considerably more than the President requested in the current year.[29]

According to Johnson, this was one reason the Reagan budget was so often considered to be "dead on arrival" when it reached the Congress since "Congress had the considerable advantage over the executive branch of knowing what it has done to the previous budget before it takes up the next one."[30]

During the course of President Reagan's second term and President Bush's four years in office, staff still used the same criteria in preparing their issue papers, but many staff in OMB perceived that budget season decision papers or other issue papers got shorter and shorter and that they received less attention from political level officials. OMB staff veterans also expressed the view that because of time constraints, there was less formal written analysis and that analysis was more often presented verbally in meetings and discussions.

These staff perceptions, however, were not universal within the program divisions. Staff under both James Miller and Richard Darman who were situated in program areas of central concern to those directors, report that they were required to prepare longer issue papers than they had in the past. Darman in particular was perceived to have grasped the importance of in-depth analysis. During his term as Director, formal awards ceremonies were held rewarding staff who produced high quality long-term analysis, with the Director publicly expressing his support for an improved analytic capacity in OMB.

The general sense within OMB at the end of the Bush administration was that even though Darman and other directors expressed a concern that OMB conduct more in-depth analysis, the time restrictions imposed by dual legislative and budgetary roles and the emphasis placed upon examining program budgets in the aggregate with one another, were the key factors preventing an improved analytic capability at that time. In addition, new responsibilities for staff promulgated by Gramm–Rudman–Hollings I and II in the late 1980s, and the Budget Enforcement Act in the 1990s, further eroded the amount of time that staff could commit to budget season as well as year-round information gathering and analysis.

The Director's Review Process

Introduction

The "Director's Review," which begins at some point from late October through late November, is a time-honored OMB procedure designed to further refine the quality of the final budgetary recommendations that appear in the President's budget. The "Director's Review Book" provides the foundation for formal Director's Review discussions. Compiled in late October through early November, the book is the outgrowth of the fact-finding and analytic processes described above. Most Director's Review Books contain analysis of major budgetary issues involving federal programs, several alternative options for resolution of each issue, and the agency's budgetary requests noted alongside the program division/Resource Management Office (RMO) recommendations for funding for the next fiscal year.

Designation of Issues to Be Considered at Director's Review

In the late 1970s, while the PADs "formally" approved which issues were to be considered Director's Review issues and which were to be dubbed "non issues," the actual decision-making process was to varying degrees a collegially determined one, involving input from the budget examiner, branch chief, and division chief. In fact, since the substantive program knowledge required to make this determination emanated from the examiner and branch chief levels, it was often the case in the past that they made this decision, with the division chief and PADs merely lending a formal stamp of approval. Moreover, since the annual federal budget was considered to be entirely too complex for all dollar decisions to be made at the political levels of OMB or the White House, the actual decision-making pattern was one in which progressively more significant issues in terms of dollars, visibility, or controversiality were decided at successively higher levels of the OMB hierarchy and ultimately the White House.

While these institutional decision-making patterns prevailed more clearly prior to the 1980s before top-down and aggregate budgeting limited OMB staff discretion by imposing ceilings and caps on budgetary recommendations, even during the 1980s and 1990s, there were opportunities for OMB career staff to influence the process. The less politically visible a program area, the more discretion afforded to program division staff. Highly complex or technical questions sometimes would not interest political appointees in OMB, so that lower-level staff had a greater opportunity to exercise discretion in such subject-matter areas. Moreover, career staff influence has always varied with the strength, experience, or political clout of particular PADs, departmental secretaries, other EOP units, or the OMB Directors who happen to be in office at the time. The less the influence of these top officials, the greater the potential role for OMB staff. Well-argued staff positions also tend to prevail when applied to less visible and/or complex issues. While less visible, such issues can still affect an agency's budgetary realities in important ways and thus prove quite significant to specific interest communities. Therefore, OMB career staff during the 1980s into the 1990s were still able to be significant participants in the budget preparation process in many instances, though not as often as in the years past.

Director's Review Sessions

Director's Reviews usually take from three to four weeks to be completed. Using the Director's Review Book as a base, they involve oral presentations before the OMB Director, deputy director, and their top lieutenants, which supplement the written issue papers and recommendations within the Director's Review Book. The sessions include not only program division staff assigned to particular accounts and programs, but also representatives from the management, regulatory, or any other OMB divisions with an interest in a particular program area.

The budget examiners are usually required to make those parts of the presentations that pertain to their particular assigned agencies. It is considered an important dimension of the budget examiner's role to personally defend the recommendations and a form of initiation rite for junior examiners experiencing their first budget cycle in OMB. Branch chiefs or division chiefs occasionally present the program division/RMO recommendations to the director if the issues involved are particularly politically charged or controversial or if the branch or division chief has a strong desire to do so.

The director and others offer follow-up questions to the presenter after the formal presentations. PADs vary in how they play into the process. Some join the adversarial position of the director and others argue on the side of their division staff, depending upon the PAD's personal style or the issues involved.

The Director's Review sessions are closed to both the public and the press. Program division staff take informal notes during the Director's Reviews, but have generally been prohibited from removing these minutes or current or past Director's Review Books from OMB premises. Information describing Director's Review topics was not to be communicated to agencies and departments at this point in the process. Leaks did, however, occasionally occur.

The timing of the formal Director's Review sessions has varied in recent years. Director's Reviews were held later in election years, in years where the previous year's budget was stalemated in Congress, or during "budget summit" meetings between the White House and congressional leadership. These delays were necessary since both the outcomes of the election and the budget parleys had to be known before the budget preparation process could move forward. The hurried Director's Reviews that occurred as a consequence sometimes compromised the whole decision-making process and ultimately perhaps the quality of budgetary decisions.

Director's Review During the Reagan and Bush Administrations

When David Stockman became OMB Director in 1981, Director's Review already had the potential to be an intimidating process, especially for young, inexperienced examiners. But prior to the 1980s examiners and other program division staff still had the advantage of understanding the internal operations of most programs with a degree of detail that few directors could fathom. That all changed abruptly with David Stockman's first Director's Review. Program division staff found his questions penetrating and his knowledge level to surpass that of recent directors. Stockman seemed to enjoy the Director's Review sessions, which were usually of long duration and were to keep staff "on their toes" during his entire tenure. A review of a single branch within a program division branch area could last for a couple of days. While some staff found these reviews intimidating and anxiety provoking, particularly during Stockman's first two budget seasons in 1981 and 1982, many staff members were happy to be able to "raise issues" and question aspects of their programs that had previously been considered politically untouchable. Even though Stockman had his own agenda with respect to the details of some programs and the dismantling of others, many staff felt that during that early period the Director's Review sessions were genuinely productive and thought-provoking exercises. Of course, the outcomes for domestic programs were usually budgetary reduction or no growth. Later on, when Stockman lost some effectiveness after the publication of his interviews with William Greider,[31] and when staff began to have less time to analyze their assigned programs and consequently less impact on final budgetary decisions, some of the initial enthusiasm surrounding those early Director's Reviews wore off.

Under James Miller's directorship, Director's Reviews changed radically. During his initial review, "division" staff, well schooled in the previous director's expectations that examiners come prepared with long lists of facts and figures, were informed soon thereafter that Miller did not wish to be confronted with such degree of detail and generally wanted to deal with aggregate issues. Consequently, Director's Review sessions became much shorter. As time went on Miller would devote more focused time and energy to certain issues of special interest to him. He also focused considerable attention on experimenting with different structural formats of Director's Review.

Richard Darman's first Director's Review surprised many OMB staff in its attention to detail and substance. Darman was generally more patient, generous with funding in his final decision making, and anxious to learn than many had expected. The first Director's Review in 1989 turned out to be the longest since the last Stockman Review in 1984. OMB staff were impressed with the fact that Darman appeared quite knowledgeable, as evidenced by his questions. Some staff felt that while Stockman had a somewhat greater grasp of the technical aspects of programs, Darman's observations were broader and hence more useful.

Darman made a few stylistic changes at the outset. Using an informal approach to Director's Review, he sometimes dispensed with the typical opening statements by the examiner and began the session by "jumping in with his own questions." Also, as Darman moved forward in his Director's Review sessions, he tended to change format instructions on a daily basis, to the consternation of many staff members.

During the fall of 1990, Director's Review was held in abeyance until the first week in November when Congress and President Bush finally reached agreement on the Omnibus Budget Reconciliation Act of 1990. Once the "Budget Talks" were completed, Darman announced that there was to be a slightly modified two-part Director's Review. First a series of "mini" Director's Reviews were staged, designed to focus on broad themes involving issues that cross-cut several programs. Program division staff were directed to prepare in-depth analysis papers for these sessions. Second, traditional Director's Review discussions were planned.

The two-part process was designed to attempt to seek solutions in major domestic problem areas that involved more than one agency by basing the Director's Review decisions on the preceding analytic exercises. However, many staff felt that there was insufficient time to prepare the kind of cross-cutting analysis Darman wanted.

It was during the 1991 budget season that Darman altered the traditional OMB budget season process most radically, announcing in early September that there was to be a drastically abbreviated Director's Review for that season. The "replacement" process was to be called the "Agency Budget Review" since Darman is said to have quipped that "the name Director's Review sounded like someone was reviewing the Director." During this "Agency Budget Review," no Director's Review book was compiled and the review consumed half the time of the reviews of the year before. The rationale for the shortened review was to give staff more time to do more thorough written analysis, but the perception among some staff was that the analysis papers either were not read or were only scanned briefly during the oral presentations.

Passback and Appeals

Following Director's Review, OMB Directors generally reach preliminary decisions and determine which issues need to be transmitted to the White House for presidential decisions. Recent Presidents have differed in the amount of time they personally devote to this task and the degree of detail used to scrutinize the budget submissions.

When the President has made decisions on the budget, the appropriate PADs and/or division chiefs officially notify the agencies of approved budgetary allotments called "marks," in a procedure known as "passback." As with many other procedures and points of communication within OMB, passback has varied from area to area. One variant might be for a formal passback from the OMB Director and PAD to the departmental secretary with the division and branch chiefs filling in details with lower-level staff. In many other cases an examiner might passback to an assistant secretary. The passback papers include policy guidance in the form of instructions to the agencies as well as general information without any specific directives for action.

After passback, the departments and agencies have an opportunity to voice any objections they might have with the decisions in a series of negotiations known as "Presidential Appeals." This process allows the agencies one final chance to influence the President's budgetary recommendations to Congress. The appeals and subsequent presidential decisions take about fifteen to twenty days on the average to complete.

During the 1980s, the appeals process evolved into an institutional procedure involving not just the White House and the OMB Director, but lower levels of the OMB as well. The response to an appeal depended upon the degree of political visibility of the issues, the dollar amount involved, and whether giving the agency what it requested would or would not involve a stated policy change. It could also hinge upon the ceilings and constraints set by deficit and budget control laws such as Gramm–Rudman–Hollings and the Budget Enforcement Act.

Traditionally, an appeal for more funding for agency salary or expenses that fell under one million dollars would usually be handled by the examiner and/or branch chief. However, an appeal for funding for a Cabinet member's "pet project" or a program with particularly congenial or adversarial relationships with the White House, regardless of dollar amount, would be resolved by the White House and/or OMB director.

Since the appeals process affords Executive Branch agencies an additional opportunity to influence the outcomes of the President's budget, there has been much strategic planning and posturing by agencies and OMB both before and during the appeal itself. It is generally known, for example, that agencies often gain some benefit from placing an appeal, since in the cases where the agency might lose on dollar amount issues, OMB will often give leeway on programmatic issues. Moreover, appeals are often resolved by "splitting the difference" or by agreeing to half of what the agency has asked for. Hence, some agencies appeal regularly. In many such cases examiners have been able to project accurately whether the agency will appeal even before Director's Review. Such examiners might be particularly generous in their recommendations in order to avoid the appeal in the first place, or, conversely, recommend an "unrealistically low mark" in order to allow for additional bargaining leverage later on in the process.

Different administrations have experimented with the use of different appeals formats as a way to try to either discourage appeals or to trim budget requests. One minor incident during Joseph Wright's short term as director occurred during the 1988 transition budget season and involved a strong memorandum issued from his office directing the agencies to constrain themselves from making any appeals, in anticipation of the 1988 election results. It became abundantly clear that Wright's pronouncement was going to be ignored when a larger number of appeals was transmitted to OMB than had been submitted in a number of years. This was not surprising, given that the transition Reagan budget requests to Congress were particularly low, presumably to give George Bush a chance to restore some token funds in his budget to create the impression that his administration was going to be "kinder and gentler," as campaign slogans had promised.

Since agencies knew that, most wanted to express on the record a deep dissatisfaction with the allotments they had received in the outgoing Reagan budget. Thus the avalanche of appeals.

Another variation of the traditional appeals process occurred during Richard Darman's first full budget season during the fall of 1989. Darman's "experiment" was driven by the unpleasant realities that the deficit had continued to mount, and that the Bush administration had repeatedly espoused increased governmental action in certain designated "high-priority" areas such as education, the environment, and homelessness.

On Friday, November 24, 1989, the following lead paragraph appeared in a front-page article of the *Washington Post* outlining Darman's "new" plan for the appeals process.

> Office of Management and Budget Director Richard G. Darman, who has a reputation as a wily tactician, is planning a novel maneuver aimed at forcing federal agencies to accept austere funding levels in the Bush administration's fiscal 1991 budget. In a letter to Cabinet secretaries earlier this week, Darman announced a "competition" in which the agency chiefs will appear before President Bush to plead for a share of a "limited pool" of money set aside to fund high-priority programs.[32]

The "novel maneuver" had been unveiled to OMB staff shortly before it appeared in the press. Career staff did not learn of it until Director's Review, while the PADs were briefed on the plan just a little bit earlier. The plan amounted to an attempt to discourage most agencies from placing any appeals at all and to involve others in a competitive process to determine which programs would be particularly favored in the President's budget.

Programs and budget accounts were to be placed into one of two categories. The first category was designated as High Priority TRACK B. These were the programs that the President had personally emphasized and that, because of their favored status, had already asked for sizable budgetary increases from the previous year. Darman and the White House were reported to have set aside an unspecified pool of "additional" funds to be divided among these programs. However, these agencies would have to compete with one another for the larger shares of the funding pool by directly arguing their cases before the President. In a letter to Cabinet secretaries in these areas, Darman pointed out that because they had been designated as high-priority agencies they could elect to avoid the "White House" competition altogether by lowering their initial requests for increases and subsequently reach some kind of compromise with OMB. No specific "passback funding mark" was included in the letters.

All other programs, designated as TRACK A, were to follow the normal process of receiving a budget mark during passback and taking the opportunity to appeal if so desired. However, TRACK A programs that appealed would then automatically become TRACK B and would have to compete with the "high-priority" programs for the pool of additional but limited funds. They would then risk having their "marks" reduced further during the course of the deliberations. Thus, the Darman plan offered a disincentive for nonpriority programs to appeal in the first place and made priority programs compete before the President for limited funds or agree to lower their requests. It also incidentally appeared to transfer certain "hard decisions" from Darman's shoulders to those of the President. The initial determinations of whether programs were to fall into TRACK A or into TRACK B were made largely by PADs and career staff with initial guidance from Darman, who described the kinds of programs that might be considered "high-priority." Staffers were also advised to define programs that were likely to appeal in the first place as "high-priority."

The outcomes of this experiment were not as clear cut as Darman may have envisioned. In its final implementation, the plan elicited a variety of responses from departments and agencies. Some, but by no means all, program administrators in both nonpriority and priority programs behaved as intended and either settled for the initial allotments they received during passback or lowered their budget requests. Many other TRACK A and TRACK B programs, however, were willing to "expose" themselves to the competition.

The outcomes in both instances were mixed. Certain high-priority programs were not asked to report directly to the President, but were required to argue for the enhanced funding before Director Darman, the PADs, and the division chiefs. Their success at getting the requested funds restored varied. Nor did all "appealing" nonpriority programs fare badly. Certain nonpriority administrators who felt they had a strong case did appeal and in some instances received hundreds of millions of dollars more than had been allotted in their "passback mark."

The TRACK B, high-priority programs that presented their arguments to the President and/or White House staff, participated in what some observers described as "staged" presentations. In most of these programs, budget requests to Congress were ultimately increased, thus allowing the President to project a magnanimous image in areas that had been dubbed high-priority. In the same vein, many agency officials began to realize that Darman's available pool of funds was "bigger" than had originally appeared.

If any overall characterization can be made about the appeals process during the Darman years, it is that decisions tended to be reached at higher institutional levels than before. Few final appeals decisions were made below the PAD level, although analytical work prepared by career staff was still considered to be somewhat influential in the process. This again appears to represent yet another example of an increasing trend toward the top-down centralized decision-making style that existed in OMB during the 1980s and early 1990s.

The Final Lap: Preparing the President's Budget Documents

For approximately six to eight weeks after passback and during agency appeals and resolution of those appeals, OMB's "Budget Analysis and Systems" and "Budget Review and Concepts" divisions prepare the final budget volumes to be transmitted to Congress. These two divisions were organized as one division called the Budget Review Division (BRD) prior to 1991. Inside OMB they are still referred to as the BRD. While the BRD assumes the lead role in this final wrap-up stage of the presidential budget preparation process, the RMOs, LRD, and agency budget office staff also enter into the often intense work effort required to produce the budget. This final phase of budget preparation is twofold; a data base that meets technical specifications and budget targets mandated by statute, and conforms with decisions reached in OMB and the White House is generated and budget documents to be transmitted to Congress are produced. The estimates and numbers cited in presidential budgets emanate from submissions by the agencies which are checked for accuracy by RMO staff. Narrative is prepared by the PADs, management staff, the Economic Policy Division, and BRD with support from the RMOs. Politically sensitive material is reviewed by the director, the deputy director, and the White House staff.

Presidential budgets have been presented to Congress in one or several volumes. The FY 1993 budget,[33] which is used as an example to illustrate the final phase of the budget preparation process, was combined by Director Darman into one volume from the seven volumes used previously. The consolidation process truncated some sections of former budget messages and intermingled others, but did not essentially change their contents. Part I of this budget, entitled "Agenda for Growth and Priorities for the Future," included a half-page budget message from the President, a twenty-page "Director's Introduction," a brief section summarizing the administration's overall economic assumptions, and about 400 pages of policy-oriented justifications for the President's budget requests to Congress.

The "Director's Introduction," which provided a polemical defense of the President's budget, was written by Richard Darman. The Fiscal Analysis Branch of the Budget Review Division had written the introduction prior to 1989, but Darman assumed the task himself in 1990. "Economic Assumptions and Sensitivities" followed the director's message and presented projections of how the administration's proposals would affect the economy. It was produced in part by staff within the Budget Analysis Branch within BRD.

The summary justification section was broken down by eighteen categorical chapter headings such as "Reforming American Education and Investing in Human Capital," "Ending the Scourge of Drugs and Crime," "Preserving National Security," and "Advancing America's Interest Abroad," to name a few. These sections were written by one or two authors per program with significant input from the PADs and relevant examiners, and were edited and printed by the Budget Systems Staff. Career staff as well as PADs put in a great deal of time in preparation of these policy positions that year, doing rewrites sometimes as many as thirty times. This part of the budget appeared to be designed to persuade Congress to accept the various components of the budget and to restate the President's general policy in each area. Studies and statistics are cited throughout in support of any new policy direction or in an attempt to illustrate how the administration's previous initiatives were meeting their objectives.

The following are two excerpts from the Summary Justifications Section, one involving tax credits for child care and the other discussing drug control programs.

> The principle of parental choice shaped the President's child care legislation which became law in 1990. . . . By insisting that the new assistance be provided through refundable tax credits and vouchers, the President assured that parents, not government employees, have maximum control over the necessary care arrangements for their own children.[34]

> The budget reflects the Administration's continuing commitment to ending the scourge of drugs and drug-related crime by expanding drug law enforcement programs, improving drug use prevention efforts, and increasing the availability of substance abuse treatment. It builds on the success made thus far, and it directs new funding to the toughest problems—dismantling drug trafficking organizations, preventing drug use by the hardest to reach users, and treating those most damaged by drug use.[35]

At the time, there was some degree of controversy surrounding the manner in which the preceding sections of the budget intermingled factual data with administration policy positions, as an outgrowth of the consolidation of the budget volumes. In previous multivolume budgets, policy-oriented arguments had been confined to one book, with the remainder of the budget volumes containing objective statistics and data. Some observers argued that the Darman format was designed as an advocacy document that made it difficult for the reader to separate opinion from fact.[36] In addition, career staff were involved to varying degrees in the drafting of this material. These findings constitute another example of the increase in politically slanted narrative that had been appearing in presidential budget submissions since 1980, and the expanded involvement of career staff in drafting such material.

Part II of the budget, entitled "Receipts," listed taxes, user fees, and other monies collected by the federal government. Part III contained special analysis and supplementary information. Both were prepared by the Budget Analysis and Systems Division of OMB.

Following Part III were three appendices of the budget—"A Budget Enforcement Act Preview," and a newly added glossary of terms and budget concepts. The main "Budget Appendix,"[37] which comprised over half of the entire federal budget volume, presented a detailed breakdown of the entire budget by department, agency, and program, and specific designations of expenditures (staffing, supplies, salaries, etc.) for the preceding, current, and upcoming years. The budget examiners, with their agency counterparts in conjunction with "Appendix Teams" from BRD, were largely responsible for preparation and final approval of the data in the Budget Appendix. Its preparation time, often surpassed that required to prepare other sections of the President's budget.

A Changing Budget Preparation Process in OMB

From 1981 through 1992, an OMB presidential budget preparation process that was once "bottom-up," agency based, and thorough became "top-down" and somewhat attenuated. Shorter issue papers, bypassing of "traditional" Director's Reviews, staff absorption with congressional tracking, and deletion of Spring Planning Reviews, all chronicled an erosion of a budget preparation process that had produced exceedingly knowledgeable advice to Presidents.

Clearly, external factors such as the need to use broad aggregate components of the budget as units of analysis in attempts to reduce the federal budget deficit, and demands that staff focus on the congressional stages of the budget process in order to influence its outcomes, explained why there was less time and incentive to prepare detailed program analysis during the budget preparation process. An important institutional dilemma that remained to the mid-1990s was that while OMB's new roles could not be abandoned, Presidents still needed a thorough and objective analytic foundation upon which to build the budgets they sent to Congress.

7

OMB and Congress, 1973–1992: Role Reversal and Stalemate

Introduction

Profound changes in the congressional budget process that began with the 1974 Budget Act were destined to alter Congress's role in what had once been presidential budgetary prerogatives, and would lead to heightened politicization, contentiousness, and visibility of budgetary policy making. During the 1980s and until 1992, both the growing budget deficit and the escalating power struggles between the Congress and the Executive that ensued, would drive OMB's missions and uses for the presidency away from their traditional roots. Much of the politicization of OMB and its surrounding environment that followed can be traced to its origin in this new decision-making arena, where the central focus would slowly shift from the Executive Branch to Congress.

OMB's Congressional Watchdog Role Is Born: 1974–1980

The budget examiner had played a "congressional watchdog" role with respect to his assigned agency programs and their relationships with Congress for many years, but the amount of congressional monitoring pursued by examiners and branch and division chiefs increased after the early 1970s.

This OMB role encompassed the tracking of authorization and appropriations committee proceedings, and gathering intelligence regarding key committee member voting patterns and personal and constituency characteristics, as well as on the nuances and history of agency relationships with relevant congressional committees. It also involved policing agency testimony and statements to be made to the Congress to make certain they conformed with or at least did not undermine administration policy. Since the above factors by definition influenced the chances for legislative passage or the outcome of the appropriations process, the examiner needed this information to assess the potential success of the various options he or she would present in issue papers and verbal analysis.

To pursue this role, examiners would use a variety of written sources to remain informed. These included certain newspapers (notably, the *New York Times,* the *Washington Post,* relevant trade journals, and industry press publications). Other frequently mentioned sources included appropriate congressional committee reports, hearings, and testimony. Many examiners also followed the *Congressional Record* and *National Journal* rather closely.

As cited in Chapter 4, in the 1970s, OMB career staff increasingly found themselves participating in personal and telephone communications with congressional staff and occasionally members of Congress, and personally attending congressional committee hearings. Unlike the general congressional monitorship that had been part of the examiner's role in the 1960s, personal OMB careerist contacts with congressional staff had been limited before the 1970s when OMB civil servants confined their congressional watchdog activities to the review of written materials and left the person-to-person contacts to agency congressional relations offices. While not an official written policy, this prohibition existed as a clearly perceived institutional norm, confirmed by those interviewees whose tenure extended back to the 1960s.

In the early to mid-1970s, "discouragement" of Hill contacts began to change to "informal encouragement." Career staff had started receiving informal policy cues during the Ford administration from the political strata (PADs and director) that ranged from encouragement of careerist "Hill" contacts to no policy at all on the subject. Ford administration PADs confirmed that there were no formal policies either requiring or prohibiting careerists from communicating with Capitol Hill staff.

What were the prime determinants of these institutional changes in OMB? First and foremost was probably the passage of the Congressional Budget and Impoundment Control Act of 1974.

The Budget and Impoundment Control Act of 1974: The Budgeting "Center" Begins to Shift

The 1970s had witnessed an effort on the part of the Congress to reassert its coequal status with the Executive Branch. One major manifestation of this climate was the passage of the Congressional Budget and Impoundment Control Act of 1974. From the Act, Congress gained additional research and staff capabilities, the Congressional Budget Office (CBO) and two budget committees, as well as a parallel budgetary process to run in conjunction with the annual appropriations cycle. CBO would become in a general sense the Congress's legislative counterpart to OMB. The new processes introduced by the Act were two budget resolutions[1] and a reconciliation procedure.

The two budget resolutions and budget committees in the House and the Senate represented an effort to introduce and enforce a measure of discipline into congressional budgeting that would force Congress to confront aggregate budgetary totals and their relationship to the growing budget deficit. Previously, the appropriations process had operated in a fragmented manner with each appropriations subcommittee specializing in particular budget accounts, but with no centralized unit or mechanism to monitor the ever-mounting budgetary aggregates, to set priorities for different segments of the budget, or to link incoming revenues with outgoing expenditures.[2]

The "budget resolution" reported out of the House and Senate budget committees was to be Congress's first effort in the annual process to set nonlegally binding guidelines for the coming year's budget and necessary revenue intake, in light of the projected deficit, public debt, and surrounding economic conditions. It also provided spending ceilings divided among nineteen functional areas to act as targets for the authorization and appropriations committees to use in their deliberations.[3] The appropriations committees were then instructed to divide up their total allocations among programs.[4]

Reconciliation was the process written into the Budget Act that was designed to obligate committees (usually authorization and tax-writing committees) to comply with the budget resolution at the end of the process. The budget committees were to report "reconciliation instructions" to any committee not complying with the specified targets and that committee would be required to report a reconciliation bill accomplishing the change.[5] According to the Budget Act, if the committees did not act on the reconciliation instructions from the budget committees, the budget committees were empowered to make the changes themselves.[6] It is interesting to note that the original idea for this compliance procedure was introduced by former OMB Director Charles Schultze during congressional testimony. He had testified that a similar procedure was used in the BOB/OMB to make certain that agencies "bring the parts of the President's budget in line with the agreed on totals before it is sent to the Congress."[7]

Until 1980, however, the reconciliation phase of the Budget Act would prove to be a paper tiger. As Stanley Collender explained, political realities in the Congress prevented its use in the 1970s.

In the early years of the budget process, reconciliation was hardly discussed, let alone attempted. The primary reason was that the budget committees were generally unwilling to risk the future of the process by antagonizing the other committees, which were highly suspicious of intrusions into their legislative jurisdictions. The concern was that an early defeat of an attempted reconciliation might have had the same effect as not including these procedures in the Congressional Budget Act at all—committees would feel free to ignore the budget resolution.[8]

This concern did come to fruition in 1979 when an attempt to pursue reconciliation caused such protest in the Congress that the reconciliation instructions were withdrawn.[9]

One of the main problems with the reconciliation process was that committees only had ten days after passage of the second budget resolution to complete the "reconciliation." In 1980, however, during passage of President Carter's last budget, reconciliation was used for the first time by making its provisions *binding during the passage* of the budget resolution. Largely because of this use of reconciliation, the fiscal 1981 budget was reduced to save a total of $8.2 billion through a combination of spending reductions and tax increases.[10]

Of particular significance to OMB was the Budget Act's creation of the CBO, which was designed to provide the Congress with its own independent source of objective, expert, and nonpoliticized budget estimates and economic projections. Thus, Congress would no longer be dependent on OMB for such information. In the coming years, OMB and CBO would alternatively act as competitors or as sounding boards for one another in their roles as providers of accurate economic forecasts.

The Budget Act and OMB

The Budget Act required OMB to prepare various economic estimates which had not been part of OMB's responsibilities before that time period. These included the presentation of updates of the projections found in the President's original budget.[11] One of these mid-session reviews was also to include information on spending and revenues during the preceding year.[12] These tasks consumed significant amounts of time for the Budget Review Division and the program divisions in the month or so before their respective due dates in July and August. The process involved BRD in collecting detailed information from the program divisions in order to provide a foundation for BRD's fiscal analysis branch to prepare the mid-session review and current services budgets. In addition, OMB was also required to prepare statements on proposed impoundments and deferrals and a presentation of the President's budget in the functional categories used by the Congress as mandated by the Budget Act.[13]

These new institutional mandates had two major effects on OMB that became more and more pronounced as the decade continued. First, they began an increase in work load for OMB that was to accelerate even further in the 1980s. Second, the Act opened the door for more OMB–congressional staff contacts since these OMB responsibilities necessitated increased interchange and communications with CBO involving technical estimating issues. As an extension, this also increased OMB staff contacts with the House and Senate budget committees, which were consumers of both CBO's and OMB's estimates. Bruce Johnson characterized the budget committees as a "window" through which the OMB could view the Congress.[14] It had been a disparity between CBO and OMB budgetary estimates that first brought staff from the two organizations together for a face-to-face meeting during the Carter administration. The meeting included BRD staff, the program division chiefs, and staff from the budget analysis division within CBO.[15]

The existence of new budget-related committees in Congress and a new congressional budget process influenced the thinking of Directors James Lynn under President Ford and James McIntyre under President Carter to expend greater efforts within OMB to influence the congressional stages of the budgetary process. Under these circumstances, it was not surprising when James McIntyre expanded OMB's congressional liaison staff from two staffers to six.[16] Any office as such designed to deal specifically with the Congress and to help sell the President's budget on Capitol Hill was relatively new to OMB. In 1973, under the Nixon administration, a two-person Congressional Relations Office had been instituted. Prior to that time, there was no organized Congressional Relations operation in BOB/OMB and any incoming inquiries for Capitol Hill were handled by one staffer within BOB's Public Affairs Office.[17]

Many OMB career staff at the time also held the view that OMB needed to be more involved in congressional monitorship because of the changes brought about by the Budget Act. One careerist said, "Once the CBO process came into existence we found we needed a far greater amount of information about congressional status at any time."

A division chief said,

> I think that congressional monitorship has increased because Congress is perceived to be a much stronger factor in the budgetary process. There are many more staff people and there is just a wider range of knowledge in the Congress. The Congress is more likely to change budget estimates than they ever were in the past.[18]

Other related factors, such as the introduction of the PAD level in 1973, played a part in accelerating OMB's congressional monitorship role. The PADs represented an important point for many OMB decisions to be finalized and were often not familiar with previous institutional norms, which had frowned upon congressional contacts with OMB. Any particular PAD who wished to pursue an aggressive congressional public relations strategy would therefore direct his or her divisions to support these goals. A related factor was that both the Ford and Carter administrations often suspected the departments and agencies of undermining administration policy on Capitol Hill. This perhaps began a trend that would increase and plateau later in the 1980s, of attempting to circumvent agency-congressional alliances by using OMB instead of the agencies to communicate with the Hill and to explain administration policies. The following observation of an OMB division chief at the time illustrates that this was already beginning to happen in the 1970s. He said,

> In a number of situations, agency people who we rely on to carry the administration's story are not very reliable people. Every agency element has a constituency that it serves and it's headed up by politically appointed managers whose appointment in the first place is somewhat beholden to that constituency and whose continuation in office is somewhat contingent upon good relations with those elements who also serve that constituency. When the President has a position which differs from the position that would best advance the interests of that constituency, the agency concerned including its political managers does not have any incentive to go up and sell that position. So, we have in effect a sort of formal policy policing job.

A final reason for OMB's move toward more frequent congressional interchange was the growth in size that the entire Executive Office of the President had experienced in recent years. With more White House and EOP units dealing with congressional committees, there were more staff and more opportunities to look to OMB staff to answer congressionally initiated questions. As one division chief said,

> You cannot examine the politicization of OMB independently of other changes in the Executive Office. The Executive Office has grown from a few individual advisors to a large group of power centers. . . . These provide a broad net to catch complaints, so the examiner gets dragged in—if not through PADs, then from the Domestic Policy staff, congressional relations staff, etc. . . . All these staffs catch the casework problems where the workings of policy as implemented by the agencies do not happen to agree with some Congressman's interest.[19]

OMB staff attitudes were divided "down the middle" with respect to the wisdom of tracking congressional action once the President's budget was transmitted to Congress.

Some staffers who did not support the increased congressional watchdog role perceived that it had begun dissipating time they would otherwise have spent pursuing agency-related analysis. To these staffers these developments also presented the potential to transform them into administration spokespeople and ultimately to bias their analysis and recommendations.

One opponent of too much contact said,

> I think our interaction on the Hill should be limited to the budget committees, but not the oversight committees. To the extent that we deal with the oversight committees we're undercutting the departmental secretary and we're intruding ourselves into that bailiwick. We became advocates for an administration position which I don't think we should.

There was little evidence at the time that career staff were being thrust into "selling" roles on Capitol Hill. All of the division chiefs, interviewed at the time, indicated that no one including themselves had ever been placed in such a position. The following is a division chief's description of what usually happened in such circumstances.

> During the Ford administration, or more so during the Carter administration at the senior level, division chiefs and maybe branch chiefs, would be called upon to sit on the rostrum with a PAD, with a director, etc., when they would make a presentation to an interest group of congressional staff and be resource people in terms of expounding on or explaining. At first I thought it was bad. It isn't our role and it wasn't our role. I guess I've become more or less indifferent to it now because I've been exposed to it for the last 5–7 years and not only that but it actually gave me an opportunity to see what it's like on the other side. If you're willing to make recommendations on program merit then you ought to be willing to defend them and discuss your rationale.

A Ford PAD described the following,

> I recall an occasion once when there was a rather critical piece of legislation involving very big bucks and it headed ultimately for the President's desk. . . . There was a juncture at which point it was just critical to sit down and talk candidly with the leading Hill staff members. Jim Lynn and I set up a lunch and asked the branch and division chiefs to join us so we could kick around with the Hill staff some of these issues. I recall being told by a branch chief it was the first time he had ever been in such a situation. He didn't open his mouth at the meeting . . . I wanted them there so they would understand what was going on, so that their subsequent analysis would be more useful to me.

Congressional Budgeting and White House–Congressional Relations: 1981–1985

The Reagan–Stockman Juggernaut

The impact of the Congressional Budget Act of 1974 turned out to be only the beginning of more momentous changes in the budget process and in OMB. When inaugurated in 1981, Ronald Reagan was determined to cut domestic spending, increase national security expenditures, cut taxes, and balance the budget deficit. David Stockman entered OMB as its new director, not only planning to lead an institution in the preparation of a drastically reduced federal budget, but to sell that budget in Congress as well. His experience as a congressman and as a congressional staff person, his keen mastery of budgetary detail, and his innate tenaciousness allowed him to do both, particularly in 1981. Throughout Ronald Reagan's first term and into the beginning of his second term, Stockman was personally a more visible presence on Capitol Hill than any BOB/OMB Director had been before.

In 1981, with Stockman in the lead, the Reagan administration extracted unprecedented domestic spending cuts from the Congress.[20] The administration was able to surmount this historic challenge to traditional "iron triangle" interest group alliances by using a number of key strategies. First, Stockman had been willing to take the President's budget to the Hill and shepherd it through the congressional process personally. The first part of his strategy had been to move quickly while a semblance of a presidential "honeymoon" with Congress, the public, and the press remained. Stockman had closeted himself in OMB fully three weeks before the Reagan inauguration,[21] preparing issue papers on programs and giving the staff free rein to challenge programs considered politically untouchable in the past. Using this information selectively, he overwhelmed potential Cabinet opposition before the inauguration.[22]

Second, Stockman was able to package domestic discretionary and mandatory budget cuts in omnibus legislation that circumvented deliberation in the appropriations and authorization processes through a radical use of the reconciliation procedure. Since reconciliation instructions were made some six weeks before they would have been made, had they been connected with the first budget resolution their instructions for three years of phased-in budget reductions had not been subjected to the usual committee examination.[23] This was significant because the ensuing cuts included entitlement expenditures that accounted for the bulk of the deficit and had been considered uncontrollable for that reason.[24] In addition, the use of budget resolutions and reconciliation procedures prevented the Senate from filibustering.[25]

Along with domestic budget cutting, President Reagan sought to cut taxes and build up military capability. The former objective was accomplished on July 29, 1981, when a three-year tax cut was passed by both houses of Congress.[26] In the defense area, the Reagan budgets had proposed increases in expenditures of over $32 billion for 1981 and 1982.[27]

Outcomes and Consequences

Instead of the promised balanced budget, the federal deficit grew to more than $200 billion by 1983. The Reagan administration attributed this to the Democratic Congress's unwillingness to reduce the domestic budget by sufficient amounts. Critics of the administration pointed to the tax cut and increases in military spending.

Several outcomes of significance to OMB grew out of the negative congressional reaction to the 1981 Reagan–Stockman juggernaut and the rapidly growing deficit. First, the presidential budget, for years the foundational budgetary blueprint for Congress, was now considered at most "the opening maneuver"[28] in drawn-out congressional–White House jousting matches beset with numerous congressionally initiated proposals and counterproposals. This became even more the case after the 1982 congressional elections, when the Republicans lost a number of seats in the House.[29]

Second, by 1983 and 1984, Stockman's successful use of the reconciliation procedure had alerted members to the dangers of such omnibus legislation. Consequently, the Hill became extremely resistant to the use of omnibus budget resolutions and reconciliation bills, which held the potential to circumvent the appropriations and authorization processes.[30] In 1983, Congress did not pass a reconciliation bill until the following year. From 1984 to 1988, budget resolutions were also voted on later in the process.[31]

This had led the administration and Stockman to switch their intense negotiating activities to the appropriations committees where the actual programmatic expenditures were being determined. Since, as Bruce Johnson wrote, the appropriations subcommittees traditionally reached decisions directly with agencies,[32] this represented the further evolution of a trend for administrations to use OMB to bypass the agencies as means of influencing congressional budget decisions.

Both partisan conflict and White House–congressional conflict continued to escalate further, leading to often drawn-out White House–congressional negotiations and summit meetings. The summit negotiations, bearing various picturesque names, often ended in further stalemates.[33] By 1985, the conflict was not only partisan but had unambiguously evolved into congressional-presidential deadlock.[34]

As a direct consequence of these developments, the congressional budget process became characterized by its complexity, its unpredictability from one year to the next, its changing rules and procedures, and its extended delays in the passage of the federal budget. In 1982 and 1983, for example, the budget resolution for fiscal years 1983 and 1984 was 39 days late, and in 1984, for fiscal 1985, it was fully 139 days late.[35] In 1985 it was 78 days late.[36] Thus appropriations bills would be crafted without the benefit of agreed upon priorities that a budget resolution might offer.[37] In every year from 1981 to 1988, Congress failed to pass all thirteen appropriations bills on time.[38]

These budget process dysfunctions led to yet another procedural change involving "Continuing Resolutions." The Continuing Resolution (CR) historically had been used to continue funding during the occasional instances when an appropriations bill or bills did not pass on time. The funding level would usually be the lowest of several potential funding rates that included the last year's appropriation, the President's request, or a House- or Senate-passed appropriation.[39] CRs of the past were meant to be temporary funding mechanisms. The fact that the funding levels were so low also had provided incentives for the appropriations committees to expedite passage of standard appropriations bills since they would presumably be higher.[40]

The continuing resolutions of the 1980s became an entirely different legislative vehicle. Many were designed to last the entire year and ultimately supplanted appropriations bills.[41] They functioned as a handy escape hatch for budget process participants because they allowed them to agree on binding specifics of the budget without agreeing on broad priorities.[42] Passed in a "seemingly" crisis-laden atmosphere to prevent government shutdowns, much of their content would not receive as much exposure as would individual appropriations or authorization bills. This vehicle therefore afforded many of the budget players political cover and facilitated a freer give-and-take horse-trading process.[43] As Aaron Wildavsky observed, "an omnibus CR does obfuscate responsibility. It is not easy to say who voted for or against what."[44] Since this became a key tactic for all participants, the potential for a CR was factored into the planning of strategy. Both appropriations and authorization committees and subcommittees would delay their work at various points in anticipation of a CR.

OMB Responses to David Stockman and a Changing Congressional Budget Process: 1981–1985

The five-year budget saga just described was to affect OMB from the very beginning. While the stage had been set for Stockman to move OMB toward increased congressional monitorship, it is important to remember that when he took over the directorship, OMB had only reached an embryonic stage in the art of providing support to political officials bent on congressional lobbying.[45] As previously noted, there were wide disparities among OMB civil servants with respect to whether they pursued personal contacts with congressional staff, and a division of opinion on the propriety of such activity. In many program division areas, while some examiners had developed a sound level of expertise with respect to congressional tracking, others had little knowledge on the legislative status of their program areas at any given time. This disparity in staff capability was the consequence of the lack of institution-wide policies encouraging or defining congressional monitorship duties among career staff.

Moreover, while expertise with regard to congressional procedures varied in the program divisions, what was clearly lacking throughout OMB was a computer capability equal to that of CBO to price out budgetary estimates in different configurations with the speed that Stockman needed.

This set of circumstances found both BRD bill trackers and program division budget examiners overburdened and working through the night in order to attempt to meet Stockman's short-fuse requests for numbers exercises which sought to convert budget authority numbers into budget outlays, or requests for comparisons between administration cost impact statements or budgetary proposals and those of congressional units such as CBO or the budget committees. One BRD official estimated that Stockman almost doubled BRD's work load.

Examiners were unable to tell the Director precisely how changes made during legislative consideration of individual programs altered the aggregate budget, nor had they been able to determine how the appropriations bills would affect the overall deficit.[46] The problem here, according to Bruce Johnson's analysis of this period, was that while the appropriations committees tracked budgetary authority on spending authorized by Congress, they didn't track outlays, or amounts actually spent.[47] Without the outlay information, it thus became easier for the committees to underestimate the amounts that would be needed for mandatory programs (generally those programs created by law and funded automatically unless laws are altered) and to shift those proposed spending authorities to discretionary programs (those funded through appropriations bills), only to request further funds for the mandatory programs later through supplemental appropriations bills.[48] It was these dilemmas that led to the first of Stockman's institutional innovations designed to provide OMB with new congressional tracking capability.

The Central Budget Management System (CBMS)

Stockman's discomfiture with OMB's lack of capability to track congressional budget resolutions and appropriations led to the creation of task groups designed to provide the director with more accurate budget estimates than OMB was able to provide at that time. These task forces led to the creation of the Central Budget Management System or CBMS.[49]

The title of the system is instructive itself in the sense of providing an understanding of its key goals and objectives. Since the traditional source of much of the information Stockman required had previously been individual agency estimates, CBMS planners envisioned a computing system that would make OMB more independent of the agencies so as not to have to reveal budgetary strategies to them.

An internal OMB manuscript appearing in February of 1982 outlined the objectives that CBMS would be required to accomplish. First, it was to be able to track different budget proposals including the administration budget, congressional budget resolutions, and appropriations bills, always keeping current on the latest modifications but maintaining "earlier versions for tracking purposes." At the same time, CBMS was to be capable of explaining disparities between each of the different proposals.[50]

Second, CBMS was to have a simulation capability in order to project outcomes based upon different existing or hypothetical budgetary options and assumptions. In short, it was designed to be able to answer the many "what if" questions Stockman was apt to pose throughout the budgetary process.[51]

Third, CBMS was charged with maintaining information on congressional and executive cost estimates of authorizing committee legislation—particularly the reconciliation bill—as well as securing within its computer memory bank the names of congressional sponsors of both bills and amendments to bills bearing budgetary implications.[52]

What ultimately evolved gradually during 1982 was a CBMS staff of ten additional professionals housed within the Budget Review Division with relatively direct access to David Stockman. These included former budget examiners with programmatic expertise and computer experts. Eventually, the distinctions between the examiners and the technical staff blurred as the former examiners became more computer literate and the computer staff became more knowledgeable about programs.

The CBMS system both as originally envisioned and as an operating entity in OMB was quite dependent upon the program expertise to be found within the program examining divisions, which were to act as the ultimate authorities on the accuracy of any numbers to be included in the system.[53]

BRD was charged with providing CBMS staff with data that tracked actions which cross-cut program areas such as budget resolutions.

The system was also designed to be used for simulation or comparative purposes by including different proposals as well as historical data dating back to 1952. The possible uses for these numbers were limited only by one's imagination and intellectual grasp, and David Stockman cannot be accused of lacking in either. CBMS permitted Stockman to compare subdivisions of the President's budget with congressional budget resolutions, budgets from previous administrations, or with cost estimates. This information was to increase Stockman's leverage in negotiations on Capitol Hill. The system also proved effective in the day-to-day or weekly tracking of presidential budget preparation as well. One BRD official estimated that CBMS allowed OMB to produce the President's budget in roughly half the time it had taken previously.

CBMS also had a variety of other uses such as providing a source for numerical citations in speeches delivered by the OMB Director or the President, in White House Policy discussions, and in response to informational requests from Republican congressional allies of the President.

The Legislative Strategy and Support Group

CBMS was only one element, albeit the major and most visible one, in efforts to create OMB staff structures designed to support David Stockman's activities on Capitol Hill. Another was OMB's Legislative Strategy and Support Group. Instituted in late November of 1982, the "group" was comprised of one major staff person supported by two newly hired administrative assistants. The initial staff person, taken from two years' service with the Legislative Affairs Office, had formerly worked for Stockman during his congressional days.

The Legislative Support Group was designed to afford Stockman immediate support in preparing presentations for meetings with White House staff members and the President, as well as for congressional negotiating sessions. To this end, it was located close to Stockman in the Old Executive Office Building. The group was designed to act as a more efficient information conduit between Stockman, the career staff in BRD, and the program divisions, when coordinating congressional information requests to the examiners. The Legislative Support Group also shield civil servants from having to assume advocacy roles by preparing advocacy material itself with informational back-up provided by the career staff.

The Legislative Support Group, along with the PADs and the Executive

Associate Director for Budget and Legislation, prepared "major themes books," which outlined comprehensive administration budgetary policy and were sent to the members of Congress. The Legislative Support Group was also charged with the coordination and preparation of another legislative lobbying tool called "talking points." Talking points were concisely stated arguments attempting to persuasively present a case against sections of bills that the administration had strong objections to. The Legislative Support Group would research legislation and would come up with a "troublesome" or "problem" bill list from which the talking points would be produced. The talking points, which would usually appear in the form of five or six of the central arguments against the bill's language or specific expenditure amounts, would be distributed to House Republican Budget, Appropriation, and Authorizing Committee members, and to general House Republican membership and leadership before floor votes.

The Legislative Affairs Office

As of June 1981, the Reagan–Stockman team increased the size of the Congressional Relations Office to eight staff members and changed the name to "Legislative Affairs." It was comprised of political-level staff, almost all of whom had significant amounts of congressional experience.

From 1981 to 1982, the Legislative Affairs Office operated more as a troubleshooting ad hoc unit attempting to support Stockman in his congressional activities, than as an institutionalized section of OMB. The staff played a role in setting strategy, designing goals and action plans, and determining whom Stockman should meet with and what kind of backup information he would need for congressional negotiating sessions. The staff was also involved in the preparation of advocacy papers.

After the first year and a half of the administration, many of the roles played by the OMB Legislative Affairs operation were transferred over to the OMB Legislative Support Group, and the Legislative Affairs Office settled into a more predictable routine. From that period until 1986, the office was generally responsible for monitoring congressional activity, attending hearings, and preparing rapid-fire analysis that would be further substantiated later on by other staff units. It would, for example, monitor appropriations committee mark-ups and prepare a summary report the same day, followed by a more in-depth analysis to be submitted by the BRD the next day.

The Legislative Affairs Office attempted to receive most incoming inquiries from Capitol Hill offices. These included questions on the administration's positions on proposed legislation, as well as constituency inquiries. Attempting to secure as much information as possible from the program divisions and responding to congressional staffers themselves, Legislative Affairs staff tried to avoid requesting that OMB program division staff respond to congressional inquiries personally. The Legislative Affairs Office also compiled and distributed within OMB a document called *The Legislative Highlight Report,* which provided a daily schedule outlining upcoming congressional appropriations and budgetary activity.

Changes in the Appropriations Bill Tracking Unit in the Budget Review Division

While there had been an appropriations bill tracking section in the Budget Review Division for some time, that unit was expanded and its functions broadened during the span of the Stockman directorship. The number of full-time appropriations bill trackers was expanded to fourteen (including five CBMS staffers).

In addition, the requirements and demands for BRD issued from the director's level changed. Prior to the Reagan administration, the appropriations bill trackers had merely prepared weekly reports on the status of appropriations bills, budget resolutions, supplementals, and continuing resolutions. During the Reagan administration, the bill tracking unit continued these functions but a much larger role came into play. In addition to bill status reports, the staff prepared statements on the administration's positions on appropriations proposals as they evolved in the Congress. These Statements of Administration Policy (SAPs), as they came to be known, were prepared at every stage of the appropriations process, namely House Appropriations, subcommittee mark-up, full committee mark-up, Senate subcommittee mark-up, and conference, and would be sent to the chairs and ranking members of the full appropriations committees and subcommittees, and sometimes to the Senate leadership. The letters were prepared for Stockman's approval about six times during each legislative appropriations cycle. In order to prepare these policy statements, the trackers received guidance from two sources—Stockman himself and the examiners within the program divisions.

While, prior to the Reagan administration, there had been some effort on the part of BRD to inform the program divisions of Hill activity, it was not as routine or constant as it had now become. Program division staff received copies of appropriations bills, committee reports, subcommittee prints, Congressional Record inserts on floor actions, computer tables summarizing bill status, and weekly Friday schedules of congressional actions planned for the coming week. They then analyzed the bills for changes from previous configurations of the President's original budget proposals in their respective account areas and determined how these squared with presidential policy. This analysis was then submitted to the PADs and the director for final decisions with BRD playing a coordinative role.

Program Division Examiner Input

While the degree to which examiners were called upon to provide staff support to Stockman, the PADs, and CBMS varied with the subject matter of the examiner's program and the degree of congressional activity surrounding that program area, the consensus among many OMB staff is that there was a net increase in the amount of time examiners spent on congressional monitorship. One former political-level policy official estimated that examiners were probably averaging about half legislative and half budgetary activity as compared with 80 percent budgetary activity and 20 percent legislative activity before 1981. The official's estimate of previous time commitments appeared to be supported by previous findings that examiners devoted an average of 22 percent of their time to legislatively related duties in 1975 and 1976.

Clear policies spelling out what kinds of OMB careerist–congressional relations would be encouraged and what kinds should be limited still did not exist. It had appeared that the institution was moving toward the creation of formal policies in 1982, but as of summer 1985 OMB again failed to implement any such proposed policies. Many examiners remained uncomfortable with the ambiguity.

OMB Legislative Responsibilities in the 1980s: Tracking, Scorekeeping, and Baseline Politics

Tracking

By the end of President Reagan's second term, many of the legislative responsibilities initiated during David Stockman's early years as OMB Director had become accepted as ongoing staff responsibilities. Appropriations bill tracking and the attendant SAP process remains to the present. Tracking of various types of omnibus legislation such as budget resolutions, reconciliations bills, and continuing resolutions also continued, and BRD and program division staff became more proficient in these new roles. BRD staff and relevant budget examiners would be responsible for explaining the differences between the President's budget and any changes made on Capitol Hill and assessing the cost impacts of each new budget proposal. The examiners were given the ultimate authority to verify the accuracy of any numbers in the budget resolution or reconciliation bill that applied to their assigned programs,[54] and BRD was charged with compiling the aggregate cross-cutting numbers for the budget resolutions or reconciliation bills.[55] This required that the examiners as well as BRD staff maintain consistent contacts with the Budget Committees including attendance at hearings and meetings with CBO staff. In both cases, these interchanges would often lead to follow-up calls from the congressional staffers to the OMB staff to answer technical questions.

Since the budget resolutions and reconciliation bills were often forged in the middle of intense negotiations between the President and the Congress, President Reagan frequently altered his original budget, thus requiring BRD and the program divisions to make the necessary adjustments to the numerical estimates. President Reagan also made changes in order to signal to the financial markets, particularly in 1981 and later after the stock market crash of 1987.[56]

OMB staff also tracked the complex continuing resolutions that were often used to fund the government in the absence of successful reconciliation and or appropriations measures.[57] Staff estimated the funding levels that had been maintained in each program and how the total continuing resolution would impact the overall deficit. This involved translating the intricate CR and appropriations bills into both budget authority and outlay estimates.[58]

Program division staff were also called upon to support the President during the congressional–White House summit meetings that occurred throughout the 1980s,[59] and to translate their broad agreements into specifics down to budget account and subaccount levels.

The Art and Science of Scorekeeping

OMB's congressional watchdog role in the 1980s was twofold: it involved tracking budgetary proposals as they worked their way through the increasingly convoluted congressional budget process, as well as estimating the potential cost impact of each in the long and short term. These cost estimates would then be compared to cost estimates in the President's original budget, current services budgets, CBO's estimates, and deficit targets. This estimating of costs of legislative proposals and their relationships to aggregate totals in part came to be known as OMB's "scorekeeping" role. The second component of the scoring role involved determining whether the estimated spending levels fit under statutory limits or within the ceilings set in a budget resolution.[60] To do so sometimes required that budget staff interpret laws and budget rules that were not always completely clear.

The Congressional Budget Office had gotten into the business of scoring and cost estimating earlier than had OMB. The Congressional Budget Act of 1974, which created CBO, mandated that it prepare estimates of cost for any legislation reported out of committee. That included estimating how much programs would cost if enacted, how long it would take to finance the expenditures, and how the spending would affect the deficit.

OMB's previously limited capabilities to estimate ultimate programmatic expenditures through projections of outlays[61] and to make projections within the parameters of "congressional rules"[62] had been addressed through the CBMS system and other Stockman-initiated OMB tracking devices. Thus, with OMB's central position in the Executive Branch, and with the CBMS system to facilitate these duties, OMB also was increasingly drawn into similar scoring responsibilities.

Whether in OMB or CBO, the scorekeeping/estimating role was not an exact science. In an article discussing CBO's cost-estimating techniques *National Journal* writer Julie Kosterlitz pointed to a number of factors that made these estimates at best only "Educated Guesswork,"[63] as the article was entitled. According to Kosterlitz, even though increasingly sophisticated computer technology and econometric models aided economists and budgeteers in making cost projections, the unpredictability of future variables that would ultimately affect real costs made completely accurate prognostication of cost extremely difficult. Also, as Kosterlitz pointed out, "because laws tend to change greatly between the time their cost is estimated and time they're enacted, it's practically impossible to compare past estimates with current realities."[64]

OMB staff expressed similar assessments when describing scoring and cost-estimating methodologies. As one OMB staff person commented, "I find that 'spend-out' rate estimates of how much an agency or program will spend over remaining parts of the fiscal year become a judgment call." The phrase "judgment call" was often used by OMB staff in describing this scoring process. A corollary of this "educated guesswork" appeared to be a certain degree of discretion for the careerist "cost estimators" and their political-level bosses. This also allowed for often appreciable differences between CBO's scoring and that prepared by OMB. Efforts to compare OMB's and CBO's long-term economic forecasts were further complicated by the fact that OMB would often assume the passage of the President's budget in its calculations when in reality there was almost no chance of that outcome occurring.

Appropriations Scoring in the Mid-1980s

From 1983 to 1985 OMB focused its tracking and scoring efforts on the appropriations process. Bruce Johnson described this development in the following way:

In the absence of a budget resolution acceptable to the president, the director of the OMB attempted to impose presidential budget targets on the various appropriations bills. Because of the implicit and sometimes explicit threat of a presidential veto, the OMB was successful in exerting such influence in an area of decision normally reserved for an agency and its appropriations subcommittees. . . . The OMB continued to be active in the appropriation process, attempting to sell pieces of the president's budget to Congress in that forum.[65]

In order for Stockman to be able to succeed at this strategy, he needed intelligence on what the appropriations proposals were and OMB estimates of their cost as opposed to relying on the appropriations committees numbers. He needed to know how the committees were moving the funds around, how they had estimated cost, and how these estimates squared with OMB's cost assessments. It was with this knowledge in hand that he was able to negotiate, to communicate veto threats, and to influence congressional decisions.

Thus, while David Stockman was negotiating with the appropriations committees, BRD and the program division staff supported his efforts by attending appropriations hearings, ferreting out information on how the committees arrived at their estimates, and preparing their own estimates on projected costs of each proposal. This information would in turn be used to prepare the administration's policy statements (SAPs) for transmission to the appropriations committees and for Stockman and the PADs to use as ammunition in congressional negotiating sessions.

The scoring outcomes and cost estimates reached by OMB and the Congress tended to differ in a direction dictated by the policy objectives of each. Wildavsky, for example, had found that OMB's scoring rules tended to lead to higher cost estimates (particularly for domestic spending) than would those of the appropriations committees.[66] As one case in point, OMB would count (score) funding authorized in a particular year even if the money was not to be spent that year.[67] It would also score unauthorized and deferred appropriations on the assumption that the appropriations would be funded in a supplemental appropriations bill,[68] while the committees would generally not score such funding.[69] OMB often resisted the congressional ploy of transferring funds from entitlement to discretionary accounts in order to create the appearance of savings in order to make the proposals fit into budget resolutions.[70] When the appropriations committees transferred unobligated balances (unspent funds) from one account to another with no actual additional money being spent, OMB scored such actions as spending increases.[71]

The Baseline "Boogie"

The increase in significance of these "scoring games" by budget process participants was closely related to a rise in the use of budgetary benchmarks known as "baselines." A budgetary baseline is a theoretical construct designed to provide a point of comparison with any executive or legislative budget proposal being considered at any given time. As Stanley Collender describes it, "A baseline is a projection of what will happen to spending and revenue based upon certain assumptions."[72]

If the assumptions differed, the predicted outcomes would differ, and the assumptions budgeteers used differed in a number of ways. Some baselines, for example, began with the actual amount spent the previous year, while others added a predicted rate of inflation for the coming year. Other assumptions that could change baselines included increases in the number of people eligible for entitlement programs, or the amount of the cost-of-living adjustments in these programs. None of these assumptions would necessarily correspond to reality when that budget was actually enacted and spent, so the baselines constituted nothing more than projections that were determined by their initial assumptions.

Baselines can be useful devices for budgeteers because they allow for necessary comparisons between past and future budgets by factoring in likely economic or programmatic changes that might affect spending in the future. They can also be helpful in charting the progress of efforts to improve upon past performance in saving and budgeting. Baselines can also be used effectively to obscure these realities as well. They can be manipulated to "muddy the waters," precisely because they are "hypothetical" projections of spending in future years, themselves based on a number of unpredictable factors that are compared with "doctored" versions of the previous year's spending. Thus the baseline does not generally represent actual spending in the previous year, but constitutes an inflated or deflated representation of what was spent depending upon "theoretical" estimates of how factors such as inflation or unemployment rates would change from that past spending in the coming year. With the "baseline" as the reference point, a budget that actually proposed spending more than was spent the previous year could be construed as saving money if an inflated baseline was used.

As with scoring, increased use of baselines can also be traced to the Congressional Budget Act, which had required that the President's budget include estimates for programmatic costs if they operated at the same level as they had during the previous year.[73] Soon after the passage of the Budget

Act, budget process participants began discovering intriguing uses for the baselines. Allen Schick writes that the Senate Budget Committee employed inflated baselines in the 1970s "to claim that it was cutting the budget even though its allocations exceeded the President's recommendation."[74]

When David Stockman became OMB Director, he came armed with an understanding of how the manipulation of baselines could allow him to claim even greater savings in the Reagan budgets than what he actually believed would materialize from them.[75] He admitted as much to William Greider in his well-publicized interview in *The Atlantic*. Greider wrote:

> He knew that much more traumatic budget decisions still confronted them. Because he knew that the budget-resolution numbers were an exaggeration. The total of $35 billion was less than it seemed, because the "cuts" were from an imaginary number—hypothetical projections from the Congressional Budget Office on where spending would go if nothing changed in policy or economic activity. Stockman knew that the CBO base was a bit unreal. Therefore, the total of "cuts" was, too.[76]

At times during the 1980s, congressional Democrats and Republicans and the White House signed on to the same baselines, but for different reasons. The Republicans were able to create the appearance that the budgets being presented were extracting significant savings without the Democrats having to agree to deep programmatic cuts.[77] At other times during the 1980s and early 1990s, there were differences in the assumptions used in the congressional and the OMB baselines that tended to serve the political goals of the respective branches and the partisans who created them. Stanley Collender, for example, reports that in some years "OMB's baseline assumed that military spending would grow by inflation plus 2 percent every year, while CBO assumed that it would only stay even with inflation."[78] Schick wrote that "by blowing up the baseline to unrealistically high levels . . . the President and Congress have exaggerated the claimed deficit reduction,"[79] and that "the rules used in constructing the baseline have enabled inventive budget makers to fabricate cutbacks by making temporary adjustments in expenditures."[80]

All of the various baselines being used on the Hill and in the Executive Branch created a process beset with complexity. Again, Stockman summed it up in his *Atlantic* interviews:

> None of us really understands what's going on with all these numbers. . . . You've got so many different budgets out and so many different baselines and such complexity now in the interactive parts of the budget between

policy action and the economic environment and all the internal mysteries of the budget, and there are a lot of them. People are getting from A to B and it's not clear how they are getting there.[81]

If Stockman claimed not to understand what was "going on with all these numbers" it became almost impossible for those who were not a part of this intricate budgetary game to fathom this baseline parlance. Schick characterized the baseline as "a dense barrier separating budget insiders, who know what the numbers mean from outsiders, including seasoned budget observers, who cannot figure out what is being done to the budget unless they uncover the assumptions behind the numbers."[82] To make matters worse, these assumptions were sometimes not published anywhere.[83]

Thus baselines would help politicians of both parties and both branches of government to please their various constituencies and to claim to be saving money to cut the deficit at the same time. Their payoff was political survival. There was also a payoff for the budget technicians in OMB, CBO, and elsewhere who crunched the numbers and spoke the baseline language. They would become much in demand by their respective institutions as part of a very small fraternity who understood the complex rules of the game and the assumptions that had driven the outcomes in any particular budgetary proposal.

With the increase in the importance of aggregate and baseline budgeting, BRD in general and its Fiscal Analysis Branch in particular became central focal points in OMB. For example, a 1992 *National Journal* article featured a picture of BRD's top career official sitting in his office with a big sign in the background that read "Baseline RD."[84] While the political appointees in OMB and other units of the administration's economic policy-making "troika" had the final say on the economic assumptions that would drive OMB's chosen baselines, the complexity of the process tended to afford the budget estimators and technicians in OMB a good deal of influence.

But there were prices to pay for this ascendancy of the "numbers crunchers," since this "climate" detracted from OMB's traditional institutional emphasis on long-term programmatic analytic capability in the program divisions as well as efforts to promote sound management practices in the agencies. In addition, when OMB's baseline assumptions and economic projections proved not to square with actual economic outcomes, OMB's institutional reputation was to suffer further damage. A larger irony can be derived from an examination of OMB's recruitment into the construction of these baselines. An institution once conceived to be a purveyor of politically untouched information and budgetary projections had been diverted into activities designed to obscure such verities.

The Era of 1986–1989: Gramm–Rudman–Hollings and Rosy Scenarios

Gramm–Rudman–Hollings I and II: The Politics of Desperation

By the end of 1985, the deficit projections for fiscal 1986 had risen to approximately $221 billion,[85] a record level even after years of unsuccessful attempts by the President and the Congress to reach consensus on a credible deficit reduction plan. It was this atmosphere of desperation that contributed to passage of the Balanced Budget and Emergency Deficit Control Act of 1985, or Gramm–Rudman–Hollings, as it came to be named after its Senate sponsors. Since the President and the Congress had not been able to agree on measures to cut the deficit, Gramm–Rudman–Hollings created automatic sanctions considered to be so unacceptable that they would force both branches of government to meet its deficit reduction targets.

Here is how it worked:[86] From 1986 to 1991 the $172 billion deficit was to be reduced by $36 billion a year until the budget was balanced in 1991. If the deficit exceeded the target amount in any of the designated years, a procedure called the "sequester" would be triggered. The sequester was a "blind" across-the-board cut in most federal program budgets equal to the amount necessary to comply with the deficit reduction schedule.

The mechanism designed to determine when and by how much the deficit reduction target had been breached, allowed both Congress and the President to shirk responsibility for the cuts that would ensue. The responsibility to determine the need for a sequester was bestowed upon CBO, OMB, and ultimately the General Accounting Office (GAO). On August 15 of each year, OMB and CBO were required to reach a "joint" estimate of the deficit for the coming fiscal year by averaging their two institutional projections together. They were then to report this estimate to GAO, which was in turn required to reach its own deficit projection largely based upon the CBO–OMB assessment. If this estimate fell below that of the legally mandated deficit reduction target, the law gave Congress and the President a month from the beginning of September to October 5 to make necessary changes to meet the deficit reduction schedule. During that time, OMB and CBO would again report to GAO by October 5 to reflect any changes that had taken place, and on October 10 the Comptroller General would send a revised order to the President. If by October 15 the necessary deficit reduction had not been taken, the President was required to issue a sequestration order on October 15. It is important to note that under the law the President had little discretion in ordering the sequestration.

In July of 1986 the Supreme Court negated GAO's role in the process.

GAO's sequestration powers were judged to be "executive" in nature, and since the Comptroller General was removable by Congress, this constituted an abridgement of separation of powers doctrine.[87] Anticipating just such a ruling, the framers of the legislation had included a fallback procedure in the law that they believed would pass constitutional muster. The provision replaced GAO's role with a temporary joint committee of Congress, composed of House and Senate budget committee members, that would authorize CBO and OMB's estimates and would present the sequestration order to the full House and Senate to be voted on. This vote would be subject to presidential veto.[88] The Supreme Court thus had refused to allow Congress and the President to avoid responsibility for the cuts that would be incurred in reducing the deficit.

Since the first full year of Gramm–Rudman–Hollings was an election year, neither Congress nor the President wished to be on the record as actually making the cuts. Thus, OMB, in its economic forecasting role, acted as political cover for both the President and the legislators. OMB's much more optimistic projections for real growth in the gross national product (GNP) when averaged with CBO's forecasts, brought the required deficit reduction needed to avoid a sequester down to $19 billion. Through government asset sales, postponement of federal pay increases, and some "creative accounting," a sequester was avoided.[89]

Gramm–Rudman–Hollings I and II: Additional Responsibilities for OMB

In December of 1985, when the Gramm–Rudman–Hollings law passed the Congress, OMB's responsibilities included preparation of numerical projections of the expected rate of national economic growth, the overall deficit, and budgetary bases for governmental programs from which budgetary reductions were to be taken. In addition, follow-up reports were to be produced in conjunction with the Congressional Budget Office. If the estimates of the two institutions did not agree, averages of the OMB and CBO estimates were to be used.[90]

CBMS played a significant role in determining the law's mandated cuts for the fiscal year 1986 budget and preparation of estimates for the 1987 budget. OMB staffers involved in the process indicated that without CBMS, OMB could not have responded as rapidly to Gramm–Rudman–Hollings mandates as it was able to do, particularly in January and February of 1986.

The fact that the wording of the law left it open to interpretation afforded OMB and CBO some measure of discretion and also led to estimating differences between the two organizations. So too did the subjectivity that was endemic to any estimating of how rapidly programs would expend funds as well as other future costs and economic outcomes. Some of the specific types of judgment calls included whether income derived by the government from the sale of government assets was to be included in defraying program costs and whether to apply sequestration to certain programs not specifically exempted but similar in nature to other nonsequestrable programs. In reaching answers to these questions, OMB tended to read the law literally and CBO to infer legislative intent, according to one OMB official commenting on the process of the time. As the examiners and CBO analysts worked through these issues, BRD would canvass the program divisions and, along with the PADs and director, would provide policy guidance.

In 1986 and 1987, issues in question between CBO and OMB had to be completely reconciled by August 15. If individual analysts and examiners could not reconcile the disputes, then the issues would be resolved by BRD staff from its Fiscal Analysis and Resources Systems Branches and their CBO counterparts. Then, from August 20 to October 6, examiners and CBO analysts had to factor any legislation enacted between August 20 and October 3 into cost estimates of outlays, revenues, and budget authority.

Legislative Clearance During the 1980s

LRD, and the legislative clearance and enrolled bill process remained relatively unchanged in the 1980s, but were often subjected to an increased work load as compared with the previous decade. These added burdens grew out of new congressional tracking responsibilities for OMB in general and the emergence of reconciliation bills in particular.

James Frey, the director of the Legislative Reference Division during the mid-1980s, was quoted by Ronald C. Moe in an article on the central clearance process as characterizing LRD as a "traffic cop" and "identifier."[91] LRD had not overshadowed the importance of the program division role nor had LRD's place in the process changed from being primarily "coordinative." This is evident from the following quote from Frey in response to the question "Do persons in the White House ask your advice on issues involving administrative management or instructions?" He responded, "We ask them for advice, not them us."[92]

While on the surface there were often fewer authorization bills and testimony that had to be cleared during the 1980s, in reality clearance-related responsibilities for both LRD and the program divisions were increasing. Behind the apparent decline in actual numbers of bills and testimony was the fact that the authorization process itself had changed.[93] It now involved the packaging of many of the authorization bills into huge omnibus reconciliation bills. This by definition cut the absolute number of bills down, but made the clearance process and the bills themselves more "complex."[94] The introduction of Gramm–Rudman–Hollings responsibilities into the process had further complicated authorization clearance.[95] Thus, it became more difficult to coordinate agency responses and to develop statements of the administration's positions on each of the aggregated bills.[96]

Another reason for a growth in LRD's work load in the 1980s was that it was more often enlisted to act as a centralized enforcer of administration policies during both the central clearance and the congressional authorization processes because of the White House's desire to keep the agencies on a shorter leash during congressional lobbying efforts. As one branch chief indicated in an interview in 1987, "the authorization process has become more centralized and the agencies are no longer in the driver's seat." This in some instances included the drafting of the bills.

According to Bruce Johnson, strains due to the deficit and "top-down" budgeting brought about enormous stress to OMB's central clearance process. He wrote in 1988, "Agencies have found the positions they must take formally before Congress so at odds with the congressional political situation and their own internal needs that informal back channels develop to communicate their real recommendations to Congress."[97] Johnson suggested that this forced budget examiners to be familiar with both the formal agency position in support of the President's policies and the less formal agency position.[98] Such requirements not only added to the "stress" of the whole clearance process, as Johnson suggested, but to the OMB staff work load as well.

More Smoke and Mirrors

If projections of the federal deficit and attendant economic projections had been points of contentious dispute between Congress and the President before the Gramm–Rudman–Hollings Act, the necessity of meeting its deficit reduction timetables only heightened the pressure on the two institutions. Each year became a desperate struggle to meet the targets, and the production of overly optimistic economic projections became a growth industry in both Congress and the Executive Branch.

By 1987, the two institutions were running out of devices and gimmicks to meet the 1988 deficit reduction goals. Faced with this crisis, the Congress changed the Gramm–Rudman–Hollings law in order to slow down its deficit reduction requirements. The Emergency Deficit Control Reaffirmation Act of 1987, or Gramm–Rudman–Hollings II, changed the fiscal 1988 deficit reduction target back to the previous year's $144 billion, thereby postponing the target date for a balanced budget from 1991 to 1993. Gramm–Rudman–Hollings II also outlawed some of the gimmickry that had been used in the past couple of years. Even so, on October 19, the stock market plunged, leading to another summit negotiation and budget agreement. This agreement allowed both Congress and the President to get through the 1988 election year without interbranch strife. The President's budget, which reflected the agreement, was for the first time in years not considered "dead on arrival" to Congress. The fact that the two branches agreed to a truce based on equally unrealistic budget assumptions can be attributed as much to weariness as to the fact that it was an election year. Procedurally, the stages of congressional budgeting operated more normally and promptly than had been the case in years. There was only one problem. By 1989, when George Bush took office, the federal budget deficit was estimated to be over $218 billion.[99]

Toward the Budget Enforcement Act: Nowhere Left to Go

The first year and a half of the Bush administration brought forth no major solution to the deficit dilemma and in fact revisited many of the same unsatisfactory prescriptions that had been tried over past years.[100] President Bush's transition budget had provided only minimal changes to Reagan's outgoing budget. In order to show that the Bush administration was going to be "kinder and gentler" than the Reagan budgets had been, there were administration claims of proposed increases in programs supporting child care, drug enforcement, the environment, housing for the homeless, Medicaid, and enterprise zones. Many of these "increases" were questionable since Bush's "flexible freeze" essentially maintained most of the non-defense budget at 1989 spending levels but did not include a percentage rise for expected inflation. In this case, according to Richard Darman's baseline of choice, the previous year's actual spending was used "to claim that the President was increasing spending even though the amount to be spent under the administration's proposal was less than was needed to maintain the same level of services."[101] This meant that most of these domestic programs would either be cut or remain at the previous year's levels under the plan. The plan in most cases did not communicate which programs were to be earmarked for increases or which were to be reduced or frozen. Those difficult decisions were left to the Congress.

The story of the White House–congressional negotiations that ensued in 1990 and led to passage of the Omnibus Budget Reconciliation Act of 1990 requires a chapter in itself. A brief outline of the progress of the negotiating process and a few particulars of the final agreement will suffice for the purposes of this study. From July of 1990 until October, Budget Director Darman, Treasury Secretary Brady, and White House Chief of Staff John Sununu negotiated with Democratic and Republican congressional negotiators only to have their initial agreement turned down by the House on October 6. After much additional posturing, the Omnibus Budget Reconciliation Act of 1990 passed on October 29. One of its main features included tax increases.

Less noticed at the time was the passage of an accompanying procedural vehicle called the Budget Enforcement Act. This law was destined to exercise a far-reaching impact on OMB's institutional stature and on the budgetary politics of the next few years.

The Budget Enforcement Act: An Overview

The Budget Enforcement Act (BEA) was a cleverly crafted political agreement devised by a very few participants in a short amount of time.[102] It was in part conceived to alleviate the pressure on both the President and the Congress to achieve fixed deficit reduction goals at least until after the 1992 election when some of its provisions would cease to apply. The BEA's aims were less ambitious than had been those of the Gramm–Rudman–Hollings laws and were therefore perhaps more realistic. It did not seek to eliminate the deficit, but merely to control discretionary spending and to ensure that legislation mandating any increase in entitlement spending be offset by either equal revenue collection *or* commensurate expenditure reduction. By setting these more realistic goals, budget process expert Stanley Collender wrote,

> White House and Congress, Republican and Democrat, Senate and House [would] avoid making any additional tough choices on spending and taxes until at least after the 1992 presidential and congressional elections were over. This meant that prior to the voting there would be none of the problems that had plagued most of the previous budget debates—no more year long stalemates, no more apparent congressional and presidential ineptitude on the budget, and no more politically hard votes.[103]

The above notwithstanding, the BEA did have maximum allowable levels for the deficit.[104] However, they were drastically higher than the Gramm–Rudman–Hollings levels had been and were, for want of a better description, extremely "flexible." For example, while in FY 1991 the Gramm–Rudman–Hollings I deficit target was to have been zero and under Gramm–Rudman–Hollings II it was to have been $64 billion under the Budget Enforcement Act the goal was set at $327 billion.[105]

While large-scale deficit reduction had seemingly been abandoned for the next couple of years, the genuine goal of the Budget Enforcement Act was to enforce spending controls. This was accomplished by creating a two-pronged approach which involved devising two separate enforcement mechanisms, one for annual discretionary spending that occurred through the appropriations process and another for mandatory entitlement spending that emanated from the authorization process.

For the discretionary spending area, the Budget Enforcement Act set caps for each year from 1991 to 1993 in each of three categories—defense spending, international spending, and domestic spending. As with the maximum deficit levels, the President was empowered to revise these caps each year when he submitted his budget to take into account changed inflation projections, cost estimates, or new technical assumptions. The cap levels could be repeatedly revised during the course of the congressional debate due to a variety of factors. These included any appropriations designated as "emergency spending" that were not required to be counted against the caps. Interestingly, the Budget Enforcement Act specified no definition of what an emergency was to entail, but Congress and the President were both required to concur in the decision to designate spending as "emergency spending." Other circumstances specified by the Budget Enforcement Act as allowing for the "cap adjustments" included needed funding for increased enforcement of IRS regulations or for contributions to the International Monetary Fund. If, after all the permissible adjusting, the Congress still had breached the discretionary spending caps, the law specified that a sequester would be triggered in the category of the breach.

The second enforcement mechanism created a pay-as-you-go (PAYGO) system for revenue or mandatory spending legislation (which usually but not always involved entitlement programs). The BEA system set controls on authorization legislation which either cut revenues or increased mandatory spending to the degree that it surpassed yet another BEA baseline. Collender defined this BEA baseline as assuming "that current law will continue and that the economic projections in the President's budget will occur."106 OMB was given the authority by the BEA to determine when legislation breached this baseline. In such cases, funding offsets would have to be proposed to make up for the amount of the breach through taxes or decreases in other mandatory spending. This differed from the discretionary appropriations caps discussed above in that revenue increases in this case were not permitted to be used to prevent a breach of the caps. The BEA designated that the sequester for all mandatory programs designated by the law would occur two weeks after Congress adjourned if the appropriate offsets had not been made.

OMB and the BEA: An Introduction

The Budget Enforcement Act was intended to enforce budgetary constraints without raising taxes or subjecting the President and Congress to the Draconian pressures that Gramm–Rudman–Hollings I and II had produced. To this end it needed an "enforcer" within the control of either the President or Congress or both. If Congress had chosen itself or a congressionally appointed unit to enforce the law, the Supreme Court would probably have invalidated the procedure as constituting an abridgement of separation of powers doctrine as had been the case in the original Gramm–Rudman–Hollings law.[107]

And so the President and OMB were granted the power to enforce the strictures of the act so much so that OMB's institutional influence precipitously increased because of this grant of authority. Howard Shuman in his *Politics and the Budget* wrote of the law, "The President, through the OMB, determines the five-year budget deficit target goals on an annual basis. The President is also the scorekeeper, umpire and judge as to whether the discretionary and direct spending goals and the pay-as-you-go provisions have been met."[108]

While CBO was to be "consulted" by OMB with respect to its BEA scoring and estimating responsibilities, it was OMB's economic assumptions and estimates that were to be binding. This was not a joint OMB–CBO effort in the same sense that Gramm–Rudman–Hollings had been. OMB's authority applied to estimates surrounding the deficit ceilings from 1991 to 1993, "to adjustments" to the caps in the three discretionary spending areas, and to cost estimates of current discretionary and entitlement programs as well as appropriations and legislation proposing changes in these programs. OMB was also responsible for totaling up these estimates and determining whether they fit under the discretionary ceilings. For proposals containing both discretionary and mandatory components,[109] and/or both domestic and military characteristics,[110] OMB was empowered to determine in which category they belonged. Through its power to decide when estimated costs of new congressional proposals would "breach" the caps and thus trigger a sequester, OMB was able to influence and alter the course of congressional action early in the process, thereby potentially being able to signal congressional committees to change the complexion of the congressional proposals under consideration.

Stanley Collender noted examples of this newly acquired clout during the 1992 and 1993 budget processes. "It [OMB] sometimes threatened a sequester early during a tax writing or appropriations deliberation if a particular provision being considered was not changed in some way more to the administration's choosing even when another provision costing the same amount was ignored."[111] Along these same lines, OMB had a significant measure of discretion to advance the Bush administration's policy objectives through its authority to determine the "classification" of programs that could not be clearly categorized as mandatory or discretionary, or domestic, international, or defense related. If the administration favored increased spending in a particular case, the program could be placed into the category with enhanced funding possibilities. In instances where budgetary constraints were favored, the program could be defined as belonging to the category with tighter discretionary caps or the entitlement area with little possibility of revenue offsets to fund it.

The complexity of the Budget Enforcement Act process in combination with the authority to make key determinations, afforded OMB significant institutional influence. If few outsiders understood the rules of the game, it became next to impossible to monitor whether the inside players were following them. Howard Shuman expressed this well, citing that the complexity of the BEA had tended to "shift attention from the macro to the micro budget activities, from an outsider's game to an insider's game, and thus to blur both action and responsibility further so that it will be difficult to determine accountability."[112]

The history of OMB had shown that the greater the focus on complex or technical issues, the more influential the career staff became. At least with respect to the BEA, this probably held true during the last two years of the Bush administration. Since parts of the BEA itself were open to interpretation, as well as many of the critical judgments required to comply with its mandates, the OMB staff who ran the numbers and made the critical calls gained a large measure of clout.

OMB Pay-As-You-Go Estimating: Who Did "What, When, and How"

OMB's new responsibilities with respect to pay-as-you-go scoring added yet another overlay to OMB's already complex congressional watchdog role. It provided an additional work load responsibility for BRD, LRD, and program division staff with relevant programs, and a new avenue of input and potential influence for OMB career staff. As part of OMB's program division tracking responsibilities, examiners with relevant program account areas were charged with examining authorization bills and determining whether the proposals required pay-as-you-go offsets.

The initial program division review and PAYGO cost estimation was triggered at various points of the legislative process. OMB's routine legislative clearance process could prompt a PAYGO review as could the preparation process for administration testimony on a particular bill. Typically, OMB PAYGO reviews would also take place after designated authorization bills were reported out of committee. In fact, any event in Congress that elicited concern in the White House or elsewhere could set the PAYGO review process in motion.

While the program divisions were charged with screening proposed authorization bills for PAYGO implications through their normal congressional tracking responsibilities, LRD also played a facilitator role in ferreting out estimates that appeared to be questionable. Again, in this process as in legislative clearance generally, LRD's role was primarily coordinative and the program divisions made the initial cost estimates. With respect to the PAYGO estimating process itself, examiners were both guided by institutional directives and allowed leeway for personal discretion and judgment. OMB examiners were encouraged to consult with CBO staff and to resolve estimating differences between OMB and CBO, but to reach their own estimates without relying on the agencies' cost estimates.

A number of staff with PAYGO-related accounts stressed that as with any cost estimating and scoring responsibility, the examiner's common sense and judgment had to enter in as an important variable. Sometimes program division staff conducted their own surveys to determine comparable costs of particular systems or services in the private sector. One veteran staffer observed that sometimes it was in the cases when he would use such "independent" estimating methods that he would find wider disparities with CBO's estimates. Such observations again underscore the subjectivity of the cost estimation process and the fact that OMB was thus able to exercise significant discretion in its enforcement. While institutional guidelines directed that PAYGO estimates were to be cleared by OMB policy officials, the PAYGO clearance process provided an opportunity for OMB career staff to exercise influence during the congressional stages of the budgetary process at the expense of departmental agency autonomy.

Another important means for influencing the BEA process was the determination of *who* proposed the offsets for proposals that suggested "new" entitlement spending, and whose proposals were ultimately enacted. The second question is beyond the scope of this inquiry but would be an intriguing area for further research. The answer to the first question is that most of the key participants in the process offered offset proposals. These included the Budget Appropriations and Authorization committees in the Congress and the agencies, OMB, and White House in the Executive Branch. Program division examiners made recommendations for offsets affecting PAYGO proposals in their areas frequently. LRD did not generally recommend offsets but would prepare memos presenting the various proposals and coordinating meetings among the key participates to discuss the recommendations.

BRD was responsible for preparing an official PAYGO report to Congress within five calendar days of enactment of legislation, an end-of-session sequester report, an account of total PAYGO estimates for the budget year and the previous year, a preview report included in the President's budget showing PAYGO implications for legislation passed up to that point, and a PAYGO sequester update report issued August 15 of each year which updated previous estimates to include legislation passed since the President submitted his budget.

The PAYGO process thus brought about significant work load increases for LRD, BRD, and those program division staff reviewing "mandatory" accounts. The PAYGO process also required that the staff examine budget increments of less than a million dollars as well as agency accounting systems to make sure that their estimates were as accurate as possible. Program division staff sometimes found deficient agency accounting systems that previously had been making technical errors amounting to discrepancies of thousands of dollars. Prior to the BEA, such problems usually did not surface and tended to be submerged in huge omnibus reconciliation bills. While in the past this level of detailed micro-accounting typically had been used for discretionary programs open to the appropriations process, smaller bills dealing with "mandatory" entitlement programs had not been examined as closely.

Enforcing the Caps on Discretionary Programs

After the President's budget was transmitted to Congress, both examiners and BRD Appropriations Committee bill trackers monitored the progress of appropriations bills for any changes to the President's budget. Examiners with accounts in discretionary areas were charged with providing cost estimates of congressional proposals affecting their areas. However, since the thirteen appropriations bills cut across many accounts areas, BRD also became involved in the discretionary scoring process. Cost estimates and scorekeeping reports were included in the SAPs that were prepared by the examiners and further compiled by the appropriations bill trackers. The scoring had to be consistent with the economic assumptions that had been stated in the President's budget. For example, if the assumption had been made in the President's budget that a certain program would require a 17 percent increase in costs for the first year and 55 percent in the second year, the examiner or BRD bill tracker could not abandon these assumptions in determining the implications of a new appropriations proposal. Scorekeeping information and cost estimates from the program divisions and the BRD bill tracker were then channeled to the Budget Review and Concepts Division staff who were charged with preparing the Preview, Update, and Final BEA reports to Congress.

OMB and BEA Designated "Emergencies"

Though the BEA required both presidential and congressional concurrence on "emergency" spending, there were avenues within the emergency designation process that placed OMB in a position to police congressional actions on supplemental appropriations bills where the "emergency money" was usually to be found.

The Budget Enforcement Act provided no definition of what comprised an emergency, leaving open the potential for disagreement on this matter. OMB developed an operational definition for emergency spending as a necessary expenditure that is "sudden," "urgent," and "unforeseen" and is "not permanent."[113] Flexibility was added to this definition by interjecting that the determination of an emergency should be made on a "case-by-case" basis, using "common sense judgment," whether the "totality of facts and circumstances indicate a true emergency" and "whether the needs can be absorbed within the existing level of resources available."[114]

During the Bush administration, the decision to ask Congress for concurrence with emergency spending was made by the President in accord with his top-level political advisors. OMB become involved in two aspects of this BEA emergency spending process: estimating the necessary costs involved, and, once Congress agreed on the emergency designation, "policing" the supplemental appropriation process to make certain that no "nonemergency" spending became hidden within the emergency categories in the supplemental appropriations bills.

With respect to the estimating responsibilities, the examiners were charged with making the determination of how much money would still be available in the relevant budget accounts, how much money would be needed for immediate use for the emergency situation, and how much would be needed in the near future to be placed in contingency funds. Their recommendations would then be approved by the PADs and the director, with BRD providing coordination to the process.

Careful OMB tracking of supplemental appropriations bills that contained *both* emergency and nonemergency spending in 1991 uncovered efforts by members of Congress to piggyback certain nonemergency spending with the "emergency" funding or to exclude nonemergency spending from being

counted under the budget enforcement caps. The first such instance occurred during the framing of HR 1281, an "emergency" supplemental appropriations bill intended to pay for the indirect costs of the Gulf War.
President Bush had requested $3.7 billion, of which $940 million was to be
considered emergency spending to be exempted from the discretionary caps. It
became evident to OMB that both the House and Senate versions of the supplemental appropriations contained spending that had not been designated by
OMB as "emergency spending." This included $1 million for the United States
Information Agency, $7 million for the Commerce Department, and funds for
dairy price supports.[115] Using the sequester threat, the administration was able
to force Congress to remove much of the illegitimate spending in the Senate
version of the bill. Some observers maintained that because of the BEA's rules,
in cases like this, the President and OMB were essentially exercising a line-
item veto, since the President did not have to veto or to threaten to veto the
entire supplemental appropriations bill in order to compel removal of features
he opposed in it.[116]

OMB showed its muscle later on during the evolution of this "Gulf War"
supplemental when the final version of the bill granted $8 million to Loyola
University of Chicago, House Ways and Means Committee Chairman Dan
Rostenkowski's alma mater. OMB refused to define the spending as part of
the emergency expenditures to be excluded from being counted under the
discretionary caps. These expenditures in turn breached the "caps," thus
triggering a "mini" sequester.

Doyle and McCaffery described the outcome:

> When Congress ignored the threat, OMB enforced its first within-session,
> mini-sequester under the BEA. Domestic discretionary accounts subject to
> sequestration were cut by a total of $2.4 million across-the-board, reducing
> programs by 0.0013 percent. That this was a political rather than an eco-
> nomic gesture is evident from the size of the program reductions. The De-
> partment of Energy's geothermal resources development fund lost $1; the
> rewards and operations fund of the Fish and Wildlife Service lost $13. A
> House aide said, "It's like sending you a bill with a 29-cent stamp to get you
> to pay 6 cents."[117]

OMB and BEA Category Changes

Another important means of influence for OMB granted by the Budget
Enforcement Act for the 1991–93 period was the authority to determine
whether a program or expenditure should be considered discretionary or
mandatory or whether a discretionary program belonged within the domestic, international, or defense categories.

In the overwhelming majority of cases, it would be clear under the BEA where programs and/or expenditures belonged and under those circumstances, OMB did not have power to move the programs around. However, some kinds of programs could be defined as either mandatory or discretionary, or domestic or defense, given that they contained elements of both. Funding for research on nuclear power could have been considered to have been designated either for military or domestic purposes.[118] A program that otherwise would have been considered discretionary could have been considered mandatory because of the financing method attached to it.

Under the BEA, OMB was able to use its authority to classify such programs as a means to discipline spending when it reflected the administration's objectives to cut (often in domestic areas) or to increase expenditures when that reflected other policy goals (usually with increased military spending.) When Congress attempted to play the same game, it generally failed. For example, in 1991 the administration wanted to extend veteran's education to Gulf War veterans. Normally such a program would be considered an entitlement subject to PAYGO limitations. In this case, however, OMB ruled that the extension was "not an entitlement because it came about as a result of a direct appropriation and thus did not need an offsetting revenue source."[119] Since OMB had the authority, that argument carried the day.

Such classification determinations were made by a variety of sources in the agencies or the program divisions when a designation of program classification was needed to interpret new legislation, or to decide whether a new financing mechanism such as a user fee might change a program from a discretionary to a mandatory category. The program division decision would then be reviewed by the Budget Analysis and Concepts Divisions of BRD, sometimes in conjunction with the OMB General Counsel to see if the change was in keeping with the Budget Enforcement Act. One BRD staffer who was questioned on this point estimated that 90 percent of such decisions would be clear cut from the reading of the Budget Enforcement Act and about 10 percent "pure interpretation."

OMB's Legislative Onslaught and Credibility Problems in the 1980s

Before the 1970s, presidential budgets had set the parameters of debate in the Congress. Congress had neither the staff resources nor the political will to fundamentally change that reality. The 1974 Budget Act affected Congress's capabilities by adding the CBO, budget committees, and new procedural mechanisms which enabled Congress to be more of an equal player in budgetary policy making. The Executive Branch responded by paying greater attention to the progress of its budgets on the Hill than it had before.

When David Stockman entered the picture and manipulated congressional procedures to work to the President's advantage, interbranch budget strife began to reach new levels. Other than a couple of temporary truces, this budgetary warfare continued throughout the 1980s until the 1992 presidential election. It had not only been based upon partisanship differences, but had persisted between presidents and congressional players of the same party as well.

The growth of the deficit in the 1980s had markedly intensified the budget wars and with time made this politicized budget process even more visible to the public. That public began perceiving the deficit to be a threat to the nation's economic well-being in the mid-1980s, but its individual interest communities and constituencies had not been prepared to sacrifice government services or to pay higher taxes individually or collectively to the degree necessary to address the problem.

Thus from the mid-1980s to the 1992 election, both presidential and congressional candidates were faced with untenable political choices. While the electorate increasingly appeared to be calling for deficit reduction, politicians soon discovered that advocacy of higher taxes or cuts in the broadly based middle-class entitlements that made up the bulk of the deficit could prove to constitute political suicide on election day. There were still some public officials who spoke up, but usually they were those whose political survivability was not at risk. Most presidential and congressional candidates responded to this climate by skirting the deficit issue during election time or distorting their opponents' views related to deficit reduction in order to score points for themselves. Once in office they devised complex procedural mechanisms such as baselining and scoring rules which facilitated budgetary restraint, but which allowed them to avoid assuming responsibility for the unpopular outgrowths of deficit reduction. The political cover that was thus afforded wrapped the budget trade-offs and choices that were being made in a haze of complex and arcane budget terminology that few could penetrate.

At each stage of this history, OMB, as the President's chief budgeteer, had been affected in profound ways. In the 1970s, when Congress became more involved in budgeting and the President decided to oversee this involvement, OMB had been called upon for assistance. When David Stockman took this process ten steps further, he did so with OMB's support. By the time of Jim Miller's directorate, OMB's congressional watchdog role had become institutionalized. Even though Miller personally was not a constant presence on Capitol Hill, OMB staff continued to pursue their congressional tracking roles.

While Richard Darman was more insular than was Stockman, and certainly more involved in direct congressional negotiations than was Miller, this did not mean that the overall trend toward OMB staff congressional monitorship decreased. Some staff in OMB perceived an increase in time spent supporting Darman's efforts on the Hill even when compared to the energy and time they expended during David Stockman's directorate. Darman was described as having demanded even more elaborate informational backup and data from staff when dealing with the Congress and as having more frequently testified before congressional committees on a variety of issues. Under Darman, some budget examiners and branch chiefs were asked to "formally" comment on reconciliation and appropriations measures, tasks formerly left to LRD and BRD. Others perceived that they were given more "short fuse" analytic assignments to support congressional negotiations.

Thus overall, legislation-related work responsibilities multiplied during the entire decade of the 1980s, with some staff estimating that as much as 50 percent of their time had become devoted to legislative responsibilities, up from 10 to 20 percent ten years earlier. At the same time, OMB budget staff numbers and resources had declined. Staff energies were further expended by the necessity of having to deal with an ever-changing budget process and ever-changing political realities. This climate was accompanied by marked variation in the levels of sophistication of program division staff with respect to new congressional oversight responsibilities and their abilities to decode the complexities of new congressional procedures. One career staff manager, who had been assigned to a new branch within the same division soon after enactment of the BEA, was surprised to find that the staff did not understand rudimentary rules in the appropriations process or scoring rules.

Traditional roles suffered as well. As Larry Haas of the *National Journal* observed:

> A half-year task of drafting the President's budget has turned into a full-year job of trying to force as much of it as possible through to enactment. Staff members can't keep up with the literature in their fields of expertise. Their analyses of programs are shorter and shallower.[120]

Even so, it can be argued that in many branches and divisions these trends were not as pronounced, since the amount of congressional monitorship activity "required" by different branches in the program divisions had always varied and continued to do so into the 1990s. Also, staff continued to be smart, analytical workaholics, so they coped by working budget season hours all year long. The author's OMB interviews during a ten-year period still support the image that most examiners were quite knowledgeable about their programs, if not a little exhausted, by the end of the process.

Nonetheless, there is no doubt that the rapidly mounting number of OMB and congressional staff tracking and scoring responsibilities described in detail in this chapter eroded the time available to seek out and analyze in-depth knowledge about their assigned program areas in order to be able to provide advice to the President.

As the deficit had escalated and the interparty and interbranch strife turned into full-scale warfare, OMB was frequently used as both a foot soldier and a political football. When the baselines, scoring rules, and statutes were devised, OMB was both formally and informally codified as their keeper for the President. Thus, in an odd reversal of roles, an institution that was designed to anonymously educate and enlighten Presidents became increasingly removed from its shield of anonymity as it became an interpreter and enforcer of procedures and laws that in part had the effect of obscuring and confusing the budget choices at hand.

Thus, the budgetary history of the 1980s had cost OMB dearly in terms of its credibility with the public. House Majority Whip Thomas Foley was not alone in the view he expressed during the mid-1980s that "OMB was not trusted to avoid politically motivated cooking of the books and skewing of the figures."[121] Perhaps this credibility problem first started entering the public consciousness when Director Stockman admitted to factoring inconsistent numbers into economic projections and generally fudging the numbers. Stockman's admissions did not, however, end the rosy scenarios. They were just the beginning. By the end of Reagan's second term, OMB was in the habit of predicting declining deficits by assuming ideal economic conditions, which frequently had proven to be incorrect and out of line with private sector estimates. For example, OMB had ranked at the bottom for the accuracy of its economic projections since 1983 in a 1987 survey of thirteen private economic forecasters and CBO.[122]

When Richard Darman became director of OMB, he paid lip service to restoring OMB's credibility in making economic forecasts. While there were improvements in some respects, the record was still somewhat mixed.[123] OMB's forecasts of economic indicators such as its growth and inflation rates were closer to the economic outcomes than were some of those of private forecasters.[124] OMB's deficit projections, on the other hand, had been less consistent. Fluctuations in OMB's 1991 deficit forecasts, which ranged from $101 billion to $310 billion, had again prompted skepticism about OMB's estimating process as well as the administration's motives.[125]

By the end of the Bush administration, OMB's energies and its credibility had become depleted and diverted. OMB still played its traditional roles for the President where possible. Some directors and PADs still began their tenures at OMB playing lip service to the goal of redirecting OMB to its traditional missions, but such intentions were usually side-tracked by the demands of the "budgetary wars." Career staff analysts and information conduits served more and more as technicians and gatekeepers of arcane budget law.

8

OMB and the Agencies: Communicating, Managing, and "Regulating the Regulators"

Introduction

The value of OMB advice to the President is in large part predicated upon whether it is based in reliable intelligence on federal departments and agencies, their budgets, the effectiveness of their programs, and how well these programs are managed. Thus, the character of OMB's relationships with the agencies it reviews will condition its capacity to serve the presidency in important ways. Chapter 8 approaches this somewhat broad topic from three vantage points: first through an extrapolation of some of the dynamics of OMB–agency communications over three decades, second by providing a history of BOB/OMB's somewhat uneven career in advancing better management in the agencies, and finally by offering an account of OMB's foray into regulatory review from 1981 until the end of the Bush administration. Each discussion only serves to scratch the surface of areas ripe for further research.

BOB/OMB Communications

OMB –Agency Relationships in the 1960s

In the mid-1960s, Ripley and Davis studied BOB–agency relationships through an examination of their points of contact, the nature of their communications, and the perceptions held by agency personnel of BOB staff.

Their findings are a useful frame of reference for a discussion of how OMB–agency relationships have changed in certain respects over the last thirty years. One of Ripley and Davis's most significant conclusions was that "access to and control over information" were "the most important internal factors affecting the bargaining process between the Bureau and the operating agencies."[1] To that can be added the point that if BOB/OMB is to fulfill its mandate of providing neutral but educated advice to the President, it must have the capability of securing and distilling a massive amount of information on bureaucratic programs and agencies.

Ripley and Davis had also found that BOB–agency contacts occurred on a daily basis and involved all of BOB's fundamental functions at the time; namely budget preparation, budget execution, legislative clearance, and various statistical, management, organizational, personnel, or related issues.[2] In addition, BOB–agency communications and contacts were also called into play at times when the President needed general information about an agency program, when agencies explained their programmatic operations to BOB, and when BOB communicated presidential policies to the agencies.[3] Communications were also directed from agencies to BOB when they required clarifications of BOB directives to them.[4]

While the level in the supervisory hierarchy where the contacts occurred varied widely and depended upon the issues being considered, the program division budget examiners were considered to be BOB's key contact point with the agencies. This was particularly true with smaller agencies. Ripley and Davis wrote that while "much of the contact between the Bureau and the operating agencies [was] maintained by men of roughly equivalent rank and position . . . it [was] also maintained by junior examiners in the Bureau and senior personnel in the agencies."[5]

Ripley and Davis reported that, since junior or mid-level agency personnel rarely if ever communicated with senior BOB officials, this brought forth some degree of resentment in the agencies. Thus they suggested that all examiners, even junior ones, played a significant role.

Other aspects of BOB–agency relationships were highly variable. These included how closely agencies tried to control contacts with BOB[6] and the nature of the characterizations agency personnel offered when describing BOB staff.[7] Agencies also varied with whether they encouraged BOB staff to make broad contacts throughout an agency or carefully attempted to limit BOB–agency communications to narrow and established channels.[8] Ripley and Davis suggested that this variation depended upon whether an agency perceived that the more information it provided BOB, the better the budgetary outcomes would be, or conversely, that more information would only undermine the agency in BOB's eyes.[9] The particular agency unit from which BOB staff sought information also varied among budget units, programs, operating bureaus, and undersecretaries' offices.[10]

In most cases, Ripley and Davis's interviewees viewed BOB and its staff as "neutral," but some agencies perceived BOB either as being an advocate of their agency mission or as being openly hostile to them.[11] These BOB–agency relationships hinged upon a number of factors. An agency's prospects and relationships with BOB tended to improve if a President's broad objectives coincided with the agency's mission and worsened if it did not.[12] Powerful Cabinet-level departments or those having clout in the Congress tended to negotiate with BOB from a stronger position.[13] Other significant factors that conditioned BOB–agency communications were the nature of the relationships among the Cabinet secretary's departmental office and those of the subordinate bureaus, the facility with which the agency was able to quantify its productivity and costs, and the personalities and abilities of BOB staffers.[14]

The positive and negative observations that Ripley and Davis's agency interviewees offered about BOB staff in the 1960s provide a useful point of comparison with current perceptions. The positive images of BOB staff revolved around a few qualities: namely, a depth of understanding and knowledge of the agency and its mission, superior intelligence, sincerity, maturity, and the ability to be savvy enough to pick up mistakes made by the agency.[15] Common to these disparate qualities was a mature understanding of the agency's functions.

Those agency staffers who viewed BOB staff in a negative light saw some examiners as brash, opinionated, unreasonable, distrustful, and suspicious. Other negatives focused on the BOB staffer's analytic approaches, capabilities, or lack of creativity.[16] These included descriptions of some BOB staff as nit-pickers, trivia-oriented, and negative, and "never . . . helpful in an inventive way."[17] Additional complaints that BOB staffers were too academic, politically naive, or did not understand the Congress focused on BOB's ivory tower orientation at the time.[18] Another general concern was that BOB interfered with agency management and subjected departments to the latest "management fad" regardless of whether the agency was already well or poorly managed.[19]

Agency-OMB Relationships at the End of the 1970s: Intelligence-Gathering Strategies and Communication Patterns

The 1970s interviews reconfirmed for the end of that decade much of what Ripley and Davis had found in the 1960s. OMB budget examiners were still playing key roles in the forefront of OMB's efforts to gather information and communicate with the agencies and generally enjoyed much discretion

with respect to the approaches they chose to use in gathering that information.[20] While incoming and outgoing OMB–agency communications took
place at all levels of OMB, examiners in the 1970s were found to exercise a
large measure of control over incoming information from their assigned
agencies. At the most basic operating level it was the budget examiner who
initially sought, received, and developed information from the agency and
acted as a conduit through which agency data was screened and processed
before being forwarded to the OMB Director and ultimately to the President. Hence, the examiners were able to influence what issues would be
raised and what information would receive maximum attention.

One division chief echoed a perception shared by supervisors and examiners alike:

> The opportunity to let a new precedent fly through or to indeed violate a basic
> principle of Federal–nonfederal relationships to be included in the budget does
> indeed rest with the examiner. If the examiner doesn't identify issues and bring
> them up, the branch chief or the division chief doesn't have the capability to spot
> them. If the examiner chooses not to raise the issue he can de facto make the
> positive decision to let the agencies go ahead on expenditures. The examiner in
> that sense has on small items a "yea" saying capability simply by ignoring them.
> He has a "nay" saying capability by raising the issue.

The division chiefs, PADs, and the director also dealt with agency officials on matters affecting their own particular level of interest. In areas
involving highly politicized and visible budgetary matters, the initial
agency–OMB communication generally took place at the division chief
level or higher. However, given the fact that there were approximately 150
examiners and branch chiefs and only eleven division chiefs and PADs, the
overwhelming amount of information still was screened and processed at
the examiner and branch level, with those staffers who had previous experience in the federal bureaucracy receiving more information.

The 1970s data were also quite consistent with Ripley and Davis's findings with respect to the high degree of variation among agencies' proclivities to limit communications flow to OMB to established and controlled
channels, or to allow more open interchange. Approximately 70 percent of
the examiners indicated they never or only occasionally had difficulty securing information from their assigned agencies.

The Intelligence-Gathering Strategies

Examiners in the late 1970s took pride in their well-honed skills in securing
information from the departments and agencies. They did so through verbal

communications over the telephone, at meetings, or in one-on-one encounters; written data were secured in the form of reports, memoranda, statistics, and correspondence informing OMB of agency policy decisions. Examiners also kept informed about the subtleties of agency programs by cultivating personal and social contacts within the agencies and by traveling outside Washington to regional field offices to investigate the implementation of programs on a grassroots level. Less overt strategies to learn what was transpiring inside their assigned agencies included the use of departmental "leaks" and selective information trading with the agency. Examiners at the time believed that they were able to obtain information they otherwise would not have received as quickly or at all through the use of these intelligence-gathering approaches.

Personal relationships with agency personnel. The importance of having reliable personal contacts at as many levels of the budget examiner's assigned agency as possible was repeatedly emphasized by the majority of the examiners interviewed. For example, one examiner observed:

> So much depends upon personal relationships. They know what you have to do on the budget and they know you're going to be at odds at times, but if you are consistent and responsible and honest, then generally you get good information.

> In order to obtain information, you need a core set of people who are friendly basically and whose judgment you can rely on *or* whose biases you are aware of.

Generally, the approaches and techniques used in developing such personal relationships with agency personnel, as well as their ultimate success, varied with individual examiners' personalities. One technique used by the examiners to meet people in the agencies was to cultivate agency personnel they knew personally before coming to work at OMB. Another technique was to visit the agency and make personal contacts. Finally, some examiners took the initiative to develop contacts when they met agency personnel at meetings.

Such contacts would sometimes develop into attendance at dinners and parties or at times become a part of the so-called Washington cocktail party circuit. While this may represent a frivolous way of obtaining data, several examiners described how many tidbits were learned in this way, which they were in turn able to use as take-off points in obtaining additional information.

Two personality characteristics and individual competencies tended to condition how successful examiners would be at establishing reliable agency contacts. Aside from the obvious requirements of being analytical, intelligent, and hard-working, the first characteristic cited was to be genuinely knowledgeable about the program and for new examiners to demonstrate that "they had already done their homework," and were not "sitting and waiting for the information to come to them." To accomplish this they needed to be willing to try to unearth as many facts and aspects of the program as possible and to demonstrate personal initiative. Second, most examiners believed that examiners needed to cultivate a sense of skepticism, but at the same time to balance qualities such as "toughness, aggressiveness, and complete self-confidence," with "not being brash," "friendliness," "tact," and the "ability to get along with people." This second personality profile was to prove particularly significant in the 1980s, when its absence in a small number of staffers was to adversely affect OMB's overall institutional image in the 1990s.

Leak sources and selective information trading. Examiners endowed with the aforementioned qualities were the ones who tended to win respect and trust among agency career civil servants. This in turn enabled them to obtain even more information through departmental leaks and through information trading. The kind of information transmitted through leaks included cost overruns, inefficient use of resources, internal agency studies, reports before they had been released by the agency, or program proposals or reports that had been suppressed within the agency. Moreover, receipt of departmental information from leak sources was not an isolated occurrence. Approximately 75 percent of the examiners in the sample were recipients of "leak" information at times. As one examiner described, "Often you have a program with serious holes in it which someone higher up is pushing for political or personal reasons. People in the agency can and do feed you this information."

To receive information, examiners had to provide some of their own. In doing so they needed to be extremely prudent not to compromise OMB or themselves. In some cases this balance could be maintained by informing agency officials of a decision not yet released but designated to be "formally" announced within a short period of time. Such an action usually would not undermine OMB's position, but could benefit the agency official by enhancing his reputation within his own agency as being a person who could extract accurate "information" from his reliable OMB contacts.

One division chief provided an assessment of where the "ethical" lines needed to be drawn in such relationships with agency personnel in the following way:

> It's dirty pool to trade compliance for information. ("As long as I know what you're doing, I'll let you do it—sort of trade. You tell me what you're doing

and I won't make an issue of it as long as I know about it.") . . . The agencies have to understand all the way along that we're free to raise an issue over anything that happens whether we gained the knowledge of it legitimately or illegitimately. This is another intriguing area of examination. There is no illegitimate channel for a budget examiner to get information except insofar as it might violate the law.

In short, selectively trading information in a way that would not be damaging to OMB appeared to have been a valuable tool for eliciting additional information from the agencies.

Other information-gathering methods. About three-quarters of the examiners interviewed also gathered information on their assigned agencies by traveling to regional agency offices, frequently during the summer, which at the time was somewhat of a slack season in OMB. Often, the examiner would personally choose the destination, and sometimes it would be determined with guidance from the branch chief. The field trips not only gave the examiners the opportunity to observe program implementation on the grassroots level, but assisted them in building up a series of contacts all over the country.

Use of private interest groups as information sources for OMB career staff was another route examiners took in the 1970s. Examiners used written material such as association news letters and trade press publications and established personal contacts through interest group membership or attendance at related professional meetings. At such meetings they obtained information that allowed them to draw comparisons between how much it cost a government agency to perform some function and the amount private businesses spent to conduct a similar activity. Many examiners valued the use of private interest groups as a useful information-gathering approach and source since they had difficulty obtaining information from their agencies.

There were no formal institution-wide policies prohibiting examiners or other career staff from contacting or communicating with interest group representatives at the time. However, not all examiners were enthusiastic about the use of interest groups as information sources. Some did not use them because there were not any well-organized interest groups related to their agency's activities. Others voiced suspicions that the lobby groups in their area were "too biased" or "self-interested" for their information to be of any use to the examiner. A third argument offered against use of outside groups as information sources was that cultivation of such groups could often generate an additional work load for the examiner that tended to become onerous. Finally, there were those examiners who simply felt that it was not the OMB examiner's role to deal with outside groups as information sources to any extent. One examiner summed this position up by saying:

> I make very little use of clientele groups. I try to avoid that situation. I don't think it is OMB's role. It should be the role of the agencies to make the grass-roots contacts. In theory, it's the bureaucrats in the agencies who are paid to deal with outside people.

Most frequently, examiners contacted these groups because they experienced difficulty gaining information from their assigned agencies and were out of necessity forced to depend on information from outside sources.

Games Agencies Play Using OMB: "Good Cop/Bad Cop" and "In Loco Parentis"

As Presidents sometimes use OMB for protective cover, so too did agencies or component units of agencies. The most common example of such maneuvering was when agency budget offices placed the onus on OMB for cutting or constraining certain programs in an attempt to avoid conflict with their constituent programs, when the impetus for the cuts actually originated with the agency budget office itself. One agency budgeteer reported that his agency did this regularly and quoted the agency's OMB examiner as advising him to "blame us when you must." Conversely, though less frequently, programs perceived as valuable and well-functioning by OMB could be protected from their own budget shops by OMB. OMB career staff sometimes also acted as arbiters between different agencies and departments by lending support to an agency that lacked "political sponsorship" on the Hill. These roles of course would be predicated upon the absence of political signals from the White House, EOP, or OMB to the contrary.

OMB–Agency Relations in the 1980s and Early 1990s

Overview

While the fundamental contours of OMB–agency relationships already described remained constant in the 1980s and early 1990s, outgrowths of the rapidly rising deficit and Congress's changing place in the budget process began to alter the agency enforcement tools and information-gathering strategies used by OMB examiners. As the deficit grew, administrations from Carter through Bush became increasingly concerned with controlling growth of the deficit through its aggregate budgetary components, and less preoccupied with budgetary policy issues in individual programs. Emphasis on agency information per se therefore became secondary to efforts to project aggregate cost outcomes and their impact on the deficit and to the machinations involved in scoring, economic forecasting, and baseline construction precipitated by Congress's ascendant budgetary powers.

OMB–agency relationships changed as a consequence of this climate. As political appointees became less interested in specific programmatic agency information, so too did incentives decline for career staff to expend prodigious energies procuring such information. Institutional rewards were to be found elsewhere. The amount of time examiners had to pursue innovative information-gathering strategies eroded precipitously as did the available resources to fund field trips to agency outposts.

As some examiners perceived themselves to have lost influence into a *budget formulation* process that had gone from bottom-up to top-down, they sought to achieve an authoritative stance with the agencies through the *budget execution* process. Even some of those who did not seek to replace lost influence nonetheless started using their budget execution authorities more strategically to replace time-consuming information-gathering techniques of the past. These examiners became more tight-fisted when apportioning appropriated monies (where allowable by law) as a means of pressuring agencies to be more forthcoming with information and of guaranteeing their compliance with OMB directives. In some cases these more punitive approaches took the place of more time consuming efforts to cultivate "trusting" relationships with personnel in the agencies. These and a few other agency control devices were to become pejoratively labeled "micro-management" by disapproving agency budget officials who would complain intermittently over the ensuing years of a generic form of OMB meddling in their agency operations.

When contrasting the nature of BOB/OMB–agency relationships in the 1960s and those in the 1980s and 1990s, the reconfigured OMB relationship with Congress that had evolved over twenty years also colored the nature of agency assessments of OMB and strategies used when dealing with OMB. While Ripley and Davis had cited agency complaints that BOB did not adequately understand the political bargaining process in the Congress, by the 1990s some agency personnel had come to view congressional information and the ability to second-guess outcomes on the Hill as capabilities they "expected" their budget examiners to have. One agency budget official believed that OMB staff earned influence and stature in his department by sharing such accurate information with agency personnel.

Along the same lines, OMB's apolitical mindset had generally ceased to be an issue. In contrast, agency displeasure with OMB would come from the opposite direction. As various pressures on OMB had eroded its ability to be as programmatically knowledgeable as it had once been, its policy recommendations were perceived to have become politicized by some agencies and to have reflected less substantive programmatic knowledge. It was not that OMB civil servants were believed to have become more politicized themselves, but that some were thought to have insufficient information to make the strong merit arguments to counter the political pressures. As one agency budgeteer observed, "good points do not get put forward so the chances of persuading anyone to the facts are slim."

In the 1980s and the 1990s, some though not all OMB staff continued to use interest groups as information sources as before. By the 1990s, some divisional areas were described by one former staff member as prohibiting career staff–interest group contacts, possibly due to the political sensitivity of the issues that they handled. Conversely, other areas formally directed their new examiners to cultivate such contacts. One branch that designed some of its own training materials for new examiners instructed the following:

> Congressional and interest group staff.—Talk to them. Even the ones the present Administration may differ with the most. You need to know them and gain their respect as an analyst. The best ones will respect your institutional need to differ with them from time to time, but distinguish that from your personal professional standing. They will talk to you because they want to influence how you think. Learn from them and in time they will learn from you.[21]

The above instructions were included in OMB-wide orientations in the 1990s. Nonetheless, there were still no hard and fast policies guiding most aspects of OMB staff–interest group contacts. A few examiners commented during the mid-1980s that they needed to pursue the outside groups then more than ever before, since they no longer had enough time to dig for information in the agencies.

As always, all of the "changes" cited above varied from agency to agency and from issue to issue. Nonetheless, the perception that the "center" had shifted from a more agency-specific focus to one directed toward aggregate budget concerns and congressional tracking duties had conditioned the nature of OMB–agency relationships as well.

The kinds of personality characteristics and capabilities that agency personnel either admired or critiqued in OMB staff in the 1990s were strikingly similar to those cited by Ripley and Davis in the 1960s. On the positive front, agency officials believed most OMB staffers to be smart and objective, but the negative descriptions of OMB staffers echoed adjectives used in the past. These included characterizations of some OMB civil servants as arrogant, hard, directive, autocratic, competitive, and the "lone ranger" description cited in Chapter 1. As before, there was great variation.

Micro-Management Through Budget Execution

"Micro-management" was the umbrella term used by some budget process participants to describe a number of forms of OMB–agency oversight, the majority of which centered around using OMB's apportionment authorities as a tool to closely scrutinize agency expenditures and policies. Most frequently mentioned as an example of this phenomena was the use of "so-called" apportionment footnotes that made the release of an agency's quarterly apportionments contingent upon whether the agency had provided OMB with requested information, answers to lengthy questionnaires, or compliance with specific instructions directing how funds should be spent. These requests, which were in some cases broken down to the individual budget account or program level, were considered by some agencies to have been one of the most egregious forms of micro-management. They were also sometimes described as onerous, time-consuming, and unworkable. OMB legend has it that one OMB manager was known for the apportionment footnotes he issued that numbered in the hundreds of pages.

Kliman and Fisher have suggested that in individual cases, such use of OMB's apportionment powers might have had several possible origins, including OMB's distrust of the agency in question, detailed congressional instructions in appropriations and authorizations regarding the use of the funding, or "departmental officials wishing to limit the authority of their own subordinates."[22]

Another form of OMB micro-management that increased in the mid-1980s involved requirements that some agencies obtain prior OMB approval before "reprogramming" or shifting monies from "one project to another within the same appropriations account." Kliman and Fisher claim that OMB was not always involved in approving reprogrammings, which had usually been negotiated informally by congressional committees and the agencies.[23]

The use of some of these agency enforcement devices by OMB began increasing in the late 1970s under President Carter, and continued on into the 1980s. Some observers believe that the origin of those agency compliance mechanisms can be traced more to the broader power struggles between Presidents and Congresses (even of the same party) and to the mounting deficit, than to Reagan administration efforts to reduce domestic spending. One career staffer had observed in the mid-1980s that while OMB enforcement efforts through the apportionment process were "all to the liking of the Reagan administration," they evolved under Carter probably as an attempt to get back some of the clout the Executive Branch lost as a consequence of the Budget Act of 1974.

In addition, this staffer believed that these uses of OMB's budget execution authorities also afforded OMB career staff a way of retrieving some of the authority "they" had lost when the PADs were added to OMB's decision-making hierarchy. He observed that apportionment was one area that allowed the examiner added discretion and power since apportionment forms normally only required the approval of the division chief, unless a politically sensitive issue was involved. Another way of interpreting these institutional trends came from one OMB career staff manager interviewed in 1995, who believed in retrospect that the fact that the Reagan administration was not all that interested in individual programmatic aspects of agencies, but chose to focus more on aggregates, had also fueled the development of OMB career staff micro-management efforts albeit in a roundabout manner. To this individual, the Reagan years actually afforded the agencies more discretion with respect to how they spent their money, as long as the spending did not extend beyond the administration's approved ceilings. Thus, since the programmatic controls had been relinquished by political-level players, OMB career staff "chose" to fill the breach by assuring programmatic controls through the apportionment process.

Whatever the predisposing factors were that spurred these uses of OMB's budget execution authorities, utilization of these oversight tools by OMB career staffers were generally in keeping with administration policy and were supported by political appointees even if not always scrutinized by them. OMB insiders thus generally maintain that the overwhelming majority of the examiners using these techniques were not pursuing independent agendas and practically always had the tacit approval of their political-level supervisors. These agency oversight activities also sometimes played useful roles for the Reagan administration as protective cover for unpleasant directives of political origin. As one observer commented, "examiners were not acting independently and were not given a free hand to do what they wanted. It was easier to not have the political levels do these things, so that the career staff could be blamed." This OMB role as lightning rod was nothing new. The caveat was that the examiners during this period still had a lot of discretion in areas of little interest to political appointees. One agency official believed this "micro-management" extended to "the 80 percent of issues at the margin [in] which the policy and political people were not involved." A couple of observers described these micro-management efforts as having peaked during the Stockman and Miller directorates and having declined a bit during Richard Darman's tenure.

Contrasting Agency and OMB Perceptions

Not surprisingly, interviewees in agencies generally viewed these issues differently from OMB program division staffers. In some agencies these OMB "oversight" devices came to be seen as stultifying and often accompanied by an increasingly "autocratic" and "arrogant" demeanor on the part of some OMB examiners. Other agency officials argued that apportionment controls in particular "put the program in handcuffs," and that voluminous information requests often distracted agency staff from pursuing essential missions. One agency official found apportionment controls to be "too blunt an instrument" for OMB's agency enforcement mandate, which he acknowledged as a legitimate OMB role. Others perceived that since career staff had increasingly been taken out of the decisional loop within OMB, they were focusing too much attention on squabbling with the agencies over "minutiae," a task better left to agency discretion.

Another critique had OMB interposing itself illegitimately into the Cabinet structure when pursuing such "micro-management of agencies." This position was advanced most often in the few cases where agency officials believed that OMB civil servants with particularly authoritarian personalities had crossed the line into pursuit of their own agendas. Such instances tended to engender much mutual distrust between OMB and the agencies in question and to ultimately impede OMB–agency communications. According to one agency staffer, agencies would become "risk averse," seal off information channels to OMB, and leak sources would "dry up" in such cases. Such mutual distrust and an increasingly rapid turnover of examiners sometimes brought forth other agency gripes of confidences broken by OMB examiners who were given information with the proviso that agency information sources not be revealed in OMB. While few of these agency critics contested the mental acuity of such OMB staff, some believed that OMB's rapid turnover created staffs often too inexperienced and lacking in self-confidence and agility to be able to perform the subtle information-trading kabuki dances that had been pursued successfully by their OMB predecessors and that had served OMB's need to secure information from the agencies.

OMB career staff viewed the "micro-management" issue differently. They maintained that such "interposition" into the Cabinet structure is merely part of OMB's role to protect the President from errant agency political officials, Cabinet secretaries, or civil servants who strayed too far from presidential policies. One agency official, for example, quoted an examiner as telling him that OMB staff did not consider "micro-management" to be a "dirty word." This contention was generally borne out by several OMB staff interviewees. One manager regularly instructed his examiners to think of themselves as bank tellers who were releasing money. He recalled, "If the agencies had to go to you six times a year to get the money, then you had a better hold and could get better information than if they only had to come to you once or twice a year." OMB career staff veterans also asserted that many agency complaints merely represented instances where the administrations in question had decided in favor of an OMB position in lieu of adapting the agencies' position.

Both OMB career staff and agency officials perceived that not all and maybe not even a majority of OMB examiners utilized these budget execution devices to control agency activities. Moreover, there was wide variation surrounding whether agencies were funded through the annual letter apportionments (which allowed for less OMB control since the agency's funds were dispensed all at once), or the quarterly apportionments, and to what degree the other oversight mechanisms were used. It appears, however, that a small group of interventionist program managers left a trail of rancor in a few domestic agencies and cast the entire OMB in an unfavorable light when the Clinton administration took office in 1993.

In addition to the individualistic style of the examiners, the "political" environment had a lot to do with the micro-management issue. Were Cabinet officials and political appointees in the agency in question perceived to have been working as team players with the President? Were agency career-level officials forthcoming with information? Did the Cabinet secretary in question have White House insider status? A department headed by a loyal White House insider during the tenure of a less prestigious OMB Director would tend to be subject to less of OMB's micro-management.

Management Roles in the Bureau of the Budget: A Checkered History

The Budget Bureau's Management Role

From its creation in 1921, the Bureau of the Budget was given the opportunity to pursue administrative management activities by virtue of key clauses within its enabling legislation, the Budget and Accounting Act of 1921. Section 209 of the Act gave BOB the authority to "make a detailed study of the departments and establishments for the purpose of enabling the President to determine what ... changes should be made in the existing organization, activities, and methods of business of such departments and establishments."[24] However, from 1921 until 1939, BOB's potential role in promoting management efficiency in the federal government was generally disregarded. This has been attributed to the small size of the agency at the time, the indifference of BOB's first three directors,[25] and the fact that the

Bureau of Efficiency in the Executive Branch and the Congressional Joint Committee on the Reorganization of the Administrative Branch for Government in the Congress already bore responsibility for administrative management.[26] Most important in explaining BOB's neglect of a management role was the emphasis placed on BOB's budgetary roles by Presidents and BOB Directors during those years.[27]

Several factors radically altered this organizational status quo, including the abolition of the Bureau of Efficiency and the rapid growth of the federal bureaucracy during the New Deal. Recognizing the fact that a greatly expanded federal management role required an upgraded administrative control mechanism for the President, the Brownlow Commission was one of the strongest proponents for developing BOB's administrative management role.[28]

Following on the heels of the Brownlow Commission Report, and the transfer of BOB to the newly created Executive Office of the President, a Division of Administrative Management was established and charged with conducting "research in the development of improved plans of administrative management, and to advise the executive departments and agencies of the Government with respect to improved administrative organization and practice."[29]

The upgrading of BOB's management arm was also enhanced by the appointment of Harold Smith, a strong proponent of centralized bureaucratic management, as BOB Director. Thus was ushered in what might be thought of as a golden era with respect to the exercise of BOB's administrative management roles. During World War II, the Division of Administrative Management grew from seventy-five staffers to over one hundred by the end of the war, and was relied upon in many cases by the President himself to handle emergencies connected with war mobilization.[30] The BOB management office also offered management advice to departments and agencies, most of whom were glad to receive the assistance because they did not as yet have their own administrative management units.[31] In more recent times, BOB/OMB management initiatives have not elicited the same praise, often incurring only resentment from the agencies.

Despite these initiatives, postwar self-studies of BOB and the first Hoover Commission Report on Budgeting and Accounting criticized the Division of Administrative Management for its lack of communications with the budget side of BOB and its alleged failure to develop a "comprehensive approach" to "organizational and management improvement."[32] On the heels of these critiques somewhat contradictory steps were taken. While in 1949 the departments and agencies were charged by President Truman with making periodic progress reports to BOB on their efforts to improve management in their respective areas,[33] the Administrative Management Division staff had been cut to half its immediate post-wartime size, perhaps undermining its capability to monitor the effort.[34]

This environment led to a period from 1952 to 1957 when BOB's management responsibilities became minimal. In 1952 Director Frederick J. Lawton abolished the Division of Administrative Management and created a more modest Office for Management and Organization (OMO).[35] It was charged with providing guidance on a government-wide basis with respect to management, procurement, and interagency relationships.[36] A number of staff from the former Division of Administrative Management were transferred to the budget divisions to work with the budget examiners.[37] During the next seven years, in spite of study commission recommendations to the contrary, BOB's management roles were clearly subsumed by budgetary pressures.[38]

The Kennedy and Johnson administrations were as little interested in developing BOB's management role as had been the Eisenhower administration, being more concerned with "new ideas, new policies, new programs, and politics, not implementation and mechanics."[39] OMO was used for narrow purposes such as analysis of data processing and work measurements during the Kennedy years[40] and LBJ's PPBS did not survive as a management tool in domestic agencies after the end of his administration.[41] The Johnson administration's neglect of management issues was not without its costs. OMO was so understaffed and received so little recognition from the White House that it was unable either to provide an adequate institutional "management memory" in planning Great Society Programs at their inception, or to offer "enough" support to the President when problems arose related to their implementation, particularly with respect to the management of programs that cut across departmental lines or involved state and local governmental units.[42] A 1967 self-study of BOB concluded that with only forty staff members in OMO, it was unable to hold onto capable management staff, much less to provide management leadership to federal agencies that themselves had management staffs superior to those housed within the BOB.[43]

The recommendations of this self-study led to an immediate BOB reorganization during the last year and a half of the Johnson administration and laid the philosophical groundwork for the 1970 transformation from BOB to OMB. The immediate change was to replace OMO with a new Office of Executive Management under a noncareer Assistant Director of the Budget.[44] A management staff was charged primarily with managing federal field offices and their relationships to state and local governments through the Federal Assistance Review (FAR) program. According to scholar Frederick Mosher, this program was quite successful at achieving its objectives[45] because it exercised so relevant a function at the time.[46] Its autonomy and detachment from the budget divisions may also have contributed to its success.[47]

OMB's Management Role in the 1970s: The Nixon Years

The Nixon administration once again attempted to move BOB/OMB's management role to center stage. The transformation from BOB to OMB represented a President's strongest attempt to elevate BOB's management function since the creation of the Division of Administrative Management under FDR. President Nixon wanted to remove BOB/OMB from the business of making policy and redirect its energies toward bringing the federal government under centralized control through management improvements. The proposal to restructure the agency was directed toward improving the management of the entire executive bureaucracy. While the new OMB still performed the key function of assisting the President in the preparation of the annual federal budget and overseeing its apportionment these functions were not intended to be its primary activity. To realize these objectives, OMB was divided into a budget side and a management arm titled the Office of Executive Management. As part of this reorganization, BOB/OMB's management staff was increased to 146.[48]

Notwithstanding all of these carefully calibrated intentions, OMB's management role would once again end up taking a backseat to its budget functions. One reason for this was that many individuals holding key roles in the management divisions were rather quickly channeled into White House "policy" jobs, thus rather rapidly depleting the talent pool in OMB's newly recharged management area.[49] Another factor was that Nixon administration policy officials began concluding that even OMB's enhanced management role needed to be brought under greater political control.[50] To this end, in 1973 Deputy Director Frederick Malek undertook yet another internal reorganization ordered by then OMB Director Roy Ash. A major outcome of the Malek study was yet another budgetary/management staff merger similar to that which occurred in 1952.[51] The new management reshuffling added a number of management "associate" positions which were generally filled by young MBA graduates who were designated to work with the budget examiners within the program divisions. Other management staff were transferred to the General Services Administration.[52] Scholar Richard Rose has argued that this reorganization was largely directed toward spearheading the Nixon administration's executive management centerpiece, Management By Objectives (MBO).[53]

While MBO was implemented in twenty-one major federal agencies, its accomplishments were limited.[54] The last effort of the Nixon administration to improve government-wide administrative management, it ended up becoming "a bottom-up catalogue of bureau chief concerns" as opposed to "a top-down White House call for objectives."[55] MBO faltered in part because OMB did not specify which particular objectives it wanted to see implemented and partially because the administration did not expend the needed energy required to keep the momentum going. Political appointees were thought to have lost interest once it became clear that MBO was only "an apolitical reform."[56] The third and obvious reason for the decline of the MBO efforts was the Watergate crisis.

The Ford and Carter Administrations

President Ford's Presidential Management Initiatives (PMI) did not change OMB's management staff size or organization, but continued the Nixon administration's efforts to link budget and management functions.[57] It consisted of a series of reviews of "decision making and departmental organization, evaluation of current programs, federal reporting and regulatory burden reduction, contracting out and controlling overhead costs and personnel management."[58] OMB was charged with preparing monthly progress reports to the President with respect to PMI's progress in the agencies.[59]

Originally, agency officials were to retain overall discretion with respect to the determination of topics to be emphasized. However, before long OMB was playing a key role in directing PMI from the top.[60] Moreover, both OMB's management staff and its budget examiners were engaged in analyzing PMI's progress, both from a crosscutting vantage point and through an agency-by-agency review.[61]

As with MBO before it, PMI encountered certain obstacles that ultimately undermined its effectiveness. First, there were no shared standards for determining an agency's progress between OMB and the agencies or between OMB's management divisions performing crosscutting analysis and the program division budget examiners who were analyzing their assigned agencies.[62] Second, traditionally well-organized and well-managed agencies submitted useful management improvement plans and those not so well managed faltered in their management improvement efforts.[63] Third, the PMI effort aroused resentment among agency personnel who considered PMI exercises to be burdensome and among the budget examiners who already had more than enough work load related to their regular budgetary responsibilities.[64] Finally, and perhaps most significant, White House staff, OMB, and agency political officials in many cases abandoned management review efforts when subjected to pressures of the budget process and the presidential campaign.[65]

Three months before Jimmy Carter was to assume office, a panel of the National Academy of Public Administration (NAPA) concluded that during the Nixon–Ford years, BOB/OMB's efforts to manage the government had declined in effectiveness and the bureau was described as "weak and fragmented."[66] The NAPA report concluded, however, that OMB's retention of its management responsibilities was preferable to their transfer from OMB to another EOP unit. The report asserted that only through the clout gained with the power of the presidency and the purse would management initiatives be taken seriously.[67] A minority of the panel, however, saw things differently. They pointed to a number of factors that undermined OMB's management efforts. These included the tendency for budget examiners to be reluctant and unable to promulgate crosscutting management efforts because of their agency-specific expertise, and the unwillingness of many agencies to share information with OMB's management staff if they perceived that it would be used against them by budget staff.[68]

Jimmy Carter entered the presidency with an inclination toward seeking "managerial" solutions to policy implementation problems after having experienced some success as a bureaucratic manager while governor of Georgia.[69] Thus, he immediately took several steps to reorganize OMB in ways he thought would help it better succeed in its managerial mission. Early in his administration, President Carter announced Reorganization Plan No. 1 of 1977, which once again separated OMB's management and budget functions.[70] The plan represented a "thumbs up" for OMB's management role, since thirty-two full-time management positions were added to the organization at a time when OMB staff as a whole was being reduced.[71] A new politically appointed Executive Associate Director for Reorganization and Management was also created as co-equal with an Executive Associate Director for Budget.[72] A management and regulatory policy division was established to oversee management improvement and evaluation, federal personnel policy, regulatory policy, reports management, information systems policy, and intergovernmental offices.[73]

One of Carter's centerpiece management reform initiatives, the President's Reorganization Project (PRP), directed a number of task forces to develop reorganization proposals for scores of federal agencies. The task forces were staffed with a combination of OMB career staff, political appointees, and temporary federal agency detailees.[74] The PRP, unlike some previous management improvement initiatives, was designed to identify bureaucratic problems within federal agencies from the "bottom-up" and to derive individualized solutions to them, but not to examine management issues from a government-wide vantage point.[75]

PRP's results, however, did not achieve Carter's goal to trim and reorganize the federal government.[76] The dozens of PRP task forces produced ten reorganization plans, which, although approved by Congress, were characterized in a 1983 GAO report as either being "of minor importance or impact," as resulting from Congressional initiatives, or as being only "a subsidiary link to policy change."[77]

While President Carter certainly devoted more personal attention to PRP than had other Presidents to their management initiatives, with time other matters became of greater priority to the President. Further, the newly reinstated separation between OMB's budget and management staff may have further distanced OMB budget examiners from the PRP effort. A GAO report suggested that the PRP did not "develop a close relationship with the budget staff and the regular processes it controlled" and "was never able to cope effectively with the knowledge or program expertise [of] the budget staff."[78]

That a substantial proportion of PRP personnel were temporary employees may also have caused agencies to take the effort less seriously. Moreover, the significance of the PRP recommendations was further undercut by the failure of the OMB to provide feedback to the agencies.[79] In addition, President Carter's limited leverage with the Congress and interest groups undermined deference he might otherwise have had for his bureaucratic reorganization efforts.[80] Agencies could more easily ward off change and reorganization by showing muscle in league with key congressional committees and interest groups. By 1980, PRP had been virtually abandoned as a major management initiative for the Carter administration.[81]

PRP was replaced with a greater focus on initiatives designed to promote management improvement activity "government-wide" and to assist in the implementation of President Carter's Zero Based Budget Initiative (ZBB).[82] Under ZBB "decision units" were to rank-order and prioritize programs "after deciding on goals and examining all available alternatives to achieve these goals."[83] Again, these efforts were beset with familiar problems, and the effects of ZBB were disappointing since no separate Executive Branch agency staff units had been created to administer it,[84] and agency personnel charged with rank-ordering their programmatic priorities did not have the authority "to decide upon goals."[85]

Management Improvement Initiatives During the Reagan Years

During the first year and a half of President Reagan's first term in office, OMB's management divisions and staff were relegated to second-class status since the main thrust of OMB's energies were directed toward budgetary concerns. The position of Executive Associate Director for Management was abolished, while the parallel budgetary position was left intact, and the management division staff were decimated in order to staff and find slots for the Reagan administration's regulatory review initiatives.[86]

Then, in the summer and fall of 1982, the Reagan administration followed the path of previous administrations and added federal management improvement to its list of priorities by launching its Reform '88 Initiative. Spearheaded by Joseph P. Wright, OMB's new Deputy Director, Reform '88 was more directly focused on achieving financial management improvements and government-wide savings than had been many of the management improvement efforts of other administrations. This included improvement of federal cash management systems and debt collection, the reduction of government paperwork, the increase of surplus government property sales, and the recovering of funds owed agencies through audits.[87]

At the same time, Wright reorganized OMB's management divisions to reflect the emphasis on financial management improvement. Functions previously placed in OMB's "M" side during the Carter administration, which did not reflect financial management related goals, were either abolished or moved elsewhere. A number of staff were also transferred to the management divisions from BRD's Financial Management Branch in order to reflect the administration's emphasis on government-wide cash and financial management."[88] Another unit, the Management Improvement Division, was charged with the chief operating responsibility for the Reform '88 Initiative as of September 22, 1982.[89]

Other groups outside of OMB were also created to advance management efficiency during President Reagan's first term. They were the President's Council on Integrity and Efficiency (PCIE), the President's Council on Management Improvement (PCMI), and the Cabinet Council on Management and Administration (CCMA). In addition, the Grace Commission, formally dubbed the President's Private Sector Survey on Cost Control (PPSSCC), looked at ways of eliminating waste in government. The prominence of these private sector and government groups was a clear indication that OMB was not intended to assume the preeminent leadership roles in the Reagan administration's government management improvement program. Chester A. Newland, for example, in his *Enforcing the Reagan Agenda,* concluded that "OMB lost much of its management policy leadership to the CCMA."[90] OMB did, however, play an important supportive role in both the President's Councils and the private sector's Grace Commission. A GAO report concluded that OMB's management side acted as a convener and coordinator[91] of information for the PCMI and the PCIE. Moreover, the "M" side of OMB was charged with monitoring the implementation of the Grace Commission's recommendations.[92]

As recommendations began emerging from all of these task forces and councils, one of the primary ways the administration attempted to implement them was by integrating management reviews into the annual budget process both within agency budget reviews and through their final budget request submissions to OMB. Management improvement plans were to be submitted alongside of and consistent with budget requests. Benda and Levine indicate that "in this way, the Reagan administration has sought to closely link its management and budget policies and to ensure that the management and budget staffs in OMB work together effectively on a common agenda."[93]

Assessments of Reform '88 and OMB's role in promulgating its objectives present a mixed picture. On the plus side, few disagree that at the time Reform '88 was undertaken, antiquated government-wide accounting systems were badly in need of modernization and a reduction in the number of agency financial and payroll systems was clearly warranted.[94] GAO also credited Reform '88 with making progress in improving financial management and debt and credit management.[95]

But Reform '88 was also criticized as too centralized to address more fundamental management problems within departments and agencies. A 1989 GAO study characterized Reform '88 initiatives in contracting out and procurement reform as "unsuccessful."[96] Moreover, the GAO study found that "in terms of basic management issues directly affecting the delivery of government services to millions of people, OMB's efforts, past and present have been much less successful."[97]

Assessments of OMB's Management Capabilities at the End of the Reagan Administration

During President Reagan's two terms in office, budgetary priorities had vastly overshadowed OMB's management efforts. In FY 1988, the management staff stood at slightly over half the size it had been in FY 1981,[98] four different associate directors had been in charge of the management divisions, and the management side had been reorganized at least six times.[99] Directors Stockman and Miller[100] had not appeared to have set a high priority on federal management initiatives. *Government Executive* magazine reported, for example, that David Stockman "would threaten to banish lackluster budget officials to the management side."[101] James Miller is quoted in the same article as arguing that "even if you moved everyone in OMB over to the management side, you still couldn't manage the federal bureaucracy."[102]

Most troubling was that the collapse of the savings and loan industry and scandals in financial mismanagement of monumental proportions at the

Department of Housing and Urban Development (HUD) had been allowed to develop in spite of the administration's emphasis on addressing financial management problems government-wide. OMB's inability to provide early warnings of these financial debacles also indicated a downgrading of its management capabilities.[103]

Harold Seidman, former assistant director for organization and management in Eisenhower's Bureau of the Budget and a senior fellow at NAPA, observed that OMB's management divisions "had virtually no impact on the savings and loan crisis," but "in the past they would have been in the middle of it."[104] In the case of the HUD scandal, a House subcommittee attributed OMB's failure to respond to its minimized resources for directing toward management oversight, after it had been overwhelmed with the task of meeting its budgetary responsibilities.[105] OMB Deputy Director Diefendorfer pointed to OMB's limited staffing of only five HUD examiners in the program divisions.[106]

In 1989, a NAPA monograph *The Executive Presidency*[107] and a GAO report entitled *Managing the Government, Revised Approach Could Improve OMB's Effectiveness,* provided assessments of OMB's managerial capabilities and deficiencies at the end of the decade of the 1980s and offered recommendations for improving them in the 1990s. Most striking were the common criticisms: dwindling professional staff, declining resources devoted to management issues,[108] the diversion of institutional forces, time, and staff energies to budget-related matters[109] and to "budgetary" interactions with the Congress,[110] and the inconsistency of support and interest of Presidents and OMB Directors in administrative management–related issues.[111]

To add to these causes of managerial ineffectiveness, the NAPA study added a pro budgetary bias among OMB staff to the charge that those engaged in management initiatives in OMB had "less than ideal relationships with OMB's budget staff."[112] A 1990 *Government Executive* article added that "the dominant budget side long had little regard or use for the management side's perspective in preparing budgets or evaluating programs."[113] The GAO study in particular found that with the exception of certain parts of OIRA, budget examiners usually did not use management division information or consider the management divisions to be good sources of information or technical assistance.[114] As a result, the "lack of close working relations between management and budget staffs [caused] miscommunications" inside OMB, as well as when OMB interacted with congressional committees.[115]

But the biases of OMB staffers were not the major deterrent to better working relationships and communications between the "M" and "B" sides of OMB. The GAO study found that the overload of program division responsibilities in the 1980s was more significant in limiting management-related activities than were attitudinal biases on the part of the examiners.[116] Along with the decline in staff and resources in OMB's program divisions was the failure of OMB's political leadership to integrate management issues into Director's Reviews[117] or to provide clear guidance to OMB staff concerning their management-related duties.[118]

Agency interviewees in the GAO study faulted OMB for a lack of consistency in its communications with the agencies, and for a lack of sensitivity to their individual differences, problems, and conditions.[119] Nonetheless, many respondents still acknowledged OMB's potential to effectively lead and assist the agencies in efforts to improve the management of their programs.[120] To be able to accomplish this goal, OMB staff were urged to show greater sensitivity to the uniqueness of different agencies.[121] More consultation between OMB and the agencies on goals and strategies was also stressed.[122]

Specific Recommendations and Options

The recommendations and action plans offered in the two studies are useful as a reference point for the future. Both the NAPA and the GAO studies recommended that another Deputy Director for Management[123] be authorized by the Congress. The NAPA report acknowledged that OMB's deputy directors, who characteristically had been delegated to direct OMB's management-related duties, no longer had sufficient time to devote to these responsibilities.[124] The GAO report also encouraged OMB to improve communications with the agencies and delegate more responsibility to agency line officers,[125] but to continue to raise issues, challenge agencies, coordinate interagency matters, provide policy guidelines, and still play Big Brother when needed to overcome resistance to change in the agencies.[126] Further, OMB was encouraged to integrate "programmatic" service delivery goals into the budget cycle and to foster better integration and communication between OMB's management and budget areas by using working "team" relationships between the management and budget sides of OMB.[127] Both studies recommended increasing OMB staff. NAPA particularly urged the adding of "talented executives with line agency experience," but acknowledged that Congress probably would not authorize such a move.[128] The GAO study recommended that OMB be urged to communicate more often and earlier with Congress with respect to the most pressing administrative management problems[129] and play an improved educative role for both the President and the Congress by explaining "the consequences" of

not pursuing long-term administrative management and financial strategies.[130] One NAPA option, that a bipartisan commission consider removing
management responsibilities from OMB altogether and create a separate
Office of Management in the EOP,[131] met with somewhat vehement opposition in two dissenting views from Chester A. Newland and Elmer B.
Staats. Newland believed such an action would "fragment authority, de-
tracting from OMB's potential effectiveness, thus diminishing EOP's capacity for coordinated leadership."[132] Staats asserted that it was "unrealistic
to attempt to separate management improvement efforts from budgetary
decisions," since "the leverage which goes with the budgetary decisions can
do much to bring about needed management improvement actions."[133]

Management Initiatives with OMB under President Bush

In October of 1989, Director Richard Darman testified before the Senate
Governmental Affairs Committee that "notwithstanding the best of intentions, the M in OMB has suffered from too little attention over the years—
too little attention within OMB, within the executive branch, and within the
Congress."[134]

By 1990, both Darman and Congress had begun taking a number of aggressive steps to upgrade the "M" in OMB. The passage of the Chief Financial
Officer's (CFO) Act in 1990 increased OMB's authority to address financial
management issues in the agencies in general, and strengthened OMB's management divisions in particular. It added new responsibilities for OMB, but
provided for the deputy directorship for management[135] that had been recommended by GAO and NAPA. It also mandated that CFOs be appointed in
departments and agencies to be responsible for tracking financial management
controls, producing annual financial statements and audits, and consolidating
and modernizing some departmental accounting systems.[136] A Chief Financial
Officer for the entire federal government was to be housed in OMB as well.[137]
With this increased emphasis on management improvement, Darman hired
about twenty new staffers on the management side of OMB.

Director Darman initiated other strategies to address administrative financial management problems and to prevent any more large-scale financial
crises from occurring under his leadership. One such initiative, OMB–
agency "SWAT" teams named after the Strategic Weapons and Tactics
Police, worked within the government to address particularly egregious
financial management problems in selected agencies.[138] Comprised of
about ten to thirty staff members from both the budget and management
sides of OMB as well as personnel from the affected agencies, the SWAT
teams tackled specific administrative deficiencies in agencies such as the

Health Care Financing Administration, HUD, the Federal Emergency Management Agency, the Bureau of Indian Affairs, the Railroad Retirement Board, and the Department of Education's Higher Education Assistance Foundation (HEAF) and the Office of Post-secondary Education.[139]

In spite of positive outcomes in the Department of Education, difficulties with the SWAT team approach included OMB–agency relations that sometimes turned contentious, and diverted OMB budget and management division personnel to other assignments.[140] Nonetheless, overall, the SWAT team approach to addressing agency financial management problems had been somewhat successful. In a symposium report, Edward J. Mazur, controller and director of the Office of Federal Financial Management, noted that 28 of 125 "high-risk" areas were considered to have been corrected by mid 1992.[141]

In order to pursue the Bush administration's management strategies, Director Darman once again reorganized OMB's management divisions. A new division, the Office of General Management, was made up of three branches—a Federal Services Branch that reviewed the General Services Administration (GSA) and government-wide administrative services, a Federal Personnel and Pay Policy Branch, and the Evaluation, Planning, and Management by Objectives Branch. The creation of the last branch had the effect of reestablishing a unit in OMB that was formally dedicated to program evaluation for the first time since 1972.[142] The management divisions integrated "management" staff and former budget examiners in the same offices as part of an effort to link both management improvement goals and program evaluation to the budget process.

In early 1992, greater congressional and Executive Branch interest in developing accurate measures of agency "performance" led OMB to tie performance measures to agency audits.[143] To this end, under the leadership of OMB Executive Deputy Director for Financial Management, Frank Hodsoll, OMB's management divisions began guiding agencies in the development of "common and agency-specific performance measures."[144] Fourteen government-funded activities were targeted by OMB staff for performance measurement.[145] The use of performance measures to evaluate federal programs did not cease when President Bush left office. In 1993, long-term performance measurement of Executive Branch agencies was to be codified in law and to become a significant mandate for OMB staff during the Clinton presidency.

The Management Role in OMB: An Overview

From 1945 on, BOB/OMB had struggled to find an appropriate place for its secondary role as a vehicle for presidential control and management of an expanding executive bureaucracy. While a few success stories can be re-counted from a number of administrations, it was still unclear whether any centralized presidential agency could improve the management of a federal workforce numbering in the millions, or if such an agency should be estab-lished apart from the currently existing OMB. If OMB was to retain this role, it was equally uncertain whether OMB's management staff should be separate from or merged within OMB's budgetary units.

The institution had vacillated between budget/management bifurcation and merger on numerous occasions. Budget/management mergers tended to result in budgetary pressures overshadowing the efforts of OMB staff to review agency management issues. Separation of budget and management staff led to duplication of functions, inadequate communications, and man-agement goals that ended up as subsidiary to OMB's budgetary demands. Moreover, presidential and political-level attention to OMB's "manage-ment" apparatus tended to wane during the life span of an administration with the growth of more politically pressing concerns and/or budgetary pressures.

Perhaps the most striking observation that can be made when surveying BOB/OMB's history as an administrative manager is the swiftness with which prescriptions for management improvement in Executive Branch agencies were altered by presidential administrations over the years, and how frequently BOB/OMB staff engaged in their implementation were moved around on the organization chart, replenished, or reduced. Such alterations almost always came with new administrations, which predictably abandoned their predecessors' management improvement methodologies and often reorganized the management units in BOB/OMB in order to institute their "own." Frequently, management-related methodologies were changed by the White House and added by the Congress once or twice *again* within one presidential term. The disruptions caused by the frequency of these fluctuations seemed to have undermined OMB's ability to pursue its administrative management roles as well.

OIRA: A Lightning Rod for the 1980s

Introduction

If the politicization of OMB's advice to the President constituted a trend that troubled students of government and public administration in the 1970s, OMB's enhanced regulatory review role through a newly enlarged Office of Information and Regulatory Affairs (OIRA) became even more ideologically charged for controversy in the 1980s. OIRA stands at the hub of disputes between agency regulators and the industries, businesses, and citizens they monitor, and in the 1980s between Republicans determined to relieve regulatory burdens on the private sector and Democrats intent on preserving federal controls to protect public safety, health, and welfare.

OMB's history as a reviewer of regulations had been much briefer than its experience as a budgeteer or manager. It can be traced back to the Nixon administration when OMB supervised an interagency review of proposed regulations before their publication. OMB set deadlines for the agencies to provide their comments on the proposed regulations. When interagency disputes arose concerning regulatory proposals, OMB determined which disagreements merited White House intervention. While the process under President Nixon had involved selected agencies, President Ford, through Executive Order 11,821, broadened the regulatory review operation to direct *all* federal agencies to provide analyses on the "inflationary" impact of major proposed rules. OMB staff orchestrated the process whereby the agencies prepared this analysis.[146]

These efforts to use OMB as a mechanism to stem the growth of regulations generated a debate similar to that which would occur during the Reagan years. Those supporting a centralized presidential regulatory review role argued that such oversight improved and sharpened the quality of the analysis. Those in the opposing camps expressed two major concerns: that OMB–White House review engendered delays in promulgating needed rules, and that too much of the decision making and too many of the communications took place "off the public record" without the benefit of an open hearing process for all interested parties.[147]

President Carter continued and expanded efforts to submit Executive Branch agencies to central EOP regulatory control. His Executive Order 12,044 stated that existing regulations were to be evaluated by two newly created organizational entities.[148] First, a loosely organized group called the Regulatory Council, composed of all department and agency heads and some representatives from independent regulatory commissions, published a list of all proposed rules agency-wide to prevent interagency duplication or inconsistencies in policies.[149] Under the Carter process, the "rule promulgating" agencies were to determine which proposed rules were considered to be "significant" and in some cases to develop analyses to measure their impacts.[150] Then the Regulatory Analysis Review Group (RARG), which included representatives from OMB, the CEA, the Departments of Treasury, Labor, and Commerce, and other economic and regulatory agencies, selected some of the agency analyses for further review and analysis.[151] These analyses were intended to become part of the public record during the "public comment" period in the rule-making process.[152]

The Ford and Carter regulatory efforts were similar in that neither vested formal authority to change proposed rules in any organizational entity outside of the affected agencies.[153] While the agencies were required to conduct the cost–benefit analyses, they still maintained the discretion to reject "outside" attempts by OMB or others to modify the proposed rules.

OIRA's Inception

The initiative that led to OIRA's creation occurred at the end of the Carter administration in large part due to the passage of the Paperwork Reduction Act of 1980. The business community's displeasure with government-inflicted paperwork burdens, which led to the passage of this legislation, was not new. To address unneeded reporting requirements associated with "price and production controls required by federal agencies" during World War II, Congress had passed the Federal Reports Act of 1942, which had attempted to reduce both the cost and burden on private industry, by eliminating duplication of required reports and questionnaires and by facilitating interagency information sharing.[154] BOB/OMB was authorized by the Act to examine how agencies gathered information and to stop any information requests that it considered duplicative or unneeded.[155] During the next three decades, federal paperwork increased exponentially, and by the late 1970s, a number of commissions and task forces had called for stepped-up efforts to further reduce the paperwork burden.[156]

Finally, in March of 1980, GAO recommended that a separate Office of Federal Information Policy be created within OMB.[157] It was this recommendation in particular that appears to have led to the passage of the Paperwork Reduction Act of 1980, and the creation of the Office of Information and Regulatory Affairs (OIRA) within OMB.[158]

Under the Act, OIRA's administrator would report directly to the OMB Director with respect to a plethora of functions related to government-wide information and paperwork reduction.[159] The Act mandated a 15 percent reduction of federal paperwork, the creation and implementation of a system to locate federal information sources, the development of more efficient systems for management of government-wide information, and the preparation of studies designed to measure how long it took individual businesses and state and local governments to prepare and organize paperwork (reports, forms, or records) requested by the federal government.[160] President Carter signed the Paperwork Reduction Act at the end of his administration,[161] but OIRA was not formally established until the Reagan administration.

From its first days, it became evident that OIRA was going to play broader roles than the framers of the Paperwork Reduction Act had envisioned. On April 1, 1981, OIRA was formally constituted as a new institutional office in OMB. It was divided into subunits specializing in regulatory review, information systems, and statistical policy. The core of its original staff was transferred from branches in the management divisions. This staff was enlarged to over eighty in 1981.[162] Unlike other units in the management divisions, which were usually organized to play government-wide management review functions, OIRA for most of its institutional life span was to have agency-by-agency "desk officers" with particular programmatic review responsibilities.

OIRA as a Vehicle for Regulatory Reform

Within weeks of President Reagan's inauguration, his Executive Order 12,291[163] was to begin to divert a large portion of the OIRA's energies away from federal paperwork management and toward expanded regulatory review responsibilities. Under the order, federal agencies would be required to conduct cost–benefit analysis known as Regulatory Impact Analysis (RIA) of proposals for new regulations as well as for the final regulations. The RIAs assessed whether the "benefits" to the public derived from the proposed regulation would outweigh the "costs" incurred by the related industries, as well as those derived from impacts to the economy at large.[164] The RIAs were also designated to provide "regulatory or nonregulatory" alternatives to the regulations.[165] OIRA entered the process as the authorized reviewer of the original regulatory proposal, the RIAs, and the final rules to determine whether they complied with Executive Order 12,291.[166] It was also authorized to review proposed regulations that the agency had deemed to be "minor" and reclassify them as "major," thus requiring the agency to prepare a RIA on the proposed rule.[167] While various time limitations were placed upon the agencies to comply with several of the order's requirements, no such constraints were placed on how long OIRA could take to review and comment on the RIAs.[168] Thus, OIRA's approvals could be delayed both during their preparation and pending an agency's response to concerns and questions OIRA had raised.[169] OIRA was also empowered to require that agencies prepare cost–benefit analysis on existing regulations and subsequently to review them.[170]

Pivotal stages of OIRA's regulatory review process remained closed to public examination. For example, OMB meetings or correspondence with the agencies in question or with "interested parties" such as industry representatives were not "on the public record of a particular rule making."[171]

OIRA's analytical formats included both written and verbal analysis. While an anti-regulatory bias is built into cost–benefit methodology since costs are easier to estimate and illustrate than are benefits, which may not materialize imminently,[172] OIRA branches varied in the degree to which the "benefits" of regulatory activity received equal consideration with the "costs."

How much input and clout relative to OIRA did the program divisions have in the development of regulatory issues? From the time of OIRA's inception, there were communications, connections, and cross-fertilization linking its regulatory review roles and staff with OMB's budgetary and legislative clearance activities and staff. However, the degree to which program division examiners were routinely involved in the analysis of regulatory issues or worked closely with OIRA counterparts varied widely, in accordance with the regulatory area they reviewed and the personal inclinations of their bosses. In some areas, it was the program divisions and not OIRA that took the lead on regulatory matters. In others, it was the other way around. The balance of power and institutional influence in cases where both OIRA and the program divisions were involved and in disagreement often hinged upon the relative clout of the relevant PAD as compared with the OIRA administrator, or on whether either position was vacant at the time.

OIRA was not a lone player in the administration's regulatory reform efforts. A White House Task Force was constituted to carry forth the objectives of the Executive Order. Formally headed by Vice President Bush, it also included the White House Assistant for Intergovernmental Affairs as well as OIRA Administrator James Miller III.

OIRA: 1981–1985

From 1981 to 1985, while OIRA played a lead role for the Reagan administration in reducing federal regulations, it also stood at the center of a maelstrom of controversy surrounding the means that were used to achieve these reductions. An examination of some comparative statistics measuring the number of proposed regulations that survived to the publication stage during President Reagan's first term yields evidence of reductions of regulations at all points in the process. Overall, between 1981 and 1984, there was over a 34 percent "reduction" in the number of proposed rules and final rules that were published in the *Federal Register,* as compared with a 16 percent "increase" in rules proposed and published during the four years of the Carter administration.[173] That OIRA review exercised an influence on slowing the rate of new rule publication was also evidenced by the fact that the number of proposed rules accepted by OIRA *without change* dropped from 87 percent in 1981 to 71 percent in 1985.[174]

Reagan administration officials perceived that this decrease in the number of regulations promulgated was indicative of a growing success in their deregulatory crusade. OIRA's institutional clout in the ensuing regulatory review process was a personal point of pride for James C. Miller III, OIRA's first administrator, who was quoted by Susan and Martin Tolchin as likening OIRA's role to "being the editor of the *Federal Register*."[175] Vice Presidential Assistant Boyden Gray linked OIRA's influence to its entry into the regulatory review at such an early stage of the process.[176] James Miller also attributed much of OIRA's early success to the speed with which the President and his top lieutenants had advanced their policy goals in this area after assuming office.[177]

Some part of this "success" may have been attributable not to an analytically thorough process designed to scrutinize proposed regulations, but instead to a sense in the agencies that efforts to propose regulations in the first place or to provide responses to OIRA comments were futile due to the anti-regulatory tone of the administration. Certain agencies such as EPA, Labor, and Energy may have been reacting to OIRA's negative scrutiny when the numbers of proposals submitted to OIRA for review dropped by over 50 percent.[178] Moreover, Tolchin and Tolchin suggested that at least in 1981, OIRA inquiries themselves might have had a chilling effect on whether an agency continued to develop agency regulatory initiatives. As evidence of this contention, the Tolchins cited a congressional subcommittee examination which found that of seven proposals sent back to agencies for responses to OIRA comments, six were never sent back to OIRA.[179]

Others, including the National Academy of Public Administration and scholar Walter Williams, also questioned whether OIRA served the Reagan administration's anti-regulatory efforts in an analytically sound way. In his *Mismanaging America, the Anti-Analytic Presidency,* Williams cited a NAPA panel finding that much of the focus in OIRA during Reagan's first term was on "nit-picking" and minutiae, while more significant issues were not adequately debated during the regulatory review process.[180] According to Williams, this prevented the Reagan administration from better accomplishing its own anti-regulatory agenda, because the agencies were able to produce far better analysis supporting the need for regulations than was OIRA questioning their costs and benefits.[181] He attributed some of OIRA's failure to the relative youth and programmatic inexperience of the OIRA staffers, and asserted that because of OIRA's newness, its staffers did not have the needed programmatic experience.[182] Unlike the program divisions, which also had young staff, OIRA did not have seasoned branch chiefs to learn from.[183] One OMB civil servant, who agreed with some of Williams's characterizations, believed that this problem was also linked to OIRA's lack of selectivity in choosing issues to analyze, observing that issues he described as "nonsense" were purportedly treated as painstakingly as were more significant regulatory quandaries. This individual also attributed this proclivity in part to the youth and inexperience of the analysts.

Obviously, there were those inside OMB, both in OIRA and in the program divisions, who did not agree with such assessments. Some staffers in both OIRA and OMB's program divisions chose to emphasize what they perceived to be strengths in OIRA's analytic process. One OIRA manager, for example, considered the "analytics" produced by OIRA to be superb and the OIRA staff to be superior in ability and background to those in the program divisions. He believed that OIRA's high level of analytical capability was due to the nature of cost–benefit analysis that required that OIRA hire more Ph.D. economists and lawyers. Another program division veteran described a healthy process of internal debate on the merits of the regulatory issues within OIRA and between OIRA and the relevant program divisions.

If there had been a downturn in the progress of the Reagan administration's regulatory agenda, other scholars did not blame OIRA. Murray Weidenbaum, for example, faulted a lack of leadership in the White House, maintaining that after the "initial burst of regulatory reform initiatives," there was little leadership for regulatory reform on the part of senior White House staff. He wrote in 1984 that "the administration's Task Force on Regulatory Relief has responded primarily to the issues presented by the OMB review process. It has exerted little independent leadership in terms of initiating reviews of existing rules or identifying needed changes in basic regulatory statutes."[184]

The Reagan administration also received ample criticism from democratic adversaries in the Congress, rooted not in the failure of its agenda, but in the substance of that agenda, and in the strategies being used to implement it. Much of this criticism surrounded the purportedly questionable legality of OIRA's processes as dictated by Executive Order 12,291.[185] At the foundation of most of these critiques was the concern that the President, through OIRA, was usurping regulatory authorities delegated to the federal agencies by the Congress. This contention, along with other concerns, spurred a number of congressional oversight hearings investigating OIRA's decision-making processes and rules during the first term of the Reagan administration. Chief among the specific focal points of critics was that decision-making processes and external communications in OIRA were not open to public scrutiny and that delays permitted by the order failed to meet deadlines for compliance issued by Congress or the Judiciary.

One case study involving EPA's regulation of the asbestos industry concluded that OMB had contradicted congressional intent through its substitution of the administration's cost–benefit guidelines in place of congressionally mandated objectives.[186] It charged that OIRA had obscured EPA's "technical, scientific, and policy judgments" through OMB "pressure" on the agency, and accused OMB of supplanting "the economic analyses required by the order" with "political considerations."[187] Eads and Fix, in a 1984 book, examined the "perception" that the Reagan administration's reform effort was not intended to make social regulation more cost-effective and coherent, but to serve as a "political filter."[188] With respect to this impression, which they attributed to "not just opponents of the administration's regulatory relief efforts," Eads and Fix concluded that "the perception may have been incorrect, but OMB's methods of operation—plus the insensitivity of the officials running the regulatory relief program to the longer-term adverse consequences of being perceived as overwhelmingly pro-business—certainly did little to alter perceptions of politicization."[189]

OIRA, OMB Politicization, and Interbranch Warfare

Scholar Terry Moe went beyond these accusations in characterizing OIRA as having been "staffed by presidential partisans."[190] Although Moe's description may have been overdrawn, it has a foundation. Many OIRA staffers were perceived by their career colleagues in other OMB units to have been "more ideological" than other typical OMB civil servants. Even so, there were other norms and practices followed by OIRA that tended to limit the politicization of analysis due to staffers' personal ideological leanings. First, OIRA did apply professional rather than partisan criteria in reaching its decisions on proposed regulations. Second, OMB guidelines prohibited using questions regarding political party affiliation in recruiting personnel. Third, the complexities of cost–benefit analysis did not lend themselves to simple ideologically based solutions most of the time.

Other charges leveled at OMB and the administration during President Reagan's first term included allegations that OIRA's political staff were often meeting privately with industry representatives and sometimes seeming to adopt their positions after the discussions.[191] Career staff did not engage in such contacts, but OIRA's Paperwork Reduction Act responsibilities *required* OIRA career staff to interact with outside groups regularly on matters covered by that law. The dilemma was that regulatory issues and the kind of issues examined when complying with the Paperwork Reduction Act often overlapped. A "safety catch" in these matters, however, was the legal requirement that all communications occurring in connection with Paperwork Reduction Act responsibilities be disclosed.

The occurrence of undisclosed White House and OIRA meetings with interest groups raised the question of whether OIRA was open to a balanced cross-section of opinion on regulatory review matters. Though the Reagan deregulation effort was presented as a process that allowed for the input of views from industry as well as public interest groups, some skeptics believed that the views of constituencies other than those of the business community were often barely factored into consideration. In one case, when OMB received a congressional subpoena to provide a list of outside groups it had met with in 1981, only two groups out of the forty-one names provided to the committee turned out to be public interest groups as opposed to industry representatives.[192] Moreover, while OIRA officials contended that any individual or group could contact OMB to express views, and that there was no "cause and effect relationship between the visits (of private sector business groups to OMB) and subsequent regulatory relief,"[193] various critics concluded that the process to communicate public views to the agencies was flawed in a number of respects. A GAO study in 1982, for example, found that there was no system in OMB to monitor whether materials submitted to it from the general public were forwarded to the relevant agency.[194] More significantly, some critics believed that the claim of an open door to OMB for any concerned citizen had proven to be a hollow one, since there was no formal process within OIRA to inform the public of key meetings where important decisions were being made.[195]

Judicial actions regarding OMB's involvement in regulatory review also faulted OMB "delays" as illegal. In *Environmental Defense Fund* vs. *Thomas,* OMB was accused of illegally delaying beyond a congressionally set deadline, "EPA's promulgation of permitting standards for underground hazardous waste storage tanks."[196] The court found in pretrial discovery that "of 169 rules submitted to OMB for Executive Order 12,291 review which were subject to statutory deadlines, OMB extended its review beyond the time limits on 76 occasions."[197] Without deciding on the constitutionality of such delays, the court disallowed OMB's authority to delay regulations in contravention of the congressionally imposed deadlines involved in the case.[198]

Both a Senate committee and GAO leveled another critique at OIRA, this time involving its Paperwork Reduction Act responsibilities. A 1982 Senate Committee faulted it for not properly implementing the duties Congress had given it, and for missing a deadline to establish a Federal Information Locator System.[199] A 1983 GAO report attributed this alleged failure to OMB's use of OIRA staff time for regulatory review functions that were not directly connected with paperwork reduction or information management.[200]

Congress Mounts a Counter-Offensive and a Standoff Is Achieved

Many of the criticisms of the Reagan administration's deregulatory tactics and OIRA's role in facilitating them led to a series of punitive actions from various congressional sources. These included withholding authorizations for OIRA and threatening to sever OIRA's appropriations.[201] In 1981, Democratic Representative John Dingell's Subcommittee on Oversight and Investigations of the House Committee on Energy and Commerce had also been particularly aggressive in probing the nature of OIRA's interest group contacts and the secrecy with which it conducted its regulatory review process. Representative Albert Gore, who was rapidly becoming known as a champion of the environmental movement, had played a vocal role in these efforts in his capacity as a member of the subcommittee.[202]

After the 1984 election, in spite of all of these threats, the Reagan administration in 1985 had promulgated a second executive order related to regulatory review that authorized OIRA to control even earlier stages of the regulatory process.[203] Agencies were required to clear any "plans" that could lead to promulgation of regulations with OIRA, by preparing annual "regulatory agenda" statements that projected such activity for the coming year.[204] Under this order, OMB was empowered to stop an agency from preparing such reports or documents deemed to be inconsistent with the administration's regulatory philosophy unless the Congress or the courts intervened.[205]

Congress responded with a more potent salvo in 1986, when the House Appropriations Committee denied OIRA's fiscal 1987 budget funding request.[206] Retreating somewhat in what was to become a "cat and mouse" game between Congress and the Executive, OMB agreed to modify some of its procedures in such a way as to become more open and responsive to public and congressional complaints. The planned "reforms" were negotiated by then OIRA administrator Wendy Lee Gramm, Senator Carl Levin (D-Mich.) and Senator David Durenburger (R-Minn.).[207] Senator Durenburger's Subcommittee on Toxic Substances and Environmental Oversight had issued a report that while not finding "concrete evidence" of legal infractions, the evidence nonetheless suggested that OMB had not been "subject to either public scrutiny or effective congressional oversight."[208]

These so-called "Gramm" reforms, named after the then OIRA administrator Wendy Lee Gramm, included eleven modifications in OIRA's operating procedure designed to open up its regulatory review process to greater public scrutiny. They included changes in procedure that would require OIRA to release certain information to the public if it was requested in writing. This information included drafts of proposed and final agency regulations under review, written communications between agency heads and OIRA involving regulations, and copies of agency submissions for regulations.[209] While some observers would later question the degree to which these reforms had been enforced, one observer who examined OIRA during the Bush administration reached the conclusion that by the end of the Reagan administration, "regulatory review had remained a comparatively accountable operation.[210]

OIRA During the Bush Administration

During the first year of the Bush administration, it appeared that both the administration and Director Darman in particular were going to de-emphasize OIRA's regulatory review activities and simultaneously address some of the charges that had been leveled against it. On May 24, 1989, Darman testified before the House Government Operations Committee that he would work to move regulation approvals in OIRA more quickly, would cooperate with Congress, and would "make an effort to present all different scientific points of view."[211] This said, it is important to note that the Gramm reforms had not satisfied all of OIRA's critics. Chief among the problems were extended delays in processing certain industry-opposed rules in areas ranging from toxic shock syndrome warnings on tampon boxes to required warnings to workers who handled toxic substances in the work place.[212] In addition, just a month before Darman's testimony, the House Committee on Education and Labor voted to support an amendment to a vocational education bill to limit OIRA's "prior review or approval" of certain documents, surveys, and reports and required OIRA to record and explain for public access any modifications it made to rules designed by agencies to implement the new legislation.[213]

In early 1990, the Supreme Court ruled that OMB had overstepped its authority in implementing the Paperwork Reduction Act of 1980. The Court in *Dole* vs. *Unified Steelworkers of America* ruled by a 7–2 majority that the Paperwork Reduction Act did not grant OMB the authority to curb agency-promulgated rules that mandated industry to make health and safety–related information concerning their products or production processes available to consumers and employees.[214] From the fall of 1990 to the following fall of 1991, efforts to negotiate a compromise between the Bush administration and Congress regarding the scope of OIRA authorities failed. The limits on OIRA that congressional members proposed were familiar: to set time limitations on regulation review and to provide information to the public with respect to the reasons behind OIRA decisions to change proposed regulations. Although it initially had appeared that the Bush administration had agreed to these modifications, "several Republican senators placed anonymous holds on the legislation and the bill died." Since the changes to OIRA's authorities were linked to the Senate's willingness to confirm the administration's chosen OIRA Administrator, James F. Blumstein, the whole agreement imploded and both OIRA's reauthorization and Blumstein's confirmation were stopped.[215]

Thus, OIRA was forced to operate with an acting career-level administrator at its helm throughout the Bush administration. A comparison of OIRA's professional staff size in different years from the beginning of the Reagan administration until the end of the Bush administration may be indicative of its beleaguered status as a result of the controversy and partisan warfare that surrounded it. By 1986, OIRA's size had dropped from its high at the beginning of the Reagan administration of about 80 professional staffers to about 50, and from 1986 to 1990 it further fell to about 40 staffers.[216]

President Bush's First Two Years: A Regulatory Presidency?

Even while the White House and Congress argued over the codification of limitations on OIRA's authorities, the confirmation of its director, and its allegedly unreasonable "delays," there were some observers such as Jonathan Rauch of the *National Journal* who cited an upswing in regulatory activity during the Bush administration.[217] Moreover, in his book on the Bush administration, Charles Tiefer expressed the view that "congressional oversight and judicial review," had "reformed the OIRA process somewhat"[218] and cited one example of a "pro" regulatory position taken by OMB's "budget operation," which prohibited municipalities from burning recyclable waste.[219] This recommendation squared well with President Bush's claim to be the "environmental" President.[220]

If there were "changes" in OIRA's decision-making outcomes from the Reagan to the Bush administrations, they can be traced to not one but several possible origins, including pressures and criticism from Congress and public interest groups and the limitations that had been imposed by court decisions. The fact that OIRA did not have a politically appointed director may also have played a role and in and of itself provided a useful opportunity to observe the functioning of this unit as a career staff entity operating under less direct political controls than had been the case before. In the case involving recyclable waste disposal cited above, it is interesting that Tiefer attributed the OMB analysis to "OMB's budget operation" and not to OIRA. Perhaps in this case it was a strong PAD in the absence of a counterpoised OIRA administrator who allowed the program division's analysis to prevail.

OMB and the Competitiveness Council

From mid-1990 to the end of his administration, President Bush shifted much of the administration's regulatory review activity to the Competitiveness Council, a previously little-used unit that had been created a the beginning of the Bush administration and was headed by Vice President Dan Quayle.[221] Tiefer suggests that in the spring of 1990, President Bush became alarmed that the increase in the promulgation of regulations in his administration was gaining attention in the press, and subsequently causing displeasure among his supporters in the business community.[222] It is also interesting to note that 1990 was when negotiations with the Congress broke down over OIRA's role and the confirmation of its administrator, thus leaving OIRA under the direction of a career administrator.[223] Tiefer further asserts that the solution to President Bush's dilemma was to activate the Quayle Council via a memorandum to Cabinet and agency heads, since the "vagueness" in the Council's mandate initially shielded it from "intensive public, congressional, and judicial scrutiny."[224] OIRA staff from that point until the end of the administration worked as foot soldiers for the Competitiveness Council.

For the next two years, until President Bush's defeat in November of 1992, the Bush administration engaged in an aggressive campaign to deregulate. The Competitiveness Council was the driving force behind these efforts. By November of 1991, Senator John Glenn's Governmental Affairs Committee reported a bill out of committee to apply many of the requirements that Congress had been attempting to use to constrain OIRA to the Competitiveness Council as well.[225] By that time, the Council had already influenced over fifty proposed rules per year.[226] In addition, the Council Director and staff refused to testify before congressional oversight committees, in contrast with OIRA officials who had regularly testified over the years.[227] At the beginning of 1992, the Bush administration declared a 90–day moratorium on the issuance of most new regulations and extended it another 120 days leading up to the 1992 election.[228] A review of existing regulations that affected the competitiveness of American industry was also undertaken.[229] The Council on Competitiveness and OIRA were responsible for supervising the moratorium and the review.[230]

Regulatory Review: A New Kind of OMB Role

As demands that Presidents gain more control over governmental regulatory activity became more pressing, those Presidents looked to OMB to assist them in this endeavor. OMB's subsequent foray into regulatory review activities was in one sense similar to its time-honored goal of helping Presidents oversee management efforts in the departments and agencies more effectively, but it also took the budget agency into uncharted waters. While OMB's other budgetary, legislative, and management-related activities encompassed the entire Executive Branch of government, OIRA's work brought it into contact with only a few regulatory agencies and pockets of regulatory activity in Cabinet-level agencies. While most of OMB's focus had been limited to the review of governmental activities, much of OIRA's regulatory review charge centered upon private sector regulations and their larger economic implications outside of the Beltway.

The key players who stood to win or lose as a result of OIRA actions (private business concerns, public interest groups, and law firms inside and outside of Washington) were different from those that figured prominently in the orbits of other units in OMB, which primarily interacted with agency personnel and certain congressional committees. Moreover, as much as OMB's other responsibilities often touched upon "politically sensitive" areas, the issues OIRA dealt with and the attendant "interested" parties linked to these issues engendered a more politically laden regulatory review climate, more often, and in more visible ways. The politicization of the process was a consequence of several factors. First, pro- and anti-regulatory forces ordered themselves along liberal/conservative or Democratic/Republican lines in a more predictable way than have some other interest group alignments. Second, complex regulatory issues were often presented in oversimplified and emotional ways by political combatants. Third, since the monetary stakes were high for private business interests, efforts to lobby decision makers could be particularly intense.

Thus, during the 1980s, OIRA was not always left to its own devices to reach ivory tower decisions. The creation of the Bush Task Force under President Reagan and the Competitiveness Council under President Bush are two examples of the reach of White House involvement with the outcomes of OIRA's "cost–benefit" analysis.

Much would change in OIRA during the first two years of the Clinton administration to open up the regulatory review process to public scrutiny. What was not to change, however, was the White House's determination to maintain central control over agency promulgation of regulations. The Vice President was to play a key role in redefining OIRA's authorities and processes. This time, however, the tables had turned and that Vice President was Albert Gore.

9

OMB Meets the Clintonites: Transitions Within Transitions

OMB on the Eve of the Clinton Election

The career staff who awaited their new political bosses were still high-quality professionals whose energies and talents had been divided among the plethora of new and often quickly changing roles they had assumed during the 1980s. Many had gotten out of the practice of preparing long-term analysis either because of lack of time or demand from political appointees, though most probably had the needed capabilities to produce first-rate analysis if so directed. Overall, the career staff had lost some degree of the influence on the formulation of budgetary policies and decisions they had experienced in the mid to late 1970s. At the same time, OMB directors during the 1980s had solicited and used staff analysis selectively when it contributed to certain policy objectives. Some staff had become conditioned to participating in agency micro-management and enforcement activities that sometimes had included the supplanting of agency–congressional liaison responsibilities.

With these roles had come ample opportunities for career staff to be "influential" in other ways, while serving the aims of the administrations of the time. However, with this source of career staff clout had come a price, since there was to be a significant residue of "greater than usual" ill will toward OMB left over in selected domestic agencies.

One source of unhappiness among some staff in the program divisions at that time, was the fact that most of the incoming staff that had been added while Richard Darman was director were located in the management divisions and entered OMB at relatively high grades. This had proved to be an irritant, given their own heavy work load and the fact that program division staff size had remained generally constant during the previous ten-year period.

Still, in the previous four years in particular, there had been "pluses" for the career staff. Largely because of outgoing director Darman's abilities and White House insider status, more than one observer had touted Darman and his OMB as having been "running the government" without major competition from other White House or EOP units. Therefore, even though many career staff felt closed out by Darman's secretive style, there was still solace to be found in the "trickle down" of influence, often exercised over agencies and on the Hill. These included the new Budget Enforcement Act authorities which Darman had cleverly negotiated for OMB.

Much of this was about to change. OMB career staff would end up paying for this reflected power long after Darman was out of office. Darman's near monopoly on intergovernmental authority would constitute an important predetermining factor in initial Clinton administration moves which signaled a potential dilution of OMB clout.

The National Economic Council (NEC) and the National Performance Review (NPR): Competing Power Centers

Actions taken by the Clinton administration during its first hundred days in office were to reverse OMB's previous hold over the departments and agencies significantly, while signaling a trend toward increased agency discretion and Cabinet-level clout in influencing presidential budgetary and management decisions and policy making in general. OMB would still be involved in the process, but as one voice among many. A number of individuals interviewed for this study, as well as press accounts, tie this trend to a determination on the part of the Clinton White House to "avoid the pitfalls of the Bush administration, where OMB Director Richard G. Darman grabbed hold of domestic policy ranging far beyond that agency's traditional boundaries."[1]

The first two manifestations of this were the creation of two new presidential advisory structures outside of OMB—the National Economic Council (NEC) and the National Performance Review (NPR). Each of these units would in part supplant or at very least share OMB mandates in a number of its important turf areas.

The National Economic Council

The NEC was designed to provide the President with a far-reaching multiple advocacy advisory body to aid in making economic policy decisions.[2] According to a March 1993 presidential directive,[3] it was initially to be composed of the President, the Vice President, seven domestic Cabinet secretaries, the Secretary of State, the OMB Director, the Council of Economic Advisors' Chair, and a selected number of the heads of EOP units such as the National Security Advisor and the Assistant to the President for Domestic Policy. The Department of Defense (DOD) Secretary was added soon thereafter. A core group, which turned out to be the more active members of the NEC, was formally designated as the NEC Principals Committee. It included the Secretary of the Treasury, the OMB Director, the CEA Chair, the Secretaries of Commerce and Labor, and the National Security Advisor as "appropriate."

The NEC was initially chaired by investment banker Robert Rubin, later to become Treasury Secretary, at which point former CEA Chair Andrea Tyson became chair. With Rubin at its helm, the council was to play a role as an "honest broker" among "more than a dozen turf conscious agencies," in the necessary trade-offs that would have to occur in reaching decisions on aggregate-level economic policies.[4] It had been designed to exercise wide-ranging involvement in economic policy making. This included acting as the principal advisor to the President with respect to both micro- and macroeconomic policy making, as well as supervising the implementation of economic policies government-wide. The NEC was also mandated to "ensure that economic policy decisions and programs are consistent with the President's stated goals."[5] To carry out its functions, the NEC was assigned a staff of about twenty professionals.

One of the obvious purposes of the NEC was to make certain that Cabinet officials (as well as key White House staff) would be able to exercise direct input into economic policy making. Since many of the NEC's functions at very least touched on OMB roles, OMB now could be said to be sharing these mandates with a new high-level EOP unit. Descriptions of the NEC's intended relationship with OMB leave little doubt that one outcome of the NEC system would be to provide a counterweight to OMB control in budgetary and economic policy making. One political-level official characterized the NEC as a "check and balance" to the "imperial OMB." This individual added that within this framework, the OMB could also act as a check on the NEC. Another official described the NEC–OMB relationship as "collegial with shared information, but with the tone set at the top." The NEC would provide the "big picture" frameworks within which OMB would provide budgetary options and recommendations.

The National Performance Review

In late winter of 1993, it became clear that OMB was also not to play center stage in the Clinton administration's lead bureaucratic reform initiative, popularly known as "reinventing government." Instead, an outside staff was to be assembled to implement the reform effort under the leadership of Vice President Gore. The decision to not position OMB in the lead on this endeavor, which was formally dubbed the National Performance Review (NPR), would prove to be a "double whammy" for OMB. Many of the original NPR staff who were largely drawn from departments and agencies came saddled with grievances against OMB which had been accrued over the past two administrations.

If the existence of the NPR and the NEC were not enough to make OMB career staff just a little nervous about how they would be regarded by the incoming administration, the President's decision to base his first budget on CBO as opposed to OMB economic assumptions would also add to the uncertainty of the initial White House–OMB adjustment period.

Perceptions of Perceptions

The Clinton administration's creation of competing power centers and OMB staff reactions to them were not entirely unpredictable. There was, after all, the history of the previous twelve years to consider. It had been marked by highly contentious budgetary and regulatory battles between Republican White Houses and congressional Democrats in which OMB career staff had often been not completely anonymous players. The constraints engendered by the omnipresent budget deficit had only heightened the adversarial environment. Now some former Democratic congressional members and staffers with whom OMB had jousted for twelve years were part of the new administration.

Further complicating OMB staff perceptions at that time was the fact that the signals they were receiving from the Clinton administration were not altogether foreboding. *In fact, in important respects they were decidedly positive.* For example, career staff were impressed and moved when the President and the Vice President made an unprecedented gesture of good will by personally visiting the New Executive Office Building in the opening days of the administration. Career staff interviewed at the time almost universally found Director Panetta and Deputy Director Rivlin to be extremely likable, approachable, and respectful of OMB career staff. Many observed from the very beginning that communications between the director and the deputy director and career staff were better than they had been for a long time. This was to continue.

So the career staff applied themselves to their traditional task of educating the administration as to how they and their institution could serve the new President. They also set out to prove themselves to their new bosses as loyal employees and objective analysts. Of course, this "educative" process went both ways in that the new administration also had to explain "what they were about." One political-level EOP official later provided an intriguing account of the other side of this process. This individual found that while some OMB staff initially tried to convert their analysis to conform to Clinton administration policy, they mistakenly perceived this to mean what the political staffer characterized as "traditional" Democratic spending orientations as opposed to the administration's "New Democratic" philosophy. The clarification of these "New Democratic" policy implications to OMB career staff took about a year, according to this official.

With the increase in the number of competing policy-making centers that were created in the Clinton administration, the potential for mixed signals to OMB career staff during this educative process was also ever present. It was perhaps one of the trade-offs that had to be made for the benefits derived from a multiple advocacy advisory system for the President.

The evolution of OMB staff relations with political-level Clinton administration officials inside OMB and with the NEC and the NPR will be chronicled throughout this chapter. A snapshot of the views of political-level OMB and EOP staff surrounding OMB career staff objectivity and analytical capabilities after three years of getting to know OMB will be presented at the end of the next chapter. But first, a word about the new directors is in order.

The Panetta and Rivlin Team: Act I

In late fall of 1992, both Congressman Leon Panetta, House Budget Committee Chair, and Dr. Alice Rivlin, the first director of the Congressional Budget Office from 1975 through 1983, were in contention for the OMB Budget Director's job. That they were considered and ultimately appointed to the two top posts at OMB attests to President Clinton's commitment to deficit reduction, since both Panetta and Rivlin had earned reputations as "deficit hawks" as well as having each crafted at least one concrete plan to eliminate the deficit. In addition, the fact that Panetta and Rivlin had publicly criticized the Clinton campaign's deficit reduction plan as being insufficiently aggressive[6] signaled the new President's openness to criticism and disagreement.

Over many years, Panetta had crusaded on behalf of genuine deficit reduction without the gimmickry he often condemned. In the interests of deficit reduction, he had been willing to put his own political survival on the line in positions he had taken and in votes he had cast. One notable example was a vote to eliminate Social Security cost-of-living increases.[7]

While Panetta's commitment to deficit reduction was considered firm, he had a reputation for flexibility in the approaches he would consider to realize that goal. For example, in 1991, a Panetta deficit reduction plan had included a mixture of tax hikes as well as spending reductions, and in 1992 he had proposed to balance the budget by 1998 by reaching yearly spending and tax adjustment targets, which if not met would force automatic cuts in spending.[8]

Alice Rivlin had been equally committed to deficit reduction, going even further in her 1992 book, *Reviving the American Dream,* by arguing in favor of actions she believed would lead to government surpluses.[9] The book, which pointed to the deficit as the "biggest single impediment to revitalizing the American economy,"[10] recommended devolving certain federal programs to the states.[11]

Leon Panetta and Alice Rivlin had each earned in his/her own way a reputation for honesty and integrity. Either nomination would have been of significant stature so as to bolster OMB's institutional credibility at the outset. Since Panetta and Rivlin could not both get the top job, the President appointed Panetta as director and Rivlin as his deputy. Bob Woodward claims in *The Agenda* that the President's decision was in part related to his favorable impression of Panetta's energy, intelligence, institutional memory with respect to the congressional budget process, and that he was "a good human being."[12] According to Woodward, Panetta portrayed himself to the President-elect as both a "deficit hawk" *and* a "traditional Democrat."[13]

In many senses, Leon Panetta was an ideal candidate for OMB Director. He had the knowledge, experience, expertise, and integrity cited above and was noted to be extremely hard-working. Panetta exhibited none of the personality drawbacks that had allegedly characterized Richard Darman. Since Stockman's days, the OMB Director had been required to be a skilled congressional negotiator par excellence. Panetta, who had been a key player in the negotiation of White House–congressional budget deals in 1985, 1987, 1989, and 1990, and purportedly "loves to negotiate,"[14] fit that description perfectly.

The Director's Dilemma Revisited

By 1993, the OMB Director's job had evolved into the equivalent of two jobs. It required an ability to serve as a key White House advisor and the skills needed to lead the "charges" on Capitol Hill for the President in often contentious budget battles, as well as the capability to assume the OMB Director's traditional responsibilities. Success or failure in the arena surrounding budgetary politics had become survival issues for Presidents because of the mounting deficit. In this atmosphere, if an OMB Director was to serve the President, he/she could not assume a neutral mantle as director of a nonpartisan think tank exclusively.

The dilemma was that Presidents needed their OMB Directors to play both roles with equal intensity, but the pressures were such that directors had tended to lean toward the former, more political role. There were more payoffs in this, such as an "empowered" OMB and few external rewards for concentrating on the "straight arrow" institutional orientation. The politicians who set the rules of the budgetary games were reflections of that reality as were most recent budget directors. It had become very difficult for one OMB budget director to balance both jobs over the course of an administration.

Rivlin: The Torch-Bearer

For these reasons, Alice Rivlin's appointment as deputy had an inherent appeal. Given the high personal stature she brought to the job, she had the potential from the early days of the Clinton administration to play almost a "co-director" role and thus to act as a genuine "backup" to Panetta with respect to the maintenance of OMB's institutional integrity. If anyone was suited in background and personality to bear the torch of neutral competence, it was Alice Rivlin. Rivlin's greatest alleged weakness was her greatest strength in this regard. Whereas Leon Panetta was a natural politician, Alice Rivlin's "political tin ear" was legendary. As CBO's first director, it was this quality along with the strength to stand her ground that enabled her to lend the new organization much credibility in the face of contrary political pressures. She had dealt up realistic economic projections and cost estimates that rained on more than a few political parades and set a precedent for honesty and credibility in CBO.[15] As a nonideological Democrat who termed herself a "fanatical, card-carrying middle-of-the-roader,"[16] she also had a reputation for being a detail person who could master complex issues with lightning speed.

And so Leon Panetta and Alice Rivlin had the potential to be a formidable team. If any duo could aid this President in crafting and selling a meaningful deficit reduction package in Congress while restoring OMB's credibility as a source of accurate estimates and analysis, they could.

Preparing the Five-Year Economic Plan and the Deficit Reduction Package: The Post-Inaugural Dilemma

From the beginning, the nation had looked to the new President to act on the economy. During the campaign, candidate Clinton had repeatedly promised that as President he would direct his efforts "like a laser beam" toward improving the economy and that there was no other priority so pressing as economic growth and the creation of new jobs. Pre-election polls had showed that demand for economic improvement and change were significant factors in the public mind, contributing to Clinton's 43 percent popular vote.[17]

But the deficit loomed ominously. Clinton had also pledged to cut the $290 billion deficit in half during his four-year term. As the Budget Enforcement Act was not designed to force overall budget deficit reduction, so it had not succeeded in this endeavor. By the time President Clinton was inaugurated in 1993, projections for the deficit in 1997 (the year the deficit would have to be reduced in half to keep the President's promise) had risen to between $305 billion and $360 billion, depending upon whose estimates were being used.[18] Between the November election and Clinton's inauguration, painful realities had come to light which increased the already monumental challenge the administration would face. Barely two weeks before Clinton was sworn in, OMB Director Darman released devastating update projections that increased the estimates for the fiscal 1997 deficit by over $60 billion from what OMB had projected in the summer of 1992.[19] Some budget process participants believed the news to be even worse than this. Senate Armed Services Chair Sam Nunn had asserted that Darman's figures had built-in assumptions that underestimated costs in the Defense budget by an additional $50 billion.[20]

Clinton's antidotes to the deficit voiced during the campaign such as taxes on the "rich," were no longer going to be enough. His promise for a middle-class tax cut was also to be sacrificed for the time being. His administration would be faced with two conflicting but, to the President, necessary goals of reducing the deficit and advancing his agenda of investing in jobs, health care, and education for the American people. The top-down process that produced the President's FY 1994 budget and Five-Year Economic Plan would both in the nature of its structure and in the views of its participants include champions of both objectives.

The Bush administration had broken with precedent and had not formally submitted an FY 1994 budget to Congress. Instead, a budget had been compiled which estimated government-wide spending projections if taxing and spending policies remained unchanged, with final decisions being left to the incoming administration.[21] The President and his economic team would have only six weeks to prepare a far-reaching economic recovery plan and to put final adjustments on the FY 1994 budget. The ensuing decision-making process used to accomplish these goals reflected both the magnitude of the task at hand and the short time frame within which participants in the process would be operating.

OMB Career Staff Role in Preparing the Economic Plan

If any one word can describe the atmosphere of that first budget preparation process, it is "top-down." However, in this case "top-down" meant not only the OMB team of Director Leon Panetta and Deputy Director Alice Rivlin, but White House staff, the newly created National Economic Council, key departmental secretaries, and clearly, the President himself.

Immediately after the inauguration, a team of the President's top economic advisors began a series of intensive meetings that would spearhead the decision-making process leading to the creation of the President's promised economic plan, which was to be outlined in the February 17th State of the Union address. The group's deliberations involved painstakingly detailed discussions of the federal budget as well as macroeconomic strategic options for reducing the deficit, with many meetings lasting hours on end.[22] The President was reported to have read through every line of the budget four times and the team to have debated virtually every program in the federal bureaucracy.[23]

The next layer of the process that directed OMB's support operations involved parallel OMB meetings, which included OMB Director Leon Panetta, Deputy Director Rivlin, their deputies, and Treasury and NEC officials such as Deputy Treasury Secretary Roger Altman, and Deputy Assistant to the President for Economic Policy W. Bowman Cutter. Again, on this level, the desire to bring combined OMB, agency, and NEC perspectives to bear on the process was evident.

An OMB career staff presence included BRD's assistant director as well as OMB program division chiefs filling in for PADs who had not yet been appointed. This did provide the division chiefs with the opportunity to present program division positions at a relatively high level of the OMB hierarchy. (However, it is important to note that as soon as the PADs were appointed in late spring, they supplanted the division chiefs in future comparable high-level discussions.)

The White House and parallel OMB meetings generated a series of three types of information and data requests to program division staff that directly reflected the President's strategies for achieving deficit reduction, job creation, economic stimulus, and investment and infrastructure building. Each was to present projections for a five-year period. First were the "savers," which were requests to career staff to try to identify any extraneous or wasteful spending in their accounts. Specific policy guidance was often included in these directives, highlighting particular program activities considered questionable by administration officials involved in the process. Second, staff were asked to recommend aspects of their programs with investment or infrastructure-building potential. Third, OMB staff were invited to suggest specific account areas where "additional" funding could result in administration efforts to stimulate the economy or could create jobs. The requests for stimulus or investment spending ideas were transmitted to OMB program division staff in the form of diffuse subject matter such as "jobs" or "children's needs" that often cross-cut familiar budget account categories. All three types of data requests were characterized by OMB staff not as bids for program analysis, but more as exercises to "price out" administration priorities and translate them into specifics.

There was little in this decision-making process that could be characterized as facilitating the "bubbling-up" of policy initiatives from the career staff levels. Most of the career staff interviewed during that period did not perceive themselves as being particularly influential in the outcomes reached, since the large number of political-level participants in the process shaped a decision-making environment that involved many more high-level "power centers" than had characterized preparation of presidential budgets in recent years.

Staff members also described the period from January 20 through April 5 as one of the most intensive ever experienced in an OMB budget preparation cycle that normally had been heavy. This was at least in part because the iterative information requests they kept receiving reflected the intensity of the detailed review and debates that were taking place among the President and his top economic advisors, and partly because they were dealing with projections for a multi-year period. Elizabeth Drew's account of the early days of the Clinton presidency offers some indication that some administration officials may not have entirely understood the mechanics of OMB's role in putting the budget and economic plan together. Drew wrote that "neither the President nor his advisors who were new to drawing up a budget understood the extreme pressure they were putting on the OMB staff."[24]

When the President delivered his FY 1994 Budget and Economic Plan to Congress on February 17, many of the details were missing and were to follow on April 5 when the President's complete FY 1994 budget was transmitted to Congress. After February 17, OMB staff worked assiduously to fill in the details in what turned out to be an unusual budget preparation phase, primarily because some agencies were given a much expanded role in determining the specifics of "who" in the agencies would "get what, when, and how." This trend to allow the agencies greater discretion in "dividing up the pot" (some would say at OMB's institutional expense) was to become a major theme during the first half of the Clinton administration.

A highly unusual passback and appeals format during the spring of 1993 first signaled these changes. Instead of a one-time passback and opportunity for appeals, there were a couple of appeals in some areas and an ongoing series of iterations in others, with agencies having a greater ability to affect outcomes. Moreover, usually in the past, passback figures had been transmitted in a very specific way by function, object class, or account. This time most agencies were given a "lump sum" and were afforded significant latitude in determining how it was to be distributed. In several departments this amounted to an unusually large divestiture of authority to newly appointed departmental secretaries to divide the funding requests, since few appointees at the assistant secretary level were in place. It also resulted in a crushing work load for high-level departmental agency career officials.

During this phase of the process, some interviewees perceived that if there were any winners in the influence game, it was departmental secretaries and whatever political-level assistants they had in place, particularly those who were part of the NEC's inner circle. The existence of the NEC had also contributed to a shift of authority from centralized OMB control toward greater agency input. As Steven Mufson of the *Washington Post* noted that spring with respect to the NEC,

> Though OMB Director Panetta sat at the center of the table, it was a striking departure from the usual budget process, in which agencies submit a budget request to OMB and then receive a written "pass back" with OMB's decision. . . . This time, thanks to the NEC process, virtually every Cabinet member sat at the same table as Panetta. Reich was able to argue about the size of the deficit. Housing and Urban Development Secretary Henry Cisneros could make a pitch for more HUD spending. . . .[25]

On April 5, when the President's detailed budget proposals were transmitted to Congress, OMB staff and the administration might have breathed a sigh of relief, but new congressional budget battles were already brewing.

OMB and Congress: Clinton's First Year

OMB career staff's congressional monitorship roles had indeed become institutionalized. The significant commitment of OMB staff required to support OMB Director Panetta's efforts to sell President Clinton's Budget and Economic Plan had not changed that much from the amount of effort required to support Richard Darman or David Stockman in the past. In some respects, however, it was to be more intense. The type of support required and its timing was to mirror the progress of President Clinton's Budget and Economic Plan on Capitol Hill.

During the fight over the President's Economic Stimulus Plan in the spring of 1993, both the OMB program divisions and the agencies had been actively involved in providing informational support for Panetta and other political officials. Panetta's efforts had taken on an even greater urgency in April, when the administration discovered that as part of the budget resolution, Congress had tightened the discretionary spending budget caps to remain at 1993 levels or below for the next five years. The immediate consequence of this development was that a large portion of the President's investment expenditures were trimmed in the House Budget Resolution in order to accommodate the more rigid ceilings. Subsequently, Panetta attempted to lobby Appropriations Committee members in person instead of merely transmitting the written Statements of Administration Policy (SAPs), in an effort to restore some of the designated "investment" funding. OMB staff were called upon to assist Panetta by providing information and tables upon which to base administration "investment" priority lists to be communicated to appropriations subcommittee chairs.

Again in the summer, OMB staff tracked the reconciliation deliberations until the dramatic "photo finish" passage of the Reconciliation Conference Report in August. During the administration's efforts to gather votes for the reconciliation package, Panetta organized joint weekly meetings including both OMB staff and agency personnel to facilitate communications among the various individuals involved in tracking any particular aspect of the negotiations. This would prove to be yet another early example of the administration's commitment to making the agencies more of a co-equal partner with OMB in both budget formulation and congressional relations.

With the Congress controlled by the President's party, OMB was given additional congressional liaison responsibilities such as the drafting of responses to congressional constituency inquiries that had been forwarded to the White House or OMB for comment. In recent past administrations, such letters, if answered at all, would usually have been handled by the White House Congressional Liaison Office or OMB's Legislative Affairs Office. In some areas, staff were also finding a shorter "turnaround" time available for legislative and testimony clearance as compared with these processes during the Bush and Reagan administrations. In part, this may be attributed to delays in the clearance process at the agency level, largely because of an apparent Clinton administration motivation to achieve as much consensus as possible among agencies, affected interest groups, and congressional members before submitting legislation. During the Reagan and Bush administrations, which had always had at least one house of Congress under opposition party control and generally had demonstrated more distrust of agency bureaucracies, OMB had been cast into more of a "nay-sayer" role of scrutinizing proposed legislation for positions that contradicted administration policy. That process had moved more swiftly and efficiently, but ultimately with less programmatic output.

The Panetta and Rivlin Team, Act II, Year One:
The View from the Top

During the crafting and selling of the 1993 budget package and economic plan, Director Panetta and Deputy Director Rivlin were credited as living up to their reputations as "deficit hawks," as they became pitted against President Clinton's political advisors in their deficit reduction efforts,[26] and as they exhibited unwavering commitment to avoiding "gimmickry" in their economic estimates even in the face of the significant constraints within which they operated.[27] These efforts were ultimately to result in kudos from Washington budget observers such as Stanley E. Collender, director of federal budget policy for Price Waterhouse, who later was quoted as saying, "It wasn't pure as snow, but last year's budget was probably the most honest budget I've seen in 12 to 15 years."[28]

Alice Rivlin had lived up to her reputation as one who reported economic projections as she believed them to be, regardless of the reactions they might incur from the President or others on the economic team, or the impact they might have on her status in the administration. This was particularly true in some of her comments with respect to cost savings the administration hoped to realize in its health care reform plan, which she had characterized as "budget neutral."[29]

Accounts of the first year of the Clinton administration also illustrate how inherent difficulties and conflicts in the modern OMB Director's role made the initial adjustment somewhat bumpy even for Washington veterans like Panetta and Rivlin. The stress came largely from the expectation that the director and in this case the deputy director play public relations roles on behalf of the President with the press, in addition to their fundamental responsibilities to provide the President with credible and honest information. As genuinely honest people, neither Panetta nor Rivlin had yet perfected the art of jousting with the press without using words or phrases that could be damaging to the administration. Panetta's error occurred on April 26 when, thinking he was speaking off the record, he told a group of reporters that he thought some administration-favored proposals were in trouble on the Hill. Shaken after seeing the headlines the next day, Panetta commented after the incident, "I suddenly realized that the truth makes big news in Washington, D.C."[30]

Rivlin got into trouble when on May 12 she described an administration "deficit reduction trust fund" as a display device, which was taken to mean a gimmick in the press.[31] Soon thereafter rumors began to appear to the effect that Rivlin's remark to the press as well as the hard-line positions she had taken on deficit reduction in the administration's inner circles would lead to her ouster. These rumors were voiced in a May 1993 *Newsweek* article which dubbed her the "living dead," and suggested that her advice was being ignored within the administration's inner circles.[32]

Another misstep occurred in Panetta's own bailiwick of congressional information gathering, when the President was unhappily "surprised" by the decimation of significant portions of his investment package due to the Budget Enforcement Act's rigid caps.[33] With the caps, as well as Congressional Budget Office estimates showing the administration budget plan to be $50 billion short of its deficit reduction goal, the House had made up the difference by cutting President Clinton's investment package. While the President had been informed about the caps, Panetta had presumed that the House would be willing to accept the administration's proposal to raise the caps to make funds available for the investment package as presented in the economic plan.[34] The error had not been in neglecting to explain budget law to the President, but in failing to gauge the increased interest in deficit reduction that existed in the new Congress.[35] This again underscores how critical a part of the OMB Director's job "up-to-the-minute" dissemination of congressional intelligence had become. This was true even for an OMB Director and a President sending an economic plan and budget to a Congress controlled by their own party.

What mattered in the end were the final results. During the summer of 1993 and into the fall, Leon Panetta was to show his mettle as a congressional negotiator in the administration's struggle to score a razor-thin victory in passing its five-year economic package. Observers would credit Panetta's congressional experience, knowledge, and personality as significantly helping the President to succeed in this effort.

Reinventing OMB: Parallel Paths

Introduction

No sooner than the President's FY 1994 budget had gone to Congress and even before the detailed version was transmitted in early April, OMB began grappling with nearly a year of the most intensive external scrutiny and internal self-assessment that it had faced in many years. During the spring and summer of 1993, research teams of the newly created National Performance Review dissected OMB's performance and evolution in the past, and analyzed what its roles should be in the future. At the same time, OMB undertook a similar self-examination, which culminated in a major OMB reorganization to be made public in March of 1994.

The Vice President's National Performance Review

The National Performance Review, the Clinton administration's centerpiece effort to streamline and reform the federal bureaucracy, was announced on March 3, 1993. Its chief missions as stated were to "make government *work better* and *cost less*."[36] The National Performance Review, while modeled after David Osbourne's prescription for reform in the private sector, was staffed primarily but not exclusively from within the ranks of the federal civil service itself. As stated in NPR's first report in the fall of 1993, "we organized a team of experienced federal employees from all corners of the government—a marked change from past efforts, which relied on outsiders."[37] While not taking the lead, OMB staff were nonetheless to be involved in the first six-month review process, staffing many of the NPR agency and "systems" teams that conducted their research during that period. Since NPR "agency" teams sought to gain an "objective" look at the various government agencies, NPR staff were assigned to teams outside their home agencies. In many cases, OMB's presence on these teams lent some foundational knowledge and expertise to the effort. In addition to the agency teams were the so-called "systems" teams, which looked at cross-cutting government-wide systems such as budgeting, procurement, and personnel.

During the six-month review period, the agency and systems teams were charged with conducting research and preparing draft working papers organized around the "central principles of making government work better and cost less." The proposals in these reports were then defended in a series of "toll-gates" during the summer of 1993 which, according to one participant, resembled Ph.D. defenses. The Vice President and his deputies and relevant Cabinet officials attended many of these sessions personally. These sessions also allowed for opposing viewpoints to be debated by teams within NPR.

The NPR–OMB Relationship, Act I: NPR Looks at OMB

As NPR set to work on its efforts to "reinvent the federal government," OMB as a central governmental agency affecting all other agencies was not to be overlooked. During the spring and summer of 1993, three of NPR's research teams were involved in examining OMB. This involved "systems" teams in areas related to OMB functions such as budget and management as well as a team reviewing the whole organization of the Executive Office of the President.

While there were some meetings between the NPR participants on these groups and OMB representatives engaged in their own self-study, the two efforts operated largely independently of one another at the staff level.

The NPR research effort pertaining to OMB involved the use of various methodologies including library research, consultation with the Council on Excellence in Government, a perusal of past studies and writings on OMB, and a series of focus groups with individuals in the agencies, some of whom had also worked at OMB in the past. The working papers and recommendations that were produced ultimately had to pass muster with the toll-gate process described above. NPR team members had to defend their recommendations regarding OMB to different participants at different times.

A look at the perceptions held by both OMB and NPR staff on what was unfolding at the time is necessary in order to understand the origins of the recommendations impacting OMB that NPR ultimately produced. From interviews with a number of participants in the NPR process at the time, it is clear that there was a wide spectrum of opinion concerning what the nature of OMB's roles should be in the future. By the summer of 1993, two generally distinguishable philosophical approaches had crystallized at the staff level. The first, which seemed to have been most vociferously expressed in the early months of NPR's existence, espoused a radically minimized OMB role in the future in terms of reductions in OMB staff size and transfer of OMB authorities to other agencies. Allegedly, "some" individuals in this group harbored specific grievances against OMB, largely derived from having worked in agencies that had been particularly affected by the more extreme instances of OMB micro-management during the 1980s.

Another group could be characterized as being more moderate in its recognition of OMB's importance as a presidential advisory system and its advocacy of various reforms within that institution in order for it to be able to carry out its missions more effectively in the future. Some of these individuals had experience both in agencies and OMB, while others had only agency or congressional experience.

On the other side of the street at OMB (the two organizations were located literally across the street from one another), perceptions were strong among some staff that the NPR meant to "minimize OMB's role to that of green eyeshade number crunchers," as one staff person commented. These perceptions came out loud and clear in interviews with OMB staff as early as the spring of 1993. An NPR official later attributed this OMB career staff displeasure to a "shock to their systems," which emanated from the serious competition they now had from NPR. This individual also believed that "the problem with OMB is what is wrong with Washington generally"—that there was not enough knowledge of programmatic implementation in the field where government services are actually delivered to the public, and that NPR was needed "to fill the void." Other NPR staff cited "arrogance" and "change resistance" as counterproductive attitudes assumed by some OMB career staff.

Some of these critiques and institutional quarrels were reminiscent of similar scenarios that had occurred in the past. The overall situation echoed past cases in which the aggrieved parties were former departmental secretaries instead of agency civil servants. These included Nelson Rockefeller (HEW Secretary under President Eisenhower) and Abraham Ribicoff (HEW Under-Secretary during that administration), who, having chafed under what they saw to be a BOB interference into their "rightful" bureaucratic turfs, later found themselves situated in positions that allowed them significant institutional platforms to limit BOB's authorities (PACGO and the Senate Governmental Affairs Committee). In both cases they had gone for the jugular.[38]

The concern that OMB staff did not have enough knowledge of regional service delivery in the field was reminiscent of critiques leveled during the Johnson administration when, after BOB had been stripped of its field offices in the 1950s and Congress had denied requests for their restoration, BOB was criticized for its failures as an intergovernmental manager—failures that might have been reversed if BOB field offices had not been dismantled. In the 1993 instance, the new roles and responsibilities exercised by OMB staff in the 1980s left them with less time to go on field trips and pursue other activities designed to gain grassroots information about the programs they reviewed, and reflected the policies and priorities of the administrations in office at the time.

Obviously, institutional self-interest and protection of turf played a fundamental role in these disputes on both sides as well. However, beneath these early NPR–OMB staff scuffles lay a debate that was not new between those supporting a "Cabinet government" model on the one hand and those skeptical of such an approach. Taken in their extreme manifestations, the former presumes that Cabinet officials and their political-level subordinates can properly implement and represent broad-based presidential policy in their departments and agencies without a need for unelected OMB civil servants to play major intervening enforcement roles. This orientation argues for a less empowered OMB, particularly as it relates to the more intrusive "policing" of areas such as agency budget formulation, execution, and legislative and testimony clearance. In keeping with this general philosophy, one senior NPR official acknowledged that one of NPR's central themes had been to reduce the interference of central control agencies like OMB in many agency activities.

On the other hand, doubters would tend to view it as unwise for the

President to place too great a reliance on Cabinet members standing firm on his behalf, particularly when presidential policies called for the sacrificing of budgetary resources or particularistic agency interests. Those supporting this position could also question whether agencies can be trusted to reduce their own personnel numbers and funding levels, or to provide their own constituency groups with fewer benefits if called for, without the intervention of "Big Brother OMB."

NPR Proposals

Two NPR proposals that were rejected at some point in NPR's decision-making process were the establishment of an "agency ombudsman" within OMB to investigate and if necessary to act as an advocate for agency complaints against OMB, and a policy change that would have mandated that departmental secretaries instead of the OMB Director sign off on Statements of Administration Policy before their transmission to Congress.

One significant NPR proposition that survived and was the focus of much contentious debate was the proposal for an "Executive Budget Resolution." One critical objective of this proposed process change was to get the President involved in setting government-wide and individual departmental ceilings early in the budget formulation process. A number of NPR participants hoped to see the whole Cabinet involved in determining these ceilings. While under the proposal, budget formulation would be "top-down" at the beginning of the process, agency employees would have a freer hand to develop their budgets and to determine how the prescribed totals would be divided among agency programs. NPR asserted that this would improve upon the then current practice of developing agency budgets without knowledge of the presidential policies or budgetary constraints that would factor into their ultimate outcomes.

With the ceilings being set at the presidential level, and the details of the budgets being worked out by the agencies, it was initially unclear where OMB fit into the process. The Executive Budget Resolution notion in fact cast OMB's entire budget review process into doubt. It is therefore not surprising that the precise wording of this proposal became a matter of no small dispute between OMB and NPR.

In spite of these internal debates within the Executive Office of the President, by the time the initial NPR report was published, OMB had been included as one among several participants who would shape the overall budgetary targets. The following wording is found in the first NPR report, published in September of 1993. It is interesting to note that no explanation is given as to what OMB's role would be in the bottom-up agency-directed phase of the process.

To develop the resolution, officials from the White House policy councils will meet with OMB and agency officials. In those sessions, the administration's policy leadership will make decisions on overall spending and revenue levels, deficit reduction targets, and funding allocations for major inter-agency policy initiatives. The product of those meetings—a resolution completed by August—will provide agencies with funding ceilings and allocations for major policy missions. Then, bureaus will generate their own budget estimates, now knowing their agency's priorities and fiscal limits. . . . Critics may view the executive budget resolution process as a top-down tool that will stifle creative, bottom-up suggestions for funding options. We think otherwise. The resolution will render top officials responsible for budget totals and policy decisions, but will encourage lower level ingenuity to devise funding options within those guidelines.[39]

The initial NPR report also had other references of significance to OMB. OMB's role in the budget execution and apportionment process that had precipitated many of the resentments harbored by some NPR staff was also discussed in the report.

It stated:

OMB will simplify the apportionment process, which hamstrings agencies by dividing their funding into amounts that are available, bit by bit, according to specified time periods, activities, or projects. Agencies often don't get their funding on time and, after they do, must fill out reams of paper work to show that they adhered to apportionment guidelines.[40]

Finally, the report took a swipe at OMB in a reference made to the role of OMB review in the cycles of agency "padding" of budgets that NPR wished to end:

OMB is especially prone to question unspent funds—and reduce the ensuing year's budget by that amount. Agency officials inflate their estimates, driving budget numbers higher and higher. One bureau budget director claims that many regularly ask for 90% more than they eventually receive.[41]

The NPR budget-related proposals in the September 1993 report would not be the last word on these and other topics, since NPR was still to publish a number of follow-up monographs that further developed its recommendations. NPR and OMB were to negotiate about some of the disputed issues for over a year in some cases before compromises would be reached and the monographs could be published. In the interim, budget process participants were about to embark on a trial run of a new budget formulation process which included elements of the NPR proposals just described.

Preparing the 1995 Clinton Budget: Constraints and Collegiality

Introduction

Due to the scope of the President's five-year economic plan and the short amount of time within which it was crafted, the plan by necessity had focused mostly on "big-picture" macroeconomic issues involving tax and spending decisions that would set the framework for budgetary decision making for years to come. The fact that the Clinton adjustments to the outgoing Bush budget were just a small part of that equation had led budget process experts to tout the FY 1995 budget preparation process as President Clinton's first genuine Executive Budget preparation experience.[42]

From the beginning, this would be an effort marked by severe budgetary constraints created by the spending reductions targeted in the 1993 economic plan, by the fact that President Clinton and the Congress decided to continue the strictures imposed in the Budget Enforcement Act, by growing entitlement costs, and "a largely spent peace dividend."[43] Since the President still wished to advance some of the investment goals that had been pared down by about 30 percent by Congress in the 1994 budget,[44] he was faced with the significant challenge of finding offsetting spending reductions to free funds needed to finance his proposals.

A New and Evolving Budget Preparation Process

This atmosphere of budgetary constraint coupled with the desire to invest money in certain domestic programs set the stage for development of a process that was both "top-down" as well as "bottom-up," as generally envisioned in the NPR proposal for an "Executive Budget Resolution." Then OMB Deputy Director Alice Rivlin described the FY 1995 budget preparation process as directed toward getting the President more involved in the budget's preparation early, and toward making relationships between OMB and the agencies less adversarial.[45]

The first major theme of this process reflected the immediate needs of a "hands-on" President who faced formidable funding limitations and would be held accountable for doing "more with less." The objectives would require a significant amount of attention from President Clinton, who had already shown the inclination to focus on budgetary details. Both of Rivlin's stated goals mirrored NPR's recommendation that the President, the Cabinet, and implicitly the NEC set broad budgetary ceilings while allowing the agencies more discretion in allocating the funds. To facilitate these ends, OMB staff were to work more collaboratively with the agencies than had been the adversarial model of the recent past. This team approach was to exist on all levels of the process, from the President and his Cabinet officers to OMB examiners and their agency budget counterparts.

Alice Rivlin later described the process that ensued as "one of the fairest, most open and most cooperative processes of any administration."[46] At its theoretical core, it reflected a notion that a modified Cabinet government could work for this President. However, as is often the case when theory meets reality, there were unexpected "wrinkles," such as the fact that President Clinton's greatest personal involvement turned out to be at the end of the process as opposed to the beginning.

This 1995 budget preparation process started during the late spring and summer of 1993 with a series of high-level meetings designed to provide a forum for the administration to communicate the need for agency budgetary restraint, to reiterate presidential priorities, and to allow departmental officials to articulate their views. They were usually attended by Cabinet secretaries and assistant secretaries on the agency side, and Panetta, Rivlin, Deputy Director for Management Phillip Lader, and relevant PADs, division chiefs, and other career staff as needed. The agency representatives had been instructed to come prepared to present their broad "visions and plans" for their agencies in the near future as well as their ideas with respect to how these agency objectives could be accommodated within general budgetary constraints. OMB policy officials, in turn, had been prepared for the discussions by program and management division staff teams. According to Alice Rivlin's confirmation documents, "a number of these meetings addressed issues that cut across several agencies."[47] Some administration officials recalled later that the level of agency preparation for the meetings had been uneven in that some agencies did not come to the discussions adequately prepared to engage in meaningful dialogue.

After the meetings, OMB program division staff wrote papers analyzing those agency plans that had been submitted in light of available resources, agency needs, presidential priorities, and budgetary constraints. The papers were intended to provide information that allowed budgetary ceilings to be determined in an informed manner. At this point in the process, the analysis was formulated at a general philosophical level and did not advise on which specific programs should be saved or cut. As one examiner described it, "the whole analysis process involved determinations of how the department's vision fit under the mark."

Based on this process, OMB transmitted "refined budget guidance to the agencies in late summer."[48] This guidance had been approved by the NEC and the OMB Directors, with instructions that the agencies submit their requests to OMB by October 1 instead of the customary September 1. OMB directives also communicated budget targets that the agency budget requests were not supposed to breach, but did not specifically direct the agencies on how to divide the funding. The exception to this was specific guidance to increase requests for funding in programs considered to be "presidential investment priorities." In these cases, OMB usually recommended ways to offset the additional funding.

From September 1 to October 1, iterative discussions between OMB and the agencies continued. Many agencies did not meet the October 1st deadline, claiming lack of time to understand the new process. Other agencies submitted budget proposals that were higher than the targets. Taken as a whole, budget requests were received $23 billion in excess of the administration's cumulative targets,[49] and a number of Cabinet members were instructed to make further cuts.

In November, Director's Reviews followed which were considered by some participants to be "serious and intensive" but were considered less detailed by others. In some areas, director Panetta reached decisions on the spot and communicated his recommendations to the President to those assembled for the review.

As a general rule, Director's Reviews during the Clinton administration had been more open to a wider range of OMB participants than was usually true during Richard Darman's tenure, and more junior career staff were given an opportunity to make presentations. But the determination of whether the PAD or the budget examiner would make the presentation was still left to the PAD level. The top-down nature of the process was evidenced by the presence of selected NEC and White House staff at the Director's Review sessions. (This excluded NEC members from the agencies.)

In December, the "Presidential Review" process was enacted through a series of meetings between the President, the Vice President, the Cabinet, agency heads, and assorted staff assistants. (OMB, the NEC, and the White House were all represented in the meetings, including but not limited to Leon Panetta and Alice Rivlin, NEC Chairman Robert Rubin, Senior White House advisor George Stephanopoulos, Counselor David Gergen,[50] and OMB PADs as relevant.) The meetings generally lasted an hour and included presentations of both OMB's recommendations and those of the Cabinet official. The President did not reach final decisions in these meetings, but determined the final disposition of agency budgets before Christmas after further consultations with his White House aides.

Both the traditional appeals and passback processes had been substantially altered. Since the meetings with the President had been designed to be the "agency's final day in court," Panetta and Rubin had sent memos instructing the agencies not to appeal after receiving their allocations. The specific passback instructions directing funding to the program or project level that agencies had generally received in the past had been replaced by more "flexible" OMB guidance which agencies were not bound to follow. The one striking exception to this rule was in presidential priority areas where the agencies were "directed" to "invest" the funding.

There were a couple of implications to these process changes that became clear during the 1995 budget process. Now that more authority had been given to agency budget staff to allot their own funding, the "budget season" work load of the agencies had increased and that of OMB career staff had temporarily declined. In some cases this may have been a mixed blessing for the agency budgeteers, who now had to approve trade-offs in funding requests among their own bureaus in a climate of extremely scarce resources. They could not use OMB for "protective cover" as they had in the past.

Another change was that in the "team-oriented" and "consensual" atmosphere that these process changes had created, some OMB career staff were having a more difficult time getting information from agency officials who no longer felt obliged to respond to all of OMB's information requests. These interpersonal dynamics represented a significant turnabout from those that had prevailed during the previous twelve years. They created difficulties for some OMB career staff who were still expected to be able to provide analysis to PADs and other political appointees quickly, but did not have their previous authoritative clout to demand the information they needed from the agencies.

In spite of what appeared to be a process which built in a number of constraints for OMB career staff, it is interesting to note that after the budget was finalized, some observers believed that the final product had in large part been influenced significantly by their input. For example, one observer cited the reduction of spending for "300 or so small programs that [had] been on OMB's hit list" for a long time.[51] President Clinton had also continued to be more involved with shaping the details of his budget proposals than had either President since Carter.[52] Due to the severe budgetary constraints that had been built into the process and the President's personal determination to find program cuts to fund his investment priorities, OMB career staff had provided a significant service to him in pointing the way to these offsets. Even a "hands-on" President can benefit from drawing upon OMB's institutional memory. In this case, once again, OMB can be observed as seeming to have an easier time serving Presidents when those Presidents need to use OMB in an informed "nay-sayer" capacity.

Toward OMB 2000

On March 1, 1994, an internal OMB memorandum signed by Director Leon Panetta and Deputy Director Alice M. Rivlin announced the spearheading of a major reorganization within OMB known as OMB 2000. The reorganizational blueprint was the product of an internal self-study conducted by a steering committee staffed by OMB career staff and political appointees.

During the summer of 1993, while NPR was reinventing government, OMB had been reinventing itself. According to the memorandum, the steering committee had been charged with making "recommendations to improve OMB's efficiency and effectiveness after two decades in which OMB's responsibilities had changed substantially."[53] It interviewed 125 professionals within OMB as well as 35 former career and political employees, agency and congressional staff, and others in the budget community. In addition to the interviews, the steering committee received over 200 recommendations from personnel throughout OMB and charged all OMB branches with preparing "work profiles" including descriptions of the nature of responsibilities assumed by each office and time allotments designated for each.[54] This was easily the most intensive self-study undertaken by OMB since the 1974 study conducted by Fred Malek.

The study was undertaken for a few basic reasons. Clearly, with Vice President Gore's National Performance Review becoming the Clinton administration's major initiative designed to reform the federal bureaucracy, and with all major agencies and departments of federal government being dissected in this effort, OMB was not going to escape examination. As the OMB 2000 memorandum explains:

> The report of the National Performance Review stressed that we need to change the way the government works. . . . The Office of Management and Budget will be at the center of these efforts and it is imperative that before we assist other agencies to achieve these goals, we examine our own way of doing business.[55]

Actually, in the spring and summer of 1993, when NPR was being organized, it was very clear to OMB staff that if OMB did not reform itself, NPR would do it for them and certainly not to their liking. If OMB had not taken the proverbial "bull by the horns" and conducted a credible and self-critical self-analysis, it ran the risk of being consigned to more peripheral roles in the future. If there had not been an NPR with its attendant anti-OMB biases, would such an intensive self-study have occurred?

Probably. Deputy Director Rivlin, who was charged with managing OMB's internal decision making and organization, might well have pursued such a study. In fact, Rivlin, after being preoccupied with the herculean effort required to support the preparation of the President's first budget during the first six months of the administration, expressed a desire to take an in-depth analytic look at the complex institution in which she found herself second in command. Coming out of a think tank atmosphere, she might well have initiated such a review. All this notwithstanding, now there was no choice.

The internal memorandum announcing OMB 2000 acknowledged that the new political leadership needed and wanted to understand OMB better: "This work profile analysis gave us a welcome snapshot of how the organization works and where its resources are expended—knowledge that was hard to come by in the early days of an administration with a dynamic, all consuming agenda."[56]

From most reports, the steering committee expended great effort in order to get an accurate picture of all viewpoints, controversies, and feelings regarding OMB and its roles over the last twenty years. The project team engaged in the self-study was comprised of both junior and senior staff members who were relieved of all of their regular responsibilities during the summer of 1993. All interviewees were assured complete anonymity to the point that when the actual Steering Committee Report and Recommendations were completed in the early fall of 1993, it was not released, since, as one participant described, "they had to find a way to sanitize it so that respondent identities would not be obvious." After the steering committee completed its recommendations and report in September, the 1995 budget process put the reform process on hold for six months.

The OMB 2000 Reorganization: The Art of the Possible

The design of the OMB 2000 reorganization represented the "art of the possible" in that it responded to a number of immediate institutional dilemmas while it also restructured the organization in a way that enabled it to "better" cope with new mandates it might be confronted with in the foreseeable future. It accomplished this within the constraints imposed by limitations on available resources that had become an almost unquestionable orthodoxy in the deficit reduction climate prevalent at the time.

How the OMB Organization Chart Changed

The major feature of the OMB 2000 reorganization was its action plan to merge OMB's budget examining divisions and its management units into new Resource Management Offices (RMOs).[57] This resulted in the elimination of several management division units and the subsequent movement of staff slots into the new RMOs. The General Management Division that had been established during Richard Darman's directorate was dismantled. The Evaluation, Planning, and Management by Objectives Branch was also abolished. The staff from the Federal Services Branch and the Federal Personnel Policy Branch were integrated into the RMOs. Branches that would no longer be on the OMB organization chart after the reorganization included the Credit and Cash Management branch in the Office of Federal Financial Management and the Office of Federal Procurement Policy's Management Controls Branch. A reduced staff was to remain in the Office of Federal Financial Management and the Office of Federal Procurement Policy, both of which had been created by statute. OIRA, BRD, and LRD remained almost completely structurally intact.

The organization of agency coverage in the new RMOs closely paralleled the structure of the program divisions with one significant exception. The Human Resources Division was divided into two areas, one retaining the Human Resources designation and covering the Education, Labor, and Income Maintenance areas, and the other named Health and Personnel, covering health programs and health financing as well as the Department of Veterans Affairs, OPM, Postal Services, and the Executive Office of the President. With the Clinton administration's emphasis on health care reform, this is not surprising. An additional PAD was designated to direct the latter area. The reorganization also included a thorough integration of "special studies" units into the RMOs. These divisions had evolved into small research offices connected to each program division from management review units established during the Nixon administration. Over the years, many of these units had become separated physically as well as conceptually from the program divisions reviewing the same agencies, and some OMB staff believed that they had lost their sense of direction for those reasons.

Work Load, Morale, and Analytic Capability

The budget–management merger represented both a response to immediate staffing shortages and "morale" problems in the program divisions, and to a broader commitment to improvement in OMB's management capability. Since both OMB's management and budget responsibilities required that staff be versed in specific programmatic knowledge, the hope was that in time a "melding" of the two areas would take place in the new RMOs.

The management divisions had grown from twenty-some staff members in 1989 to almost sixty in 1993, while the program divisions had remained generally constant in size during that period.[58] This and the fact that some of the new management "hires" had entered the institution at higher entry-level salary grades than were generally applicable in the program divisions, made this "budget–management imbalance," the topic of much heated discussion during the self-study interviews. The reorganization served the purpose of addressing some of these resentments.

But program division staff egos and morale were not the only consideration in this regard. The program divisions had for years been the "heart of the institution," the place to which other staff offices looked in order to find in-depth knowledge and institutional memory regarding federal programs. As new roles had been added to OMB's "plate" over the past fifteen to twenty years, the program divisions, as a repository of programmatic information, often found themselves either completely shouldering new burdens or to some degree sharing them with other units in OMB. Consequently, program division staff often found themselves lacking the time to prepare as many programmatic studies as they had prepared in the past. Perhaps this was not a fundamental problem to the Reagan administration, which had emphasized "shrinking government," not "shrinking and reinventing what was left," but to a Democratic administration still holding firm to its vision of selective investment in government programs while at the same time reducing the deficit, OMB's long-range analytic capability was of greater importance. That directors Panetta and Rivlin subscribed to this view can be seen in the OMB 2000 Memorandum, which points to a need for more "longer-term" analysis defined as the consideration of long-term "cost and implications of policy decisions," "analyses of policy and program issues that can aid in policy development for the President," and analysis that could provide an early warning system to alert Presidents to "potential economic, budgetary, or institutional problems that are looming on the horizon."[59] The OMB 2000 memo further cites the finding that "OMB had the staff expertise to do 'mid-range' analyses," but the "pressure of immediate requirements" made such long-term analysis "often a second priority."[60]

The hope was that the integration of the budget, management, and special studies units would allow for more time to pursue such analysis, as well as to enrich staff with new perspectives which in turn would improve their analytic capabilities.

It should be noted that some observers evaluated the budget management merger as a mere ploy to garner added troops for the program divisions or to provide the opportunity to "shake out" individuals from key management positions who for one reason or another were not "producing" for the current administration. While my interviews yielded accounts of a few individuals who would have fit the latter description, those two or three cases would not have warranted a major institutional reorganization of the scope of OMB 2000.

While the program divisions did in general need additional staff, the integration of the budget and management staffs in the RMOs had the potential to be much more. In its design it provided a useful holistic approach to solving a number of OMB's problems without seeking the extra funding or staffing that was unattainable at the time. The OMB 2000 memorandum summed up its vision for these "new" units in the following way:

> The new Resource Management Offices (RMO) we will create will be neither the current budget divisions augmented by more people, nor the current management offices. In time, they will by mission, training, staffing, and operating style, be new entities unlike anything now in OMB.[61]

To this end, the RMOs were to be responsible for budget formulation and execution, "program effectiveness and efficiency," annual, mid- and long-term policy and program analysis, "implementation of government-wide management policy . . . and program evaluation."[62]

A New Kind of Budget–Management Merger: Can It Work?

As Chapter 8 concluded, the debate over whether OMB's management capability flourishes best under bifurcated or merged management and budget units has a long history as does the debate over whether any centralized institution can score large-scale improvements in managing the federal bureaucracy at large. After reviewing this history, the choice of the merger option as configured in the new RMOs can be supported for a number of reasons.

There is a large body of opinion and evidence to support the position that unless compliance with management improvement efforts are somehow linked to budget planning, such initiatives do not receive serious attention among federal managers. Richard Darman appeared to subscribe to this view when budget and management staff were brought together in his MBO and SWAT team efforts as described in Chapter 8. In that sense the OMB 2000 budget–management merger could be viewed as a natural outgrowth of some of his pilot efforts. A 1989 GAO study appraising OMB's management effectiveness during the 1980s had also concluded that "teams comprised of budget examiners and management staff blending program and management expertise" were one important way of helping OMB to understand "the problems agencies have and what it takes to solve them."[63] The GAO study cited the views of a majority of its interviewees which were made up of OMB management and budget staff as well as twelve assistant secretaries that "supported linking management issues to the budget process." Some interviewee comments "reflected the staff's view that the only really effective way to get agencies to improve their management operations is to get their considerations raised as an integral part of the budget formulation and execution processes, where OMB has the agencies' attention."[64] Both the GAO study and the self-study leading to OMB 2000 cited inadequate communications between separated budget and management divisions as leading to duplication of work efforts and the transmission of conflicting signals to Congress or the agencies.[65] To these unwelcome outcomes of budget–management staff separation can be added the tendencies for the management divisions to lack in-depth knowledge of individual programs (due to their typical involvement in government-wide management issues), and conversely for the program divisions to resist cross-cutting program analysis due to turf consciousness or the tendency for cross-cutting analysis to lead to greater overall expenditures and to consume much time.[66]

Budgetary constraints imposed by the Budget Enforcement Act may also have precipitated moves toward fusing the budget and management functions, since they forced a much greater focus on much smaller spending increments, thus magnifying the importance of "wise" management of tight funds through more careful budget execution. The Clinton administration's desire to offset costs for the President's investment priorities also argued for this approach.

Finally, "unsuccessful" budget–management mergers in both 1952 and 1973, where the demands of the budget cycle tended to subsume management-related activities, may not turn out to be applicable to the OMB 2000 reorganization. In both cases, those reorganizations failed to live up to expectations because of a lack of long-term commitment at the political levels of BOB/OMB and the White House. In the 1973 instance, the "management associates" brought into OMB's program divisions still functioned as "separate units" alongside the relevant program divisions and therefore could not be thought of as being actually merged in the same sense as was signaled in the OMB 2000 design.

OMB 2000 Parallels with NPR: Cross-Cuts and Collegiality

Certain directives in the OMB 2000 memorandum were characterized by their consistency and similarity with those found in the National Performance Review report. One such theme is a commitment in the OMB 2000 plan to formulate budgets, to the degree possible, through functional policy areas that cross-cut traditional agency account areas.[67] The emphasis in related NPR analyses was on the advancement of collaborative approaches to reaching "informed choices across program lines."[68] In other words, certain significant public policy issue areas would be considered in a holistic way by jointly reviewing all relevant agency budgets.

Another theme that the OMB 2000 reorganization had in common with NPR's recommendations was the stated intent to transform the essential character of OMB–agency relationships from the "adversarial" to the "collegial," and to change budget preparation processes into quasi agency–OMB team endeavors, an approach that had also already been given a trial run in the 1995 budget process. The OMB 2000 memorandum's admission that "we have responded to concerns raised by the National Performance Review about OMB–agency relations," suggests that this OMB–agency "collegiality" recommendation may have been included at least in part in deference to the Vice President and NPR.[69]

To this end, the OMB 2000 memorandum gives OMB staff very specific guidelines to govern their behavior when communicating with or eliciting information from federal agencies. While it recognizes the sometimes intrinsic adversarial nature of OMB–agency relations, it also communicates disapproval of the "alleged" arrogant demeanor of some OMB staff by articulating sanctions for such behaviors. OMB staff performance evaluations would thus include an "additional element on maintaining good relations with agencies," and "promotions, bonuses, and awards" would be denied to staff who were "consistently the subject of valid agency complaints," and some of these staff would be ultimately asked to leave OMB.[70]

A Long-Needed "Internal" Management Committee

Finally, the OMB 2000 reorganization addressed an important area too often neglected in BOB/OMB's seventy-five-year history when it established an internal management committee structure that was designed to outlast the tenure of any one administration. The committee included two non-career staff, seven career managers and professional staff, the Assistant Director for Administration, and one support staff person. It was to advise the director and the Office of Administration on matters related to personnel, organization, and hiring. The OMB 2000 memorandum stressed that it would "serve as an institutional memory on internal management."[71]

OMB 2000: Congressional Relations and Politicization

The OMB 2000 memorandum also addressed the issues of OMB's congressional monitorship role and potentially politicizing trends related to it. It is worthwhile to note what it did not do. It did not turn back the clock and remove the reconstituted RMOs from the congressional tracking functions that had evolved over the previous twenty years. In fact, the memorandum pondered "how OMB can improve its decision making processes to parallel more closely those in Congress, and how it can more effectively make the case for an administration's policies."[72] It not only acknowledged OMB's congressional monitorship role, but sought to improve its capacity to perform this function without compromising career staff.

To this end, it pointed to two areas where its authors had concluded that OMB had fallen short. The first was structural in the sense that it centered around the fact that OMB program division organization did not parallel that of the appropriations subcommittees. This organizational structure often resulted in making several examiners in different program division branches responsible for the account areas that comprised a single appropriations bill. The memorandum faulted this arrangement for leaving OMB without a coordinated intelligence-gathering capacity in each appropriations area. The second dilemma was an outgrowth of this problem, in that OMB was criticized for not having the ability to foresee competing "policy trade-offs" among and within the appropriations subcommittees.[73]

These concerns, of course, reflected the centrality of the appropriations committees in the congressional budget process after the Budget Enforcement Act. In addition, the fact that Director Panetta had labored so assiduously to save pieces of the President's investment package during the 1993 congressional appropriations process provided further impetus for an enhanced predictive capacity in OMB with respect to the dynamics of political "horse trading" in the appropriations committees. So did the reality of scarce resources under increasingly rigid discretionary budget caps.

The OMB 2000 memorandum, however, stopped short of reorganizing OMB's RMOs along parallel lines with the appropriations committees, opting instead for what it called a more "process-oriented" approach. OMB was then charged with devising a process whereby it would better be able to advise the President as to potential Appropriations Committee trade-offs, before passback and before his final review of OMB decisions.[74] The memo also prescribed a more thorough BRD tracking process involving appropriations action to include "periodic rack-ups of agency requests and tentative decisions by subcommittee jurisdictions."[75]

How did the OMB 2000 approach plan to accomplish all of this "quasi-political" information gathering without further politicizing OMB? To resolve this question, the self-study group questioned a cross-section of OMB staff and outside experts on the issue of OMB politicization. According to the memo, the findings presented an array of opinion on this matter, and confirmed that staff attitudes still varied widely in this regard. The OMB 2000 Memorandum observed that "most agree that staff should provide

information or technical assistance to Hill staff on an administration's policies. Advocacy, however, is the other extreme and most career staff agree
that it is inappropriate."[76] The Director and Deputy Director then staked out
their middle-ground verdict on this issue.

> We tend to agree that OMB career staff can actively support enactment of a
> President's agenda without becoming "politicized." Staff should be able to
> explain an administration's policies, but should not get into the business of
> making deals or trades on policy issues or legislation. The latter are clearly the
> domain of those appointed by a President to represent an administration.[77]

Finally, the memorandum espoused a commitment to instituting consistent institution-wide policies to guide OMB staff in their interactions with
Congress. In this and in its other directives, the OMB 2000 blueprint endorsed the advancement of OMB's congressional monitorship role. OMB's
management team seemed to be saying that career staff should be able to
explain the President's policies, to know the politics, anticipate the politics,
but not assume "deal-making" or negotiating roles better left to political
appointees. And this was to be accomplished with consistent "rules of engagement" throughout the institution.[78]

"Building Bridges Between the Two Buildings":
OMB 2000 and Communications Lines

Overall, there had been a pronounced improvement in the communications
between OMB career staff and the office's director, deputy director, and
most other political-level staff. Much of this change can be attributed to
Panetta and Rivlin's personalities and their stated commitment to seeking
ways to build bridges between the New Executive Office Building, which
housed OMB career staff, and the Old Executive Office Building housing
the PADs and OMB Directors. This emphasis on advancing better internal
OMB communications had been observed by a number of OMB career staff
interviewees and was documented by a number of the Directors' written
statements in the OMB 2000 proposal. These included the stated preference
for both junior and senior career staff to attend meetings with political-level
officials and the endorsement of the practice of having individual career
staffers personally sign analytic papers to provide the opportunity for political-level officials to become aware of OMB staff expertise on particular
subjects of interest to them.[79] Another indication of improved internal communications was the fact that Directors' Reviews now included more career
staff than had generally been the case under Richard Darman.

To further gauge the degree to which internal OMB communications were allowed to advance from career staff levels to that of the OMB Director, four PADs were questioned to determine whether they presented OMB career staff information and views to the directors in cases where those positions tended to run counter to their personal conclusions on the topic at hand. On this issue, all of the PADs interviewed indicated that they did communicate information and positions under such circumstances to the director, with half responding that they generally did so, and half explaining that they only transmitted those views they considered "reasonable."

While internal communications appeared to have taken a turn for the better in OMB, OMB career staff communications with the White House and other EOP offices presented somewhat more of a mixed picture. For example, in one case an RMO branch chief found such communication "better than in any other administration," while another career staff manager perceived much "less of a direct line to the White House" than had existed in his area in the past. Another communications problem that can be generated in a multiple advocacy advisory system such as that found in the Clinton administration is the tendency for career staff to sometimes receive different "signals" from the various political-level advisory offices while attempting to garner policy guidance from political-level officials. Whether this constituted a significant problem in OMB–EOP communications dynamics during the first two years of the Clinton administration is unclear.

The Clinton Transition: Changes Within Changes

The first year and a half of the Clinton administration presented challenges for OMB from a number of sources. The change in the President's party after twelve years represented just one transformation for OMB. The Clinton administration's philosophy regarding the departments and agencies and its decision to create new units to share power with OMB were perhaps more significant to OMB's institutional status. From the administration's new perspectives grew experimentation with modified budget preparation procedures, an institutional self-study and reorganization for OMB, and different prescribed stances for OMB staff to assume when they communicated with Executive Branch agencies. Some of the dynamics in the relationships between political appointees and OMB career staff during the transition had mirrored behavioral cycles from past administrations. In all, a lot had happened.

OMB staff did not have much time to theorize about the implications of these changes. Within the next year, they would experience the reality of the reorganization itself; Alice Rivlin would become OMB Director; Leon

Panetta would move to the White House to become President Clinton's chief of staff; and the November 1994 Republican takeover of both houses of Congress would reinstate the budget process dynamics of divided government. Each of these developments in its own way would alter the nature of OMB's work, its usefulness to and clout with the White House, and its relationships with the agencies and the Congress.

10

Beyond the Deluge:
The Clinton OMB after the
1994 Election

Transitions: Summer and Fall of 1994

Panetta and Rivlin Move Up a Notch

In late June of 1994, not long after the OMB 2000 reorganization, Leon Panetta was appointed to be President Clinton's chief of staff. While rapid turnover of associate or deputy directorships due to promotion to White House or other positions had posed a problem at OMB for many years, tenures of recent directors had been more stable. Panetta's year and a half stint in the position was the shortest since Bert Lance left the institution after only eight months. However, while Lance was forced to resign under the shadow of conflict-of-interest charges, Panetta was rising to the most critical staff position in the White House as something of a hero.

Leon Panetta had won both the President's and the Congress's respect and admiration by projecting an image of honesty and being willing to give the President accurate economic facts. An inscription to Panetta from the President that hung in Panetta's office at the time is telling: "To Leon, who taught me things that turned my hair grey—but who shows no visible wear and tear himself."[1]

Panetta's pedagogical role for the Chief Executive was probably not the main motivator for the promotion. His talents as a congressional negotiator were of critical importance in bringing him into a key White House position, as the administration's health care plan appeared to be foundering on Capitol Hill. Then there was the issue of establishing order and central control in a White House staff organization composed in large part of young professionals who lacked Washington and Executive Branch experience. Since OMB's process-oriented disciplines had sharply contrasted with other more loosely organized EOP and White House units, the hope had been that Panetta could offer some of this discipline in his new job.

Alice Rivlin, dubbed by Leon Panetta as the "conscience of the budget process,"[2] was getting the top OMB job in spite of her misstatements to the press and at least one reported clash with the President himself over the elimination of farm subsidies.[3] Rivlin, whom *Congressional Quarterly's Weekly Report* characterized as representing "the most hawkish end of the spectrum"[4] of administration opinion on deficit reduction, was to face an easy confirmation process.

The 1994 "Pre-Election" Budget Process

Meanwhile, at the time of the OMB directorship transition, the beginning of the FY 1996 budget process was rapidly moving forward. At that point it was looking a lot like a "modified" version of the 1995 process. Alice Rivlin's preconfirmation responses to the Senate Committee on Governmental Affairs' questions described that process in the following way:

> The new direction in budget decision making, emphasizing more communication and interaction, has continued to be refined and improved for the FY 1996 budget. Agencies again received early guidance of their allocations for FY 1996 under the discretionary spending and FTE limits established in the law. OMB has also continued budget meetings with other elements of the White House and Treasury to discuss cross-cutting budget issues for the FY 1996 budget and the longer term.[5]

One change from the previous year was evident. While the practice of providing early guidance to the agencies had survived from the 1995 process, there is no mention of the formal meetings including Cabinet and agency officials that had occurred at the beginning of the process the year before. This change, in addition to an observation in Bob Woodward's book, *The Agenda,* suggests the somewhat speculative conclusion that the President's experiences during the 1995 process may have alerted him to some of the limitations of Cabinet government, especially when it involved departmental competition over scarce funds. Woodward wrote,

> Panetta was fielding requests from the departments for their 1995 budgets. Secretary of State Christopher requested an additional $2 billion. "What is he doing?" Clinton asked Panetta. "There's no way we can suddenly find $2

billion out of thin air." Panetta felt that Clinton was beginning to catch on, and he was glad when the President rejected the request.[6]

Two priority areas were to play increasingly significant roles in early planning for the 1996 budget. They were the NPR-initiated "streamlining" of 272,900 Executive Branch positions by 1999, and the beginning of OMB's efforts to comply with an important new statute, the Government Performance Review and Results Act of 1993.

OMB and Streamlining

In 1993, NPR had recommended the elimination of approximately 250,000 Executive Branch personnel slots. This proposal was later codified in statute and increased to about 272,900 reductions by 1999, by the Federal Work Restructure Act of 1994. A "buyout" program to encourage federal workers to retire or leave their jobs voluntarily in return for payments of up to $25,000 had also been authorized by Congress to ease the personal dislocation of this downsizing process.

While agencies were to designate their own "streamlining" and "buyout" plans within the strictures imposed by the law, by September of 1994 OMB was nonetheless intensively involved in reviewing agency plans in both areas. According to Alice Rivlin's confirmation testimony, OMB was at that time in its "third cycle of receipt and review of agencies' streamlining plans," which were considered to be "an integral part of the Fiscal Year 1996 Budget Process."[7] Through this process, OMB was assuming a traditionally directive enforcement role with the agencies. By the end of September of 1994, OMB had only approved a small percentage of the potential agency buyout plans, since allegedly many agencies were proposing to offer significant numbers of buyouts without presenting credible plans for commensurate downsizing. OMB and NPR appeared to be working in tandem on this effort. A press report that the "streamlining plans" had not satisfied the Vice President cited an immediate follow-up memorandum to the agencies from Rivlin indicating that their "revised" streamlining and buyout plans would play a critical role in 1996 budget decisions.[8]

The Government Performance Review and Results Act (GPRA): Yet Another OMB Mission

In the summer of 1993, while OMB was conducting its self-study and OMB and NPR were covertly jousting over OMB's future role, Congress passed yet another bureaucratic reform package that was signed by President Clinton. It had been spearheaded by Senator William V. Roth, Jr. (R-Delaware), who had nurtured the idea of "a smaller, more efficient government built on performance measurement and accountability since the early 1980s."[9] As its title suggests, the GPRA aimed at revitalizing bureaucratic missions through systematic linkages of clearly defined agency goals with measurements of how well those agencies were realizing the intended results. The act set out an action plan and schedule for implementing these goals. All agencies were responsible for preparing overall strategic plans by September of 1997 and a minimum of ten agencies would be required to participate in pilot projects to determine agency missions and to design indicators to determine if agency objectives were being met. All agencies were required to submit annual performance plans by fiscal 1999, and to actually begin preparing annual performance reports by March 31, 2000.

OMB was given a pivotal role in this legislation in that it, in conjunction with the affected agency, was made responsible for designing the pilot projects, for reviewing their outcomes, and for reporting conclusions to Congress by May of 1997. OMB was also designated with the responsibility for submitting a performance plan for the entire Executive Branch.

While GPRA had been Senator Roth's brainchild, newly confirmed OMB Director Alice Rivlin embraced it wholeheartedly both before and after the 1994 congressional elections. Rivlin testified at her confirmation hearings that if there had not been a GPRA during her tenure at OMB, she would have been trying to advance performance measurement anyway. She also endorsed GPRA as being "a very well designed law."[10]

In August of 1994, in order to begin to determine a process for implementing GPRA as well as to discuss the agency streamlining and downsizing issues, virtually the entire OMB professional staff participated in two days of discussion and brainstorming in small groups. These "dialogues," as they were called, reflected the Clinton administration's emphasis on "teamwork" and had been carefully planned and organized for several weeks in advance by the new Deputy Director for Management, John Koskinen, and his staff. Eighty to ninety percent of staff from OMB's RMOs and statutory offices attended the sessions,[11] which featured "team leaders" and "recorders" and allowed for inputs from different institutional perspectives to be aired. The conclusions that were derived from these discussions were then transmitted to the agencies in order to give them initial guidance in their efforts to develop performance measurements and downsizing plans to be included in their FY 1996 budget requests.

NPR–OMB Relations: Act II

By the fall of 1994, the temper of relations between NPR and OMB had improved somewhat, at least on the surface. A year had passed since the publication of the initial NPR report, the 1995 budget process had exposed NPR-derived alterations in the budget process to a reality test, and OMB had reorganized itself. With the streamlining of the bureaucracy and the supervision of the government buyouts, OMB and NPR were now working hand in hand, with OMB playing a more directive role toward the agencies than had been the case in 1993.

Threats of diminishing OMB's overall raison d'être seemed far reduced. One NPR staffer observed that once the original NPR report had been published, thus becoming "presidential policy," OMB career staff "fell into line and became good soldiers" by playing an important role in securing congressional passage of NPR-backed proposals. Another NPR official later acknowledged OMB's contributions toward implementing the streamlining processes. The fact that OMB staff seemed to be generally supportive of their future involvement in the "Performance Review" process and that NPR had also envisioned this as an appropriate OMB role had helped to ease the tensions. Many of the more emotional "OMB-bashers" had left NPR and had returned to their agencies. Those who remained were purportedly quieter about OMB.

This changed environment is evident in the tone taken in some of the more recently released budget process monographs. For example, an NPR Status Report published in September of 1994, briefly summarized and endorsed the OMB 2000 plan by quoting highly favorable assessments of the OMB 2000 reorganization by Donald Kettl of the Brookings Institution, and cited Kettl's characterization of the reorganization as a " 'transformation within people,' not a reshuffling of boxes."[12]

The discussion of the so-called Executive Budget Resolution in NPR's "Mission-Driven, Results-Oriented Budgeting," the follow-up budget process monograph that took about a year to be released, appeared to have represented a compromise between NPR and OMB after many months of negotiating. Its complimentary wording toward OMB is illustrative. For example,

> Revisions to the traditional process were piloted shortly after President Clinton took office. This process was more open; it set broad policy priorities; and it considered cross-cutting policy initiatives affecting each agency. OMB expanded the roles of the White House staff and other policy groups, such as the National Economic Council, the Domestic Policy Council, and the National Security Council. OMB went to great lengths to involve Executive Branch leaders in budget decisions and to communicate priorities.[13]

OMB had also won some degree of respect among those attempting to further NPR's goals of "making government work better and cost less," and for "being very good at fostering discipline in the agencies," as a high-level NPR official explained.

However, all of this did not mean that NPR was willing to endorse or encourage OMB to exercise a broad level of discretion in micro-managing the agencies. This latter point is evident from other excerpts from the NPR monograph where political-level and White House and agency officials are recognized for their teamwork, but OMB and agency staffs are told that they would be expected to "work collaboratively in budget development as well. . . ."[14]

Also on the unpopular "apportionment footnotes," NPR continued to recommend changes. The monograph stated:

> Policy decisions should be relayed by OMB policy officials by means other than apportionments. . . . Any exceptions to the letter apportionments process should be explained to the affected agency. . . .[15]

This would not be the final chapter in the evolution of OMB relationships with NPR or the agencies during the Clinton administration. There would be new twists and turns after the upcoming election.

OIRA During the Clinton Administration: A New Chapter?

The Clinton administration's use of OIRA during its first year had clearly reflected its interest in pursuing a middle-of-the-road course with regard to regulation. As one observer opined with regard to OMB regulatory review under President Clinton, "They want win-win solutions."[16]

While immediately after his inauguration President Clinton had abolished the Competitiveness Council and rescinded all Bush administration regulations not yet published in the *Federal Register,* Clinton administration actions did not suggest a desire to divest the administration of the ability to centrally control the regulatory process through OIRA. Accordingly, OIRA had been one of the few units in OMB that was not disturbed by the OMB 2000 reorganization.

Executive Order 12,866, which had delineated regulatory review procedures for the Clinton administration, retained centralized regulatory review responsibilities, but under clear new guidelines designed to allow for expanded public disclosure of OIRA's internal decision-making processes and its communications with interest groups and agencies. The Executive Order that was promulgated on September 30, 1993, to replace Reagan–Bush order 12,291, had been developed by an ad hoc working group headed by new OIRA Administrator and Vice President Gore's chief of staff. The group had consulted with representatives from both public interest groups and industry.[17] It cited the restoration of openness, "integrity and legitimacy of regulatory review and oversight," and the "primacy of federal agencies in the regulatory decision-making process" as fundamental objectives.[18]

To these ends, the order addressed most of the alleged deficiencies of OIRA during the Reagan–Bush years. For example, all oral and written communications between OIRA and any outside groups or individuals were to be shared with the involved agency within ten days, and agency representatives were to be invited to meetings between outside parties and OIRA.[19] OIRA was required to keep logs recording the status of rule reviews, written communications to the agency, and a record of oral communications with outside parties.[20] The order dictated that documents exchanged between OIRA and the agency were to be made available to the public upon completion of the review process.[21] Agencies were instructed to choose regulatory approaches that would take into account quantifiable as well as qualitative measures of costs and benefits of proposed regulations, and to "select those approaches that maximize net benefits including potential economic, environmental, public health and safety. . . ."[22] Finally, to address the dilemma of extended delays in the regulatory process, OIRA was to be bound by a ninety-day deadline for completion of most rule reviews.[23]

One year after the promulgation of the Executive Order, a study of regulatory oversight in the Clinton administration found the regulatory review process to be "more open, timely, and rigorous," and both "less contentious,"[24] and less disproportionately driven by business as opposed to public interest representatives.[25] The study also documented a reduction of delays in the process. From November 1993 through March of 1994, only three regulatory reviews were found to have been extended beyond the ninety-day deadline.[26]

However, the study's author was not without qualifications in his praise of the recent changes in regulatory review in the Clinton administration. One concern was that the Executive Order did not require OIRA to disclose its communications with the President and the Vice President, thus creating an opening for interest groups to view the White House as a "backdoor" avenue through which to influence decisions.[27] The author cautioned that this could give interest groups "an incentive to harden their positions with the agency writing the rules."[28] Another difficulty identified in the study was that OIRA did not always have enough time to meet the regulatory review deadlines, particularly when dealing with certain complex and detailed regulatory issues.[29]

The October Leak: A Pre-Election Tremor

In October, about a month before the 1994 congressional election, an internal administration deficit reduction options paper under Director Rivlin's signature was leaked to the press. The document, which was only intended for review by a very few administration insiders, demonstrated that maintenance of the projected FY 1995 deficit levels of $168 billion until the year 2000 would require $184 billion in new spending reductions or tax increases over the five-year period.[30] The paper also outlined six potential budgetary action plans and some of their projected implications. Three of these continued the momentum of deficit reduction "on a downward track."[31] One of the other plans presented a $719 billion price tag in additional savings or revenue that would be required to provide for much of the investment spending the President had envisioned for his administration.[32] Other scenarios provided formulas for actually bringing the budget into balance by the year 2000, but showed commensurate projected cuts or needed revenue increases of about $690 billion.[33]

The paper also presented a series of strategies for achieving different degrees of deficit reduction or budget balance including cuts in discretionary spending, entitlements, and tax increases, all of which were standard focal points in deficit reduction discussions among budget policy experts. The memo then pointed out the potential "political" perils of pursuing some of these strategies. For example, it warned that the "90 percent of savings [would] come from Social Security and Medicare, and would probably be labeled by opponents as tax increases."[34]

Rivlin was later quoted in the press as saying that no recommendations were given to the President in the memo and that the purpose of the document had been "to bring the President up to speed on the debate" and that the options "are not necessarily our options."[35]

According to columnist Hobart Rowan of the *Washington Post,* the closest the memo came to offering an implicit recommendation was through one of the options that was designed to "build on our commitment to make life better for the average citizen in New Democrat style by taking on the special interests and eliminating tax loopholes and spending giveaways that favor the few while hurting growth."[36]

Soon after the memo was leaked to the press, a Republican National Committee press release entitled "The 'Big Lie' Exposed," characterized by Rowan as a "truly wicked distortion," claimed "that Rivlin and the administration favored getting 90 percent of spending cuts from Social Security and Medicare.[37] Rivlin was criticized for writing the memo and the administration was portrayed as having *decided* "politically" unacceptable options two weeks before the election.

It became clear soon after the leak occurred that it had not emanated from OMB, and it was traced to the Treasury Department.[38] The contents of the memo, particularly as framed by administration opponents, were viewed as placing the administration at political risk so close to the November election and later as foreclosing the President from using some of the deficit reduction strategies outlined in the options paper in the near future, since he would feel compelled to renounce some of them during the election.[39]

There are a couple of ironies connected with this incident that are worth noting. The first highlights OMB's specific difficulties finding a place for itself within the decision-making structures created by the Clinton administration. The irony here is that the damaging leak originated not from OMB, which had allegedly been viewed with suspicion by some Clinton White House newcomers, but from the Cabinet component of the President's economic team that was supposed to serve as a "check" against OMB. The second irony is related to the long-standing dilemma of what OMB's appropriate role should be in the increasingly politicized atmosphere within which budget and economic policies are forged. In this case, the potentially provocative options listed were not "presidential policy." Alice Rivlin's preparation of the deficit reduction options paper represented an OMB Director doing her job, or for that matter, the OMB carrying out its most fundamental mission—that of presenting objective information and options to the President based on the most up-to-date statistics available at the time.

This incident raises troubling questions. Given the adversarial and visible climate within which budget decisions were reached at the time, should Director Rivlin have declined from putting pen to paper so soon before an election, or should the administration have directed her not to do so? Does this institutional arm of the presidency now have to internally censor the very information and advice that defines its fundamental utility for the President? The affirmative response to either of these questions (which many observers of the political process today might offer) calls into question whether it is possible for OMB to operate as a purveyor of objective guidance without risking the political survivability of the Presidents it serves. While such risks and conflicts have always surrounded BOB/OMB's role for the presidency, the contentious environment created by recent "deficit" politics heightened it considerably.

Former CEA Chair Herbert Stein came to Alice Rivlin's defense after the incident, commenting that "her sin had been to tell the truth."[40] However, in the climate that surrounded deficit reduction debates in the 1994 congressional elections, being associated with the "truth" and its unavoidable policy-making implications could easily be misrepresented to an electorate unwilling to make "personal" sacrifices for the deficit reduction it demanded be accomplished with *someone else's* nickel. In this instance, the entire brouhaha surrounded not even the memo in question, but a distortion of the memo.

And, of course, the environment was to become even more charged. In November 1994, the Republican Party recaptured a majority of the Senate and the House of Representatives.

Its "Contract with America" pledged a balanced budget in seven years. Now deficit solutions would once again be left to a divided government. OMB would be operating under familiar conditions experienced in the 1980s, with the partisanship of the key protagonists reversed. It would find itself able to be useful to the President in ways it perhaps had not foreseen.

Initial Reaction to the Election

While political analysts and pundits continue to disagree on the precise nature of the message being communicated by the voters in the 1994 Republican takeover of both houses of Congress, one observation of relevance to the topic at hand can be safely offered. The first sustained deficit reduction since a 1986–87 decline driven by the Gramm–Rudman–Hollings Act was either not being credited to the Clinton administration or was not salient enough to the electorate to supersede other voter dissatisfactions. While some in the media and some budget experts later attributed at least partial kudos for the 1993–94 deficit decline of roughly $100 billion to the administration's 1993 budget package,[41] public reaction could still be characterized as demanding deficit reduction, but not being willing to pay for it. These perceived political realities would factor into the administration's actions in the months to come. Polls at the time indicated that many voters were not even aware that the deficit had dropped.

The outcome of the November 1994 plebiscite would also alter OMB's status among presidential budgetary and economic advisory units as it would offer OMB a greater incentive to recommend cuts, a task some would say it does best. But with a Republican Congress determined to dismantle, privatize, or devolve responsibility for whole program mandates to the states, OMB was not to constitute the primary threat to the survival of many programs. OMB and NPR would increasingly work as a team in sifting through "the basic missions of government to find and eliminate things that don't need to be done by the federal government and sort out how best to do the things the federal government should continue to do."[42] To accomplish these goals would be to demonstrate that the administration was paying heed to perceived anti–big government sentiments in the electorate and at the same time protecting against potentially unwise excesses should they be proposed by the Congress.

Post-Election Restructuring and "REGO II"

The election, which occurred during the first Director's Review process of Alice Rivlin's directorship, had forced an administration-wide rethinking of the FY 1996 budget. Regarding the budget, the Clinton administration's initial reaction and response to the election was twofold: First was to be the unveiling in mid-December of a proposed $60 billion tax cut directed at "middle-class" Americans and a modest $16 billion deficit-reduction package, to be paid for by significant downsizing in five domestic agencies—the Department of Housing and Urban Development (HUD), the Department of Transportation (DOT), the Office of Personnel Management (OPM), the Department of Energy (DOE), and the General Services Administration (GSA). Second was the announcement of a second phase of Vice President Gore's "Reinventing of Government" (REGO II), an initiative that extended beyond REGO I in its assertion that government agencies needed to question the utility of their fundamental missions. As part of this effort, collaborative working groups with representatives from the agencies, NPR, OMB, the President's Management Council,[43] and White House policy staffs[44] were to examine ways in which some agency functions could be privatized, devolved to state and local government, or completely eliminated.[45] For those activities in which a federal presence was deemed essential, the teams were to investigate how service to the public could be improved.

Soon after the election, OMB's RMOs were submerged in a period of intensive activity to produce analysis, to clarify issues, and to facilitate communication between the White House and the agencies as part of the effort to derive adequate savings for the President's proposed tax cut and to support the more formalized REGO II process. There is anecdotal evidence that the analysis produced by OMB staff during this period engendered new respect for its ability to serve the Clinton administration among NPR staff as well as other political appointees.

The "First" 1996 Budget

On February 6, 1995, President Clinton submitted a $1.6 trillion budget proposal to Congress that included $140 billion in spending cuts over a five-year period, the $60 billion package of tax cuts that had been proposed in December, and an additional $80 billion in cuts from "freezes or reductions in some domestic programs," and from the elimination and consolidation of "130 small programs and agencies."[46] Even so, the budget, which did not reduce Social Security, Medicare, Medicaid, or raise taxes, projected continued deficits of about $200 billion in each of the coming seven years.[47]

During White House discussions in December of 1994, OMB Director Alice Rivlin was characterized by Elizabeth Drew as being virtually the only top-level advisor to argue forcefully in opposition to the tax cut.[48] There were also indications that the "institutional" OMB had cloaked itself in its budget-cutting mantle as well during this period. Paul Light had written that the President had been "pushed hard by the Office of Management and Budget to come up with cuts to match those floated by Republicans in Congress."[49]

Other advisors, some of whom had been deficit hawks during the previous two budget processes, offered economic as well as political arguments counter to that approach and were more supportive of the actual 1996 budget proposal submitted to Congress. These included White House Chief of Staff Leon Panetta, outgoing Treasury Secretary Lloyd Bentsen, Treasury Secretary designate Robert Rubin, and CEA Chair Laura Tyson.[50] A substantial portion of the motivation for this position was linked to the supposition that the administration had received almost no credit for its previous efforts at reducing the deficit.[51] Continuing this line of reasoning, some observers interpreted the President's 1996 budget proposal as a tactic intended to throw the gauntlet to Congress to support its claims that it could balance the budget in seven years by producing a budget plan with the politically unpopular cuts that would be required to realize that objective.[52]

OMB Staff Status Undergoes "Perceptible Shift"

To some degree, it seemed that OMB's place in the Clinton administration's "pecking order" had risen in the months that followed the November election. OMB staff had been providing the administration with valuable services in a variety of ways after the election. While decisions on "which" agencies or departments were to be downsized were made at the White House, the RMOs were able to make genuine contributions to the development of the plans. In some of REGO II's "team" efforts with NPR and the agencies, OMB was able to facilitate communications between the White House, NPR, and the agencies. A number of Clinton political appointees contrasted the high quality of OMB's input into this "restructuring" effort with what they considered to be inferior proposals produced by the affected agencies. One high-level NPR official credited the OMB PADs for much of the high-quality work that was produced. Those PADs interviewed for this study, in turn, expressed ample praise for their career staffs in this regard.

When the new Congress assumed office, many of the OMB career staffers had played a useful role by establishing initial communications between the staffs of incoming new members, the Republican leadership apparatus, and the administration. Perceived as relatively objective intermediaries, OMB career staff were able to assist congressional staff newcomers on procedural questions and thereby pave the way for the communications with the Clinton administration PADs that would follow. These contacts would also be valuable in the coming months in 1995 as RMO staff became increasingly involved in tracking legislative developments on the Hill.

The election and the subsequent REGO II effort also further precipitated the evolution of better working relationships between OMB and NPR with an outright acknowledgment on the part of one NPR interviewee of the necessity that OMB take the lead in some administration initiatives due to its established institutional structure. In addition, OMB–agency relationships continued to change. With many programs vulnerable to *congressional* targeting, there were greater incentives for agencies to cooperate with OMB and NPR's efforts to defend at least some agency functions as being both essential and efficiently and economically implemented. In this endeavor, according to some OMB staff, there even were instances during the REGO II restructuring process in which OMB had intervened to protect smaller programs from being sacrificed by their own agencies. As one staffer explained, these programs performed important functions, but had few political constituencies to support them.

Though it may have been coincidental, beginning in December of 1994, OMB career staff started receiving invitations to the White House. (Two more such invitations followed in the coming months: one in August of 1995 and one in October for the First Lady's birthday.) Coincidental or not, some though not all OMB interviewees perceived themselves to be more appreciated, valued, and listened to than ever before during the Clinton administration. Some interviewees described outright positive feedback from political appointees as evidence of this.

Some part of this new "appreciation" of OMB was attributed to the fact that Leon Panetta's presence in the White House had elevated OMB's status in the eyes of top administration officials and the President. Others perceived that this increased understanding and esteem of OMB was already taking hold well before the fall election, as the President had become more familiar with OMB career staff. One high-level OMB career staff person attributed the White House invitations entirely to Panetta and Rivlin's desire to reward OMB staff for their work efforts.

Spring Review Restored

Even while the White House and OMB coped with the aftermath of the elections, Director Rivlin and her chief deputies did not allow momentum on the implementation of the Government Performance and Results Act to falter. There were now political incentives as well to "keep the ball rolling." The GPRA legislation had been conceived by Senator Roth, who was now the new Chair of the Senate Committee on Governmental Affairs, the committee most involved in overseeing government-wide management issues as well as OMB operations. Using the GPRA process could provide objective evidence to protect well-performing programs from arbitrary cuts, suggest better ways to manage scarce funds, and rationally determine what activities had outlived their usefulness.

Two important objectives for then Deputy Director Rivlin even back in 1993 had been to enhance OMB's long-term analytic capability and as part of that effort to restore the Spring Planning Review process that had been abandoned during the early 1980s (see Chapter 6). Now under the rubric of attending to the difficult process of guiding the agencies in their efforts to produce strategic plans and develop performance measures, OMB held a Spring Review in March of 1995.

The process of developing performance indicators that were hand-tailored to specific programs was complex and initially required a narrowing of the virtually limitless criteria upon which program performance could be judged. The RMOs were charged with this task in preparation for the OMB Spring Review, which was designed to further refine the criteria to be considered in the performance measures. Some, but not all, agencies were able to schedule meetings with OMB to offer their initial guidance to OMB with regard to this task. One agency interviewee believed that the preliminary meetings between his agency and OMB had precipitated an elevation in the level of analysis and sophistication of thinking in his agency. While the RMO staff were given broad discretion in preparing their analysis for the Spring Review, they did receive guidance that the evaluation techniques should be clear and understandable enough to be "explainable to the typical taxpayer."

The Spring Reviews held in March of 1995 resembled Director's Reviews in their format, with the PADs and the Director working with a Director's Review book and RMO staff presenting recommendations. Decisions reached through this Spring Review process were then communicated to the agencies in "Strategic Guidance" letters directed toward giving the agencies detailed programmatic guidance to be used in preparing their 1997 budget proposals. One agency budget staff interviewee described this guidance as "good stuff and not micro-management." This guidance was then to be used to evaluate agency requests during the Director's Review in the fall. In order to afford the RMOs broader perspective of issues that cross-cut their agency turf areas, each was given a copy of the Spring Review book for the other RMOs.

Though some interviewees observed that various performance measures had been part of their repertoires for evaluating programs for many years, most of those interviewed expressed positive views of GPRA's methodology and the fact that the director had emphasized it. One long-time OMB staffer commented, "We've been doing this kind of analysis for years here, but the advantage of this process is to drive home new realities to the agencies and actually get the Assistant Secretaries to listen."

The June Balanced Budget Plan

By the spring, both the House and Senate Republicans had produced but not agreed upon plans to balance the budget in seven years. The House plan included a $353 billion tax cut as well, while the Senate version proposed $170 billion in tax cuts, which were only to go into effect upon passage of their deficit reduction plan.[53] While there was not unified Democratic support for the President to produce his own budget balancing proposal, a White House determination was made that the President now had to generate a plan of his own.

According to OMB career staff, as the administration decided to examine the potential contours of its own "ten-year" budget balancing proposal, the White House was unusually apprehensive over the prospect of a leak to the press occurring before the plan was fully formulated, perhaps because of the experience of the previous October. Consequently, at first only the PADs and BRD were included in the initial "running of the numbers" on the broad options that had been determined in the White House. However, after this point it became necessary for the RMOs to join yet another intensive work effort to fill in estimates for individual programs. It became a point of pride in a number of 1995 career staff interviews that there had been absolutely no leaks to the press during this agency "blackout" period when units other than OMB had not been involved in the process. There was a tone among OMB career staff of again trying to prove their trustworthiness and utility to the White House. After the agency "blackout," the RMO estimates had then been submitted to the agencies for review before receiving final approval in the White House.

The balanced budget plan announced by President Clinton on national television on June 13 involved an effort to balance the budget in ten as opposed to the Republicans' seven years, through $128 million in cuts from Medicare, $54 billion in savings from Medicaid, about $197 billion in reductions from discretionary nondefense programs, and $3 billion in cuts from defense spending.[54] While this "second 1996" budget proposal trimmed much more spending than had the February budget, its cuts in

Medicare and Medicaid were less drastic than were either the House or Senate proposals.[55] The proposal's $105 billion tax cut was about $250 billion less than was the House of Representative's revenue reduction plan. That and the ten- as opposed to seven-year "deadline" allowed for increases in spending in certain designated "priority" areas including education, training, environmental protection, and medical research.[56]

Another difference between the White House and the Republican proposals were their economic assumptions and the future projections they were based upon. The Presidents' June balanced budget plan was almost immediately dismissed by Congress, allegedly because of its "rosy" economic assumptions.[57] This rejection of the plan was to be the first shot in what would become another OMB–CBO estimating war reminiscent of those in the 1980s, but with greater implications.

OMB 2000: Early Verdicts

Introduction

The OMB 2000 reorganization had yet to pass the reality test of meeting its key objectives while coping in OMB's typical atmosphere marked by "firefighting" and crisis management. The twenty-month period after the reorganization was announced was to be no exception, with changes in OMB's top political slots, reemergence of divided government after the election, and the making and remaking of the 1996 budget and long-term deficit reduction plans. This background was hardly an ideal setting upon which to launch an ambitious plan to fundamentally transform institutional attitudes and behavior, and should be factored in when rendering early judgments of its success or failure. While the overall tone of staff observations in my sample was positive, there were also some mixed perceptions with respect to how rapidly OMB 2000's objectives were being addressed.

How OMB 2000 Looked a Year Later

The budget–management integration and movement of additional staff slots into the RMOs had varied from area to area since the individual RMOs required different types of personnel expertise. The new RMO staff members brought either financial management, economic, procurement, or legal expertise to the newly constituted units. Overall institutional slot vacancies had allowed for some new staff hires from outside of OMB to bring other specialized knowledge to certain RMOs. While RMO staff size had increased by 26 percent over the previous program division numbers (from

241 to 304),[58] the scope of the program examiners' (the new title for the budget examiners) job responsibilities had been significantly increased over previously designated budget examiner duties.

A number of the new tasks were clearly related to the mandate to focus increased attention on management-related issues. As stated in the examiner's updated job description,[59] these included reviewing reorganization plans, developing strategies for improving management systems, and determining the most cost-effective methods of management and program service delivery.[60] Other additional duties were related to GPRA implementation (determining performance and results and recommending approaches for strategic planning),[61] or to the objective of facilitating more long-term analysis ("[synthesizing] highly complex and voluminous materials" and "[helping] to develop and initiate long range-plans and goals.")[62] The new written requirements that an RMO program examiner "assists in the review and clearance of reports to Congress," and "reviews, comments on and leads negotiations on policy issues,"[63] codified already existing examiner responsibilities in certain RMO areas.

Program division staff had received some training for their new roles in procurement, financial management, and other areas of specific concern to certain areas. Conversely, former management staff moving to the RMOs were offered training on "budget concepts, laws, and procedures."[64] Several staffers in my sample cited a need for additional training, some of which was anticipated in the near future.

The core staff remaining in the three management branches were responsible for assuming leadership roles in compliance with the statutory requirements of the Chief Financial Officers Act, the Federal Manager's Financial Integrity Act, and the Financial Standards and Reporting Act as before. These units were designated to provide expertise to the RMOs on these government-wide statutory responsibilities to facilitate RMO staff in implementing them in individual program areas. It should be noted that the strong leadership offered by the new Deputy Director for Management John Koskinen and Controller Edward DeSeve helped keep the momentum continuing on management–budget integration in spite of the budget process tumult of 1995. Koskinen had brought skills to bear from the private sector, where he had for years headed a company that specialized in restoring private businesses with financial and management problems to solvency. This had proved to be a useful background for his mandate at OMB to improve financial management systems in the Executive Branch. As the newly appointed Controller of the United States, Edward DeSeve had served as Chief Financial Officer for the State of Pennsylvania and Director of Finance for Philadelphia.[65]

In the procurement area, ten Office of Federal Procurement Policy staff members had been moved into the RMOs. Several of these staffers were "jointly managed under a 'matrix management' approach in which they were made responsible for working on both the agency-specific issues in their RMOs and cross-cutting procurement issues on an OFPP team."[66]

Early Staff Perceptions of OMB 2000

Better communications between the core management and RMO staff was cited by a number of interviewees as one positive outcome of the reorganization. Staff viewed this as having led to less duplication of work efforts and therefore fewer conflicting signals to the agencies. Progress with the OMB 2000 goal of producing more cross-cutting analysis was uneven, but not without several encouraging examples of cases where OMB and agency staffs were able to break through programmatic and departmental barriers to reach trade-offs and produce common legislative initiatives. In addition, Alice Rivlin in her confirmation testimony had reported more "cross-pollination" between OIRA and the RMOs through regular joint meetings including both staffs.

A number of interviewees believed that both the RMO structure and the high level of commitment of the Director and Deputy Director for Management had ensured that management-related issues had been integrated into budgetary planning, even with the budget-related work load demands that existed in 1995. In addition, while GPRA had not been mentioned in the OMB 2000 Memorandum, the RMO structure was turning out to be well suited for its implementation and in turn was providing a focus and a process within which to link budget and management issues. As had long been the case, initiatives that were supported in statute had a better chance of being taken seriously by both OMB and the agencies. In discussions with OMB staff regarding how well they had been able to connect budget and management issues in their budget formulation duties, examples were often cited as they related to GPRA responsibilities.

These findings, that management issues were receiving more consideration in budget planning, and that GPRA mandates were facilitating this trend, were replicated by a GAO study released at the end of 1995. The study found that "the quantity and quality of information about management issues presented during the budget process increased after the reorganization."[67] This improvement specifically manifested itself in more qualitative information in the FY 1996 documents on how streamlining plans would relate to agency performance in the future, and more attention to financial management issues than had appeared in the FY 1995 documents. For example, for FY 1995 both the Department of Justice and OMB budget analyses had framed issues involving Bureau of Prison overcrowding as "strictly resource issues," while for FY 1996, budget document discussions extended much further into a consideration of "trends in state and county prison systems, operating costs at the Bureau's medium and low security facilities compared to private facilities, and issues involving the quality of confinement and the adequacy of security."[68]

Another positive sign from a couple of managerial-level careerist RMO staffers was enthusiasm over a particular additional staff person or two who had been hired for some specialized knowledge and were making it possible to produce the longer-term analysis that the OMB 2000 Memorandum had cited as one of its goals. Other career mid-level managers had found the integration process a daunting task, given the presence of so many other institutional demands during this period. In this regard, the GAO study also found skepticism among some of their OMB interviewees who believed that their work load had increased since the reorganization and had "left . . . little time for long term analysis."[69] It attributed this increased work load to budget process pressures and agency restructuring efforts, as well as new responsibilities related to the OMB 2000 reorganization.

In my interviews, this concern was expressed more among a couple of PADs who described themselves as having struggled with the day-to-day challenges that evolved from the typical OMB overload syndrome. The RMOs, while deriving some assistance from the core OFFM and OFPP staffs and the delegation of some budget-related duties to the agencies, were now at least in part responsible for integrating CFO, GPRA, and procurement-related activities into their budget formulation and congressional tracking duties in addition to all of their other responsibilities. While RMO staff numbers had been significantly increased, OMB's size had remained generally constant from what it had been at the beginning of the Clinton administration. At the same time, by virtue of the program examiners' formal job elements, institutional expectations for them had increased. Short-term information requests from the White House and other EOP units such as the NEC in particular had also been very heavy, as had requests for responses to constituent inquiries from congressional offices.

As usual, not everyone interviewed found an overly heavy work load to be problematic. In one case a PAD felt strongly that the staff were stretched too "thin," while subordinate career staff did not agree. The PAD attributed this to an attitude among some OMB career staff that drove them to take on any amount of work and not complain, a "bravado" I had also witnessed among many OMB civil servants over the years.

The OMB 2000 goal of creating an atmosphere of greater collegiality with the agencies probably had been realized to as great a degree as possible in a relationship where one institution is mandated to oversee the other. Reactions to the OMB collegiality issue did not appear to constitute an irritant to staff in the sense it had a year earlier. In some cases where OMB staff had felt that the agencies had been withholding needed information from them a year earlier, they now indicated that this was no longer a problem since, as one staffer described it, "the agency had learned that collegiality cut both ways." Some agency and OMB staff interviewees also cited more teamwork with the agencies and efforts on OMB's part to be more respectful to agency staff, but a few interviewees in the agencies expressed skepticism over how long this would last.

In sum, in spite of the difficulty of achieving an ambitious transformation on top of the tumultuous budgetary routines staff had to contend with after the 1994 election, the RMO and core management staffs generally seemed to be "trying hard to make it work." GAO's overall conclusion that"OMB staff generally had a positive view of OMB 2000" supports these findings.

End Game

Forecasting Wars Redux: A Politician's Game

With the renewal of divided government, it had not been long before Congress and the President began accusing one another of producing skewed economic estimates, often with barbs questioning the credibility of the "other" institution's chief forecasting units. It was difficult not to experience a sense of déjà vu from the 1980s, as OMB's projections were once again denounced as being overly "optimistic."

It had begun soon after the 1994 election when Director Rivlin had characterized Republican proposals that CBO assume a change in its economic estimating procedures known as "dynamic scoring," as "tantamount to 'cooking the books.' "[70] The Republican Congress cast its first stone when President Clinton's "first" 1996 budget was transmitted to Congress. Even though the administration had made no claims that this proposal would bring the budget into balance in the foreseeable future, its economic assumptions and projections had still been criticized as being overly rosy, and of producing larger deficits than the administration had predicted.

But the forecasting wars between the two parties in the Congress and the Executive really began in earnest when President Clinton presented his plan to balance the budget in June. While according to the administration's economic assumptions, the Clinton plan produced a balanced budget in ten years with fewer programmatic cuts necessary than were required in the

Republican proposals, when CBO's more pessimistic economic assumptions were factored into the Clinton proposal, the deficit had added up to $400 billion at the end of the same ten-year period.

The irony here is that the differences between the OMB and CBO assumptions on the individual economic indicators that produced these projections were exceedingly small, and much closer to each other than had been true at many points in the past. Alice Rivlin had testified before the Joint Economic Committee that in seven of the eleven years from 1995 to 2005, OMB and CBO projections of economic growth were just 0.1 percent apart and for three other years the difference was a mere 0.2 percent.[71] Rivlin had added that "differences in other economic indicators are a bit larger, but mostly offset one another. OMB projects lower unemployment rates, which lower the deficit, but higher interest rates which raise the deficit."[72]

The "early" deficit forecasts were also very similar, with CBO predicting an FY 1996 deficit of $210 billion and OMB forecasting a $201 billion deficit for the same period. But with each tiny disparity compounding in each succeeding year, the differences became huge.[73]

The rhetorical debate on the forecasting disparities continued to gather momentum. In August of 1995, during Rivlin's testimony before the House Budget Committee, Committee Chair John Kasich interpreted the administration's adaptation of CBO numbers in the 1993 budget as the creation of a precedent to do so in the future that had now been broken by the President. During her June testimony before the Joint Economic Committee, Rivlin had already refuted this point by explaining the 1993 action as only resulting from the President's wish to "take any dispute over economics off the table," and that OMB projections had been used since then because, "we have restored the credibility that OMB's economic assumptions had lost under earlier Administrations."[74] During the August exchange, Rivlin replied flippantly to Kasich, "You didn't notice that?"[75]

This acrimonious rhetoric continued to the point in November when these forecasting differences appeared to be a key stumbling block to a congressional-presidential agreement on balancing the budget, even as the federal bureaucratic workforce was experiencing its first four-day shutdown. During this period, a perusal of press accounts and even more probing news analyses could lead casual observers to the conclusion that differences between the arcane protocols of two "green eye-shade" numbers crunching agencies were playing a central role in bringing the government to a standstill. To support this impression, this first impasse was only to be broken when the White House agreed to use CBO assumptions in future deficit projections after CBO had consulted with "OMB and other outside experts." (The agreement also specified that the budget would protect Medicare, Medicaid, education, environmental programs, and the Earned Income Tax Credit for the working poor.)[76]

Much of this focus on OMB–CBO estimating disparities ultimately proved to be a smokescreen for seemingly irreconcilable ideological and politically motivated disagreements that persisted between the President and the House Republicans in particular. Later, when the President produced a plan to balance the budget in seven years that was "certified" by CBO as had been demanded by the Republicans, these differences remained and there was still no deal.[77]

The "scoring wars" between the legislative and executive branches that took place from 1994 to 1996 had changed from those in the 1980s in some respects. As illustrated in Chapter 7, gaps between OMB's and CBO's forecasts had already narrowed in the latter part of the 1980s. During the Clinton years, OMB's forecasts had proven to be much more in line with CBO's estimates.[78] Not only had OMB not been a purveyor of rosy scenarios, but its forecasts had at times been more pessimistic (as had CBO's) than some actual economic outcomes.[79] By these measures, OMB's track record during the Clinton administration had been at least as credible as that of CBO.

Nonetheless, many of the press accounts of this period could be interpreted to convey subliminal portrayals of the "institutional" OMB as being intrinsically less honest, overly optimistic in its projections, and less capable of foretelling future economic trends than CBO and other estimating organizations.[80] Some part of this characterization may have emanated from a perceptual lag left over from OMB's excessively "rosy" scenarios of the early and mid-1980s, when broad disparities prevailed between the two agencies.

Of this dilemma, it could be said that OMB serves a useful role as a "heat shield" for the President in such circumstances. However, the long-term problem with using OMB in this way is that it destroys its institutional credibility while undermining its utility to serve as a "protective cover" for the next President to come along. These dynamics are well illustrated by what happened at the beginning of President Clinton's term, when OMB's "image" problem prompted the President to take scoring disputes off the table by using CBO instead of OMB estimates in calculating the five-year Economic Plan, for what some may consider to be understandable political reasons. However, OMB's public image was further eroded. OMB cannot operate as a very effective "heat shield" without an adequate reservoir of public credibility.

OMB "Certifies" the Welfare Study

Another by-product of the brand of divided government that existed in the fall and winter of 1995 was OMB's involvement in the preparation of a number of "distributional analyses" of Republican proposals to restructure entitlement programs such as Medicare, Medicaid, and Aid to Families with Dependent Children (AFDC), and/or to devolve some of their responsibilities to state control. "Distributional analysis" forecasts the future economic impacts of proposed policies in selected populations. The "populations" might be categorized by income level, age, or other criteria.

In mid-October, Director Rivlin had called a press conference in the White House briefing room to unveil the results of an analysis of projected outcomes of House "proposed cuts in an array of programs, including AFDC and food stamps."[81] The conclusions of this analysis as explained by Rivlin at the briefing was that there would be "nearly $40 billion in cuts to families with children."[82] She cited that this "roughly" equaled the House GOP–proposed tax break to the top 5 percent of American households as measured by family income.[83] A press account of this briefing implied skepticism as to the objectivity of the report.[84]

OMB also worked with distributional analysis when it was called in to "verify" a Health and Human Services (HHS) study that had concluded that more than a million additional children would fall below the poverty line as a consequence of a Senate Welfare Reform plan the President had purportedly signaled support for. It was unclear whether the President had seen the study before the Senate had added amendments that ostensibly had eased the effects of the proposal on increasing child poverty. Using the HHS study as evidence in support of their position, Senator Daniel Patrick Moynihan and Marian Wright Edelman of the Children's Defense Fund urged the President to recant his support for the Senate Welfare Reform Plan.[85]

Once all of this had been aired in the press, the administration responded by directing OMB to conduct a "new analysis of 'the impact of this bill on children entering or leaving poverty,'" according to a letter from Alice Rivlin to Moynihan and eleven other Democratic conferees on the welfare bill.[86] Rivlin promised the analysis would be completed in a week's time.[87]

On November 9, 1995, a twenty-nine-page report entitled "Potential Poverty and Distributional Effects of Welfare Reform Bills and Balanced Budget Plans" was released from OMB as "presented by the Office of Management and Budget prepared with the Department of Health and Human Services, the Department of the Treasury, and other agencies." According to an OMB official, the report was crafted through an intensive effort by RMO staff in the Human Resources area to scrutinize the HHS data through an analysis of a series of OMB computer runs. OMB career staff then presented a "range" of potential economic impacts to OMB political-level staff for their approval and review.

The OMB report provided "an analysis of the potential impact on poverty of the House and Senate Welfare Reform bills, and Senate Democratic alternative," as well as a distributional analysis of how the overall Senate and House budget plans and the administration plan would affect different income groups.[88] It began in an advocacy style with three pages commending and defending administration actions and positions to date related to the topic at hand.[89] This was followed by a presentation of estimates of numbers of children who would fall below the poverty line under the various proposals and lists of a number of administration-backed changes that had already been incorporated into the proposal in question and others that the administration urged be added.[90] Another section presented the so-called distributional analysis.[91] The report took on academic trappings when it explained the components of the measures it used and its methodologies, and the intrinsic variability of the projected outcomes.

The study thus appeared to be an amalgam of a scholarly examination of a complex topic not easily lending itself to simple conclusions, as well as an advocacy piece intended to persuade observers to a particular point of view. The latter element potentially undermined the credibility of the former. OMB had been brought in as the "objective" evaluator; a well-constructed assessment was produced in short order, and OMB's long-standing image problem made it easier for critics to call the analysis into question if they wished. The skeptical comments in the press with regard to the Rivlin presentation of the earlier study highlighted the same dilemma.

This incident was but one manifestation of the larger role conflict that had existed within OMB for a number of years. This conflict lies between OMB's more recent mandate to provide the best and most honest information and analysis available *in support* of the President's preset positions, and its traditional role to provide the best and most reliable information available to the President before he determines his positions. In the last fifteen to twenty years, there has been less of the latter and more of the former.

Credibility issues aside, OMB might well find itself conducting more impact and distributional analyses in the near future. In former Labor Secretary Reich's account of his experiences during the first term of the Clinton administration, Reich recalls one occasion when the President expressed frustration that he was not receiving such distributional analysis from OMB and the Treasury Department quickly enough.[92] Distributional and other forms of impact analysis could prove to be one valuable way of evaluating outcomes for the public brought forth by privatization or devolution of federal programs to state control. So too, it could be useful as one means of determining whether existing federal programs or new initiatives are serving the public as intended.

Yet Another Management Office Proposal

OMB's economic estimates were not the only focus for critics, as OMB found itself in the political crossfire of divided government. At the end of 1995, OMB's "management record" became another "political football" in contention between some House Republicans and Democrats. The Republican majority on the House Committee on Government Reform and Oversight had issued a report, part of which had called for OMB to be relieved of its management responsibilities, which were to be transferred to a new EOP Office of Management. It may be recalled that such proposals had been made a number of times in past years.

Under the proposal, OMB would revert to functioning as an "Office of Budget," which would remain coequal with the new management office.[93] While acknowledging the current OMB Director and Deputy Director for Management as "competent" and "underutilized," the committee based this recommendation on its view that OMB's capacity to effectively address federal bureaucratic management issues had "steadily declined and now barely [existed]."[94] The House Committee majority also proposed a "program resolution" office within OMB to supervise the dismantling of large agencies and the redistribution and consolidation of retained federal government functions. This "program resolution" role was then suggested as an appropriate function for the new Office of Management.[95]

The attached minority report, signed by practically all the committee's Democrats, disputed many of the report's claims, including those related to OMB's federal management capabilities, and based its conclusions in part on the 1989 GAO study that had argued for "more" as opposed to "less" linkage between budget and management tasks.[96] The Democrats further chastised the majority committee members for failing to give credit to the Clinton administration's OMB 2000 initiative for implementing several of those same GAO recommendations, which purportedly had been ignored by the Bush administration.[97] The 1995 GAO report's generally positive early assessment of OMB 2000's outcomes was also presented to counter the proposal to create a separate management office.[98]

The House Committee proposal and the follow-up commentary offered by its opposition party critics present yet another example of a potentially substantive discussion of OMB's federal management role becoming partially obscured by partisan sparring. The Democratic response, in its effort to lay much of blame for OMB's "past" ineffectiveness as a manager at the feet of the previous two Republican administrations, at times tends to confuse where Reagan administration policies ended and OMB's "institutional" role began. Sometimes the two are appropriately separated and at other times they are blurred.

For example, when referring to OMB under the Bush administration, the Democratic follow-up report properly separated Bush administration actions from OMB's institutional performance when it held the Bush administration responsible for what it contended to have been little progress with OMB's surveillance of high-risk programs due to the assignment of only three OMB employees to track ninety-nine programs.[99] But when looking back to the Reagan years, OMB is made to appear responsible for failures in bureaucratic management that at least in part reflected Reagan administration priorities. OMB is cited as leading the "drive to deprive agencies of the tools they needed to manage, cutting audit and enforcement resources, failing to plan for the long term and ignoring rip-offs in government, health care, defense, loan and other programs."[100] With respect to the HUD scandal, an "embarrassed OMB" is described as taking action only after being forced to do so by Congress.[101]

Substantive issues are also confused by each party's attempt to score points at the expense of the other, by deleting "part" of the relevant history. The Democrats were correct in complaining that OMB 2000 reforms were not factored into the discussion by the Republican majority, but they in turn failed to acknowledge Richard Darman's efforts to bolster the effectiveness of OMB's management divisions.

End Game with No End: "The Longest and Most Chaotic Budget Season in Memory"

In September of 1995, OMB's RMOs had begun a modified budget review process in preparation for the transmission of the 1997 budget to Congress. These "budget briefings" constituted more of an internal OMB process than had other Director's Reviews during the Clinton years in their general exclusion of NEC or other EOP staff. One career staffer described the review as a "thoughtful and analytical process," which had presumably been enriched by the performance reviews held the previous spring.

From November of 1995 through January of 1996, the most sustained presidential-congressional impasse in twentieth-century budget history and its attendant shutdown of large portions of the federal government derailed these efforts. Unlike previous congressional-executive budget deadlocks in the 1980s when continuing resolutions had kept the government funded until agreements could be reached, the Republican Congress had attached significant substantive policy changes to continuing resolutions that President Clinton subsequently vetoed. Thus funding for those programs without signed appropriation bills had ceased.

OMB staff had attempted to be prepared for what would face them in the fall of 1995. Even in mid-summer as talk of the possibility of a potential "trainwreck" in budget negotiations began appearing in the media, some RMOs had started analyzing the logistics that would be required to ensure an orderly and even-handed furlough process in their individual agencies should such a government stoppage occur. As the earlier fears became realities and many federal agencies and departments were forced to cease many of their activities due to lack of operating funds, the unpleasant task of reviewing and approving agency shutdown plans fell to OMB as did the task of estimating lost revenue to the government brought on by the lack of an appropriation. (During the first work stoppage, most OMB employees had been furloughed, but by the second shutdown, OMB had received its appropriation.)

As appropriations bills, continuing resolutions, and long-term proposals and counterproposals to balance the budget had moved back and forth between Congress and the Executive, OMB was charged with "costing-out" the implications of each. This analysis involved the preparation of a changing series of estimates of the aggregate economic implications and programmatic effects of the different proposals. One high-level career official described these "drills," which were often requested on a daily basis, as "mentally tortuous." In early January of 1996, OMB political-level officials met with congressional staff to structure the face-to-face discussions between the President and the congressional leadership that were to prove fruitless as a means of reaching consensus. This "longest and most chaotic budget season in memory," as one RMO branch chief described it, continued for almost three months until the President's State of the Union address, at which point prospects for a balanced budget agreement seemed increasingly remote. OMB staff had once again been foot soldiers in a budget war, this time with a new set of combatants.

Political Appointees' Perspectives on Career Staff Analytic Capability and Objectivity

Three years into the Clinton administration, a sample of OMB and EOP political-level officials elicited some enthusiastic perceptions of a still top-notch OMB career staff offering analysis unrivaled by departmental agency analytic units. To these officials, the overall intellectual level of OMB career staff was excellent. One PAD captured the general observations of others in describing the career staff as "a remarkable gifted group who absolutely serve the Presidency as a generic." Another EOP official observed that the "weakest OMB examiner would be a star in the agencies." A third NEC staffer marveled at the dedication that motivated OMB staff to "pull all-nighters at OMB and be willing to field 11:00 P.M. work-related phone calls at home." In speaking with these officials there was no indication of any of the erosion in the capabilities of career staff recruits that observers had long feared.

Nor were there perceptions of career staff having absorbed the ideological predispositions of the two previous Republican administrations. One political official (outside of OIRA), for example, who recalled some concerns about the objectivity of OIRA's career staff at the beginning of the Clinton administration, three years later was characterizing OIRA's career analysts as objective, helpful, and as having been able to provide the Clinton administration with valuable institutional memory regarding regulation review.

Still, there were occasional responses that were less than positive and that sounded very much like some of those that had surfaced and resurfaced at times throughout BOB/OMB's seventy-five-year institutional history. Consider the following assessment by a PAD who found

> a form of analytical inertia in cases—absent policy guidance—to decide issues "the way we did before." It was less a matter of value commitments or ideological positions than a tie to consistency which mitigated against revisiting positions taken before. This resistance was not based on "Reaganite" views but on their conception of OMB's institutional role.

Another slant on this characterization was offered by an EOP political-level official who had interacted extensively with OMB over three years. This individual concluded that "the thing OMB does best is to bring discipline to the agencies and to run processes once they have been instituted. They are worst as innovators or change agents." These political-level staff described an institutional role orientation that could be likened to an almost identical one critiqued by Johnson administration political-level officials years earlier. In both instances, career staff were perceived to have proven resistant to accepting "program development" as opposed to "nay-sayer" orientations.

With a huge deficit to contend with, Clinton administration policy objectives mirrored those under President Johnson only in the minority of selected areas designated as "presidential priorities." The prevailing preoccupation was with "cutting" and "downsizing" by necessity. The Clinton administration's "mixed" administration goals perhaps explain in part a very different observation offered by another PAD, who described a "program advocacy" among some staff that had initially predisposed them to be resistant to "administration directed" cuts that they perceived would impair agency services and missions.

In trying to evaluate how these seemingly contrary role orientations affect OMB's ability to serve the presidency, the follow-up comments of the two PADs proved to be illuminating. In each case, after forcefully expressing their positions and showing some initial resistance to "new ways of thinking," as one PAD put it, the career staff in question proved to be both flexible and ultimately competent enough to produce the kind of analysis the PAD had been looking for. One of the PADs described the final work output as "terrific." In neither case did the career staff "engage in hiding the ball, even if they might have wanted to," as one of the PADs described it. It could also be argued that these so-called nay-sayer and program advocacy role orientations in some cases represented little more than staffers reporting program-related conditions as they found them.

Socialization of PADs, and Views on Congressional Liaison Roles

Do the PADs and other political appointees come into OMB with a sophisticated understanding of OMB norms of neutral competence, and if not, how do they become socialized into an appreciation of OMB's institutional constraints? One way used to assess whether the political staff appreciated certain limitations in what OMB staff could be asked to do was to determine what kinds of career staff activities "they" considered to "cross the line" into politicizing roles.

Political appointees in the sample had not received any formalized institution-wide training on OMB's institutional norms of neutral competence. Just like entry-level career staff, they were socialized by their top career staff division chiefs. They nonetheless appeared to have had a relatively sophisticated understanding of OMB's institutional role to serve the presidency since most had become relatively familiar with OMB in their past professional pursuits.

However, with that caveat, there remained broad discretion among the PADs to call the question on what constituted appropriate activities for the OMB careerists working under them. While none of the four PADs questioned on this issue were of the belief that they could ask their career staffs to participate in virtually any potentially politicizing activities, there were subtle differences among them with respect to where they "drew the line" separating appropriate from inappropriate behavior and how they reached that determination. For example, one of the PADs would not demand that career staffers participate in any activity they did not feel comfortable with, while another consulted with senior branch and division personnel as well as BRD's senior career official when ambiguities presented themselves.

Career staff were expected to present the issue options to a third PAD who factored in political considerations himself. This PAD personally wrote all "advocacy" sections of the budget in his area, but sent it back to career staff to check on factual sections. The PAD who probably came closest to placing career staff in "advocacy" roles saw no problem with careerists "advocating" presidential policies on the Hill or writing speeches in an advocacy style. The delimitation to this PAD was twofold: to never communicate or advocate policies that were not clearly stated administration policy, and to never distort facts to reach a desired outcome.

Of the PADs interviewed, none considered that the OMB career staff–congressional monitorship roles exercised under the past two Republican administrations had either "tainted" OMB staff in their current efforts to play information conduit roles in the Congress, or rendered them unable to serve different administrations in similar capacities. In fact, one PAD considered this career staff role as one of the most valuable services offered by OMB, commenting,

> The fact that these career people are known and respected by both Democrats and Republicans as knowledgeable and honest with long-term institutional memory, allows them to play a catalytic role in reaching consensus between the White House, Congress and different agencies.

Two other PADs wished their career staff had more time to pursue congressional monitorship. They expressed the view that career staff were more effective on the Hill as information conduits than were political staff because of their combination of institutional memory, program expertise, and knowledge of the congressional process. In addition, a number of political-level interviewees enthusiastically credited the chief career staff person in the small Legislative Affairs Office for his vast store of congressional knowledge and his ability to serve Presidents of either party with equal effectiveness and impartiality. One PAD believed that each PAD area needed to have its own similarly experienced career staff to guide relations with Congress, since in his area, the analysts did not have sufficient time to devote to this role. To this individual, a political staff person would not be as useful and effective in this role.

A fourth PAD was surprised at the broad scope of congressional tracking and liaison activities that OMB career staff now engaged in, and while not finding them "compromising," was concerned that they eroded time that could be devoted to staff analytic responsibilities.

With the expression of these views from most PADs, it was therefore not entirely surprising to find that the consistent institution-wide policies recommended in the OMB 2000 Memorandum to "provide guidance to OMB career staff on appropriate interactions with the Hill" had not been implemented in a formal sense. One OMB career official explained this by asserting that the unpredictable nature of recent presidential-congressional budgetary relations, coupled with changing administrations and conditions, tended to alter the rules of engagement between OMB and Congress, thus making "cookbook" guidelines and prescriptions for all staff untenable. Therefore, the substantive guidance to direct OMB career staff–Hill interactions had continued to originate in the individual RMOs, and OMB's "secondary" congressional monitorship staff role had survived and in some instances increased during the Clinton administration. This was true even from the beginning of President Clinton's first term, when some program division branches not traditionally involved in such activities were asked to begin to pursue such information gathering. This demand increased in some areas after the Republican-controlled Congress assumed office. At least according to some political appointees, this staff capability had served the Clinton presidency. If its consensus-building potential is considered, it could even be argued that it serves the "institutionalized" presidency as well.

The Rivlin–Panetta Team: Act III

OMB Director Alice Rivlin had argued for more aggressive deficit reduction in early 1995, and at the end of the year had supported the completion of a budget balancing deal before, as opposed to after the 1996 election. In the summer and fall of 1995, she had been a highly credible team player as she defended the President's balanced budget plan on various news programs. Rivlin had also attended to OMB's institutional needs by advancing the performance review process and improving internal OMB communications.

Nonetheless, there were some observers who believed that while Leon Panetta's ascent to the White House had led to an elevation of OMB's stature in the President's eyes, Panetta had, in effect, continued to maintain control of OMB from the White House, thereby consigning Rivlin to an extended deputy director role. This view was expressed in print when Al Kamen of the *Washington Post* wrote, "word is that Rivlin has been frustrated, treated at times like Panetta's special assistant. Also, there is the widely held suspicion that Rivlin is the good soldier, defending the administration's policies, but that her heart's not always in it."[102] Following the same line of reasoning, there were those who speculated that by naming Rivlin as opposed to an individual with more highly developed political skills to the director's position, the President was in effect relegating OMB to a second-tier position.

The assumptions supporting this argument can be questioned. Whether

OMB and its Director are "powerful" or not at any given point is not necessarily an indication of whether OMB is in fact serving the presidency, and may under some conditions actually undermine OMB's ability to do so, by politicizing both its activities and image. Under Stockman, OMB was perceived as being extremely influential and at the same time its "institutional" health had been left unattended. During the Darman era, OMB was believed to be "running the government," when in fact it was Richard Darman and a few "selected" OMB officials who were allegedly doing so. That assumed concentration of "power" allegedly had so alarmed some Clintonites that they had entered office determined to clip OMB's institutional wings, a development which in most respects could scarcely be considered a boon to OMB's ability to serve the presidency in a generic sense.

Whether intentionally or by accident, together, Leon Panetta and Alice Rivlin had been able to meet the dual and often conflicting requirements of the "traditional" and "modern" OMB directorates in a way that had supported both President Clinton and OMB's long-term ability to serve the presidency.

First, Panetta. His profile had fit and he had lived up to the "modern" director's job description perfectly, even as it turned out after he became the President's chief of staff. During the winter budget impasse of 1995–96, Panetta had played the "game" with enormous skill, both trying to serve the President's political interests, and trying to achieve the deficit reduction he had sought for so long. At the same time, it was well that the following exchange between Panetta and Senate Budget Committee Chair Pete Domenici, as reported by Michael Weisskopf and David Maraniss, did not take place from the "traditional" director's seat. Domenici is quoted as asking Panetta,

> "I just have to ask you: Weren't you a little embarrassed with the offer that you brought in on the 15th of December that did absolutely nothing?" There was a moment of silence before Panetta responded. "Not as a negotiator, I wasn't embarrassed," he said.[103]

It is precisely because of situations like that recounted above that OMB needs a "traditional" director as well. This reason alone would have made Alice Rivlin's presence of far greater importance than that of a "special assistant" to Panetta. While some had questioned the extent of Rivlin's "power" in the hierarchy of presidential decision making, literally no one questioned her intellectual capacity, her integrity, or her willingness to speak her mind to the President at the same time that she remained a loyal team player for him.

And so in the final analysis, the Panetta–Rivlin team "worked" for this President as did the institution called OMB. It did not matter whether the President always accepted their counsel or the administration chose to have competing power centers. What mattered was that OMB was there "ready and able to serve."

Yet the "director's dilemma" will not disappear in the future. Moreover, it can be viewed as a metaphor for one of OMB's overall institutional paradoxes, since the whole organization also has been compelled to assume dual and sometimes contradictory sets of services, which to Presidents of this deficit era were nonetheless imperative. Chapter 11 will offer some prescriptive thoughts and recommendations for Presidents, OMB's "political" leadership, and OMB career staff to help OMB better meet its seemingly impossible demands in ways that serve the presidency and individual Presidents alike.

11

Beyond OMB 2000:
One Bridge to the
Twenty-First Century

OMB During the Clinton Administration: 1990s Onslaught and Rapid-Fire Changes in Institutional Demands

During President Clinton's first term in office, OMB had been driven by accelerated and intensified versions of some of the same pressures and external conditions that had affected it during the previous twelve-year period. Further exacerbating these stresses, and continuing the trend of institutional overload, were alterations in OMB roles and processes introduced by the new administration. In 1993, after twelve years of Republican presidencies, OMB staff had had to adjust to a Democratic administration that expected it to share some of its major responsibilities with other EOP units. This had come after it had served Director Richard Darman, who was said to have been "running" the entire domestic bureaucratic establishment singlehandedly. At the same time, it had been called upon to transform itself from an agency "enforcer" into a collegial "facilitator" that was to determine budget recommendations for the agencies through team arrangements with the departments and agencies in question.

Another set of challenges that faced both the federal agencies in general and OMB in its agency oversight role in particular emerged when the realization of NPR's objective of government doing "more with less," and the implementation of the first stages of performance review, were impeded and complicated by the downsizing and the buyout process that was simultaneously taking place in the agencies.

The "numbers crunching" emphasis of the 1980s, which had come at the expense of programmatic intelligence-gathering efforts, had left OMB less prepared to serve certain Clinton administration goals. The Clinton administration's emphasis on programmatic service delivery at the grass-roots level differed from the previous administration's focus on financial management and thus also represented a change in demands on OMB.

In mid-1994 after the OMB 2000 plan was unveiled, OMB was reorganized to merge its budget and management staff and to introduce a "culture change" that aimed to transform it into a more "holistic" organization. Around the same time, Leon Panetta left OMB to become chief of staff in the White House and Alice Rivlin became director.

Having just become accustomed to tracking budgets in a Congress completely controlled by the President's party for the first time since the 1970s, in late 1994 OMB had to reorient itself to demands growing out of the Republican takeover of Congress. These included participation in REGO II exercises, preparation of a modified FY 1997 budget and of the President's ten-year budget-balancing plan and its repeated reconfiguration into more rapid seven-year road maps toward balancing the books. In the middle of all of this, OMB managed to pursue a Spring Review exercise geared toward facilitating the development of performance measurements.

A "mother of all battles" between Congress and the President from early November 1995 until well beyond the New Year in 1996, and its attendant government shutdowns, created an atmosphere in OMB reminiscent of the early months of the Stockman era in which rapidly changing demands for numbers exercises required continual estimates of evolving congressional proposals. In some government agencies, it was unclear whether the uncertain atmosphere that ensued would allow operations to continue at even a minimal level, let alone to foster the spirit of entrepreneurial enthusiasm of customer service for which NPR's designers had hoped in 1993. As the institution chosen to facilitate the downsizing, buyouts, performance reviews, and strategic plans of other agencies, OMB was in the midst of these upheavals. By this point, OMB had also agreed to prepare its own strategic plan.

Surprises and changes that would continue to alter OMB's future equations went on well into the summer of 1996. In the late spring, President Clinton appointed Alice Rivlin to a fourteen-year term as Vice Chair of the Federal Reserve Board and Vice Chair of Fannie Mae Corporation, and former Carter administration PAD Franklin Raines to be the new OMB Director. By August, the short-term deficit projections for 1996 were also looking far better than had been foreseen a year earlier, as they hovered around $116 billion.[1] Democratic legislators who were reported in the press to have argued a year earlier for "using the more optimistic projections of the Office of Management and Budget," were portrayed as having had "little sympathy" for Republican members who "complained . . . that one reason the deficit [would] spike next year" was that CBO was "vastly underestimating projected revenue."[2] According to former Director Rivlin, by the time she left, the "institutional" OMB had become highly valued at the White House.[3] At least at that moment, OMB's familiar posture as everybody's favorite political football had placed it in a better light.

Continuing Trends from the 1980s: Centrality of the Budget Deficit and Politicization of the Budget Process

The budget and the budget deficit had continued to be central defining issues for the Clinton administration as they had been during the Bush and Reagan presidencies, only more so. In 1993, with the deficit reaching "peak" levels of almost $300 billion and "deficit fever" taking hold among increasing numbers of legislators, deficit reduction had become a top presidential priority along with health care reform. The genuine deficit reduction that was painfully forged became a major though largely uncredited accomplishment during the President's first two years. Later, after the Republican Congress upped the ante by producing budget "balancing" plans, the administration countered with a competing proposal that reflected the President's priorities.

In this climate, the President became personally involved with budgetary details more often than had Presidents Reagan and Bush, and new high-level budgetary and administrative advisory units were created which competed with OMB for the President's attention along with selected Cabinet members and political consultants. Thus the "top-down" decision making that had reduced OMB career staff influence in the 1980s had continued during the Clinton administration. At the same time, OMB career staff were brought in to "work around the clock" during crisis periods as supporting players in familiar capacities, including the presentation of data to support policies that were predetermined at political levels, and the preparation and reconfiguration of economic forecasts and cost estimates as determined by the dictates of the Budget Enforcement Act.

Increasing pressure on the President and the Congress to make the politically difficult choices required to reduce the deficit continued to heighten the politicization of the broader budget process, particularly after the 1994 election. This, in turn, perpetuated a number of the institutional demands and strains that OMB had experienced during the previous twenty years. These included the need to continually upgrade OMB's congressional tracking capabilities, assaults on OMB's reputation for neutral competence and role conflicts for OMB Directors.

A Continuing Congressional Liaison Role

During President Clinton's first term, OMB's assistance to the White House during the congressional stages of the budgetary process had continued to be critical. OMB's political appointees soon realized that they needed OMB to continue pursuing its congressional tracking and liaison roles and to improve its capacities to do so in a number of respects. Thus, OMB career staff continued to track the Congress, prepare their cost estimates, and pursue their information gathering on the Hill. Former director Alice Rivlin observed that they had performed an invaluable service in this regard. Believing that OMB's informational base contributed significantly to the President's success in the budget negotiations, she stressed OMB's importance in serving the President during White House–congressional negotiations in 1995–96. "The Hill has nothing comparable," she observed.[4]

In the spring of 1996, Congress had passed a line item veto bill that bestowed significant "new" budget-trimming authorities on the President and OMB, to take effect after the election. In the tradition of the Budget Enforcement Act, the threat of exercising this authority armed OMB with the ability to further influence earlier stages of the congressional budget process.

The law allowed the President to cancel certain categories of spending after congressional passage, though Congress could still veto the President's "disapproval."[5] The President's veto power extended to discretionary budgetary authority (appropriations), "new" direct spending, and tax breaks that aided fewer than 100 beneficiaries.[6] The law allowed the President only five days after the enactment of an appropriations bill to notify the Congress of the line item veto and required that he submit other information along with the dollar amounts vetoed.[7] These included the reason for the vetoes, the fiscal, economic, budgetary, and programmatic implications of the funding cancellations, the departmental programs affected, and the states and congressional districts involved.[8]

OMB was to be responsible for assembling the required information in a short period of time. The nature of the time constraints set forth in the statute created the potential for an intolerable burden on OMB and the White House after appropriations enactment. The requirement that OMB delineate those states and congressional districts that were affected by the vetoes generated conditions that could blur the line between appropriations tracking for informational purposes and the need to do so strategically with particular political outcomes intended. Thus, the law could potentially pull OMB career staff even further into the political thicket of congressional activity in the future.

OMB began planning for its new line item veto responsibilities and conducted external discussions with the agencies on the topic during the summer of 1996. OMB staff were adopting a "wait and see" attitude as to the implications of the law for their institution. Some observed that if the veto were to be used sparingly, the law's reporting requirements would probably not constitute a major burden. One staffer believed that OMB would have to "build a data base to be able to report the state and congressional district outcomes."

Continuing Challenges to OMB's Credibility and Maintenance of Neutral Competence in a Politicized Budget Climate

Continuing assaults on the credibility of OMB's economic projections as well as its managerial capabilities, often leveled at least in part to advance partisan ends, had also followed from the increasingly politicized atmosphere in which budget decisions were reached. So too, did the pressures of role conflicts for the OMB Director and challenges to her heretofore pristine reputation for objectivity.

In one incident, Rivlin was purportedly accused by White House staffers of being a Republican sympathizer when one of her special assistants while she served as deputy director later went to work at the Republican National Committee and another aide wrote articles criticizing the administration's budgetary policies after he left his position.[9] Rivlin took a second, more significant "hit" in the political crossfire during her confirmation process for appointment to the Federal Reserve Board, when a Republican-initiated movement in the Senate postponed and threatened to derail her confirmation.[10] Rivlin was later confirmed by a slim margin.[11]

The politically charged atmosphere that surrounded OMB threatened to politicize OMB career staff, but as in the preceding administrations, they continued to be viewed by most administration appointees, agency civil servants, and congressional staff as neutral brokers of information. Aside from the additional PAD in the health area, the numbers of political appointees and noncareer staff assistants had stabilized at about twenty. OMB's "policy officials" continued to respect the agency's nonpartisan status during the Clinton administration as they had during the Bush and Reagan administrations. So, too, in all three administrations when political-level staff occasionally attempted to engage OMB staff in analytic, information gathering, or congressional liaison activities considered to be clearly inappropriate, both OMB career and political-level officials usually resisted, drawing the necessary "lines in the sand."

Seeds of Change and Transformation

From the upheavals and turnabouts that had marked President Clinton's first term, the beginnings of positive changes had begun to bear fruit. In the summer of 1996, OMB had held two institutional retreats, which allowed for a level of institutional self-evaluation that had not occurred regularly if at all in recent years. Also, in the spring of 1996, BRD had held monthly informational meetings of a Budget Officers' Advisory Committee composed of agency budget officials, and BRD and RMO personnel, to discuss issues of mutual concern such as procedures required to comply with the line item veto law. By mid-fall of 1996, "details" of OMB staff to work in the agencies were being encouraged. Also by the fall of 1996, OMB's management committee had spearheaded an effort to update and rewrite OMB's staff training manual.

OMB's political leadership had made commendable strides in attempting to break down barriers between different parts of OMB and to foster more of a cohesive team spirit for the whole institution, but none of these first steps would be easily transformed into permanent institutional norms.

Seeds of Change: An Educative Role for OMB?

In 1995, OMB began taking action to increase public understanding of the budget process, the deficit, and OMB. Hints of a new educative role for OMB appeared in early 1995 as some staff began receiving guidance that the reasoning behind their recommendations for performance review measurements be made understandable enough to be "explainable to the average citizen." Preparation of a fifteen-page booklet "The Citizen's Guide to the Budget,"[12] was also an early manifestation of a desire on Director Rivlin's part to increase public awareness of the nature of the budget choices that the President faced. The book was primarily a straightforward presentation of factual material. It opened by posing the rhetorical question, "How much do you know about the federal budget? If your answer is 'not much,' you're not alone. . . . That's why we created this Citizen's Guide to the Federal Budget."[13]

A second action taken by OMB was the development of a home page on the Internet in late fall of 1995. The page accessed a menu that allowed users to retrieve budget materials such as the President's Budget Proposals, the "Citizen's Guide to the Budget" described above, and biographical information on OMB's Director, Deputy Director, and Deputy Director for Management, as well as job openings in OMB. It also provided new OMB circulars, and information on the status of proposed regulations under review in OIRA. While the OMB home page came into existence at the same time as did the White House home page, it had been conceived in part in response to demands from law firms and interest groups that OMB circulars and information concerning regulatory review status become more accessible to outsiders. NPR had also expressed similar concerns. In early fall of 1996, OMB staff continued to upgrade the home page so that it would be more user friendly to the general public, particularly with respect to the indexing of regulation review. According to one OMB official instrumental in developing the home page, it also "forced" a deliberate and well-paced review of old circulars and was beginning to increase the applicant pool for OMB job vacancies, in addition to pursuing the broader goal of increasing public information and understanding of government.

Grist for the Mill: Prescriptions for Addressing OMB's Institutional Dilemmas

Institutional Role Conflicts and Politicization

For many years, BOB/OMB has been performing a delicate balancing act by responding to "some" of the President's political needs as well as to his need for information and analysis of a kind that can only come from a career service institutional staff. The strain of exercising these dual roles has at times affected different strata within the institution, from its directors and other political appointees to its career staff, and has colored the reports, recommendations, and economic projections they have produced.

The dilemma is that neither of these institutional roles can or should be abandoned at *this* time. OMB cannot now retreat to an ivory tower mentality. In doing so, it would be rendered irrelevant in the politicized budget process that is now driven by the Congress and its "budget wars." On the other hand, if the effort to retain OMB's role as an objective source of presidential advice is abandoned, a unique support and perspective for Presidents will be lost. Over the years, *too many* ill-conceived policy decisions have been reached without the benefit of adequate vetting of their long-term implications, costs, and the requirements for their implementation. Without OMB to exercise a check and balancing role, the incidence of unconsidered policies will just increase.

OMB's role conflicts are closely related to the politicization of OMB advice and potentially of its career staff. While part of this politicization mirrors an actual institutional struggle that has existed in OMB for many years, and part represents only a "potential" threat, it still needs to be addressed to whatever degree possible.

The PAD position has been one of the chief targets for those who have decried an increasing OMB politicization over the last twenty years. Groups like NAPA have suggested that elimination of the PAD level in OMB would be one means of restoring its unfettered objectivity.[14] Such recommendations, however, appear to have had little chance of being seriously considered because they would deprive the President of one significant coping device to use in dealing with Congress's increased clout in the budgetary process. Moreover, there is a school of thought among some OMB political appointees and career staff that the existence of the PADs does not politicize the institution, and may do precisely the opposite by shielding career staff from having to reach politically based recommendations. Also, a top political echelon can effectively "take on" Cabinet secretaries who have strayed from the President's agenda, and lead the way in the President's political battles on the Hill.

The down side of keeping the current configuration of political layering between OMB's career staffs and the directors includes many of the same concerns voiced by Hugh Heclo and others twenty years ago. These include the "potential" for PADs to screen out objective information that does not support politically favored positions, or to lead career staff into the acceptance of blatantly political roles. Another concern is that some PADs might have strong personal incentives to pursue independent agendas that diverge from the President's interests and policy positions, particularly when those PADs are coming from and returning to the interest communities they review. The relatively short average tenure of PADs over the past twenty years has further exacerbated this potential problem. For the same reasons, PADs can also be in a position to undercut the director, depending upon how skillful the director is in wielding internal institutional power.

One possible solution to the PAD dilemma (real or potential) as related to the larger issues of OMB role conflict and politicization would be to make certain organizational adjustments that would retain the PADs, would continue to allow them to do the heavy "political lifting" in the Congress and elsewhere, but would minimize their ability to undermine OMB's role as an objective advisor. This could be accomplished by simply removing the PADs from their "line" supervisory authorities in the RMOs and by placing them in charge of an "enhanced" OMB Congressional Liaison Office that would continue to work closely with the RMOs. In terms of processing information and advice, the RMOs would then report directly to a newly constituted "institutional" Director's position, which will be discussed in the next section.

In an upgraded Congressional Liaison Office, each PAD would "direct" one or more new civil service support staffers with significant congressional and programmatic experience. Several of the PADs I spoke with desperately needed such staff support. Thus, OMB could better serve the needs brought forth by a new congressional budget process, while at the same time moving toward a de-politicization of presidential advice. Some noncareer support positions throughout the institution might also be replaced by senior career staff with proven institutional track records and career incentives that assure honest assessments within the institution and the integrity to be "good soldiers" outside of it. Such staffing arrangements might make it easier for new Presidents to trust OMB's counsel from the beginning and to feel secure in hashing out the pros and cons of policies without the fear of having their ultimate decisions castigated publicly.

A second way to address problems incurred by the existence of the PAD position would be to institute more standard training and socialization procedures for all new incoming PADs. One of the underlying causes of the diversity of PAD behavior is that in most administrations, PADs operate with great discretion and receive no formal "institutional training" upon coming to OMB. Like career staff, they are briefed and broken in by their division chiefs so that the institutional norms and cues they receive will vary by divisional culture. As one PAD commented, "PAD roles evolve separately and PADs do not get much help from other PADs." Once they assume their positions, they generally are free to set the tone in their division(s). This discretion, plus the generally short average tenure of PADs, frequently results in significant vacillations in the "marching orders, leadership styles, and policy signals" career staff receive one or more times during a single four-year term.

A third proposal that might help maintain neutral competence in a politically realistic way involves that "second most important job in Washington"— OMB's Budget Director. One possible way of addressing the role conflict that modern OMB Directors face is to divide the director's two jobs among two officeholders. Both Directors would need to be persons of top-level stature, both should report directly to the President, and both should have direct communications channels, albeit different ones, to every activity pursued by OMB. The Deputy Director and the Associate Directors over Budget and Management that have existed in the past, or the current deputy director for Management, will not meet the need here, since they have had and will continue to have more than enough to do. The missions of the two positions would be conceptually different from any that currently exists in OMB.

The "political director" would head an upgraded OMB Congressional Liaison Office and would serve as a policy advisor and policy implementer. The "traditional or institutional director" would be centrally responsible for facilitating a steady flow of objective information upon which to base "merit" judgments consistent with the President's positions. The official occupying this position would make certain that information that was not distorted by political considerations was reaching the political director as well as the President. When recommendations were being aired to the President, both individuals would be present, and when major disagreements occurred between the two directors, the President would hear both positions.

The lines of hierarchical authority would be driven by the requisite functions of the two directors. The PADs would report directly to the "political" director and the RMO career division chiefs, and the career heads of BRD *and* LRD would report to the "institutional" director. So, too, would the statutory officers—the deputy director for Management and the heads of OIRA and the Office of Federal Procurement Policy, since another fundamental function of the "traditional" director would be to keep management and procurement issues from fading into oblivion in the White House. The political director and PADs would still be in a position to benefit from OMB's knowledge base, since the RMOs would continue to work closely with the PADs and the Congressional Liaison Office in an informational capacity, but without creating opportunities for that information to be screened out of the communications loop. Promotion and career-track decisions for OMB civil servants would remain under the purview of the "traditional" director.

The traditional director would conduct Director's Reviews, which would emphasize more "bottom-up" policy development than has occurred in recent years, and the political director would serve as a liaison to the White House political and legislative affairs units. Both directors would be appointed by the President and subject to Senate confirmation with the understanding of the different career profiles necessary for each. Leon Panetta and Alice Rivlin provide useful role models to lead the way. Even if the clout of the traditional director becomes subsumed by the political director and merit arguments lose out, the presence of the traditional director will provide built-in supports for the maintenance of OMB's institutional service to the presidency without depriving the President of the *informed* support needed to be able to govern in the politicized budget process.

Institutional Overload and the Maintenance of Analytic Capability

It was not surprising that OMB's staff size had dropped from approximately 560 in 1993 to about 520 in 1996,[15] during a time of deficit cutting. Once again the institution had taken its own "medicine."

While the crush of OMB's many mandates has constituted a challenge to this relatively small organization for many years, it has managed to cope reasonably well with its external demands. Though strategically targeted increases in staff size *could* enhance OMB's ability to shoulder its many responsibilities, the prospects are dim for such a personnel expansion in the current climate of government downsizing. Thus, OMB will need to find other ways of maximizing the utility of its staff at current levels.

The OMB 2000 reorganization was a step in the right direction, but could be further improved by the continuation of efforts to facilitate teamwork among LRD, BRD, OIRA, and the RMOs. Budgetary, management, and regulatory decision making would be enriched as a result of clearer communications and the sharing of information among OMB's constituent units.

Another way of dealing with OMB's multifarious and changing missions without significant staff increases is to create temporary "visiting" positions that are targeted toward meeting specific institutional needs as they arise. The Clinton administration set a precedent for such short-term hires when an expert on performance review was brought into OMB in just such a capacity.

The potential erosion of OMB's analytic capability and its informational base is related to its institutional overload. There is a mixed verdict on whether OMB's programmatic knowledge has become depleted over the past twenty-five years as OMB staff expended much time and energy on mastering new skills. Thus, efforts to bolster OMB's analytic capacity require the institution's immediate attention. Programmatic knowledge is at the core of what OMB does. If OMB analysis and advice is going to have breadth, depth, and long-term reliability, it must be supported by empirically based knowledge of the programmatic areas in question. This holds whether the information is used for program evaluation, performance review, or to determine whether to eliminate programs, downsize them, or expand them.

If there is a wholesale erosion of OMB capability in this regard, then the institution's utility to the President and the public becomes questionable. Obviously only the agency program and budget managers know all the specific details surrounding agency operations. However, unless OMB is known to have attained a reasonably sophisticated level of programmatic knowledge regarding agency activities, it tends to lose credibility and the respect of the agency under review. Without substantive information as a counterweight, superficial politically based options will all too often carry the day.

The incentives, career paths, and institutional turnover rates of OMB employees are closely interconnected with OMB's ability to maintain its institutional memory and high-quality analytic capability. Turnover rates at the junior staff and branch levels in the 1990s remained generally comparable to what they had been in the mid to late 1980s, as had OMB's ability to maintain its institutional memory at the branch chief level. OMB officials and managers perceive that they are still able to attract top-notch staff to OMB. Most of my political-level interviewees were impressed with the mental acuity and knowledge levels of the career staff as well.

These observations, however, do not negate a parallel conclusion that certain changes in OMB's organizational status quo related to turnover, career patterns, and staff recruitment could contribute toward making OMB an even more effective presidential advisory system and prevent further problems from developing in the future. A moderate increase in the "average" three-year turnover rate for entry-level staff to five years would allow staffers to become even more adept at their multi-faceted jobs, and would further improve OMB's institutional memory, but would be brief enough to prevent rigidification of staff attitudes or biases. It would also create a larger talent pool in terms of institutional experience, for senior-level positions.

Such an increase in the institutional longevity of entry-level staff will not be an easy objective to achieve since junior examiners have strong incentives to leave OMB after a few years for reasons above and beyond intense work load. First and foremost among these is the fact that many talented OMB employees face a situation in which they rapidly "top-out" in salary rates because branch chief positions are so infrequently vacated. Second, if career staffers remain in OMB too long, some are unable to qualify for executive-level positions in the agencies since as "senior" examiners they do not get the managerial experience required to qualify for such jobs.

A number of possible OMB actions might provide junior staff with incentives to remain in OMB a few more years. First, a small number of "new" executive-level career positions could be created to support political appointees and to replace noncareer support staff such as special assistants to the directors. Junior staff could aspire to these positions, and might therefore be willing to remain in OMB a little longer. Second, prospective hires could be apprised at the onset that a slightly longer tenure would be expected of them. Third, the institution could provide these staffers with ongoing guidance to assist these junior staffers in their own career planning.

The emphasis on hiring entry-level professional staffers with few ties or little expertise in the programs they review needs to be augmented by aggressive efforts to attract more mature and experienced individuals to OMB as well. Such hiring should be implemented selectively and strategically and should draw individuals with needed specialization or skills from federal and state government as well as academe, think tanks, and private industry. The use of temporary "visiting" positions, described earlier, would be useful in this regard as well.

OMB can enhance its analytic capability by committing more time and resources to the pursuit of some of its time-honored information-gathering activities such as field trips. There might also be brief rotations through the agencies for incoming staff, and more extended ones for staff who plan to remain in OMB beyond a five-year period.

A related recommendation that has appeared more than once in OMB self-studies and has not been implemented in any major way is for more frequent staff rotations within OMB. These could serve several purposes, such as facilitating the necessary teamwork and exchange of knowledge required to better prepare "cross-cutting" analysis. Such rotations could also play a role in making OMB's discrete units more institutionally cohesive as they broaden OMB staffers' skills and areas of expertise, and thus enhance their career potentials.

Training and Staff Socialization

White House and Political-Level Staff

BOB/OMB was created to serve the presidency in various capacities, yet all too often new presidential administrations do not understand how it can best be used to advance presidential objectives. Moreover, White House staffers are frequently suspicious of OMB civil servants after a party change has taken place in the White House. Yet as one interviewee commented, "the more the President trusts OMB, the more OMB can help the President."

Thus, more systematic actions need to be taken to educate new political appointees whether in OMB, the EOP, or the White House about OMB's values, culture, and traditions. There is some historical precedent for pursuing this notion of "educating" or socializing new White House staffs about OMB's roles and its utility to the President. Veteran OMB staffers recall such structural and organizational training sessions, which fell into disuse at some point prior to the Reagan administration. While LRD does some of this kind of work, there should be more efforts in this direction. These should include sessions that candidly allow political appointees and civil servants to share their varying perspectives with one another. For many individuals in both "populations," there needs to be a greater understanding and appreciation of the demands and pressures faced by the other group. My impression is that during the course of most administrations many such frank exchanges occurred between political officials and career staff, ultimately contributing to greater mutual understanding. Such communications should be institutionalized.

Career Staff Training

For many years, OMB has needed to undertake a serious examination of how it can better provide both specific and generalized training and professional career development for its employees. It is well that it now seems to be moving in that direction.

The training issue reflects a broader "internal" management weakness in the institution at large. As senior analysts moved into "management" positions in the branches, many came without any academic background or experience in managing professional staff and/or have not always been offered such training by the organization. Some had personal qualities well suited to the management of professionals and others did not. Thus, it is not surprising that OMB projects an image of an institution populated by smart "lone rangers" where new managers and staff "both sink or swim" in their new positions. This approach may quickly weed out less than competent staff, but falls short in its capability to support overall institutional cohesion.

On the need for better training, career development, and internal management, there appears to be more general consensus among those within the institution than on many of OMB's "other" institutional issues. These areas are never adequately addressed for some of the same reasons that other of OMB's institutional problems remain unsolved—the institution is too busy providing its many services for the President to have time to do so. Taking all of these obstacles into account, upgraded training in OMB that is hand-tailored to specific institutional objectives would be well worth its cost. The enhancement of OMB training has already begun. Development of an upgraded week-long staff orientation was a step in the right direction, as was the creation through the OMB 2000 reforms of the Internal Management Committee. During both the Bush and the Clinton administrations, staff spoke of more frequent "brown bag" lunch sessions where current institutional topics were discussed by relevant speakers. As of late summer of 1996, a new training manual was being assembled. The staff retreats that were held during the summer of 1996 were also a hopeful sign that in spite of all of its current pressures, OMB is showing great initiative in trying to plan for the future.

A number of further means to improve upon the quality of OMB training might also be considered. First, since the RMO areas differ in so many respects, perhaps they should follow the lead of those that have developed their own structured training materials. These could also include area-specific guidelines on congressional and interest group contacts, which three administrations have been unable to provide on an institution-wide basis. Second, Hugh Heclo's description of neutral competence should be emphasized as a central creed for OMB in all staff training. Such discussions do not have to deny the institution's highly politicized environment to begin to imbue staffers with the sense of mission and esprit de corps that existed in OMB many years ago. It could contribute toward building a larger vision for OMB and its staff, toward motivating staff to integrate their own programmatic expertise into a larger framework, and to maintaining a balance between institutional service to the presidency and service to the President in his political battles with Congress.

Training should also not shy away from addressing OMB staff behaviors and stylistic images that have been counterproductive to the institution in the recent past, particularly those that have tended to impede the clear flow of communications from the agencies to OMB. For example, the boundaries of appropriate behavior when interacting with agency staff should be discussed. The lines should fall somewhere between "buddy-buddy" collegiality, which ends up encouraging agency personnel to ignore OMB, and rigidity and arrogance, which impede innovation in agency missions and information flow from the agencies to OMB. Other subtleties of the job should be emphasized as well. While OMB career staff need a high level of assertiveness and self-confidence in order to do their jobs, these personal qualities must be fine tuned to prevent that "assertiveness" from crossing the line and becoming an "arrogance" that could undermine another requirement of the job—the ability to fall in line when one's recommendations are not adopted.

The Budget–Management Conundrum

BOB/OMB has not been able to find an ideal solution to its "budget–management" conundrum for the past fifty years. On the questions of whether budget and management staff should be separated or merged within OMB, of how many OMB staffers should be exclusively engaged in handling administrative management issues, or whether the central management function should be removed from OMB entirely, unequivocal answers have not been found.

Proponents of large, separated OMB units devoted entirely to management issues argue that integration of budget and management staffs will result in the demands of the budget functions overshadowing the pursuit of the management objectives. They also point to occasional historical instances when such bifurcated offices have yielded good results by engendering the trust of Executive Branch agency staff. On the other hand, critics of this approach believe that duplication of efforts, and communications and coordination problems, are common outgrowths of the separation of budget and management units in OMB. They also attribute the failure of management initiatives in the agencies to their separation from budgetary controls, and point to deficiencies in the management divisions' knowledge of individual programs.

This debate seems to recycle every few years, but with a few exceptions, satisfactory centralized management approaches have remained elusive. Thus, some scholars and practitioners have concluded that Presidents just cannot effectively assume a posture as manager in chief through OMB or any centralized EOP unit.

This does not, however, have to be the final word on this matter. Perhaps with OMB 2000's new variant of budget–management merger, OMB can avoid some of the pitfalls it experienced with similar organizational arrangements in the past, since it will be working within the dictates of the Government Performance and Results Act of 1993. GPRA might in itself provide a unique historical opportunity for OMB to "evolve" as both a manager *and* a budgeteer. GPRA could act as a catalyst in this respect, since by definition it ties together budgeting and management through OMB review of performance measures to determine whether the agencies' self-chosen strategic goals are being met. Since GPRA links and integrates budget, management, and performance measurement, so it requires an integrated organizational vehicle with the requisite institutional memory and programmatic knowledge to help guide its implementation in the agencies.

Thus, in spite of all the historical pitfalls, a holistic and integrated OMB is the best way to go. Only by linking the budgetary, management, and performance-related components of programmatic issues in easily understandable ways can OMB offer the high-quality counsel Presidents will always need. Staff offices with different agendas which are located all over the EOP map cannot produce a conceptually sound and broadly based problem-solving capability in OMB. In a compelling argument for a "holistic" OMB, OMB veteran Bernard Martin expresses the view in a published interview that separation of budget and management functions ensures "that budget will always win,"[16] the very opposite of what advocates for better bureaucratic management hope for; he believes that by integrating performance review into budget analysis, budgetary and management issues will become genuinely integrated. Moreover, he argues that "management" cannot be separated from OMB's other core roles such as program review and still receive adequate attention, and that the program divisions in differing degrees had always been involved in management-related activities to some extent anyway.[17]

There are several other conditions that will enhance the prospects for OMB 2000 and GPRA to achieve their desired results. First, if the budget–

management merger is to produce an effective advisory structure for the President, there have to be sufficient numbers of "troops" in the RMOs equipped with appropriate educational and experiential backgrounds, or trained on the job to be able to synthesize agency-specific budgetary, management, legislative, and regulatory issues as well as to prepare analysis and recommendations on issues that cross-cut agency boundaries. Second, members of Congress of both parties should refrain from using the issue of OMB's management capability to score political points or to achieve political objectives. They should instead seek to find ways to "support" OMB in its efforts to facilitate better management and performance of government programs. Third, and perhaps most important, the White House needs to maintain genuine and committed attention to administrative management issues and programmatic service delivery. The "political" personalities that frequent the White House tend to become bored with such issues over time, and consequently the agendas they espouse tend to lose their direction as they are translated into specifics during their implementation.

The National Performance Review and OMB

The creation of the National Performance Review with no less an influential player than the Vice President at its helm to forge an enduring campaign to make government serve the public "better" for "less," had been a highly appropriate action to take in an era of massive public discontent with government. The Vice President's leadership of NPR helped maintain focus on these issues at the highest levels of government.

As President Clinton's first term drew to a close, OMB and NPR continued to have their differences from time to time, but generally had been able to resolve them and to be mutually supportive in advancing the administration's objectives. As of spring of 1995, NPR's recommendation to limit OMB's discretion in its budget execution activities had not been acted upon. Purportedly, a determination had been made in NPR that its recommendation on this contentious issue needed to be implemented on a case-by-case basis, taking into account the views of the pertinent agencies, OMB, and relevant appropriations committees.[18]

Though the relationship between NPR and OMB had sometimes been a "challenging" one in the early days of the administration, the two organizations have the potential to complement each other. NPR can initiate "reinvention," while "OMB maintains the discipline and constant pressure to keep reinvention going," as one NPR official characterized the relationship between the two groups. One strain of opinion that supports this viewpoint in the agencies and in OMB is the assessment that NPR had been pro-active in raising many of the "right" issues, but that many of NPR's initiatives had "gotten lost" during their implementation in the agencies. If this is the case, then it is critical to cast OMB as an NPR "partner" in maintaining the necessary follow-through. That both groups (NPR and OMB) seem to agree on a pro-active role for OMB in the performance review process may be one means to that end. Moreover, Vice President Gore's leadership of the National Performance Review can prevent administrative management issues from fading into obscurity.

A Final Word

The OMB of the twenty-first century will need to be flexible enough to pursue the budgeting and management of funds in federal agencies, the development and implementation of policies, and the preparation of cost–benefit analysis on regulatory matters and long-term economic projections. Continued congressional liaison work may also be part of the future picture, even if the "budget wars" between Congress and the Executive subside and the budget is balanced, since Congress is not likely to retreat to its more limited pre-1974 role in the budget process.

Regardless of the partisanship of future occupants of the Oval Office, Presidents will be forced to grapple with weighty issues that will require sophisticated informational support. These include, but are not limited to, the measurement of the outcomes of the devolution of welfare programs to the states, and the pursuit of ways to preserve the Social Security and Medicare programs as the baby boomer generation nears retirement age. With so much at stake, Presidents will need reliable impact and distributional analysis *before* policies are made as well as during their implementation, in order to track their outcomes. OMB could still be one of the best places for them to get such honest analysis.

If OMB is to meet these challenges and to display peak performance in serving the presidency, it will have to be equipped to operate as a consummate information and analysis center for Presidents to draw on. The realization of such an OMB is not beyond reach, but will require long-term and consistent institutional innovation, vision, and planning. It will call for a career staff that is motivated by a sense of institutional mission, a passion for anonymity, and, in the tradition of Harold Smith so long ago, a motivation to serve the public by serving the presidency. Such staffers will have to leave their egos and "their need to win" at the door along with their partisanship and private agendas, and still be motivated to work long hours on behalf of lofty public service objectives. OMB's career staff leaders need to recruit such people and when they come to OMB remind them often of the unique and important missions that OMB can serve. In that way, OMB's culture will continue to evolve to meet the demands that it will face in the future.

Epilogue

To chart OMB's evolutionary course over the last twenty years has been to follow a moving target. True to form, alterations in OMB's world continued to occur since the summer of 1996 when the research for this book was concluded.

New Statutory Responsibilities

OMB's mandates continued to increase as a number of new statutes went into effect. These included the Cohen-Clinger Act of 1996, which gave the OMB Director responsibility for upgrading government-wide acquisition and utilization of new information technology,[1] and the Government Management Reform Act of 1994, which mandated that OMB guide federal agencies in preparing their financial statements.[2] The reauthorization of the Paperwork Reduction Act in 1995 further increased OMB's charges from what they had been under the 1980 Act by requiring that the OMB Director, in conjunction with departmental officials, "reduce information collection burdens imposed on the public."[3] Moreover, in anticipation of the year 2000 and beyond, OMB in general and OIRA in particular became involved in overseeing a government-wide "Year 2000" Project, which had been established to recalibrate government computers to adapt to new configurations of dates beyond the year 2000.[4]

The Budget Agreement

The culmination of the budget-balancing agreement between President Clinton and the Republican Congress, in combination with a precipitous plunge in the deficit,[5] affected OMB operations by freeing institutional personnel from some of the uncertainties they had coped with in recent years when attempting to plan budget formulation schedules and processes. However, in the short term, these developments are unlikely to ease OMB's congressional tracking responsibilities sufficiently to free up the additional time needed for OMB staff to implement their analytic and information-gathering roles. This is the case for two reasons. First, many of OMB's congressional tracking duties are derived from statutes such as the Budget Enforcement Act and the Line Item Veto Act, and thus will continue to place demands on the time and resources of OMB staff. Second, the combination of tax cuts and new spending that are part of the budget agreement create tight constraints on appropriations for many government programs in the next few years, but leave resolution of the details of "who will get what, when, and how" for later. Even assuming a federal budget surplus for 1998 and beyond,[6] the political tug-of-war over the disposition of that surplus is likely to continue. These debates could determine whether Congress and the President agree to further tax cuts, enactment of legislation with spending increases, the restructuring of Medicare and/or Social Security, or some mix of all three. Thus, congressional-presidential posturing and sparring in the appropriations arena will not soon abate, nor will the need for OMB to track the congressional budget process.

The Line Item Veto Act

The early experiences with implementation of the Line Item Veto Act provide further evidence that OMB's congressional tracking role is here to stay, at least for the foreseeable future. The Supreme Court's refusal to rule on the constitutionality of the statute during the summer of 1997 allowed President Clinton to implement the law during the following fall.[7] OMB's role in supporting the President after the appropriations bills reached the White House was twofold: to obtain information on the nature, beneficiaries, and sponsors of vaguely described appropriations, and to recommend uniform criteria to use in determining which spending would be item vetoed. The magnitude of effort required to perform these tasks promised to be formidable at the time the Line Item Veto Act was signed into law, because of the short amount of time the law allowed for OMB to obtain the back-up information that the President would need to make veto decisions and to transmit the required information to Congress once the veto actions had been taken.

The work load generated by the fall 1997 line item veto process did in fact place a substantial burden on the RMOs involved. The aforementioned time constraints were further exacerbated for several reasons. First, it was not always clear whether the appropriations items in question had been added during committee action or during the final conference stage of the appropriations process. In the latter case, the only way to glean information regarding the purposes and beneficiaries of the spending was through conference reports that did not reach OMB until days after the appropriations bills in question had been passed. Compounding this dilemma was the difficulty of tracing the purposes, beneficiaries, and congressional districts affected by the designated spending.[8] Second, the information gathering and decision making on the item vetoes occurred while OMB was preparing the President's budget proposal for the following year, always its most intensive period of activity. Third, during the same period, OMB was deluged with telephone inquiries from legislators concerning the status of *their* individual projects vis-à-vis potential item vetoes. Fourth, even though the quality and magnitude of agency-based information on the "last-minute" appropriations add-ons often surpassed that of OMB, it was frequently difficult for OMB to engage assistance from the agencies. As one official noted, "The politics of it all would have made the agencies' relations with the appropriators very difficult." For all the foregoing reasons, this first experience with the item veto process led one OMB PAD to characterize it as a "huge addition to OMB's responsibilities" and the process as causing the "worst time sump ever to hit OMB."

If the Line Item Veto Act ultimately survives further scrutiny by the Supreme Court, OMB and the White House will have to engage in expanded and earlier tracking efforts to avoid the time crunch at the end of the process that occurred in 1997. One OMB participant in the process believed that there would have to be increased OMB tracking of the Congress during the appropriations process as well as negotiating by the White House and OMB's political echelons to reach consensus on proposed appropriations *before the final appropriations bills are transmitted to the White House.* In a White House press briefing, Director Raines seemed to agree. Speaking for himself and the President, he asserted that "the most important part of changes in future behavior is to have greater communication between the appropriators and the administration so that we're quite clear on what our views are on various subjects and that we are part of the discussions that go on. I think that if we can do that successfully in the future, there will be fewer and fewer line item vetoes because we will have worked out these issues and our concerns would have been adequately represented in their deliberations."[9]

OMB's experience with the line item veto process in 1997, and the lessons OMB leadership seem to have drawn from it, thus portend more OMB involvement in the politics of appropriations than ever before; this will only increase the work load and potential politicization of OMB career staff in the future. Again, OMB's most significant and time-honored resource of agency programmatic information and its more recent currency of congressional information will continue to require close staff attention to serve the needs of the Presidency in the near future.

The Strategic Plan

A third development to be noted is the publication of OMB's Strategic Plan. By the time the plan was published on September 30, 1997, it had been thoroughly reviewed by all of OMB's internal constituencies and revised after a first draft of the plan had been assessed by the General Accounting Office, the Congressional Research Service, the House Government Reform and Oversight Committee, the Senate Governmental Affairs Committee, and the House and Senate Appropriations Committees.[10]

The strategic plan in final form set forth four broad goals, which were further broken down into sixteen overall objectives. A brief summary of the means and strategies to be used to realize each objective and how each related to the broader performance goals was outlined. So too was a short discussion of "external factors" that could affect OMB's ability to realize these goals.

Three of the overriding goals were organized along the lines of OMB's major mandates. The first of these was OMB's *budgetary, economic, and regulatory advisory role* to recommend policies to the President that fulfill his "policy goals and promote sustainable economic growth."[11] The second involved the implementation of OMB's management role, which was to be derived from "faithful execution of the enacted budget, programs, regulations, and policies."[12] In light of OMB's struggles over agency discretion in the early days of the Clinton administration, this statement represents a clear reassertion of OMB's *oversight authority over the agencies.* Third, the plan emphasized OMB's long-range demographic, fiscal, and economic analytic and advisory roles.[13]

OMB's internal management issues and some of the dilemmas related to its organization, personnel patterns, training, and institutional overload are addressed in the fourth goal, which seeks the improvement of OMB's ability to carry out its responsibilities by better utilizing and developing its "human resources and information systems."[14] The fourth goal makes the strongest commitment to achieving an improvement of the status quo. The first three imply a continuation of current roles while making efforts to apply performance measures to certain work activities, in order to demonstrate high standards in implementing OMB mandates.

The sixteen specific objectives for the most part involve responsibilities and activities which BOB/OMB has engaged in for much of its institutional life. These include but are not limited to: efforts to produce "timely, accurate" and "high quality" budget documents;[15] assessments of the financial condition of the federal government;[16] "complete, objective and high quality analyses" on priority policy issues;[17] long-range economic forecasts;[18] and an "effective interagency legislative and executive order coordination and clearance process."[19]

Congressional tracking responsibilities acquired since the 1970s and GPRA responsibilities assumed in the mid-1990s are also well represented in several objectives and the strategies offered to achieve them. These are: to provide prompt and accurate "scoring for legislation that affects the budget";[20] to track in order to "implement the five year budget agreement to reach balance by 2002";[21] "to ensure that agency performance plans are . . . integrated into the budget process";[22] to "prepare a government-wide performance plan"; and to finish reviews of GPRA pilot projects.[23] With respect to OMB's regulatory review responsibilities, the Strategic Plan commits to further development of the "benefit" side of its cost–benefit analysis by finding ways to develop better measurements of the net benefits of federal regulations.[24]

Partnership with the National Performance Review is cited in several of the objectives which themselves represent a few of NPR's core goals. These include improving savings and customer satisfaction in agency procurements[25] and the resolution of issues that cross-cut agencies.[26]

A number of the Strategic Plan's objectives are strikingly parallel to those offered in Chapter 11 of this book. For example, the first objective— "recruit, develop, and retain a high quality and diverse staff"[27]—involves the specific strategy of developing a plan to improve the effectiveness of mid-level recruiting, and obliquely acknowledges that overly rapid turnover of entry-level staff is an institutional problem.[28] OMB staff development and enhancement of its analytic capability are addressed by seeking to increase internal OMB and external staff rotations in the agencies and by developing division-specific and institution-wide staff training and development programs.[29] One promising approach for improving staff capability and cutting down on junior staff turnover is to "continue and enhance mentorship programs, and [to encourage] highly qualified senior staff members to serve as mentors."[30] Other useful strategies include the development of measurements to assess staff diversity based on gender, ethnicity, and disability as well as turnover rates of entry-level staff.[31]

Finally, the Strategic Plan realistically assumes that OMB will remain at its current staffing levels, but acknowledges that it should seek to address its overload problem through use of improved technology to increase work-load efficiency. Some specific strategies cited to achieve this end are a broader use of OMB's internal home page to make necessary information more readily accessible to staff;[32] an emphasis on keeping OMB's computer technology up-to-date; the advancement of computer-based inter-change between OMB and the agencies; and the development of " 'work from home' via personal computers."[33]

The General Accounting Office's observations on a first draft of the Stra-tegic Plan provide a thoughtful examination of OMB's current roles and challenges and thus merit brief mention. Moreover, the interchange between GAO and OMB on the substance of the Strategic Plan illustrate the continua-tion of some of OMB's relational behavior patterns with groups external to itself.

Through a series of letters to the Director of OMB, compiled into a single document titled "Observations on OMB's Draft Strategic Plan,"[34] GAO urges OMB to explain more carefully "how" it intends to demonstrate high performance standards. GAO appears most concerned with assessing those of OMB's organizational capabilities that are directly related to its ability to implement both its government-wide management roles and cer-tain related statutes. These capabilities include: the ability to deal with agencies on a cross-cutting basis;[35] the need for OMB to better foster coop-eration and coordination of purpose in the departments and agencies and with Congress;[36] the capability of OMB's internal units to work in a team-like fashion;[37] and the need for OMB staff training to provide technical and other competencies necessary to realize its own goals and those imposed by statute.[38] Along the same lines, GAO asserts that the Strategic Plan could be improved by providing more concrete and specific examples of its "ex-pected results" and the strategies that will be used to determine whether its objectives and goals have been achieved.[39] GAO requests, for example, that OMB specifically assess its performance and results with respect to the OMB 2000 goal to integrate management issues into the budget process.[40]

GAO's "observations" also provide a testament to the institutionalization of OMB's congressional tracking role in the acknowledgment that "OMB plays a key role in both the presidential and congressional budget pro-cesses" ... "preparing and submitting the President's budget to the Con-gress, it monitors the congressional budget process to assess how congressional budget decisions address presidential policies."[41] This asser-tion by an arm of the Congress is striking when referring to a presidential budget office that had refused to allow its examiners to communicate with congressional staff before 1970.

This "congressionalization" of OMB cuts both ways. Although Congress periodically complained to BOB/OMB before the mid-1970s, it was none-theless recognized as an agency that almost exclusively served the presi-dency. As Congress claimed Senate confirmation power over OMB Directors, Deputy Directors, and some Associate Directors, and vested OMB with various additional responsibilities in statutes initiated by the Congress, OMB increasingly became answerable to Congress. Thus, it is not surprising that GAO, in its assessment of the Strategic Plan, is more concerned with Congress's uses for OMB than for its presidential advisory responsibilities. GAO asserts, for example, that "for the most part, the draft plan focuses much more on OMB's responsibilities to advise and assist the President and on its managerial and policy-making roles than it does on the specific statutory requirements OMB must carry out."[42]

Moreover, while GAO recognizes OMB's multifarious responsibilities and burdens and its relatively limited staff size,[43] it fails to factor in the relevance of these limitations in its critiques of OMB's Strategic Plan. Perhaps this is why OMB digs its heels in with respect to two of GAO's critiques: that OMB does not use program evaluations to chart its prog-ress,[44] and that it needs to provide more specificity in illustrating "the relationship between general goals and objectives and annual performance goals."[45] On the former point, OMB maintains in a follow-up letter and in its final strategic plan that, since it does not "run programs," it has no need to use program evaluations "to develop its plan."[46] On the latter point it asserts that more specifics will be presented in the performance plans that it is required to submit to Congress annually.[47]

OMB Redux

As the fall of 1997 turned into the winter of 1998, there were elements of déjà vu to be found in OMB's world. In September 1997, when "Year 2000" computer adjustments appeared to be faltering in some agencies, three Republican members of Congress called on President Clinton to ap-point a special White House assistant to supervise the "Year 2000 Proj-ect."[48] One of these members acknowledged that OMB had "done a 'good job' on Year 2000 policy," but still asserted that "they need someone for whom this is a full-time job."[49] In response, OIRA Administrator Sally Katzen fended off the establishment of new units (outside of OMB) and asserted that the individual agencies themselves must stand accountable for their slow progress on the Year 2000 Project.[50] OMB, according to Katzen, would step-up its watchdog efforts and would "reestablish priorities for these agencies."[51]

The passback process for the President's FY 1999 budget also reinforced the time-honored adage that there is nothing new under the sun. In November 1997, as agencies received their passback decisions, OMB announced a "new" passback and appeals format strikingly reminiscent of Richard Darman's 1989 appeals competition described in Chapter 6 of this book. At least some agencies were informed in their passback guidance from OMB that the estimates that constituted OMB's passback decisions would be placed in one of two categories. Some programs were designated by OMB to be candidates to compete for funds in a Presidential Priority Reserve fund. The President would make the final decision on these funding allocations. Other programs received funding decisions to maintain their "base operations" and other activities the administration had favored in past budget cycles. OMB informed these programs that if they chose not to appeal these decisions, the funding level designated in the passback letter would be maintained in the President's 1999 budget. However, agencies in this category that did choose to appeal for increased funding for base program operations or other initiatives were forewarned that, while their funding levels could be increased, they could also be decreased or remain unchanged. As with the Darman appeals "experiment" nine years earlier, these agency appeals for more funding would be placed in competition with new initiatives OMB had already determined would be funded by the Presidential Priority Reserve.

Nineteen ninety-eight ushered in a striking new development. The new year had barely begun when the President announced his plans to send a balanced budget to Congress for the first time in almost thirty years, three years earlier than the 1997 budget agreement had mandated. The events directly leading up to this historic announcement once again illustrate how important it is for a President to be able to count on prompt and accurate fiscal and budgetary information and how congressional–executive competition for such credible data and projections can tilt the direction that public policy making takes.

On the day after Christmas 1997, Budget Director Raines informed the President of higher than predicted tax collections and lower Medicare expenditures for the previous twelve months.[52] By the end of the first week of January, as more detailed information became available, press accounts reported that the Budget Director and top OMB staff "concluded that they were within striking distance of a balanced budget—provided the Congress and the Administration stayed within the discretionary spending caps set in last year's budget agreement and offset future tax cuts with other savings."[53] With the determination that federal revenue intake had been greater than expected, they decided that a balanced budget for 1999 could be proposed with only minor adjustments to the budget proposal that had been prepared in the fall.[54] The prompt decision to do so allowed the President to take the lead in transmitting the first balanced budget since 1969, and purportedly was also intended to head off efforts by the Republican Congress to pursue further tax cuts.[55] Moreover, since the White House had the information that government coffers would be fuller than expected just days before CBO was expected to make its projections, the President was able to "go first."[56] But the funding had to come from somewhere. Such "minor adjustments" often exert an impact on someone's job, funding, or ability to deliver services. As is usually the case, OMB bore the brunt of delivering the news to the affected programs.

OMB was also there to provide the President with the final assurances that the goal of budget balance was within reach. Purportedly it took only forty-five minutes after meeting with Budget Director Frank Raines, deputy Jack Lew, and NEC chair Gene Sperling for the President to reach a decision.[57] A press account describes the President looking to his Budget Director for final assurance. "How sure are you?" President Clinton reportedly asked Raines. With Raines's reply that he was "sure enough to announce it" that day, the President made his decision.[58] Later that week CBO announced even rosier economic forecasts of federal budget surpluses reaching to the next ten years.[59] Press accounts found it ironic that CBO, which just three years before had been portrayed as the more cautious of the two agencies, was now the more "optimistic" forecaster.[60]

Will a balanced budget and revenue surpluses change OMB's significance and roles? Maybe OMB's roles will be modified, but not its significance. In the long term, an environment free of deficit constraints and unduly contentious budget battles could help OMB assume enhanced information-gathering, analytic, program-planning, and presidential advisory roles. Such an OMB could genuinely serve a presidency pursuing "activist government with fiscal constraint,"[61] envisioned by some observers as a way for President Clinton to bring disparate factions of his party together in a post-deficit environment.[62]

In an April 1998 interview,[63] OMB Director Franklin Raines gave cause for optimism in this respect. Raines observed that once OMB was freed from having to scrutinize each issue's impact on the magnitude of the deficit, it would be able to focus more intensively on the merits of any particular action. Raines hoped that release from a constant focus on the deficit would, in fact be "liberating," but cautioned that in light of tight budget caps, there would still be pressure on government programs to demonstrate that they were meeting their intended objectives through performance measurement.

According to Raines, OMB had also been educating itself on the pros and cons of different strategies for preserving the Social Security system in the future. For several months before a series of presidentially initiated forums on the Social Security issue were launched in early April, OMB had been conducting internal seminars to better inform OMB staff on various aspects of the issue. Moreover, OMB had been a significant player along with the National Economic Council in the planning of the 1998 public debates on the Social Security system.

OMB continues to be a moving target. Six days after the April 1998 interview, Raines resigned as OMB Director to accept an offer to become Chairman of Fannie Mae. The President characterized Raines as having been a "brilliant OMB director,"[64] and nominated Deputy Director Jacob J. Lew to replace him as Budget Director. So began another changing of the guard at OMB's pinnacle, another confirmation process, and another period of uncertainty for OMB.

Yet, in spite of the unpredictability that often surrounds this multi-purpose institution, much also seems to remain unchanged in OMB's world. Presidents require OMB's rapid delivery of accurate economic forecasts, agencies spar with alleged "nay-sayers" at OMB, and congressional committees question whether OMB "can do it all." Presidents also need OMB to tell them how the public's collective will is being translated into executive governance, with what cost, and with what degree of efficiency.

That requirement, most of all, is not likely to change in the future.

Notes

Notes to Preface

1. Paul H. O'Neill, Presentation to Office of Management and Budget Staff (Mimeographed Copy), September 6, 1988, p. 2.
2. There is one exception to this and it involved an interview that dealt only with procedural questions and technical issues.

Notes to Chapter 1

1. O'Neill speech, p. 5.
2. Virginia A. McMurtry, "OMB's Role in the Federal Budgetary Process," in *Office of Management and Budget: Evolving Roles and Future Issues.* Prepared for the Committee on Governmental Affairs, U.S. Senate, by the Congressional Research Service, Library of Congress (February 1986), pp. 24–25.
3. O'Neill speech, p. 3.
4. For a more thorough discussion of the origins of politicization in BOB/OMB, see Chapter 3 of this volume, pp. 54–56.

Notes to Chapter 2

1. These are estimates for budget authority and staff numbers in full-time equivalents (FTEs) for 1997 as they are presented in the budget appendix for fiscal year 1998. See Executive Office of the President, *Appendix. Budget of the United States Government, Fiscal Year 1998,* pp. 59–67.
2. Ibid.
3. *1997 Summer Federal Staff Directory.* Congressional Quarterly Staff Directories, Inc. Alexandria, Virginia, pp. 31–34.
4. Bernard H. Martin, Joseph S. Wholey, and Roy T. Meyers, "The New Equation at OMB: M + B = RMO," *Public Budgeting and Finance* 15, no. 4 (Winter 1995), p. 92.
5. BRD and OMB's General Counsel are usually the first units in OMB to attempt to decipher congressional budgetary fixes such as the Gramm–Rudman–Hollings Acts I and II, the Budget Enforcement Act, and the Line Item Veto Act and determine the

scope of OMB authority under these laws. Often there are aspects of such legislation that are open to interpretation or contradictory. Former director James Miller attests to this reality with regard to Gramm–Rudman–Hollings II in his book, *Fix the U.S. Budget: Urgings of an "Abominable No-Man."* He writes "despite having the best and the brightest in the Budget Review Division of OMB, we were unable to understand the bill fully in all its details. In some areas the legislative language contained outright contradictions. In other areas, there was a great deal of ambiguity, . . it was difficult to understand the intent of Congress as to how the law would apply" p. 56.

6. Executive Office of the President, Office of Management and Budget, Training for New Employees and the FY 1997 Budget Season. TAB E Appropriations Bill Tracking, p. 4.

7. See Chapter 7 for a more thorough discussion of the evolution of the SAP process.

8. Ronald C. Moe, "Central Legislative Clearance," in *Office of Management and Budget: Evolving Roles and Future Issues.* Prepared for the Committee on Governmental Affairs, U.S. Senate (February 1986), p. 180.

9. Ibid., p. 181.

10. Executive Office of the President. Office of Management and Budget, Training for New Employees and the FY 1997 Budget Season. TAB E Basic Elements of the Work of the Legislative Reference Division. Basic Elements No. 2. Clearance of Agency Legislative Proposals.

11. Moe, "Central Legislative Clearance," p. 181.

12. Ibid.

13. Ibid.

14. "Work of the Legislative Reference Division," Basic Elements No. 3.

15. Ibid.

16. Ibid.

17. Ibid.

18. "Work of the Legislative Reference Division," Basic Elements No. 2.

19. General Accounting Office, "Office of Management and Budget. Changes Resulting from the OMB Reorganization" (Washington, DC, December 1995), GAO/GGD/AIMD-96–50, p. 17.

20. Ibid.

21. Stephanie Smith, "OMB and Procurement Management," in *Office of Management and Budget: Evolving Roles and Future Issues* (February 1986), p. 259.

22. "Changes Resulting from OMB 2000 Reorganization," p. 18.

23. Ibid., p. 3.

24. "Appropriations Bill Tracking," p. 5.

25. Miller, *Fix the U.S. Budget,* p. 26.

26. Hugh Heclo, "OMB and the Presidency—the problem of neutral competence," *Public Interest* 38 (Winter 1975): 83–84.

27. For example, Richard Nixon wrote the following to Richard Darman upon his appointment as budget director: "You have the toughness & political skill to handle the most difficult job in government." See Richard Darman, *Who's in Control? Polar Politics and the Sensible Center* (New York: Simon and Schuster, 1996), p. 200.

28. U.S. Senate. Hearings before the Committee on Governmental Affairs on Nomination of Leon Panetta for Director of the Office of Management and Budget, 103rd Congress. First Session. January 11, 1993, p. 1.

29. See, for example, U.S. Senate Hearings before the Committee on Governmental Affairs on the Nomination of Richard G. Darman, Nominee to be Director, Office of Management and Budget. January 19–23, 1989, p. 3.

30. Kathryn Waters Gest, Rhodes Coak, and Larry Light, "Reagan Claims Nomina-

tion; Picks Bush as Running Mate after Deal With Ford Fails," *Congressional Quarterly Weekly Report* 38, no. 29 (July 19, 1980), p. 1983.

31. Personal interview with Alice Rivlin, February 11, 1997.

32. Ibid.

33. See Walter Williams, *Mismanaging America: The Rise of the Anti-Analytic Presidency* (Lawrence, KS: University of Kansas Press, 1990), pp. 31–34. Williams cites three qualities that he considers to be of paramount importance, "at the top of the presidential process," that also seem to be particularly desirable qualities for budget directors to attain. They are integrity, loyalty, and neutral competence. Williams defines integrity as "an unswerving adherence to high moral principles—an individual (not an institutional) code of honor that guides behavior." Loyalty in the case of the OMB Director would apply personally to the President he or she serves, while in the OMB institutional sense would apply to the "Presidency" as a generic concept.

34. Frederick C. Mosher, *A Tale of Two Agencies: A Comparative Analysis of the General Accounting Office and the Office of Management and Budget* (Baton Rouge: Louisiana State University Press, 1984), p. 175.

35. Ibid., p. 187.

36. See Steven Mufson, "Papers But Where's Policy?" *Washington Post,* June 13, 1993, p. H-6.

37. Darman, *Who's in Control?* pp. 219–222.

Notes to Chapter 3

1. For a description of the public reform movement that led to the formation of an "executive budget system," and its underlying causes, see Frederick C. Mosher, *A Tale of Two Agencies: A Comparative Analysis of the General Accounting Office and the Office of Management and Budget* (Baton Rouge: Louisiana State University Press, 1984), pp. 19–21.

2. For a thorough description of these exceptions, see Louis Fisher, *Presidential Spending Power* (Princeton, NJ: Princeton University Press, 1975), pp. 9–35.

3. Mosher, *A Tale of Two Agencies,* p. 20.

4. Ibid.

5. Fisher, *Presidential Spending Power,* pp. 29–31.

6. Ibid., pp. 31–33.

7. Larry Berman, *The Office of Management and Budget and the Presidency, 1921–1979* (Princeton, NJ: Princeton University Press, 1979), pp. 3–4.

8. Mosher, *A Tale of Two Agencies,* pp. 27–31.

9. Ibid., p. 31.

10. Berman, *The Office of Management and Budget and the Presidency,* p. 4.

11. Ibid., pp. 4–5.

12. Mosher, *A Tale of Two Agencies,* p. 43.

13. Charles G. Dawes, *The First Year of the Budget of the United States* (New York, 1923), pp. 8–9, as cited in Mosher, *A Tale of Two Agencies,* pp. 40–41.

14. Mosher, *A Tale of Two Agencies,* pp. 36–37.

15. Ibid., p. 43.

16. Ibid., pp. 42–43; see also Berman, *The Office of Management and Budget and the Presidency,* p. 6.

17. Ibid.

18. Berman, *The Office of Management and Budget and the Presidency,* pp. 7–8.

19. Ibid., p. 12.

20. Mosher, *A Tale of Two Agencies,* pp. 45–46.

21. Berman, *The Office of Management and Budget and the Presidency,* p. 9.

22. Mosher, *A Tale of Two Agencies,* p. 71.

23. Ibid., p. 75.

24. Ibid.

25. Berman, *The Office of Management and Budget and the Presidency,* pp. 11–12.

26. Mosher, *A Tale of Two Agencies,* pp. 65–66.

27. Mosher describes the structure in *A Tale of Two Agencies,* p. 69. See also Berman, *The Office of Management and Budget and the Presidency,* pp. 19–20.

28. Berman, *The Office of Management and Budget and the Presidency,* pp. 20–21.

29. From the Diary of Harold Smith, May 25, 1940, Franklin D. Roosevelt Library, as cited in Berman, *The Office of Management and Budget and the Presidency,* p. 20.

30. Ibid.

31. Ibid., p. 22.

32. Richard Neustadt, Roosevelt's Approach to the Budget Bureau (Mimeo, attachment B of Memorandum from Richard Neustadt to President-elect John Kennedy, October 30, 1960), p. 3, as cited in Berman, *The Office of Management and Budget and the Presidency,* p. 22.

33. Mosher, *A Tale of Two Agencies,* p. 68.

34. Berman, *The Office of Management and Budget and the Presidency,* pp. 23–24.

35. Ibid., p. 24.

36. Ibid., p. 37.

37. Ibid., pp. 27–28.

38. Mosher, *A Tale of Two Agencies,* p. 70.

39. Ibid., p. 192.

40. Berman, *The Office of Management and Budget and the Presidency,* p. 33.

41. Ibid., pp. 31–32.

42. From the Diary of Harold Smith, January 31, 1946, as cited in Berman, *The Office of Management and Budget and the Presidency,* p. 35.

43. Berman, *The Office of Management and Budget and the Presidency,* p. 34.

44. Ibid., p. 40.

45. Ibid., pp. 40–41.

46. Ibid., p. 41.

47. Ibid., p. 43.

48. Ibid., p. 42.

49. Berman, *The Office of Management and Budget and the Presidency,* p. 42.

50. Transcript, Roger Jones Oral History Interview, January 1970, p. 3. Harry S. Truman Library, as quoted in Berman, *The Office of Management and Budget and the Presidency,* p. 42.

51. U.S. Congress. Commission on Organization of the Executive Branch of the Government, *Task Force Report on Fiscal, Budget, Accounting Activities* (January 1949), pp. 52, 40, as cited in Mosher, *A Tale of Two Agencies,* p. 105.

52. U.S. Congress. Commission on Organization of the Executive Branch of the Government, *Report on Budgeting and Accounting* (February 1949), 81st Congress, First Session, p. 23, as cited in Mosher, *A Tale of Two Agencies,* p. 105.

53. Berman, *The Office of Management and Budget and the Presidency,* pp. 44–46.

54. Ibid., p. 45–46.

55. Ibid., p. 46.

56. Mosher, *A Tale of Two Agencies,* p. 106.

57. Ibid., pp. 106–107.

58. Berman, *The Office of Management and Budget and the Presidency,* p. 51.

59. U.S. Congress, House Committee on Appropriations, Independent Offices Appropriations (Washington, DC: Government Printing Office, 1954), p. 615, as cited by Berman, *The Office of Management and Budget and the Presidency,* p. 53.

60. Berman, *The Office of Management and Budget and the Presidency,* pp. 57, 58.

61. Transcript, Matthew Nimetz Oral History interview, January 7, 1969, p. 41. Lyndon Baines Johnson Library, as cited in Berman, *The Office of Management and Budget and the Presidency,* p. 78.

62. Aaron Wildavsky, *The Politics of the Budgetary Process* (Boston: Little, Brown, 1964), p. 36.

63. Berman, *The Office of Management and Budget and the Presidency,* p. 55.

64. Ibid., pp. 53–54.

65. Ibid., p. 53.

66. Ibid., pp. 72–73.

67. For a full description of the Johnson Task Forces, see Norman C. Thomas and Harold L. Wolman, "The Presidency and Policy Formulation: The Task Force Device," *Public Administration Review* 24 (September/October 1969), no. 5.

68. Berman, *The Office of Management and Budget and the Presidency,* pp. 75–77.

69. Ibid.

70. Ibid., pp. 77–78.

71. Ibid.

72. Ibid.

73. Mosher, *Tale of Two Agencies,* p. 107.

74. Ibid., pp. 108, 110.

75. Ibid., p. 108.

76. Ibid.

77. Berman, *The Office of Management and Budget and the Presidency,* p. 59.

78. Ibid., pp. 61–62.

79. Ibid., p. 63–64.

80. Mosher, *A Tale of Two Agencies,* p. 108.

81. Ibid.

82. Berman, *The Office of Management and Budget and the Presidency,* p. 82.

83. Ibid., p. 102.

84. Berman, *The Office of Management and Budget and the Presidency,* p. 83.

85. Ibid.

86. Ibid., p. 85.

87. Mosher, *A Tale of Two Agencies,* p. 109.

88. Berman, *The Office of Management and Budget and the President,* pp. 83–84.

89. Mosher, *A Tale of Two Agencies,* pp. 123–124.

90. Ibid.

91. Allen Schick, "A Death in the Bureaucracy: The Demise of Federal PPB," *Public Administration Review* 33 (March/April 1973), p. 148.

92. Mosher, *A Tale of Two Agencies,* p. 126.

93. Ibid., p. 110.

94. Ibid., p. 111.

95. Berman, *The Office of Management and Budget and the President,* pp. 96–97, 64.

96. Ibid., pp. 65–66, 93–94.

97. Ibid., p. 94.

98. Ibid., p. 93.

99. Merrill T. Collett "The Management of Professional Staff in the Bureau of the Budget," June 1967, p. 11.

100. "The Work of the Steering Group on Evaluation of the Bureau of the Budget," February–July 1967, p. 6–9.

101. Merrill J. Collett "The Management of Professional Staff," pp. 4–5.

102. Mosher, *A Tale of Two Agencies,* p. 111.

103. Ibid.

104. Berman, *The Office of Management and Budget and the Presidency,* p. 102.

105. Ibid.

106. Ibid.

107. Ibid., p. 108.

108. Compilation of Presidential Documents, March 16, 1970 (Washington, DC: Government Printing Office, 1970), pp. 355–357.

109. Mosher, *A Tale of Two Agencies,* p. 112.

110. Richard Nathan, *The Administrative Presidency* (New York: Wiley, 1983), p. 9.

111. Berman, *The Office of Management and Budget and the Presidency,* p. 109–110.

112. Ibid., pp. 108–110.

113. U.S. Congress. Senate Sub-Committee on Executive Reorganization and Government Research, Committee on Government Operations, *Hearings on Reorganization Plan 2 of 1970,* 91st Congress, Second Session, May 7, 1970, p. 35.

114. Berman, *The Office of Management and Budget and the Presidency,* p. 111.

115. Richard Rose, *Managing Presidential Objectives* (New York: Free Press, 1976), p. 67.

116. Peter M. Benda and Charles H. Levine, "OMB's Management Role: Issues of Structure and Strategy," in *Office of Management and Budget,"* *Evolving Roles and Future Issues,* prepared for the Committee on Governmental Affairs, U.S. Senate, by the Congressional Research Service, February 1986, p. 97.

117. Berman, *The Office of Management and Budget and the Presidency,* Appendices, Fig. 1970.

118. Ibid., p. 116.

119. Mosher, *A Tale of Two Agencies,* p. 113.

120. Nathan, *The Administrative Presidency,* p. 7, as quoted in Benda and Levine, "OMB's Management Role," p. 98.

121. Berman, *The Office of Management and Budget and the Presidency,* p. 118.

122. Mosher, *A Tale of Two Agencies,* p. 113–114.

123. Ibid.

124. Benda and Levine, "OMB's Management Role," pp. 103–105.

125. Rose, *Managing Presidential Objectives,* p. 58.

126. Berman, *The Office of Management and Budget and the Presidency,* p. 119, taken from "The Senate Watergate Report," *The Final Report of the Senate Select Committee on Presidential Campaign Activities* (New York: Dell Books, 1974), p. 332.

127. Fisher, *Presidential Spending Power,* pp. 174–177.

128. Berman, *The Office of Management and Budget and the Presidency,* p. 122.

129. Ibid.

130. Ibid., p. 123.

131. Ibid., pp. 123, 127.

132. Hugh Heclo, "OMB and the Presidency—The problem of neutral competence," *Public Interest* 38 (Winter 1975), pp. 84–85.

133. Under the newly reinvigorated and "separate" management units, an OMB-sponsored management improvement conference was attended by over 300 managers from 34 departments and agencies in the federal government. Of the conferees only 35

percent believed that OMB gave more emphasis to management issues than did BOB, as cited in Berman, *The Office of Management and Budget and the Presidency*,   pp. 113–114.After the budget–management merger orchestrated by Fred Malek, a panel of the National Academy of Public Administration (NAPA) characterized OMB's managerial capabilities as "weak and fragmented" in 1976. See NAPA, *The President and Executive Management*; summary of a symposium, (Washington) National Academy of Public Administration, 1976, pp. 19–20.

134. Berman, *The Office of Management and Budget and the Presidency*, p. 128.

135. Ibid.

136. Mosher, *A Tale of Two Agencies*, p. 115.

137. Ibid., p. 131.

138. Executive Office of the President, Office of Management and Budget, *Seventy Issues for FY 1977* (Washington, DC, January 1976).

139. For other discussion and research on politicization in OMB during the mid to late 1970s, see Fisher, *Presidential Spending Power*, pp. 55–58. Stephen J. Wayne, Richard L. Cole, and James F.C. Hyde, Jr., "Advising the President on Enrolled Legislation," *Political Science Quarterly* 94 (Summer 1979), pp. 303–317. Also, Berman, *The Office of Management and Budget and the Presidency*, pp. 118–130.

140. Mosher, *A Tale of Two Agencies*, p. 130.

141. Ibid.

142. Heclo, "OMB and the Presidency—The problem of neutral competence," pp. 80–98.

143. Ibid., pp. 81–82.

144. Ibid., p. 90.

145. Ibid., p. 92.

146. See Berman, *The Office of Management and Budget and the Presidency*, p. 129. Colin Campbell, *Managing the Presidency: Carter, Reagan, and the Search for Executive Harmony* (Pittsburgh, PA: University of Pittsburgh Press, 1986), p. 176.

147. Berman, *The Office of Management and Budget and the Presidency*, p. 129.

148. Colin Campbell, *Managing the Presidency*, pp. 175–176.

149. Ibid., p. 197.

150. Benda and Levine, "OMB's Management Role," p. 112.

151. Walter Williams, *Mismanaging America: The Rise of the Anti-Analytic Presidency*, p. 56.

152. Ibid.

153. Berman, *The Office of Management and Budget and the Presidency*, p. 129.

154. Mosher, *A Tale of Two Agencies*, p. 132.

155. Berman, *The Office of Management and Budget and the Presidency*, p. 129.

156. Allen Schick, "The Problem of Presidential Budgeting," in Hugh Heclo and Lester M. Salamon, eds., *The Illusion of Presidential Government* (Boulder, CO: Westview, 1981), p. 105.

157. Mosher, *A Tale of Two Agencies*, p. 132.

158. Schick, "The Problem of Presidential Budgeting," pp. 103–104.

159. Ibid., pp. 104–105.

160. Ibid., p. 104.

161. Ibid., p. 107.

162. Ibid., pp. 107–108.

163. Ibid., p. 105.

164. Ibid., p. 108.

165. See Aaron Wildavsky, *The Politics of the Budgetary Process*, 2d ed. (Boston: Little, Brown, 1974), pp. xvii–xx.

166. Campbell, *Managing the Presidency,* p. 266.
167. Ibid., p. 267.
168. Ibid.

Notes to Chapter 4

1. Much of the material in pages 65–72 was later published. See Shelley Tomkin, "Playing Politics in OMB: Civil Servants Join the Game," *Presidential Studies Quarterly* 15, no. 1 (1985), pp. 160–163.
2. Larry Berman, *The Office of Management and Budget and the Presidency, 1921–1979* (Princeton, NJ: Princeton University Press, 1979), p. 120.
3. Hugh Heclo, "OMB and the Presidency—the problem of neutral competence," *Public Interest* 38 (Winter 1975), p. 93.
4. Much of the material in pages 80–82 was later published. See Shelley Tomkin, "OMB Budget Examiner's Influence," *The Bureaucrat* (Fall 1983), pp. 43–47.

Notes to Chapter 5

1. Howard E. Shuman, *Politics and the Budget: The Struggle Between the President and the Congress,* 3d ed. (Englewood Cliffs, NJ: Prentice Hall, 1992), p. 273.
2. *Official Proceedings of the Thirty-Second Republican National Convention* (Washington, DC: Republican National Committee, 1980), p. 304.
3. Colin Campbell, *Managing the Presidency: Carter, Reagan, and the Search for Executive Harmony* (Pittsburgh, PA: University of Pittsburgh Press, 1986), p. 156.
4. Ibid., p. 187.
5. Shelley Tomkin, "OMB Budget Examiner's Influence," *The Bureaucrat* 15, no. 1 (Fall 1983), p. 46.
6. Ibid.
7. Ibid.
8. Campbell, *Managing the Presidency,* p. 185. See also Hugh Heclo, "Executive Budget Making," in Gregory B. Mills and John L. Palmer, eds., *Federal Budget Policy in the 1980s* (Washington, DC: The Urban Institute, 1984), pp. 255–291.
9. Aaron Wildavsky, *The New Politics of the Budgetary Process,* 2d ed. (Berkeley, CA: HarperCollins, 1992), p. 187.
10. Bruce Johnson, "From Analyst to Negotiator: The OMB's New Role," *Journal of Policy Analysis and Management* 3 (Summer 1984), p. 505.
11. Bruce Johnson, "OMB and the Budget Examiner: Changes in the Reagan Era," *Public Budgeting and Finance* 8 (Winter 1988), pp. 11–12.
12. Frederick C. Mosher, *A Tale of Two Agencies* (Baton Rouge: Louisiana State University Press, 1984), p. 185.
13. Stockman admitted in his account of his experiences as budget director that both his ideological fervor and his ego probably got the best of him. He wrote, "Had I been a standard policymaker and not an ideologue with a Grand Doctrine for changing the whole complexion of American government, I would have panicked at this point" (when the emerging deficit projections started appearing) "and said, This won't work. . . ." "But I had my own agenda. Four weeks of nonstop budget cutting, congressional briefings, press interviews and Washington show stopping had given me an exaggerated sense of power." See David A. Stockman, *The Triumph of Politics: How the Reagan Revolution Failed* (New York: Harper & Row, 1986), p. 132.

14. Writing of the first weeks of Reagan's term and speaking of the fact that the anticipated budget plan was "raising defense and cutting taxes on a multi-year basis," Stockman pondered, "How much of the 15 percent of GNP that went to inherited domestic spending had to be shrunk so that the defense increase and tax cuts wouldn't swell the deficit?" "History cannot blame the President for not considering this crucial question; I never provided him with a single briefing on this. There simply wasn't time." Stockman, *The Triumph of Politics*, p. 91.

Later in early February, when OMB staff had begun forecasting a $130 billion deficit by 1984 with the defense buildup and the Kemp–Roth tax cut factored in (ibid., p. 122), Stockman recalls that "the President of the United States was not even given the slightest warning that his economic policy revolution was bursting at its fiscal seams" (ibid., p. 127). Further, he pondered, "How many congressional horses do you need to cut $40 million more—on top of the black book full of cuts already proposed? . . . This essential feasibility question was never asked. Our team had no serious legislative experience or wisdom. Most of them had no comprehension of the numbers, and I didn't really care. Mowing down the political resistance was the whole purpose of the Reagan Revolution" (ibid., p. 128).

In fairness to Stockman, he shows at various points in the book that his superiors were not an easy group to educate as to the intricacies of budgetary or economic concepts and terminologies (ibid., pp. 12, 129). Stockman admits to being "worried to death about where my numbers were going" (ibid., p. 270). He was worried that given congressional and political realities, the domestic programmatic cuts that had a chance of being approved by Congress would not be enough to avoid staggering deficits unless the defense increases were "slowed," and/or domestic spending was drastically reduced and/or taxes on imported oil, alcohol, and tobacco were imposed. It was at this time that he communicated his bad news to the President and his advisors forcefully enough and began to acknowledge to himself that President Reagan was comfortable with and in agreement with only half of Stockman's vision (ibid., pp. 270–276).

15. These interviews culminated in publication of an article that caused quite a furor inside the Reagan administration, received a good deal of attention in the press, and led to President Reagan's "woodshed talk" with Stockman. See William Greider, "The Education of David Stockman," *The Atlantic* 248, no. 6 (December 1981), p. 27–54.

16. Stockman admits at the end of his own book, "since no one in the White House wanted to propose the first triple-digit budget deficit in history, I finally did what the *Atlantic* story seemed to accuse me of. I out and out cooked the books, inventing $15 billion per year of utterly phony cuts in order to get Ronald Reagan's first full budget below the $100 billion deficit level. As on prior occasions, I rationalized this as a holding action. When the President finally came around, we would substitute new revenues for the smoke and mirrors." Stockman, *Triumph of Politics*, p. 353.

17. Ibid., p. 376.

18. Allen Schick, *The Capacity to Budget* (Washington: Urban Institute Press, 1990), p. 162.

19. Shuman, *Politics and the Budget,* pp. 272–273.

20. Executive Office of the President, Office of Management and Budget, *A Citizen's Guide to the Federal Budget* (Washington, DC, FY 1996), p. 17.

21. Schick, *The Capacity to Budget,* p. 169.

22. Bruce Johnson, "The OMB Budget Examiner: Changes in the Reagan Era," paper prepared for the Ninth Annual Research Conference of the Association for Public Policy Analysis and Management, Bethesda, Maryland, October 30, 1987, p. 8. See also, Bruce Johnson, "From Analyst to Negotiator: The OMB's New Role," *Journal of Policy Analysis and Management* 3, no. 4 (1984), pp. 510–511.

23. Lawrence J. Haas, "After Stockman," *National Journal,* June 27, 1987, p. 1690.

24. Ibid. See also Lawrence J. Haas, "Budget Guru," *National Journal* 22, no. 3 (January 20, 1990), p. 114.

25. Bruce Johnson, "The OMB Budget Examiner and the Congressional Budget Process," *Public Budgeting and Finance* 9, no. 1 (Spring 1989), p. 10.

26. Ibid., p. 11.

27. James C. Miller III, *Fix the U.S. Budget: Urgings of an "Abominable No-Man"* (Stanford, CA: Hoover Institution Press, Stanford University, 1994), p. 39.

28. Lawrence J. Haas, "Budget Guru," *National Journal* 22, no. 3 (January 20, 1990), pp. 111, 112.

29. U.S. Senate. Committee on Governmental Affairs on Nomination of Richard G. Darman, to Be Director, Office of Management and Budget, 101st Congress, First Session, January 19, 23, 1989, p. 197.

30. Ibid., p. 40.

31. Lawrence J. Haas, "Darman's OMB," *National Journal* 24, no. 5 (February 1, 1992), p. 261.

32. Richard Darman, *Who's in Control? Polar Politics and the Sensible Center* (New York: Simon & Schuster, 1996), p. 233.

33. Haas, "Budget Guru," p. 112.

34. Ibid., p. 114.

35. Darman, *Who's in Control?* p. 238.

36. Haas, "Budget Guru," p. 111.

37. Darman, *Who's In Control?* p. 291.

38. Haas, "Darman's OMB," p. 261.

39. Ibid.

40. See Elizabeth Drew, *On The Edge: The Clinton Presidency* (New York: Simon and Schuster, 1994), p. 33. Drew characterized the image of Darman held by some Clintonites as "free wheeling and talkative [to the press]."

41. Darman, *Who's In Control?* p. 107.

42. Ibid., p. 233.

43. Ibid., p. 234.

44. Ibid., p. 242.

45. Ibid., p. 240.

46. Ibid., p. 297.

47. Ibid., p. 298.

48. Macon Morehouse, "Darman Reassures, But Panel Wary," *Congressional Quarterly Weekly Report,* May 27, 1989, p. 1253.

49. U.S. Congress. House Committee on Appropriations, Treasury, Postal Service, and General Government Appropriations for Fiscal Year 1986. Hearings before Sub-Committee, 99th Congress, 1st Session, Part 3, Executive Office of the President, April 23, 1985, p. 551.

50. Darman Confirmation Testimony, p. 42.

51. Ibid.

52. General Accounting Office (hereafter GAO), "Managing the Government: Revised Approach Could Improve OMB's Effectiveness," GAO/GGD-89-65 (May 1989), p. 20.

53. Darman Confirmation Testimony, p. 42.

54. GAO, "Managing the Government," p. 21.

55. Ibid.

56. The Budget of the United States Government Fiscal Year 1990. Part Four, p. 278.

57. The Budget of the United States Government Fiscal Year 1991. Appendix One, p. 209.

58. The Budget of the United States Government Fiscal Year 1992. Appendix, p. 223.

59. The Budget of the United States Government Fiscal Year 1993. Appendix, p. 95.

60. GAO, "Managing the Government," p. 20.

61. Walter Williams, *Mismanaging America: The Rise of the Anti-analytic Presidency* (Lawrence: University Press of Kansas, 1990), p. 97. To Williams, these skills meant "less than meets the eye," if "substantive area specialization" was lacking.

62. Ibid., p. 94.

63. *Presidential Management of Rule Making in Regulatory Agencies,* report by a Panel of the National Academy of Public Administration (Washington, DC: National Academy of Public Administration, 1987), p. 38, as cited in Williams, *Mismanaging America,* p. 94.

64. Ibid.

65. Ibid., p. 95.

66. Irwin Goodwin, "Exodus of Five OMB Science Staffers Leaves Gaps in Key Science Policies," *Physics Today* 45, no. 9 (September 1992), pp. 56–57.

67. Ibid., p. 56.

68. Ibid., p. 57.

69. "The Executive Presidency: Federal Management for the 1990s." Report by an Academy Panel for the 1988–89 Presidential Transition of the National Academy of Public Administration (Washington, DC: National Academy of Public Administration, 1988), p. 38.

70. Ibid.

71. Williams, *Mismanaging America,* p. 91.

72. Ibid.

73. Haas, "Darman's OMB," pp. 259–260.

74. Johnson, "OMB Examiner and Congressional Budget Process," p. 12.

75. Ibid., pp. 12–13. Bruce Johnson asserted that OMB either needed to expand its staff (budget examiners in particular) or scale down its responsibilities. He further recommended that OMB institute separate staffs to handle legislative tracking and cost estimation duties and to perform in-depth analysis of Executive Branch programs, citing a similar arrangement in CBO as a model. Johnson's position is well taken, but the realistic prospects of enlarging OMB staff to any significant degree were not good at the time, and were to be less so in the 1990s. Thus institutional overload continued to be a significant dilemma for OMB.

Notes to Chapter 6

1. See Allen Schick, *The Capacity to Budget* (Washington, DC: Urban Institute Press, 1990), pp. 162–169.

2. Shelley Tomkin, "OMB Budget Examiners' Influence," *The Bureaucrat* (Fall 1983), p. 46. Shelley Tomkin, "Playing Politics in OMB: Civil Servants Join the Game," *Presidential Studies Quarterly* 15, no. 1 (1985), pp. 168–169. Bruce Johnson, "From Analyst to Negotiator: The OMB's New Role," *Journal of Policy Analysis and Management* 3, no. 4 (1984), p. 512; Bruce Johnson, "OMB and the Budget Examiner: Changes in the Reagan Era," *Public Budgeting and Finance* 8 (Winter 1988), p. 8.

Bruce Johnson cites a number of factors that have eroded the amount of time available for budget examiners to produce in-depth analysis and gather information with respect to OMB's traditional role of preparing the President's budget. A number of these factors are discussed in Chapters 5 and 7 of this book. They include an increase in the magnitude of information Congress requires as part of the President's annual budget submission to Congress and the time necessary to support "top-down budgeting."

3. Tomkin, "OMB Budget Examiner's Influence," pp. 46–47. See also Hugh Heclo, "Executive Budget Making," in Gregory B. Mills and John L. Palmer, eds., *Federal Budget Policy in the 1980s* (Washington, DC: Urban Institute Press, 1984).

4. Tomkin, "Playing Politics in OMB," pp. 160–163. Bruce Johnson, "From Analyst to Negotiator, pp. 512–513.

5. Schick, *The Capacity to Budget,* p. 169.

6. Viveca Novak, "Previewing Bill Clinton's First Budget," *National Journal* 25, no. 2, January 9, 1993, p. 83.

7. See Chapter 9.

8. U.S. Office of Management and Budget, *Examiner's Handbook* (Washington, DC: Office of Management and Budget), p. 301.

9. Ibid., p. 305.

10. Johnson, "OMB and the Budget Examiner: Changes in the Reagan Era," p. 10.

11. See Executive Office of the President, Circular A-11, *Preparation and Submission of Budget Estimates,* July 1992.

12. Executive Office of the President, Office of Management and Budget. *Training for New Employees and the FY 1997 Budget Season.* TAB Q, Agency Budget Submissions.

13. Ibid.

14. Executive Office of the President, Office of Management and Budget. *Training for New Employees and the FY 1997 Budget Season.* "FY 1997 Agency Budget and Policy Reviews/Fall Scorekeeping." TAB K unnumbered.

15. Ibid.

16. U.S. Office of Management and Budget, *Examiner's Handbook,* p. 305.

17. Executive Office of the President, Office of Management and Budget. *Training for New Employees and the FY 1997 Budget Season.* TAB Q. "Policy Analysis at OMB and Writing an Issue Paper—Basics For New Examiners," pp. 1–6.

18. Ibid.

19. Ibid.

20. *Training for New Employees and the FY 1997 Budget Season.* TAB Q. "Policy Analysis at OMB and Writing an Issue Paper—A Few Things to Look For When You Review a Decision Paper." Unnumbered.

21. Ibid.

22. Ibid.

23. *Training for New Employees and the FY 1997 Budget Season.* TAB Q. "Policy Analysis at OMB and Writing an Issue Paper—Basics For New Examiners," p. 4.

24. Ibid., p. 6.

25. Ibid.

26. See Shelley Tomkin, "The Role of the Budget Examiner as Political Analyst." Paper presented at the Southern Political Science Association Meeting, Atlanta, Georgia, November 6–8, 1980.

27. Tomkin, "OMB Budget Examiner's Influence," p. 46.

28. Ibid.

29. Johnson, "OMB and the Budget Examiner: Changes in the Reagan Era," p. 16.

30. Ibid.

31. See Chapter 5 and also William Greider's "The Education of David Stockman," *The Atlantic,* vol. 248, no. 6 (December 1981).

32. Paul Blustein and Bill McAllister, "Budget Director Devises a Novel Plan to Constrain Spending, Agencies Would Have to Compete for Pool of Money," *Washington Post,* November 24, 1989, p. A-1.

33. *The Budget of the United States Government, Fiscal Year 1993* (Washington, DC: Government Printing Office, 1992).

34. *The Budget of the United States Government,* 1993, Part One. "Agenda for Growth and Priorities for the Future," Investing in the Future 8. Providing Hope to Distressed Communities, p. 175.

35. Ibid. Investing in the Future 9. Ending the Scourge of Drugs and Crime, p. 189.

36. Lawrence J. Haas, "Darman's OMB," *National Journal* 24, no. 5 (February 1, 1992), p. 261.

37. *The Budget of the United States Government,* 1993, Appendix One, "Federal Programs by Function, Agency, and Account."

Notes to Chapter 7

1. Now there is only one budget resolution. The second budget resolution was later dropped because the required deadlines for this procedure could not be met by the Congress. See Howard E. Shuman, *Politics and the Budget,* 3d ed. (Englewood Cliffs, NJ: Prentice-Hall, 1992), p. 240.

2. For a discussion of the principles and intentions of the Budget Act, see Shuman, *Politics and the Budget,* pp. 230–246.

3. Ibid., pp. 237–239.

4. Stanley E. Collender, *The Guide to the Federal Budget, Fiscal 1994* (Washington, DC: The Urban Institute Press, 1993), p. 52.

5. Ibid., pp. 53–54.

6. Ibid.

7. Shuman, *Politics and the Budget,* p. 241.

8. Collender, *Guide to the Federal Budget,* p. 54.

9. Shuman, *Politics and the Budget,* p. 256.

10. Ibid., p. 257.

11. Bruce E. Johnson, "From Analyst to Negotiator: The OMB's New Role," *Journal of Policy Analysis and Management* 3 (Summer 1984), p. 503.

12. Collender, *Guide to the Federal Budget,* p. 195.

13. Johnson, "From Analyst to Negotiator," p. 503.

14. Ibid., p. 504.

15. Shelley Tomkin, "Office of Management and Budget (OMB) Congressional Relations During the Reagan Administration." Prepared for delivery at the 1985 Annual Meeting of the American Political Science Association, New Orleans, August 29–September 1, 1985, p. 6.

16. Jonathan Rauch, "Stockman's Quiet Revolution at OMB May Leave Indelible Mark on Agency," *National Journal* 7, no. 21 (May 25, 1985), p. 1213.

17. Tomkin, "OMB Congressional Relations," p. 6.

18. Shelley Tomkin, "Playing Politics in OMB: Civil Servants Join the Game," *Presidential Studies Quarterly* 15, no. 1 (Winter 1985), p. 162.

19. Ibid., p. 163.

20. Shuman, *Politics and the Budget,* p. 273.

21. William Greider, "The Education of David Stockman," The *Atlantic* 248, no. 6 (December 1981), p. 30.

22. Ibid., p. 33.

23. Shuman, *Politics and the Budget,* pp. 258–266.

24. Ibid., p. 261.

25. Ibid.

26. For a discussion of the strategies and politics involved in the passage of the Reagan 1981 tax cut, see Shuman, *Politics and the Budget*, p. 266–270, and Greider, "The Education of David Stockman," pp. 35–50.

27. Shuman, *Politics and the Budget*, p. 271.

28. Allen Schick, *The Capacity to Budget* (Washington, DC: Urban Institute Press, 1990), pp. 162–163.

29. Aaron Wildavsky, *The New Politics of the Budget Process*, 2d ed. (New York: HarperCollins, 1992), pp. 183–184.

30. Ibid.

31. Schick, *The Capacity to Budget*, pp. 174–175.

32. Johnson, "From Analyst to Negotiator," p. 504.

33. For example, in 1982, White House negotiations with a group of congressional leaders known as the "Gang of 17" included sparring over the Reagan-initiated tax cuts and proposed cuts in Social Security and did not resolve the differences. In 1983 partisan conflict had reached such a high point that White House negotiations took place mostly between the White House and Senate Republicans. Talks in 1984's "Rose Garden Summit" did not strike immediate bargains. For a review of these summits, see Schick, *The Capacity to Budget*, pp. 184–186.

34. Shuman, *Politics and the Budget*, p. 280.

35. Schick, *The Capacity to Budget*, p. 174.

36. Ibid.

37. Ibid., p. 173.

38. Ibid., p. 180–181.

39. Ibid.

40. Ibid.

41. Ibid.

42. Ibid., p. 182.

43. Ibid., p. 183.

44. Wildavsky, *The New Politics of the Budget Process*, p. 235.

45. The material in pages 148–153, unless otherwise noted, was taken from Shelley Lynne Tomkin, "Office of Management and Budget (OMB) Congressional Relations during the Reagan Administration." Prepared for delivery at the 1985 Annual Meeting of the American Political Science Association, New Orleans, August 29–September 1, 1985. The paper was later published in abridged form. See Shelley Lynne Tomkin, "Reagan OMB's Congress Watchers," *The Bureaucrat* 16, no. 2 (Summer 1987), pp. 55–60.

46. Bruce Johnson, "The OMB Budget Examiner and the Congressional Budget Process," *Public Budgeting and Finance* 9, no. 1 (Spring 1989), p. 6.

47. Ibid.

48. Ibid.

49. See *Centralized Budget Management System (CBMS) Requirements Analysis and Management Plan* (hereafter *CBMS Plan*) (Washington, DC: Office of Management and Budget, February 4, 1982).

50. Ibid., p. 3.

51. Ibid.

52. Ibid.

53. Ibid., p. 43.

54. Ibid.

55. Ibid., p. 45.

56. Bruce Johnson, "OMB and the Budget Examiner: Changes in the Reagan Era," *Public Budgeting and Finance* 8 (Winter 1988), p. 4.

57. Johnson, "OMB Budget Examiner and the Congressional Budget Process," p. 5.

58. Ibid., p. 6. Johnson shows how OMB did not have the capability to perform all these functions, when Stockman first became director.

59. For a description of summitry during the 1980s, see Schick, *The Capacity to Budget,* pp. 185–189.

60. Allen Schick, *The Federal Budget. Politics, Policy, Process* (Washington, DC: Brookings Institution, 1995), pp. 91, 214.

61. Johnson, "OMB Budget Examiner and the Congressional Budget Process," p. 6.

62. Hugh Heclo, "Executive Budget Making," in Gregory B. Mills and John L. Palmer, eds., *Federal Budget Policy in the 1980s* (Washington, DC: Urban Institute Press, 1984), p. 281.

63. Julie Kosterlitz, "Educated Guesswork," *National Journal* 23, no. 40 (October 5, 1991).

64. Ibid., p. 2408.

65. Johnson, "From Analyst to Negotiator," p. 504.

66. Wildavsky, *The New Politics of the Budgetary Process,* p. 185.

67. Ibid.

68. Ibid.

69. Ibid.

70. Ibid., pp. 184–185.

71. Ibid., p. 185.

72. Collender, *Guide to the Federal Budget,* p. 10.

73. Schick, *The Capacity to Budget,* p. 97.

74. Ibid., p. 98.

75. Ibid.

76. Greider, "The Education of David Stockman," p. 51.

77. Schick, *The Capacity to Budget,* p. 99.

78. Collender, *Guide to the Federal Budget,* p. 11.

79. Schick, *The Capacity to Budget,* p. 99.

80. Ibid., p. 100.

81. Greider, "The Education of David Stockman," p. 38.

82. Schick, *The Capacity to Budget,* p. 99.

83. Ibid.

84. Lawrence J. Haas, "Darman's OMB," *National Journal* 24, no. 5 (February 1, 1992), p. 261.

85. Shuman, *Politics and the Budget,* p. 283.

86. For a basic description of the workings of the Gramm–Rudman–Hollings process, see Shuman, *Politics and the Budget,* pp. 286–290.

87. See Bowsher v. Synar et al., Supreme Court of the United States, July 7, 1986.

88. Shuman, *Politics and the Budget,* pp. 291–292.

89. Ibid., pp. 292–293.

90. Ibid., pp. 288–289.

91. Ronald C. Moe, "Central Legislative Clearance," in *Office of Management and Budget: Evolving Roles and Future Issues,* prepared for the Committee on Governmental Affairs, U.S. Senate (February 1986), p. 181.

92. Ibid.

93. Ibid., p. 182.

94. Ibid.

95. Ibid.

96. Ibid.

97. Johnson, "OMB and the Budget Examiner," p. 12.

98. Ibid., pp. 12–13.

99. Shuman, *Politics and the Budget,* p. 305.

100. For an account of events leading up to the 1990 budget talks, see Shuman, *Politics and the Budget,* pp. 305–314.

101. Collender, *Guide to the Federal Budget,* p. 12.

102. Ibid., pp. 21–22.

103. Ibid., p. 22.

104. For a discussion of maximum allowable deficit levels in the BEA, see Collender, *Guide to the Federal Budget,* pp. 23–25.

105. Ibid., p. 23.

106. Ibid., p. 28.

107. Shuman, *Politics and the Budget,* pp. 338–339.

108. Ibid., p. 338. For other discussion of OMB's "enforcement" powers under the BEA, see also Susan F. Rasky, "Substantial Power on Spending Is Shifted from Congress to Bush," *New York Times,* October 30, 1990, p. A-1; and Richard Doyle and Jerry McCaffery, "The Budget Enforcement Act in 1991: Isometric Budgeting," *Public Budgeting and Finance* 12, no. 1 (Spring 1992), pp. 3–15.

109. For examples of how this was implemented, see Doyle and McCaffery, "The Budget Enforcement Act in 1991," pp. 8–10.

110. Rasky, "Substantial Power on Spending Is Shifted."

111. Collender, *Guide to the Federal Budget,* p. 29.

112. Shuman, *Politics and the Budget,* p. 337.

113. I obtained these definitions through a Xeroxed sheet that I was given during the course of interviewing in OMB. This sheet was titled "Introduction" to a report fulfilling "the requirements of Public Law 102-55, which provides dire emergency supplemental appropriations for humanitarian assistance to refugees and displaced persons in and around Iraq and for peacekeeping activities," p. ii.

114. Ibid.

115. Doyle and McCaffery, "Budget Enforcement Act in 1991," p. 11.

116. George Hager, "Supplemental Spending Bills Bolster OMB Budget Clout," *Congressional Quarterly Weekly Report* (July 6, 1991), p. 1820.

117. Doyle and McCaffery, "Budget Enforcement Act in 1991," pp. 11–12.

118. Rasky, "Substantial Power on Spending Is Shifted."

119. Doyle and McCaffery, "Budget Enforcement Act in 1991," pp. 9–10.

120. Lawrence J. Haas, "What OMB Hath Wrought," *National Journal* 20, no. 36 (September 3, 1988), p. 2190.

121. Wildavsky, *The New Politics of the Budgetary Process,* p. 259.

122. Lawrence J. Haas, "After Stockman," *National Journal,* June 27, 1987, p. 1690.

123. Lawrence J. Haas, "Darman's OMB," *National Journal* 24, no. 5 (February 1, 1992), p. 261.

124. Ibid. See also Paul Blustein, "OMB Chief Wielding Knife on Budgetary Explanations," *Washington Post,* December 13, 1989, p. A-23.

125. Haas, "Darman's OMB," p. 261.

Notes to Chapter 8

1. Randall B. Ripley and James W. Davis, "The Bureau of the Budget and Executive Branch Agencies: Notes on Their Interaction," *The Journal of Politics* 29, no. 4 (1967) p. 768.

2. Ibid., pp. 751–752.

3. Ibid., pp. 752–753.

4. Ibid., p. 753.

5. Ibid., pp. 767–768.

6. Ibid., pp. 758–759.

7. Ibid., pp. 760–761.

8. Ibid., pp. 758–759.

9. Ibid., p. 759.

10. Ibid., p. 755.

11. Ibid., p. 761.

12. Ibid., p. 765.

13. Ibid., pp. 765–766.

14. Ibid., pp. 766–767.

15. Ibid., pp. 760–761.

16. Ibid., pp. 760–763.

17. Ibid.

18. Ibid., pp. 762–763.

19. Ibid., p. 764. The latter concern came from one of Ripley and Davis's agency interviews.

20. See Shelley Tomkin, "Decision-making Within OMB: The Role of the Budget Examiner" (Ph.D. diss., George Washington University, 1981), pp. 160–207.

21. Executive Office of the President, Office of Management and Budget, *Training For New Employees and the FY 1997 Budget Season.* TAB Q. "Policy Analysis at OMB and Writing an Issue Paper, Basics for New Examiners," p. 5.

22. Albert J. Kliman and Louis Fisher, "Budget Reform Proposals in the NPR Report," *Public Budgeting and Finance* 15, no. 1 (1995), pp. 30–31.

23. Ibid., p. 31.

24. Public Law 67-13, June 10, 1921, Sect. 209.

25. Larry Berman, *The Office of Management and Budget and the Presidency, 1921–1979* (Princeton, NJ: Princeton University Press, 1979), pp. 5–8.

26. Frederick C. Mosher, *A Tale of Two Agencies* (Baton Rouge: Louisiana State University Press, 1984), pp. 45–46.

27. Peter M. Benda and Charles H. Levine, "OMB's Management Role: Issues of Structure and Strategy," in *Office of Management and Budget: Evolving Roles and Future Issues.* Prepared for the Committee on Governmental Affairs, U.S. Senate, by the Congressional Research Service (February 1986), p. 79.

28. Ibid., pp. 81–82.

29. Ibid., p. 82.

30. Benda and Levine, "OMB's Management Role," pp. 82–83. Berman, *OMB and the Presidency,* pp. 28–29; and Mosher, *A Tale of Two Agencies,* p. 70.

31. Allen Schick, "The Budget Bureau That Was: Thoughts on the Rise, Decline, and Future of a Presidential Agency," *Law and Contemporary Problems* 35, no. 3, p. 529.

32. Mosher, *A Tale of Two Agencies,* p. 105.

33. Benda and Levine, "OMB's Management Role," p. 85.

34. Marver Bernstein, "The Presidency and Management Improvement," *Law and Contemporary Problems* 35 (Summer 1970), pp. 506, 508.

35. Benda and Levine, "OMB's Management Role," p. 86.

36. Mosher, *A Tale of Two Agencies,* p. 106–107.

37. Benda and Levine, "OMB's Management Role," p. 86.

38. Ibid., p. 86–87. This tendency was criticized by the second Hoover Commission, which recommended expanding BOB's management staff. Rockefeller's PACGO, which had shown some hostility to BOB, proposed creating a separate Office of Management or reorganizing BOB and upgrading its management capabilities.

39. Mosher, *A Tale of Two Agencies,* p. 108.

40. Bernstein, "Presidency and Management Improvement," p. 512.

41. Benda and Levine, "OMB's Management Role," p. 91.

42. See Chapter 3, pp. 44–46.

43. U.S. Bureau of the Budget. The Work of the Steering Group on Evaluation of the Bureau of the Budget, July 1967, as cited in Benda and Levine, "OMB's Management Role," p. 93.

44. Mosher, *A Tale of Two Agencies,* p. 111.

45. Ibid.

46. Ibid.

47. Ibid.

48. Richard Rose, *Managing Presidential Objectives* (New York: Free Press, 1976), p. 67.

49. Benda and Levine, "OMB's Management Role," p. 97.

50. Ibid., pp. 98–99.

51. Mosher, *A Tale of Two Agencies,* p. 113–114.

52. Ibid., p. 114.

53. Rose, *Managing Presidential Objectives,* p. 67.

54. Ibid., pp. 67–68.

55. Ibid.

56. Ibid.

57. Benda and Levine, "OMB's Management Role," p. 105.

58. Ibid., p. 106.

59. Ibid., p. 107.

60. Ibid.

61. Donald Haider, "Presidential Management Initiatives: A Ford Legacy to Executive Management Improvement," *Public Administration Review* 39 (May/June 1979), p. 250.

62. Ibid., p. 254.

63. Ibid., p. 255.

64. U.S. General Accounting Office (hereafter U.S. GAO), "Selected Government-Wide Management Improvement Efforts—1970 to 1980," GAO/GGD-83-69 (Washington, DC, August 8, 1983), p. 18.

65. Ibid.

66. "The President and Executive Management." Summary of a Symposium, (Washington) The National Academy of Public Administration, 1976, pp. 19–20.

67. Ibid.

68. Ibid.

69. Benda and Levine, "OMB's Management Role," p. 110.

70. Ibid., pp. 111–112.

71. Ibid., p. 112.

72. Ibid.

73. Ibid.

74. John R. Dempsey, "Carter Reorganization: A Mid-Term Appraisal," *Public Administration Review* 39 (January/February 1979), p. 74.

75. Benda and Levine, "OMB's Management Role," pp. 113–114.

76. Dempsey, "Carter Reorganization," p. 35.

77. U.S. GAO, "Selected Government-Wide Management Improvement Efforts," p. 20.

78. Ibid., p. 21.

79. Ibid.

80. Dempsey, "Carter Reorganization," p. 75.

81. Benda and Levine, "OMB's Management Role," p. 117.

82. Ibid., pp. 118–119.

83. Ibid., p. 120.

84. Ibid.

85. Ibid.

86. Chester A. Newland, "Executive Office Policy Apparatus: 'Enforcing the Reagan Agenda,'" in Lester M. Salamon and Michael S. Lund, eds., *The Reagan Presidency and the Governing of America* (Washington, DC: The Urban Institute, 1985), p. 166.

87. Benda and Levine, "OMB's Management Role," p. 123.

88. Ibid., p. 123.

89. Ibid.

90. Newland, "Executive Office Policy Apparatus," p. 166.

91. U.S. GAO, "Selected Government-Wide Management Improvement Efforts," p. 35.

92. Benda and Levine, "OMB's Management Role," p. 126.

93. Ibid., p. 127.

94. Mark L. Goldstein, "The Flickering 'M' in OMB," *Government Executive* 22, no. 3 (March 1990), p. 28.

95. U.S. Congress, General Accounting Office (hereafter GAO), *Managing the Government: Revised Approach Could Improve OMB's Effectiveness,* GGD-89-65 (May 1989), p. 3.

96. GAO, *Managing the Government,* p. 3.

97. Ibid.

98. Ibid., p. 21. This figure included all management offices except for OIRA.

99. Ibid., p. 71.

100. In his book, *Fix the Budget,* Miller admits that the "budget problem . . . left little opportunity for fundamental reform of government organization." However, he cited success during his tenure with efforts toward reduction of government waste, privatization, and productivity improvement goals. See James C. Miller III, *Fix the Budget: Urgings of an "Abominable No-man"* (Stanford, CA: Hoover Institution Press, 1994), p. 22.

101. Goldstein, "The Flickering 'M' in OMB," p. 32.

102. Ibid., p. 31.

103. GAO, *Managing the Government,* p. 3.

104. Goldstein, "The Flickering 'M' in OMB," p. 31.

105. U.S. Congress, Senate Committee on Banking, Housing and Urban Affairs. HUD/Mod Rehab Investigation Subcommittee, *Final Report and Recommendations,* Committee Print 124, 101st Congress, Second Session (Washington, DC: Government Printing Office, 1990), p. 194.

106. Goldstein, "The Flickering 'M' in OMB," p. 31.

107. National Academy of Public Administration (hereafter NAPA), "The Executive Presidency: Federal Management for the 1990s." A Report by an Academy Panel for the 1988–89 Presidential Transition, NAPA, (Washington, DC, September 1988).

108. NAPA, "The Executive Presidency," pp. 28, 31; GAO, *Managing the Government,* pp. 4, 94, 95.

109. NAPA, "The Executive Presidency," p. 28; GAO, *Managing the Government,* pp. 2, 63–67.

110. NAPA, "The Executive Presidency," p. 28; GAO, *Managing the Government,* pp. 63–67.

111. NAPA, "The Executive Presidency," p. 27.

112. Ibid.

113. Goldstein, "The Flickering 'M' in OMB," p. 32.

114. GAO, *Managing the Government,* pp. 79–80.

115. Ibid., pp. 79, 81.

116. Ibid., pp. 66–67.

117. Ibid., p. 67.

118. Ibid., pp. 79–81.

119. Ibid., pp. 85–86.

120. Ibid., p. 83.

121. Ibid.

122. Ibid., pp. 58, 83–84.

123. NAPA, "The Executive Presidency," p. 28; GAO, *Managing the Government,* p. 99.

124. NAPA, "The Executive Presidency," p. 28.

125. GAO, *Managing the Government,* p. 4.

126. Ibid., p. 96.

127. Ibid., pp. 4, 7.

128. NAPA, "The Executive Presidency," p. 28. See also Elmer Staats's remarks, p. 31.

129. GAO, *Managing the Government,* p. 90.

130. Ibid., p. 4.

131. NAPA, "The Executive Presidency," pp. 28, 30.

132. Ibid, pp. 28.

133. Ibid., p. 31.

134. Goldstein, "The Flickering 'M' in OMB" p. 26.

135. Christopher G. Wye, "The Office of Management and Budget: A Continu-ing Search for Useful Information," in Christopher G. Wye and Richard C. Sonnichsen, eds., *Evaluation in the Federal Government: Changes, Trends, and Opportunities,* no. 55 (Fall 1992), Jossey-Bass Publishers, Publication of American Evaluation Association, p. 70.

136. L.R. Jones and Jerry L. McCaffery, "Implementation of the Federal Chief Financial Officers Act," *Public Budgeting and Finance* (Spring 1993), p. 68.

137. Ibid. Frank S. Hodsoll was OMB's Chief Financial Officer in 1989, and Presi-dent Bush appointed him as the first deputy director for management in 1991.

138. Mark L. Goldstein, "Darman's Raiders," *Government Executive* 23, no. 11 (November 1991), p. 22–23.

139. Ibid., pp. 22–26.

140. Ibid., p. 23.

141. Edward I. Mazur, "Vision of Federal Financial Management," Part II, Sympo-sium: Federal Financial Reform, in *Public Budgeting and Finance* (Spring 1993), p. 65.

142. Wye, "The Office of Management and Budget," pp. 68, 69. Wye also explains that "over one hundred high-risk areas susceptible to fraud, waste, and mismanagement" had been found by OMB in keeping with its reporting requirements under the Federal Managers' Financial Integrity Act of 1982. The SWAT teams were created to address the most serious of these problem areas.

143. See Jones and McCaffery, "Implementation of the Chief Financial Officers Act," pp. 72–74.

144. Ibid., p. 73.

145. Ibid.

146. Morton Rosenberg, "Regulatory Management at OMB," in *Office of Management and Budget: Evolving Roles and Future Issues.* Prepared for the Committee on Governmen-tal Affairs, U.S. Senate, by the Congressional Research Service (February 1986), p. 199.

147. Ibid., pp. 198–199.

148. Rosenberg, "Regulatory Management at OMB," p. 199.

149. Ibid.

150. Ibid.

151. George C. Eads and Michael Fix, *Relief or Reform? Reagan's Regulatory Dilemma* (Washington, DC: The Urban Institute Press, 1984), p. 55.

152. Rosenberg, "Regulatory Management at OMB," p. 200.

153. Ibid.

154. Stephanie Smith, "OMB and Paperwork Management," in *OMB: Evolving Roles and Future Issues*. Prepared for the Committee on Governmental Affairs, U.S. Senate, by the Congressional Research Service (February 1986) p. 237.

155. Ibid.

156. Ibid., pp. 238–239.

157. U.S. Congress, General Accounting Office, Report to the Congress by the Comptroller General. "Program to Follow Up Federal Paperwork Commission Recommendations Is in Trouble." Washington, U.S. Government Printing Office, GGD-80-36. March 14, 1980.

158. Smith, "OMB and Paperwork Management," pp. 239–240.

159. Ibid., p. 240.

160. Ibid.

161. Ibid., p. 235.

162. GAO, *Managing the Government*, p. 21, Table 1.2. OMB's Employees (Fiscal Year 1981 vs. FY 1988).

163. 3 C.F.R. 1981., p. 127, 46 *Federal Register*. 13,193 (1981).

164. Rosenberg, "Regulatory Management at OMB," p. 200.

165. Robert J. Duffy, "Regulatory Oversight in the Clinton Administration." Prepared for delivery at the annual meeting of the American Political Science Association, New York Hilton, September 1–4, 1994, p. 4.

166. Rosenberg, "Regulatory Management at OMB," pp. 200–201.

167. RIAs were required only for "major" rules though all rules had to be submitted to OIRA before being published in the *Federal Register*. Agencies had the discretion to classify the proposals as "major" or "minor," but had to submit them to OIRA ten days before publication. OMB could reclassify them during that period. Rosenberg, p. 205, from Executive Order (hereafter E.O.) 12, 291, Sec. (c)(3) and Sec. 3(f).

168. Rosenberg, "Regulatory Management at OMB," p. 205.

169. Ibid.

170. Ibid., p. 206.

171. Rosenberg, "Regulatory Management at OMB," pp. 205–206.

172. See Richard A. Harris and Sidney M. Milkis, *The Politics of Regulatory Change: A Tale of Two Agencies* (New York: Oxford University Press, 1989), pp. 105–106. Also see Walter Williams, *Mismanaging America: The Rise of the Anti-Analytic Presidency*, pp. 92–93.

173. OMB Regulatory Program of United States: April 1, 1985–March 30, 1986 (August 8, 1985), pp. 581, 583, in Rosenberg, "Regulatory Management at OMB," pp. 210–211.

174. Rosenberg, "Regulatory Management at OMB," p. 211.

175. Susan J. Tolchin and Martin Tolchin, *Dismantling America: The Rush to Deregulate* (Boston: Houghton-Mifflin, 1983), p. 57.

176. Ibid., p. 61.

177. Ibid., p. 57.

178. These statistics—EPA, 58.9 percent; Labor, 57.8 percent; and Energy, 52.8 percent—were cited in Rosenberg, "Regulatory Management at OMB," p. 211, as being taken in part from the testimony of OMB Director James C. Miller III before the

Subcommittee on Intergovernmental Affairs, Senate Committee on Governmental Affairs, January 28, 1986 (1985 statistics).

179. Tolchin and Tolchin, *Dismantling America,* pp. 63–64.

180. From *Presidential Management of Rulemaking in Regulatory Agencies* (Report by a Panel of the National Academy of Public Administration (Washington, DC: NAPA, 1987) pp. 37–38, cited in Williams, *Mismanaging America,* p. 94.

181. Williams, *Mismanaging America,* p. 94.

182. Ibid., pp. 94–95.

183. Ibid., p. 95.

184. Murray L. Weidenbaum, "Regulatory Reform under the Reagan Administration," in George C. Eads and Michael Fix, *The Reagan Regulatory Strategy: An Assessment* (Washington, DC: Urban Institute Press, 1984), p. 18.

185. For a discussion of the legal issues involved, see Eads and Fix, *Relief or Reform? Reagan's Regulatory Dilemma,* pp. 112–117.

186. "EPA Asbestos Regulations: Report on a Case Study on OMB Interference in Agency Rulemaking," by the Subcommittee on Oversight and Investigations of the House Committee on Energy and Commerce, 99th Congress, First Session 109 (1985), (Comm. Print #99–V), as cited in Rosenberg, "Regulatory Management at OMB," p. 214.

187. Ibid.

188. Eads and Fix, *Relief or Reform, Reagan's Regulatory Dilemma,* p. 138.

189. Ibid.

190. Terry Moe, "The Politicized Presidency," in John E. Chubb and Paul E. Peterson, eds., *The New Direction in American Politics* (Washington, DC: The Brookings Institution, 1985), p. 262.

191. Harris and Milkis, *Politics of Regulatory Change,* p. 105.

192. Executive Office of the President, OMB list of non-governmental groups represented along with subject and data accompanying letter from James C. Miller to Representative John Dingell, April 28, 1981, in Tolchin and Tolchin, *Dismantling America,* p. 64.

193. Ibid., Tolchin and Tolchin, *Dismantling America,* p. 65.

194. General Accounting Office. "Improved Quality, Adequate Resources, and Consistent Oversight Needed of Regulatory Analysis as to Help Control Cost of Regulation," 53—554 (November 4, 1982), as cited in Rosenberg, "Regulatory Management at OMB," p. 206.

195. See Tolchin and Tolchin, *Dismantling America,* p. 77. In one instance, Tolchin and Tolchin appear to have questioned a high-level OIRA staffer's credibility in his claim to have been meeting with Ralph Nader "all the time," when they quoted Nader as claiming to have never personally met with him (p. 60), though he acknowledges that one of his "groups" had met with the OMB official once or twice. Further, they suggested that when Vice President Bush sent a letter to business and governmental lenders eliciting recommendations for regulatory reform, OMB never systematically analyzed the thousands of responses that came into OMB, p. 58.

196. Rosenberg, "Regulatory Management," p. 216.

197. Ibid.

198. Ibid., pp. 216–217.

199. U.S. Congress, Senate, Committee on Governmental Affairs, Subcommittee on Federal Expenditures, Research, and Rules. Implementation of the Paperwork Reduction Act of 1980. Hearings. 97th Congress, Second Session. April 14, 1982. Washington, U.S. Government Printing Office, 1982, p. 65.

200. U.S. General Accounting Office, Report to the Chairman, Committee on Government Operations, House of Representatives by the Comptroller General of the United States, "Implementing the Paperwork Reduction Act: Some Progress, But Many Prob-

lems Remain." Report No. GAO/GGD-83-35. Washington, U.S. Government Printing Office. April 20, 1983, p. 29.

201. Kitty Dumas, "Congress or the White House: Who Controls the Agencies?" *Congressional Quarterly Weekly Report,* April 14, 1990, p. 1133.

202. Tolchin and Tolchin, *Dismantling America,* pp. 63–66.

203. 50 *Federal Register* 1036 (1985).

204. Rosenberg, "Regulatory Management at OMB," p. 201.

205. Ibid.

206. Dumas, "Who Controls the Agencies?" p. 1133.

207. Ibid.

208. Harris and Milkis, *Politics of Regulatory Changes,* p. 112.

209. Ibid.

210. Charles Tiefer, *The Semi-Sovereign Presidency: The Bush Administration's Strategy for Governing Without Congress* (Boulder, CO: Westview Press, 1994), p. 64.

211. Macon Morehouse, "Darman Reassures, But Panel Wary," *Congressional Quarterly Weekly Report,* May 27, 1989, p. 1253.

212. Dumas, "Who Controls the Agencies," p. 1134.

213. Phil Kuntz, "Democrats Take a Swipe at OMB," *Congressional Quarterly Weekly Report,* April 29, 1989, p. 972.

214. Dumas, "Who Controls the Agencies?" p. 1135.

215. "Paperwork Reduction Renewal Stymied," *Congressional Quarterly Almanac* 413, 1990.

216. See GAO, *Managing the Government,* p. 21, for 1981 figures. Figures for 1986 and 1990 were derived from a comparison of OMB staff directories during those years.

217. Jonathan Rauch, "The Regulatory President," *National Journal,* November 30, 1991, pp. 2902–2903.

218. Tiefer, *Semi-Sovereign Presidency,* p. 64.

219. Ibid., p. 68.

220. Ibid.

221. Officially named the Council on Competitiveness, this unit had originally been established in April of 1989 to examine regulatory issues and issues that affected the "competitiveness of the U.S. economy." During its first year, it "neither met nor had any staff." Tiefer, *Semi-Sovereign Presidency,* p. 65.

222. Tiefer in *Semi-Sovereign Presidency,* p. 65, cites two press accounts that suggested this conclusion. They were Bob Woodward and David Broder, "Quayle's Quest: Curb Rules, Leave 'No Fingerprints,' " *Washington Post,* January 9, 1992, A-1; Michael Duffy, "Need Friends in High Places? For Industries Trying to Skirt the Law, Dan Quayle's Council on Competitiveness Is a Good Place to Start," *Time,* November 4, 1991.

223. Tiefer, *Semi-Sovereign Presidency,* p. 77.

224. Ibid, p. 66–67.

225. Holly Idelson, "Glenn Trying to Shed Light on Rulemaking Process," *Congressional Quarterly, Weekly Report,* November 23, 1991, p. 3449.

226. Tiefer, *Semi-Sovereign Presidency* p. 81.

227. Ibid. p. 86.

228. Tiefer in *Semi-Sovereign Presidency* discusses the moratorium at length on pages 82–88.

229. Elizabeth Palmer, "White House War on Red Tape: Success Hard to Gauge," *Congressional Quarterly, Weekly Report,* May 2, 1992, p. 1155.

230. Ibid.

Notes to Chapter 9

1. Steven Mufson, "Papers, but Where's Policy?" *Washington Post,* June 13, 1993, p. H-6.

2. President, Presidential Decision Directive/NEC-2, "Organization of the National Economic Council," The White House, Washington, DC, March 24, 1993. Photocopy.

3. Ibid.

4. Mufson, "Papers, but Where's Policy?" p. H-6.

5. "Organization of the National Economic Council," p. 2.

6. Lawrence Haas, "Leon E. Panetta: Jumping Through the Budget Hoops," *Government Executive* (February 1993), p. 53. See George Hager, "Rivlin Brings Independent Streak to Director's Chair at OMB," *Congressional Quarterly Weekly Report* 52, July 2, 1994, p. 1770.

7. Haas, "Leon E. Panetta: Jumping Through Budget Hoops," p. 53.

8. Ibid.

9. Alice M. Rivlin, *Reviving the American Dream: The Economy, the States, and the Federal Government* (Washington, DC: The Brookings Institution, 1992), p. 17.

10. Ibid., p. 13.

11. Ibid., p. 17.

12. Bob Woodward, *The Agenda: Inside the Clinton White House* (New York: Simon and Schuster, 1994), p. 73.

13. Ibid.

14. Haas, "Leon E. Panetta: Jumping Through Budget Hoops."

15. Hager, "Rivlin Brings Independent Streak."

16. Rivlin, *Reviving the American Dream,* p. 4.

17. Woodward, *The Agenda,* p. 56.

18. George Hager, "Time Bombs for Clinton Seen in Bush's Final Budget," *Congressional Quarterly Weekly Report* 51 (January 9, 1993), p. 68.

19. Ibid. The final Bush budget projected a $305 billion deficit for 1997, while Clinton and some congressional Democrats estimated it at $350 to $360 billion.

20. Ibid.

21. Ibid.

22. Dan Balz and Ann Devroy, "Clinton Navigated Politics, Deficit to Craft Plan," *Washington Post,* February 21, 1993, p. A 16.

23. Ibid.

24. Elizabeth Drew, *On the Edge: The Clinton Presidency* (New York: Simon and Schuster, 1994), p. 68.

25. Mufson, "Papers, but Where's Policy?" p. H-6.

26. Woodward, *The Agenda,* pp. 125, 126, 130.

27. Ibid., pp. 125, 126, 170.

28. Janet Hook, "Budget Will Test Panetta's Reputation as an Affable and Honest Operator," *Congressional Quarterly Weekly Report* 52 (February 5, 1994), p. 223.

29. Woodward, *The Agenda,* p. 86.

30. Hook, "Budget Will Test Panetta's Reputation," p. 223.

31. Rivlin later clarified her comments as having been distorted when they were quoted. She explained that she did use the word "display" but that it was not meant as a criticism, Woodward, *The Agenda,* pp. 187, 294.

32. William F. Powers, "Alice Rivlin's Apolitical Pitch," *Washington Post,* August 9, 1994, p. C-6.

33. The Drew and Woodward books both provide accounts of the President's sur-

prise and frustration with this development. Both cite that the President felt the ramifications of the BEA caps had not been adequately emphasized to him. Drew wrote that "aides said he had been told—clearly—on at least two occasions." "Leon Panetta, the OMB director, had plainly told him." Drew, *On the Edge*, p. 166.

34. Ibid. From Woodward's book came the explanation that Panetta had said he would get the House to rewrite the caps to accommodate the proposed investments. (*The Agenda*, p. 163.) However, "they" had underestimated the degree of "deficit-mania," in the Congress. (*The Agenda*, p. 163).

35. Ibid.

36. Vice President Al Gore, *From Red Tape to Results: Creating a Government that Works Better and Costs Less* (Report of the National Performance Review, Washington, DC: GPO, September 7, 1993), p. i.

37. Ibid.

38. See Chapter 3, pp. 43–46.

39. Gore, *From Red Tape to Results*, pp. 16–17.

40. Ibid., p. 19.

41. Ibid., pp. 15–16.

42. Lance T. LeLoup and Patrick T. Taylor, "The Policy Constraints of Deficit Reduction: President Clinton's 1995 Budget," *Public Budgeting and Finance* 14, no. 2 (Summer 1994), p. 8.

43. Ibid., p. 3.

44. Viveca Novak, "The Long Brawl," *National Journal* 26 (January 8, 1994), p. 59.

45. Alice M. Rivlin, interview by author, Washington, D.C., March 4, 1994.

46. U.S. Senate Committee on Governmental Affairs, *Hearing Before the Committee on Governmental Affairs on Nomination of Alice M. Rivlin to Be Director, Office of Management and Budget*, 103rd Congress, Second Session, September 27, 1994, p. 20.

47. Ibid.

48. Ibid.

49. Lawrence J. Haas, "Skating on the Hard Freeze," *Government Executive* (February 1994), pp. 25–26.

50. Novak, "The Long Brawl," p. 59.

51. William Niskanen, edited transcriptions of symposium on "President Clinton's Budget and Fiscal Policy: An Evaluation Two Budgets Later," University of Virginia, April 14, 1994; Panel 2: "The Economic Aspects of President Clinton's Budgetary Politics," printed in *Public Budgeting and Finance* 14, no. 3 (Fall 1994), p. 23.

52. LeLoup and Taylor, "The Policy Constraints of Deficit Reduction," pp. 9–10.

53. Office of Management and Budget Office Memorandum No. 94-16 (March 1, 1994), p. 1.

54. Ibid., pp. 1–2.

55. Ibid., pp. 2–3.

56. Ibid., p. 2.

57. Ibid., p. 4.

58. See Chapter 4, pp. 103, 105; chapter 8, p. 201.

59. OMB Office Memorandum No. 94-16, p. 11.

60. Ibid.

61. Ibid., p. 4.

62. Ibid., pp. 4–5.

63. General Accounting Office, *Managing the Government, Revised Approach Could Improve OMB's Effectiveness*, GAO/GGD-89-65 (May 1989), p. 4.

64. Ibid., p. 78.

65. See GAO, *Managing the Government,* pp. 79–81; OMB Office Memorandum No. 94-16, p. 4.

66. OMB Office Memorandum No. 94–16, pp. 10–11.

67. Ibid., pp. 11, 93.

68. Al Gore, *From Red Tape to Results: Creating a Government That Works Better and Costs Less: Mission-Driven, Results-Oriented Budgeting* (Report of the National Performance Review, Washington, DC: GPO, September 1993), p. 54.

69. OMB Office Memorandum No. 94-16, p. 2; NPR's monograph, *Mission-Driven, Results-Oriented Budgeting* urges more collegiality and team approaches. See pp. 54–55.

70. Ibid., p. 18.

71. Ibid., p. 17. The OMB Director would appoint the chair of the committee and both deputy directors would be ex-officio members. Members of the director's immediate staff with administrative responsibilities would also be on the committee.

72. Ibid., p. 12.

73. Ibid.

74. Ibid.

75. Ibid.

76. Ibid., p. 13.

77. Ibid.

78. Ibid.

79. Ibid., pp. 14–15.

Notes to Chapter 10

1. Beth Donovan, "Calling Dr. Panetta," *Congressional Quarterly Weekly Report* 52 (July 2, 1994), p. 1794.

2. William F. Powers, "Alice Rivlin's Apolitical Pitch," *Washington Post,* August 9, 1994, p. C-6.

3. Bob Woodward, *The Agenda (Inside the Clinton White House)* (New York: Simon and Schuster, 1994), pp. 127–128.

4. George Hager, "Rivlin Brings Independent Streak to Director's Chair at OMB," *Congressional Quarterly Weekly Report* 52 (July 2, 1994), p. 1771.

5. U.S. Senate Committee on Governmental Affairs, *Hearings Before the Committee on Governmental Affairs on Nomination of Alice M. Rivlin to Be Director, Office of Management and Budget,* 103rd Congress, Second Session, September 27, 1994, p. 20.

6. Woodward, *The Agenda,* p. 324.

7. *Hearings on Nomination of Alice M. Rivlin to Be Director of OMB,* p. 23.

8. Stephen Barr, "OMB Approves Modest Number of 'Buyouts,'" *Washington Post,* September 30, 1994, p. A-27.

9. Stephen Barr, "Roth Aspires to Be Architect of Smaller, More Efficient Government," *Washington Post,* January 4, 1995, p. A-13.

10. *Hearings on Nomination of Alice M. Rivlin to Be Director of OMB,* p. 9.

11. General Accounting Office, "Office of Management and Budget, Changes Resulting From the OMB 2000 Reorganization," GAO/GGD 96-50 (December 1995), p. 16.

12. Donald F. Kettl is so cited from *Reinventing Government? Appraising the National Performance Review* (Washington, DC: Brookings Institution, August, 1994), p. 42, in Gore, *Creating a Government That Works Better and Costs Less, Status Report of the National Performance Review* (Washington, DC: GPO, September 1994), p. 56.

13. Vice President Al Gore, *From Red Tape to Results: Creating A Government That Works Better and Costs Less, Mission-Driven Results-Oriented Budgeting.* Accompanying Report of the National Performance Review (Washington, DC: GPO, September 1993), p. 54.

14. Ibid., p. 55.

15. Ibid., p. 34.

16. Viveca Novak, "The New Regulators," *National Journal* 25, no. 29 (July 17, 1993), p. 1802.

17. Ibid., p. 1801.

18. Presidential Document Executive Order No. 12,866, 58 *Federal Register* 51735, September 30, 1993.

19. Robert J. Duffy, "Regulatory Oversight in the Clinton Administration." Paper presented at the annual meeting of the American Political Science Association, New York, NY, September 1994, p. 11.

20. Ibid.

21. Ibid.

22. Executive Order No. 12,866,58 *Federal Register* 51735.

23. Duffy, "Regulatory Oversight," p. 11.

24. Ibid., p. 12.

25. Ibid., p. 14.

26. Ibid., p. 13.

27. Ibid., pp. 14–15.

28. Ibid., p. 15.

29. Ibid., p. 13.

30. Ann Devroy, "Memo Outlines Fiscal Options for President," *Washington Post,* October 23, 1994, p. A10.

31. Ibid., p. A-1. See also Hobart Rowen, "The Rivlin Reality Check," *Washington Post,* October 26, 1994, p. A-23.

32. Devroy, "Memo Outlines Options," p. A-10.

33. Ibid.

34. Rowen, "The Rivlin Reality Check."

35. Devroy, "Memo Outlines Options."

36. Rowen, "The Rivlin Reality Check."

37. Ibid.

38. Clay Chandler, "In Pursuit of the Mystery Memo Leak," *Washington Post,* October 29, 1994, p. C-1.

39. George Hager, "Political Flap over Deficit Memo Could Hamstring Clinton," *Congressional Quarterly Weekly Report* 52 (October 29, 1994), p. 3089.

40. Herbert Stein, "Don't Ask Alice: Budget Chief Rivlin is Apt to Tell the Truth— and Who Wants That?" *Washington Post,* October 30, 1994, p. C-5.

41. Some observers believed that at very least the President deserved credit for creating greater confidence in the financial markets by taking difficult steps to move the deficit on a downward trend which in turn led to lower interest rates. See Lance T. LeLoup and Patrick T. Taylor, "The Policy Constraints of Deficit Reduction: President Clinton's 1995 Budget," *Public Budgeting and Finance* 14, no. 2 (Summer 1994), p. 22.

The president's deficit reduction package was bitter medicine requiring a hard sell that was both risky and narrowly achieved. But the early results were impressive, with deficits falling by $100 billion over projections in the first year alone and leveling off at a more acceptable 2 percent of GDP. Can the administration take credit? To some extent it can, because despite the fact that the recovery was already underway, the deficit reduction package reassured Wall Street and the Federal Reserve, giving the Fed the confidence to keep interest rates at historic lows.

See also John M. Berry, "Clinton's Rising Tide? Many Economists Give President Partial Credit for Economy's Growth," *Washington Post,* February 18, 1996, H-1, H-5.

42. National Performance Review, "National Performance Review: Phase II, Putting It Together" (Washington, DC, February 1995, mimeographed), p. 1.

43. The President's Management Council was chaired by OMB's Deputy Director for Management, which included Chief Operating Officers from 15 major agencies, 3 other agencies designated by the Chair, and the heads of GSA, OPM, and the President's Director of Cabinet Affairs. Its agenda included

Setting priorities, identifying and resolving cross agency management issues; establishing interagency task forces to reform government wide systems such as personnel, budget, procurement, and information technology; and soliciting feedback from the public and government employees.

As described in Gore, *From Red Tape to Results,* p. 90.

44. "NPR, Phase II: Putting It Together," p. 2.

45. Ibid., pp. 2–5.

46. Ann Devroy and Clay Chandler, "New Budget to Continue U.S. Deficits," *Washington Post,* February 4, 1995, p. A-1.

47. Ibid.

48. Elizabeth Drew, *Showdown: The Struggle Between the Gingrich Congress and the Clinton White House* (New York: Simon and Schuster, 1996), p. 70.

49. Paul Light, "Fear and Loathing Meet Reinvention," *Government Executive* (March 1995), p. 56.

50. Devroy and Chandler, "New Budget to Continue Deficits," p. A-4.

51. Drew, *Showdown,* pp. 69, 71.

52. Ibid., p. 69.

53. George Hager, "Clinton Shifts Tactics, Proposes Erasing Deficit in 10 Years," *Congressional Quarterly Weekly Report* 53, no. 24 (June 17, 1995), p. 1716.

54. Alissa J. Rubin, "Details of the Clinton Proposal," *Congressional Quarterly Weekly Report* 53, no. 24 (June 17, 1995), p. 1718.

55. Hager, "Clinton Shifts Tactics," pp. 1715, 1717.

56. Ibid., p. 1715.

57. Ibid., p. 1720.

58. See Appendix II, "Staffing Profile, Before and After OMB 2000," in GAO, "Changes Resulting from OMB 2000 Reorganization," p. 34.

59. Appendix IV, "Program Examiners' Major Duties and Performance Standards," in GAO, "Changes Resulting from OMB 2000 Reorganization," p. 41.

60. Ibid.

61. Ibid.

62. Ibid.

63. Ibid.

64. GAO, "Changes Resulting from OMB 2000 Reorganization," p. 16.

65. Shannon S. Gravitte, "Financial Management Insiders," *Government Financial Management Topics* 35, no. 6 (July/August 1995), p. 3.

66. GAO, "Changes Resulting from the OMB 2000 Reorganization," p. 18.

67. Ibid., p. 20.

68. Ibid., p. 22.

69. Ibid., p. 24.

70. Alissa J. Rubin, " 'Dynamic Scoring' Plan Exposes Deep Divisions Within GOP," *Congressional Quarterly Weekly Report,* December 10, 1994, p. 3501.

71. Alice M. Rivlin, "Testimony of Alice M. Rivlin, Director, Office of Management and Budget Before the Joint Economic Committee" [U.S. Congress] June 22, 1995 (Washington, DC: Office of Management and Budget, mimeographed), p. 6.

72. Ibid.

73. Hager, "Clinton Shifts Tactics," p. 1720.

74. "Rivlin Testimony Before the Joint Economic Committee," p. 6.

75. George Hager, "Republicans, White House Still Far Apart on Budget Issues," *Congressional Quarterly Weekly Report* 53, August 5, 1995, p. 2346.

76. Ann Devroy and Eric Pianin, "Clinton and Congress Agree on Outlines of Budget Goals; Workers Return Today," *Washington Post,* November 20, 1995, p. A-10.

77. Ann Devroy, "Bills Signed to Fully Reopen Government," *Washington Post,* January 7, 1996, p. A-1.

78. See, for example, Clay Chandler and Steven Pearlstein, "A Budget Clash, by the Numbers," *Washington Post,* November 15, 1995, p. A-17. They quote one economist who concluded that the forecasts OMB and CBO reached were "essentially the same"—"one is as likely to be true as the other." CBO had also acknowledged the similarity between its economic projections and those offered in the President's first budget. See Congressional Budget Office, *An Analysis of the President's Budgetary Proposals for Fiscal Year 1996,* p. 3, as cited in Rivlin testimony before the Joint Economic Committee, June 22, p. 6.

With respect to the long-term forecasts to the year 2000, the initial differences between the two agencies on important economic indicators such as economic growth and the consumer price index had been infinitesimal. For example, the White House's July 1995 forecast for gross domestic product was $9.25 trillion and CBO's March 1995 estimate was $9.13 trillion. The White House's and CBO's estimates for total taxable income as a percentage of gross domestic product were 77.2 percent and 76.1 percent, respectively. The estimates for inflation-adjusted growth were 2.5 percent (White House) and 2.3 percent (CBO), and for the consumer price index 3.1 percent (White House) and 3.2 percent (CBO). See David Wessel, "The Art of Tweaking: White House's Altered Forecast on Economy Underlies Capitol Hill Budget Duel," *Wall Street Journal,* November 3, 1995, p. A-16. It was only when projected seven to ten years into the future that these small differences compounded and created the large gaps in future projections of the deficit.

79. The overly "optimistic" economic forecasts that some observers thought "both" organizations had been predisposed to reach in the early to mid-1980s seemed to have shifted in the reverse direction for both agencies. In July of 1994, OMB's estimate for the FY 1995 deficit was $167 billion and an "informal" CBO estimate had dropped to $170 billion. See George Hager, "White House, CBO Both Foresee Lower Deficits for '94 and '95," *Congressional Quarterly Weekly Report* 52, July 16, 1994, p. 1911.

The actual 1995 deficit came in still lower at $164 billion. See John Berry, "U.S. Budget Deficit Falls for Third Year," *Washington Post,* October 26, 1995, p. D-1. In July of 1994, OMB had projected an FY 1994 deficit of $220 billion See Hager, "White House, CBO." The "actual" 1994 deficit had turned out to be $203 billion. See Steven Pearlstein, "Economy Rebounds Surprisingly," *Washington Post,* October 28, 1995, pp. A-1, A-15.

80. Throughout the budget negotiations and stalemate between the Clinton White House and the Republican Congress, press accounts of the unfolding events frequently referred to OMB's economic projections as "rosy" (see, for example David Maraniss and Michael Weisskopf, "Personalities Shaped Events as Much as Ideology, Inside the Revolu-

tion," *Washington Post,* January 20, 1996, p. A-12), and to CBO as "the more conservative" of the two (see Eric Pianin, "Revised Congressional Forecast Narrows Gap for Budget Talks," *Washington Post,* December 11, 1995, p. A-1). Such descriptions presumably meant that OMB's projections were overly optimistic with respect to the future well-being of the economy. However, in light of OMB's credibility problems developed in the early to mid-1980s, these pejorative terms conveyed an impression that OMB's forecasts were somehow markedly and intrinsically less reliable than were those issued by CBO.

81. Eric Pianin and Judith Havemann, "GOP Drops Medicaid for Disabled," *Washington Post,* October 14, 1995, p. A-4.

82. Ibid.

83. Ibid.

84. Ibid.

85. Ann Devroy and Barbara Vobejda, "Clinton Faces 'Huge Heat' on Welfare," *Washington Post,* November 4, 1995, pp. A-1, A-10.

86. Judith Havemann and Ann Devroy, "Clinton Agrees to New Welfare Study, *Washington Post,* October 28, 1995, p. A-4.

87. Ibid.

88. Office of Management and Budget, prepared with the Department of Health and Human Services, the Department of the Treasury, and other Agencies, "Potential Poverty and Distributional Effects of Welfare Reform Bills and Balanced Budget Plans," November 9, 1995, p. 1.

89. Ibid., pp. 1–3.

90. Ibid., pp. 4–10.

91. Ibid., pp. 14–23.

92. Robert B. Reich, *Locked in the Cabinet* (New York: Alfred A. Knopf, 1997), p. 287.

93. U.S. House Committee on Government Reform and Oversight, *Making Government Work: Fulfilling the Mandate For Change,* 104th Congress, First Session, December 21, 1995, p. 8.

94. Ibid., p. 5.

95. Ibid., p. 27.

96. Ibid., p. 42.

97. Ibid.

98. Ibid., pp. 42–43.

99. Ibid., p. 45.

100. Ibid., p. 44.

101. Ibid., p. 45.

102. Al Kamen, "In the Loop Fed Update," *Washington Post,* February 5, 1996, p. A-19.

103. Michael Weisskopf and David Maraniss, "Personalities Shaped Events as Much as Ideology," *Washington Post,* January 20, 1996, p. A-12.

Notes to Chapter 11

1. Eric Pianin, "Report Shows Deficit Diving to $116 Billion," *Washington Post,* August 16, 1996, p. D-1.

2. Eric Pianin, "Senate Grudgingly Backs Budget Plan," *Washington Post,* June 14, 1996, p. A-4.

3. Interview with Alice Rivlin, February 11, 1997.

4. Ibid.

5. S. 4, "Line Item Veto Act," Sec. 1023 a.

6. House of Representatives Report 104-491, "Line Item Veto Act," March 21, 1996, Conference Report to Accompany S. 4 Sec. 1021 p. 1–2 and Sec. 1026 (9)i pp. 10–11.

7. "Conference Report," pp. 2–3.

8. Ibid.

9. See Al Kamen, "Courting Clinton's Reconsideration," *Washington Post,* March 11, 1996, p. A-17. This morsel of Washington insider gossip says more about the need to convert some of OMB's politically appointed support positions to career status than it does about any of Rivlin's political party loyalties. Noncareer appointees of short duration with no other permanent positions to return to *will have incentives* to trade off their OMB insider information for upward mobility in the Washington marketplace to a far greater extent than mid-career OMB officials. The individual who went to work at the RNC was a young graduate research assistant of Rivlin's at George Mason University, brought in as a special assistant when she first came to OMB. The other had been assigned to coordinate the OMB 2000 self-study among other duties. Again, the "traditional" director had gotten caught in the crossfire of a politicized environment.

10. John M. Berry, "Election Year Politics Stall Votes on Fed Nominations," *Washington Post,* June 12, 1996, p. F-1.

11. John M. Berry, "Senate Confirms Fed's Greenspan to Third Term," *Washington Post,* June 21, 1996, p. D-1.

12. Executive Office of the President, Office of Management and Budget, *A Citizen's Guide to the Federal Budget,* Fiscal 1996.

13. Ibid., p. 1.

14. National Academy of Public Administration, "The Executive Presidency: Federal Management for the 1990s." A Report by an Academy Panel for the 1988–89 Presidential Transition (Washington, DC: September 1988), p. 38.

15. *Fiscal Year 1994 Budget Appendix and 1997 Budget Appendix.*

16. Bernard H. Martin, Joseph S. Wholey, and Roy T. Meyers, "The New Equation at OMB: M + B = RMO," *Public Budgeting and Finance* 15, no. 4 (Winter 1995), p. 90.

17. Ibid., p. 88.

18. Albert J. Kliman and Louis Fisher, "Budget Reform Proposals in the NPR Report," *Public Budgeting and Finance* 15, no. 1 (Spring 1995), p. 31.

Notes to Epilogue

1. See United States General Accounting Office. GAO/AIMD/GGD-97-/69R, *The Results Act: Observations on the Office of Management and Budget's July 1997 Draft Strategic Plan,* p. 4.

2. Ibid., p. 3.

3. Ibid., p. 4.

4. The "Year 2000" effort was necessitated by the fact that many large-scale computer systems in the departments and agencies were programmed such that, without reworking or replacement, the systems would register the year 2000 as 1900. See Stephen Barr, "Year 2000 Report Flunks 3 Agencies," *Washington Post,* September 16, 1997, p. A-15. Barr reports that if the systems are not fixed, "malfunctions could jeopardize the tax-processing system, payments to veterans with service-connected disabilities, student loan repayments, and perhaps even air traffic control."

5. The fiscal 1997 deficit of $23 billion turned out to be $100 billion less than the White House and CBO had predicted a year earlier. See Clay Chandler, "Economy Shaves Deficit, Spurs Dreams of Surplus," *Washington Post,* October 4, 1997, pp. A-1, A-12.

6. Ibid. See also Eric Pianin, "Pressure Grows to Cut Taxes in '98," *Washington Post,* December 26, 1997, p. A-1.

7. The President was viewed as having used the power sparingly by only vetoing a small percentage of the items that might have qualified as "pork barrel" spending. (See "Wielding a Tiny Pen" [Editorial], *Washington Post,* October 16, 1997, p. A-18; also Eric Pianin, "Going Light on the Line Item Veto," *Washington Post,* November 10, 1997, p. A-19.) Nonetheless, the House and Senate voted to override the President's item vetoes in a military construction bill. Several of the initial military construction vetoes had to be pulled due to "erroneous" information from the Defense Department. (See Eric Pianin and Helen Dewar, "House Vote Seals Override of Military Line-Item Veto," *Washington Post,* November 9, 1997, p. A-6.) (See also Eric Pianin and Bradley Graham, "Clinton Tempers Line Item Approach," *Washington Post,* October 15, 1997, p. A-4. Guy Gugliotta and Eric Pianin, "Line Item Veto Tips Traditional Balance of Power," *Washington Post,* October 24, 1997, pp. A-1, A-6.)

The President was also criticized by different observers for not vetoing enough. (See John McCain, "Line Item Furor," *Washington Post,* Editorial Page, November 7, 1997; also Pianin and Graham, "Clinton Tempers Line-Item Approach.") Another critique was that the vetoes were motivated by partisan political considerations. (See McCain "Line Item Furor." McCain finds these charges "somewhat off the mark," but asserts that the administration had "no established consistent and objective criteria against which all programs are evaluated . . . .")Director Raines denied that there had been partisan motivations for the vetoes and maintained that there had been uniform criteria used for determining the item vetoes. In a White House Press briefing, he asserted that there were three criteria used to determine the vetoes of military construction projects: that the spending was not in the President's 1998 budget request; that the design work for the construction projects was not started; and that the projects would not make "a substantial contribution to the well-being and quality of life of men and women in the Armed Forces." Raines stated that "these criteria were tough, but they were also objective." He further asserted that they were "not partisan," that "no decision was made based on political party or location of the project," and that they represented "the President's commitment to the careful stewardship of the nation's defenses." (See the White House, Office of the Press Secretary. "Press Briefing. Chair of the President's National Economic Council Gene Sperling, and Franklin Raines, Director of the Office of Management and Budget," October 6, 1997, p. 2.)

8. *Washington Post* writer Guy Gugliotta illustrated how difficult and time-consuming it could be to obtain the kind of information that OMB needed to provide the President before he could make a line item veto. He described the efforts involved in identifying a $450,000 "transportation emergency preparedness response demonstration project" and where it would be located. Gugliotta reported that "it took one reporter five days and 27 phone calls to a half-dozen federal agencies and seven congressional offices to find out that the center is supposed to be located in Arab, Ala., and that Sen. Richard C. Shelby (R-Ala.) is its patron." (See Guy Gugliotta, "Veto is Making 'Pork Barrel' a Shell Game," *Washington Post,* October 18, 1997, pp. A-1, A-4, A-6.)

9. White House, Office of the Press Secretary. Press Briefing. OMB Director Frank Raines, NSC Senior Director for Defense Policy and Arms Control Bob Bell, and Deputy Defense Secretary John Hamre on the Line Item Veto," October 14, 1997, pp. 8, 9.

10. Executive Office of the President. Office of Management and Budget, "Strategic Plan FY 1998–FY 2002," September 30, 1997, p. 21.

11. Ibid., p. 1.

12. Ibid.

13. Ibid.

14. Ibid.

15. Ibid., p. 6.

16. Ibid., p. 14.

17. Ibid., p. 16.

18. Ibid., p. 15.

19. Ibid., p. 13.

20. Ibid., p. 6.

21. Ibid., p. 5.

22. Ibid., p. 9.

23. Ibid.

24. Ibid., p. 12.

25. Ibid., p. 10.

26. Ibid., p. 9.

27. Ibid., p. 17.

28. Ibid. The plan cites external factors that might make it difficult to address this problem. It states: "The training and experience of OMB staff make them highly attractive in the job market. Despite the importance of work done at OMB and the high value placed on it, a substantial upward change in the current private-public sector pay differential for OMB staff with highly valued analytic and knowledge-based skills in certain high-demand business areas, e.g., health care economics, could offset OMB's initiatives to improve retention."

29. Ibid., pp. 17–18.

30. Ibid., p. 17.

31. Ibid.

32. Ibid. p. 18. Some of these uses include transmission of background information on legislation, status reports on paperwork and regulatory reviews, economic information, and analyses of technical budget and long-term economic forecasts.

33. Ibid., p. 19

34. See "Observations on OMB's Draft Strategic Plan."

35. Ibid., pp. 5–6, 14–15.

36. Ibid., p. 19.

37. Ibid., pp. 17, 19.

38. Ibid., p. 19.

39. Ibid., pp. 7–12.

40. Ibid., p. 8.

41. Ibid., p. 3.

42. Ibid., p. 14.

43. Ibid., p. 4. For example, it admits that "OMB faces perennial challenges in carrying out these management responsibilities in an environment where its budgetary role necessarily remains a vital and demanding part of its mission."

44. Ibid., pp. 12–13.

45. Ibid., pp. 23–24.

46. Ibid.

47. Ibid.

48. Barr, "Year 2000 Report Flunks 3 Agencies."

49. Ibid.

50. Ibid.

51. Ibid.

52. John F. Harris and Eric Pianin, "Year End Figures Turned Budget Fancy into Fact," *Washington Post,* January 7, 1998, p. A-4.

53. Ibid.
54. Ibid.
55. Ibid.
56. Ibid.
57. Ibid.
58. Ibid.
59. Eric Pianin, "Seeing Budget in Balance, CBO Projects a Decade of Surpluses," *Washington Post,* January 8, 1998, p. A-15.
60. Ibid.
61. Al From, president of the centrist Democratic Leadership Council, is quoted as characterizing activist government with fiscal restraint as an appropriate ideological ground for the Clinton administration to be occupying at this time. See Peter Baker and John F. Harris, "To Boost His Presidency and Party, Clinton Leaps into the Policy Void," *Washington Post,* January 11, 1998, p. A-1.
62. Ibid. Baker and Harris speculate that pursuit of activist government with fiscal restraint might exert a unifying effect on the Democratic Party.
63. Telephone Interview with Franklin Raines, April 8, 1998.
64. Clay Chandler, "Raines Departing As Chief of OMB," The *Washington Post,* April 15, 1998, pp. A-1, A-6.

How to Learn More
About the Office of
Management and Budget

How to Contact OMB and Request OMB Information

The internet has made OMB and the information services it provides much more accessible to the public. OMB's home page at http://www.white-house.gov/WH/EOP/omb is an excellent place to begin to examine the range of information that OMB can offer as well as to learn more about the institution itself. Information on OMB includes brief descriptions of its roles and missions, organization, and the names of its current Director, Deputy Director, and Deputy Director for Management.

For those looking for employment at OMB, the OMB home page provides vacancy announcements, selected position descriptions, and application procedures. Information on temporary employment in OMB, including internships for graduate students and "details" to OMB for federal agency personnel through programs such as the Presidential Management Intern Program and the Women's Executive Leadership Program, is also available on the OMB web site.

The OMB home page also provides guidance on how to access a wide variety of government documents, including but not limited to the President's budget, Government-wide Performance Plan, copies of the testimony of the OMB Director or Deputy Directors before congressional committees, Statements of Administration Policy (SAPs), OMB's Strategic Plan, OMB memoranda to federal agencies, and OMB financial management policies. OMB circulars, which provide federal agencies with instructions or information expected to "have a continuing effect of two years or more," are listed by number and agency category. For some circulars and additional selected forms and documents, OMB provides a 24-hour-a-day fax-on-demand service which can be contacted at (202) 395-9068, or for hard copies, (202) 395-7332. Moreover, interested citizens can obtain lists of regulations under review that are updated daily, as well as copies of proposed and final rule submissions to the *Federal Register*. The OMB home page also affords access to a number of selected reports and documents under a section titled "Miscellaneous Documents."

The OMB home page includes a four-page section titled "Public Handbook for Gaining Access to OMB Information." This section, which summarizes menu selections of the OMB home page and OMB's fax-on-demand service, also cites three other sources of information from and about OMB: the publications office for the Executive Office of the President, the EOP Library, and an OIRA Docket Library. Holdings in the Docket Library include records related to regulatory review actions including telephone logs and "materials from meetings with the public attended by the OIRA Administrator," and records concerning information collections conducted by the federal government and reviewed by OIRA under the Paperwork Reduction Act of 1995. Individuals interested in using the public reading room in the EOP Library or the OIRA Docket Library are advised to write or telephone to make an appointment, since visitors must be cleared into the building in advance. The Executive Office of the President Library can be contacted by calling (202) 395-7250 and the OIRA Docket Library can be reached at (202) 395-6880. Both are located at 725 17th Street N.W., Washington, DC, 20503.

Finally, the information handbook offers guidance to persons wishing to request information or records that might require a Freedom of Information Act inquiry. Such information requests should be made through the Deputy Assistant Director for Administration, Office of Management and Budget at 725 17th Street N.W., Washington, DC, 20503; Tel. (202) 395-5715.

Selected Bibliography

The following is a "selected" bibliography of published books, articles, or government documents that primarily focus on some aspect of OMB or BOB's historical development or operations, including accounts by three of OMB's Directors.

Berman, Larry. *The Office of Management and Budget and the Presidency, 1921–1979.* Princeton, NJ: Princeton University Press, 1979.

Congressional Research Service. *Office of Management and Budget: Evolving Roles and Future Issues.* Senate Committee on Governmental Affairs, February 1986.

Campbell, Colin S.J. *Managing the Presidency, Carter, Reagan, and the Search for Executive Harmony.* See Chapter 6, "Coping With Cyclical Forces Affecting the Budget and Management," pp. 153–98. Pittsburgh, PA: University of Pittsburgh Press, 1986.

Darman, Richard. *Who's in Control? Polar Politics and the Sensible Center.* New York: Simon and Schuster, 1996.

General Accounting Office. *Managing the Government, Revised Approach Could Improve OMB's Effectiveness.* GGD-89-65. May 1989.

———. "Office of Management and Budget, Changes Resulting From the OMB 2000 Reorganization." GGD-96-50. December 1995.

Goldstein, Mark, L. "The Flickering M in OMB." *Government Executive* 22 (March 1990): 26–32.

Greider, William. "The Education of David Stockman." *The Atlantic* 248, no. 6 (December 1981): 27–54.

Haas, Lawrence J. "What OMB Hath Wrought." *National Journal* 20, no. 36 (September 3, 1988): 2187–191.

———. "Budget Guru." *National Journal* 22, no. 3 (January 20, 1990): 110–114.

———. "Darman's OMB." *National Journal* 24, no. 5 (February 1, 1992): 256–261.

Heclo, Hugh. "OMB and the Presidency—the problem of neutral competence." *Public Interest* 38 (Winter 1975): 80–98.

———. "Executive Budget Making." In *Federal Budget Policy in the 1980s,* edited by Gregory B. Mills and John L. Palmer, 255–291. Washington, DC: The Urban Institute.

Johnson, Bruce. "From Analyst to Negotiator: The OMB's New Role." *Journal of Policy Analysis and Management* 3, no. 4 (1984): 501–14.

———. "OMB and the Budget Examiner: Changes in the Reagan Era." *Public Budgeting and Finance* 8 (Winter 1988): 3–21.

———. "The OMB Budget Examiner and the Congressional Budget Process." *Public Budgeting and Finance* 9 (Spring 1989): 5–14.

Martin, Bernard H.; Wholey, Joseph S.; and Meyers, Roy T. "The New Equation at OMB: M + B = RMO." *Public Budgeting and Finance* 15 (Winter 1995)

Miller, James C. III. *Fix the U.S. Budget! Urgings of an "Abominable No-Man."* Stanford, CA: Hoover Institution Press, 1994.

Moe, Ronald C. "The HUD Scandal and the Case for an Office of Federal Management." *Public Administration Review* 51, no. 4 (July/August 1991): 298–307.

Mosher, Frederick C. *A Tale of Two Agencies: A Comparative Analysis of the General Accounting Office and the Office of Management and Budget.* Baton Rouge, LA: Louisiana State University Press, 1984.

Ripley, Randall B. and Davis, James W. "The Bureau of the Budget and Executive Branch Agencies: Notes on Their Interaction." *The Journal of Politics* 29, no. 4 (November 1967): 749–69.

Schick, Allen. "The Budget Bureau That Was: Thoughts on the Rise, Decline, and Future of a Presidential Agency." *Journal of Law and Contemporary Problems* 35 (Summer 1970): 519–39.

———. "The Problem of Presidential Budgeting." In *The Illusion of Presidential Government,* edited by Hugh Heclo and Lester M. Salamon, pp. 85–111. Boulder, CO: Westview Press, 1981.

Stockman, David A. *The Triumph of Politics: How the Reagan Revolution Failed.* New York: Harper and Row, 1986.

Tomkin, Shelley L. "OMB Budget Examiner's Influence." *The Bureaucrat* 12 (Fall 1983): 43–47.

————. "Playing Politics in OMB: Civil Servants Join the Game." *Presidential Studies Quarterly* 15, no. 1 (1985): 158–69.

————. "Reagan OMB's 'Congress Watchers'." *The Bureaucrat* 16, no. 2 (Summer 1987): 55–60.

Wayne, Stephen J; Cole, Richard L.; and Hyde, James F.C., Jr. "Advising the President on Enrolled Legislation: Patterns of Executive Influence." *Political Science Quarterly* 94 (Summer 1979): 303–17.

Wayne, Stephen J. and Hyde, James F.C., Jr. "Presidential Decision-making on Enrolled Bills." *Presidential Studies Quarterly* 8 (Summer 1978): 284–96.

Wye, Christopher G. "The Office of Management and Budget: A Continuing Search for Useful Information." In *Evaluation in the Federal Government: Changes, Trends, and Opportunities,* edited by Christopher G. Wye and Richard C. Sonnichsen. San Francisco: Jossey-Bass.

Index

About the Author

Shelley Lynne Tomkin is Associate Professor of Political Science at Trinity College, Washington, DC, and has served as an adjunct professorial lecturer at the George Washington University. For the past twenty years, she has conducted research on the Office of Management and Budget and the federal budget process. She has lectured for governmental and private organizations on these topics. Dr. Tomkin's articles on OMB have appeared in *The Bureaucrat* and *The Presidential Studies Quarterly*.